AFRICAN AMERICAN
PREACHERS AND POLITICS

African American Preachers and Politics

THE CAREYS OF CHICAGO

Dennis C. Dickerson

University Press of Mississippi / Jackson

www.upress.state.ms.us

Margaret Walker Alexander Series
in African American Studies

The University Press of Mississippi is a member of the
Association of American University Presses.

First printing 2010

∞

Library of Congress Cataloging-in-Publication Data

Dickerson, Dennis C., 1949–
African American preachers and politics : the Careys of Chicago /
Dennis C. Dickerson.
p. cm. — (Margaret Walker Alexander series in African
American studies)
Includes bibliographical references and index.
ISBN 978-1-60473-427-0 (cloth : alk. paper) — ISBN 978-1-60473-428-7
(ebook) 1. Carey, Archibald J. (Archibald James), 1868–1931. 2. Carey,
Archibald J. (Archibald James), 1908–1981. 3. African Americans—
Illinois—Chicago—Politics and government. 4. African American
clergy—Political activity—Illinois—Chicago. 5. African American
clergy—Illinois—Chicago—Biography. 6. African Methodist
Episcopal Church—Illinois—Chicago—Biography. 7. Chicago
(Ill.)—Politics and government—To 1950. 8. Chicago (Ill.)—Politics
and government—1951– 9. Chicago (Ill.)—Race relations. 10. Chicago
(Ill.)—Biography. I. Title.

F548.9.N4D53 2010
270.092—dc22

[B]   2009047212

British Library Cataloging-in-Publication Data available

To
Nicole, Valerie, Christina, and Dennis Jr.
From
Your Very Proud Father

CONTENTS

PREFACE

This book reflects three major currents in the African American religious experi-ence. The first pertains to the historic role of black clergy initiatives and programs for black advancement. These normative expectations drive most assessments of the effectiveness of black preachers and parishioners and how well they served their surrounding communities. The second relates to the emancipatory ethos of the African Methodist Episcopal (AME) Church and its tradition and reputation for staunchly defending black people. This study examines the complicated forces that determined whether AME clergy and congregations met with either success or stale-mate in achieving liberationist objectives. The third refers to the development of the clergy/politician. While most observers applauded preachers' activities in innumer-able efforts to protect black human and civil rights, others eschewed the presence of men of the cloth in political office. In the late nineteenth and twentieth centuries, various black leaders believed that ministers who entered the rough-and-tumble of politics disrespected their sacred calling and compromised their independence.

During most of the twentieth century, Archibald J. Carey Sr. (1868–1931) and Archibald J. Carey Jr. (1908–81), father and son, stood in the public square as defenders of black civil rights, as political officeholders, and as AME clergy com-mitted to their denominational ethos of social activism. They thought that politics enhanced their ministerial effectiveness and enabled them to fight for better jobs, housing, and other amenities crucial to their churches and communities. They were practitioners of public theology, which approached church and civic affairs as inter-related spheres in which ministers pursued liberationist goals beneficial to the black population. Moreover, the Careys, both of whom were admirers of AME founder Richard Allen, emulated his espousal of Wesleyan social holiness, through which spiritual renewal among believers spilled over to efforts to renew society in the direction of equity and justice. To accomplish their aims, the Careys defined public theology as a praxis with politics at its core. They convinced their religious com-munities to empower them to bargain with white politicians. The give-and-take of political involvement placed the Careys in circumstances in which undesirable alliances and associations tainted their reputations. They thought, however, that these affiliations were both necessary and inescapable if they wanted to achieve a larger good for their communities. Their poor choice of allies and their pursuit of selfish goals at times undermined their efforts, but their accomplishments convinced them that public theology pursued through politics ultimately improved the condition of African Americans.

Numerous debts are owed to the archivists and librarians, interviewees, and scholars whose cooperation made this book possible. The staffs at the Chicago Historical Society, the Library of Congress Manuscript Division, the Dwight D. Eisenhower Library, and the Dirksen Congressional Center facilitated the research and made the work easier. The staffs at the Robert Woodruff Library at the Atlanta University Center, the Swarthmore College Library's Peace Collection, the John Hope and Aurelia Franklin Library at Fisk University, the Moorland-Spingarn Research Center at Howard University, and the Interlibrary Loan Department at Vanderbilt University also were very helpful. A Freedom of Information request to the FBI yielded important information. Interviews with the Careys' family members and associates played a crucial role in the research. I have received ongoing cooperation from Dr. Elizabeth Bishop Trussell and Dr. Dorothy E. Patton, the granddaughters of Bishop Archibald J. Carey Sr. and the nieces of Reverend Archibald J. Carey Jr. They gave informative interviews and shared valuable family memorabilia.

Colleagues in various disciplines read insightfully and critiqued rigorously the manuscript either wholly or in part. They include Kenneth M. Hamilton of Southern Methodist University, Reginald F. Hildebrand of the University of North Carolina, Chapel Hill, Annetta L. Gomez-Jefferson of the College of Wooster, Barbara Dianne Savage of the University of Pennsylvania, Hanes Walton of the University of Michigan, and Robert H. Reid Jr., the retired editor of the *Christian Recorder*. I am grateful to President Larry E. Rivers of Fort Valley State College, an accomplished historian, for inviting me to his institution to speak about the Careys as part of the John Davison Lecture Series in 2006. I received useful responses and critiques from this attentive audience. Two leaves from Vanderbilt University enabled me to conduct research and write, as did a Religious Institutions Sabbatical Grant provided by the Louisville Institute. I appreciate the generosity of both institutions.

My family remains an unfailing source of support and encouragement. Without Mary A. E. Dickerson, my wife and partner, this project would not have reached fruition. She provides stability, patience, and love, all of which are indispensable elements of any research and writing effort. My children, Nicole, Valerie, Christina, and Dennis Jr.; and my granddaughters, Melanie and Morgan, cheered the project in multiple ways. My mother, Oswanna Wheeler Dickerson, passed away on January 18, 2009, but before her serious illness, she read parts of the manuscript and validated what she recalled about the Careys. She also spoke on behalf of my late father,

Carl O. Dickerson. My brothers, Carl and James, were supportive, and our late brother, Dr. Charles E. Dickerson, my history professor, would share their pride. Craig Gill, editor-in-chief of the University Press of Mississippi, always believed in this project, and to him I owe a large debt. The shortcomings of the book, of course, are all mine.

AFRICAN AMERICAN
PREACHERS AND POLITICS

INTRODUCTION

In a 1932 memorial address about Bishop Archibald J. Carey Sr. (1868–1931), his Episcopal colleague and fellow Georgian, William A. Fountain Sr., commended the deceased prelate in the African Methodist Episcopal (AME) Church for his long career as an "evangelical preacher" and for his "unique position as a public officer who devoted himself wholeheartedly and unselfishly to the service of the public." Carey, Fountain said, "never feared taking a stand in church or state that he believed to be for the best interest of his racial group," adding that "the church loved him because he loved the church; the race loved him because he loved the race." Fountain also understood Carey's belief in politics as a means for clergy to advance the social and economic interests of their congregations and communities. Wesley J. Gaines, another Georgia-born bishop who knew Carey, had affirmed this view in an 1899 publication, *The Gospel Ministry*. Though Gaines admonished clergy against partisan affiliations, he observed that a minister "should be alive to what is transpiring around him, and interpret all events in light of divine revelation." Gaines continued, "Christ advocated the cause of universal liberty, and proclaimed with fiery denunciation against the hypocrisy of the ruling classes both in the church and in the state."[1]

William J. Walls, a bishop in the AME Zion Church who lived in Chicago, declared Archibald J. Carey Jr. (1908–81) an heir to the same commitment to ministry and politics that defined his father's career. In the aftermath of a 1949 battle for fair housing, Walls observed that the junior Carey had made a "great fight" for black advancement: "I know you now as never before in the light of your renowned father. Indeed his spirit is marching on in your honored self." Other contemporaries expressed similar sentiments about the younger Carey and his blended ministries in church and civic affairs. Daniel G. Hill, the dean of the divinity school at Howard University and a fellow AME, admired Carey's civil rights speech at a national GOP convention and hoped that Carey would "be spared for many years of usefulness and service to the AME Church and the community of city and nation." In 1961, a contributor to the *Christian Recorder* called Carey "the top civic leader of the world" and "one of the brilliant theological minds of the church."[2]

These comments demonstrate that leading clergy reached a consensus that political involvement was integral to ministry and necessary for effective church and community leadership. Moreover, Eric L. McDaniel has noted that "clergy facilitated the connection between religion and politics" and that pastors play "an integral role" in politicizing churches toward shared goals in achieving black advancement. These observations accurately describe the Careys.[3]

During the first three decades of the twentieth century, Archibald Carey Sr. became a significant figure in Chicago politics. He accepted appointive positions that opened municipal employment opportunities to local blacks. Moreover, his national visibility as a bishop in the AME Church made him a spokesman for the broader interests of black people. In succeeding decades, his son and namesake, also a pastor, achieved local and national elective and appointive offices. African Americans in Chicago and beyond credited the younger Carey with winning important gains for blacks in jobs and housing and praised his role in the criminal justice system. Both Careys pursued politics as intrinsic elements to their clerical responsibilities, moving easily from proclamations in the pulpit to public pronouncements on issues crucial to African American advancement.

When Richard Neuhaus published *The Naked Public Square: Religion and Democracy in America* (1979), he decried the exclusion of religious ideas in the making of public policy, noting that the seeming absence of Judeo-Christian perspectives in shaping public debate deprived the American body politic of valuable views that could enrich democratic discourse.[4] Neuhaus, however, neglected to point out that scholars of the African American experience had written numerous works about the crucial role of black preachers and black congregations in the struggle for civil rights and their influence on public policy. From Richard Allen, Absalom Jones, Henry Highland Garnet, and others in the late eighteenth and nineteenth centuries to Martin Luther King Jr., Jesse Jackson, Al Sharpton, and their contemporaries in the twentieth and twenty-first centuries, black clergy have long condemned the racial subjugation of African Americans and offered theological commentaries on civic justice and equality for this oppressed minority. Similarly, women such as Harriet Tubman, Sojourner Truth, Anna Arnold Hedgeman, Fanny Lou Hamer, among others, without the benefit of ordination but motivated by the same spiritual fervor as their male counterparts, pushed their religiously based activism to the forefront of the black freedom struggle. Black liberation was integral to the theology of these religious leaders and provided a core element of their civic consciousness. Through these themes, they denounced slavery, condemned segregation, and argued for the humanity of African Americans on both biblical and constitutional grounds. Black religious leaders thus have long provided important voices in civic discourse.[5]

David Howard-Pitney has classified black clergy who pursued public roles according to three categories. Those who believed in a "nation under God" contended that public issues should reflect theological and biblical principles. Members of the prophetic category evaluated public behavior in light of a "sacred ideal." A third group, called progressives, adopted perspectives and programs of liberal/left activists to change the subjugated situation of African Americans. Clergy are not limited to membership in only one of these categories but can combine elements of multiple perspectives. Whatever precise approach they followed, black clergy raised their voices in public places in behalf of the black communities and congregations they represented.[6]

Howard-Pitney's paradigms explain the blend of religion and politics in the careers of Archibald J. Carey Sr. and Archibald J. Carey Jr. Both Careys articulated views that generally combined elements of all three categories. Both believed that if American society adhered to biblical and constitutional principles, African Americans would become citizens fully free from discriminatory laws and practices that relegated them to second-class status. The Careys did not advocate a Christian commonwealth, where theology would replace civic discourse. Rather, they argued for the values of equity and justice that reflected biblical teachings and the equal rights rhetoric embedded in the Declaration of Independence and the Bill of Rights. Though they eschewed leftist ideology and socialistic solutions, they thought that vigorous federal intervention in state and local affairs was necessary to protect black civil rights. To understand the Careys and how they viewed the relationship between religion and politics, however, requires further explanation. A heritage of black political involvement during Reconstruction and its aftermath, the role of black clergy as race leaders, and the influence of the Social Gospel show why the Careys viewed their civic involvements as integral to their calling as African American clergy.

The enfranchisement of African Americans in the postbellum South brought blacks into the body politic. As they made the transition from chattel to citizens, former slaves cast ballots in the same southern states where they had previously been held in bondage. Combined with the right to vote was the opportunity to run for political office. Hence, black voters, often in coalition with transplanted northern whites and cooperative southern whites, either elected or caused the appointment of 1,465 fellow African Americans to local, state, and federal positions between 1866 and 1877. These black politicians came disproportionately from the military, missionary groups, and the ministry. Clergy comprised a minority among black politicians but constituted a significant segment of black civic leadership. In South Carolina, for example, 487 African Americans, including nearly 40 clergymen, held office during Reconstruction. Perhaps the most prominent among them was Richard H. Cain, the pastor of Emanuel AME Church in Charleston, who was elected to the U.S. House of Representatives and later to the bishopric.[7]

The disputed 1876 presidential election put Republican Rutherford B. Hayes into the White House with a commitment to withdraw the remaining federal troops from the former Confederacy. This symbolic gesture formally ended Reconstruction but did not immediately stop black political activity. Not until the spread of disenfranchisement and political violence in the 1890s and early 1900s did black voters and politicians disappear from the southern scene, as alliances with various partisan groups enabled blacks to maintain a presence in southern politics through the late nineteenth century.

Political activity, however, never proved a panacea for a peasant people recently manumitted from slavery. Black elected officials served their constituents by establishing public schools; addressing punitive penalties for debt, peonage, and vagrancy; and protecting African American civil rights. These leaders proved less effective in regulating matters pertaining to land redistribution, admonishing blacks about the dangers of the emerging crop lien system, and championing other labor concerns of their ex-slave constituents. Thomas Holt, a historian of South Carolina Reconstruction, has observed that black officeholders, including those who were clergy, failed to use their political power for the maximum benefit of the poor and landless. Similarly, Canter Brown Jr. has noted the political ineffectiveness of Florida's black politicians in the 1880s and 1890s. Factional fights and uneasy alliances with white Democrats and white Republicans limited the impact of black political activity. For example, one politician, George Washington Witherspoon, an unsuccessful GOP nominee for Congress in 1880 and an AME minister, "grappled with virtually insurmountable problems," according to Brown. "His own actions" subsequently "split the black community and undermined black and Republican political strength."[8]

When the Careys pursued ministry and politics, they embraced the model of the preacher/politician that Cain, Witherspoon, and others had embodied in the postbellum period. The uncertain legacies of these dual engagements, however, proved problematic. Church critics believed that politics compromised the clergy's moral and ministerial standing. Daniel A. Payne, the senior bishop of the AME Church, blamed clergy who were Reconstruction officeholders in the Carolinas and Georgia for inserting secular political practices into the proceedings of the denomination's 1880 General Conference, particularly targeting Cain. For this reason, Payne opposed Cain's election to the episcopacy. Witherspoon's activities drew derisive declarations from A. J. Kershaw, a fellow AME Church pastor, regarding the "dirty world of politics" that claimed so much of Witherspoon's energies. Each Carey received the same criticisms that Cain and Witherspoon encountered. They inherited both the paradigm and its problems.[9]

One problem pertained to black politicians' policies that favored elite African Americans under the guise of service to the peasant poor. Holt argues that the elevated class status of numerous black officeholders in South Carolina, for example, differed from the economic condition of the majority of their constituents. Hence, the initiatives that these politicians supported did not always address the electorate's core concerns. Moreover, some officials possessed skin privilege and leveraged their light complexion in intraracial settings as a sign of superiority and as a claim to African American leadership. As a result, most blacks found their interests poorly served because specific policies aimed at the black entrepreneurial elite superseded issues that would benefit the laboring class. Political ineptitude expressed in intraracial and interracial factional fights also limited efforts to improve the black masses' condition. Though the Careys chose politics as a means for more effective ministry, they built on a flawed foundation for dual religious and political leadership. Moreover, despite their altruistic desire to improve blacks' social and economic conditions, the Careys as officeholders yielded to alliances and compromises that had some injurious effects on African Americans. Though public square involvements were defensible and even desirable, holding public office at times led to ambiguous results. Moreover, the Careys were ambitious men. Sometimes they were more selfless than ambitious; at other times, they were more ambitious than selfless.

Southern white Democrats' return to power in the 1870s and 1880s and their successful crusade to disenfranchise black voters in the 1890s and early 1900s removed African American politicians from their important public role. Although a few late-nineteenth-century blacks received federal appointments—mainly from GOP presidents—and a scattering of others attained elective office in various states in the Northeast and the Midwest, the public voice of African Americans at the turn of the twentieth century increasingly came from new sources of leadership. Nonpolitical black clergy, editors, educators, physicians, and lawyers, in their status as an educated elite or the "talented tenth," articulated issues related to African American advancement. As race men and bourgeois black women, they became public advocates for black people.[10] Whether they were national figures such as Booker T. Washington, W. E. B. Du Bois, and Ida B. Wells or institutional leaders such as Robert S. Abbott, Alexander Walters, and Mary Church Terrell, they replaced black politicians as the principal spokespersons and brokers for African Americans. Though the Careys followed the model of the earlier preacher/politicians, they also adopted a role as race leaders who fought for the interests of blacks in the public square.

In addition, both Careys used the Social Gospel to enhance their public ministry. Though Walter Rauschenbusch, a Congregational clergyman, developed the idea of the Social Gospel in New England in the 1870s, key ministers and social settlement practitioners popularized it in Chicago. That churches should provide a variety of social services to the urban poor and industrial workers became a firm feature of numerous Chicago congregations, including Reverdy C. Ransom's Institutional Church and Social Settlement. Ransom, an experienced AME pastor, aligned with Graham Taylor, Jane Addams, and other Social Gospel and settlement house practitioners and served as a mentor to Monroe Work, Richard R. Wright Jr., and other black divinity students eager to learn this new form of ministry. The senior Carey, Ransom's contemporary and a fellow Chicago pastor, imitated him by adopting Social Gospel programs for his pastorates. Archibald J. Carey Jr. pursued similar ministries during the 1930s and 1940s. Both Careys found the Social Gospel to be compatible with their vision of their ministerial and political roles. Politics, the Careys believed, provided the means through which the Social Gospel could be advanced. They also believed that Social Gospel ministries made their churches attractive to black migrants newly arrived from the South. The Careys and other clergy thought that the availability of various social services would increase their church membership and provide them with enhanced political influence. They hoped that ministers' support would persuade newly enfranchised parishioners to vote for certain candidates.

The Careys had dual relationships with those who benefited from their political involvements. As church officials, the Careys drew support from their congregations, but as black community leaders they viewed their pastoral and political positions as intertwined. They mobilized ministers and members in their function as political activists, and these persons provided a reliable pool of people who endorsed the Careys' public stands and affirmed their authenticity as African American spokesmen. These grassroots supporters, specifically in black churches and generally in the black electorate, regularly validated the Careys' leadership.

The Careys, however, belonged to an elite. Family members maintained their fair complexion through careful choices in marriage partners, passing this physical attribute across the generations. But this seeming skin privilege, highly regarded by mulattoes and blacks alike, was not enough to sustain them in leadership positions. Their power derived from two interactive relationships. Their position as clergy in the AME Church, the oldest of Chicago's black denominations and one of the largest black religious bodies nationwide, provided the Careys with sizable support for their public stands; however, unlike professional black politicians, neither man could guarantee large groups of voters to either the Republicans or the Democrats. Nonetheless, their grounding in an influential black institution also made them attractive allies for white politicians eager for votes from whatever source. This reciprocity enabled the Careys to deliver a broad range of social and economic benefits to the city's black residents. Moreover, the Careys extended their involvement from this municipal base to state and federal affairs and thus became influential national leaders.

Despite similarities between the two Careys, they belonged to different generations and functioned as leaders in changing circumstances. Archibald Sr. was a part of a black elite born during the Civil War and Reconstruction era whose

members became spokespersons for African Americans at the turn of the twentieth century. These black professionals—doctors, lawyers, educators, editors, and
ministers—comprised what sociologist E. Franklin Frazier has called a "responsible
elite." These persons, "among the first generation of educated Negroes," according
to Frazier, "were products of missionary education." They "had a sense of responsibility toward the Negro masses and identified themselves with the struggles of the
masses to overcome the handicaps of ignorance and poverty."[11] These professionals
gained leadership and credibility from numerous institutions established to serve
African Americans. From their positions of power within these institutions, educated blacks became brokers for African Americans and interacted with influential
whites, articulating constituent's social, economic, and political interests.

This brokerage role, which this first generation of black leaders typified, defined
how Archibald J. Carey Sr. operated in the public sphere. Though black leaders
had previously derived their power from black voters, the demise of Reconstruction and the rise of disenfranchisement shifted African American leadership away
from southern black politicians to institutional leaders in religious, educational,
business, professional, and fraternal organizations. These black leaders negotiated
with whites, who ultimately decided what social and economic benefits African
Americans would receive. Hanes Walton, a scholar of the black political experience,
has argued that the senior Carey demonstrated how "community substantiated an
institutional base of followers to replace the voter base of followers that disappeared
with the coming of disenfranchisement."[12]

The next generation of black leaders, born in the 1890s and early 1900s, were
often scions of the earlier group of African American spokespersons, emulating
their predecessors' leadership strategies. In the 1930s and 1940s, having pursued the
same professions as their fathers, this second generation of black leaders, especially
clergy, used politics as a proxy for their Social Gospel commitments. When these
second-generation spokespersons witnessed the success of grassroots protest and
activism in pursuit of civil rights, they fully embraced these tactics and modified
their roles as brokers. Archibald J. Carey Jr. adapted himself to the increased reli-
ance on grassroots protest and mobilization that characterized strategies for black
advancement during his era. His endorsement of the March on Washington Movement and the Congress of Racial Equality (CORE) in the 1940s and his support
of the Southern Christian Leadership Conference (SCLC) in the 1950s and 1960s
marked his transition from brokerage leadership to a role as background benefactor
to grassroots black and interracial civil rights organizations.

The Careys thus combine to constitute a case study that delineates the history of clergy activists in the public square. The rationale for their civic careers
is reflected in Paul A. Djupe's and Christopher P. Gilbert's *The Prophetic Pulpit:
Clergy, Churches, and Communities in American Politics* (2003), which argues that

the pressing public issues that concerned congregations and communities pushed pastors toward extensive civic and political participation. The authors also ask hard questions about these preachers, declaring that "the mere finding that clergy are active in politics does not indicate for whose benefit the action is performed. Are clergy just one more vendor hawking ideological wares to a marketplace of citizens? Are they pursuing their own goals? Or are clergy acting in the interests of their congregations and communities? The answer matters and the truth is elusive, but asking the question is most important." Moreover, in "Theocratic, Prophetic, and Ecumenical: Political Roles of African American Clergy" (2001), Mary R. Sawyer contends that the overall history of slavery and segregation imposed on African Americans required a politicized clergy. Such ministers, Sawyer argues, operated in "a black religious tradition that holds as its ultimate values communalism, the welfare of the collectivity, the integral relation of the spiritual and the material, and the moral obligation to pursue social-political concretization of the theological principles of equality, justice, and inclusiveness." The Careys' careers illustrate all of these themes.[13]

Politicized black ministers also theologized their roles in the public square. The Careys, lifelong Wesleyan clergy, belonged to a historically black Methodist denomination. Embedded in this religious and racial heritage were two activist and complementary theologies. One was reflected in a pastoral paradigm surrounding "practical divinity" and the "new creation," both of which mandated their presence in the public square. "Practical divinity" required practitioners to actualize their religious commitment through activities that "help effect the love of God and neighbor." These endeavors offered visible evidence of the fruits of faith and sought to relieve the suffering of the poor, to achieve the manumission of slaves, and to meet the needs of the marginalized. The essence of Wesleyan theology lay in "transforming personal life and social relations." The "new creation" refers to God's will to renew humankind to conform to the image of the Creator. God's love is shown within humanity and spreads to all creation. This idea finds fruition in "a vocation or calling to which human beings are called" to "renew" creation. The renewal can be developed through efforts to serve and liberate the oppressed and disadvantaged, which helps to restore humankind to the perfect state in which it was created.[14]

The Careys understood this Wesleyan legacy through their embrace and emulation of Richard Allen, the founder of the African Methodist Episcopal Church, as their model minister. Allen developed an emancipationist ethos that included championing the manumission of slaves, giving assistance to escaping fugitives, and protecting the rights of free blacks. In *Black Theology and Black Power* (1969), James H. Cone, an AME minister and theologian, examines this black liberationist legacy, asserting that the ministry of Jesus "is essentially one of liberation" and that the "message" of empowerment is similarly derived from "Christ himself." Cone views

Allen as operating within this basic Christian and Wesleyan understanding of liberation. Hence, Cone contends, the rise of independent African American churches shows that blacks developed views about Christianity that differed from the views held by slave masters. In Cone's words, "As early as 1787 Richard Allen and his followers walked out of St. George Methodist Episcopal Church at Philadelphia because they refused to obey the dictates of white superiority."[15]

Wesley's "practical divinity" and the "new creation" were communicated to the Careys through Allen's emancipationist ministry. Moreover, Wesleyan and black liberationist theology, as realized in Allen's public ministry, justified and compelled the Carey's participation in politics and their involvement in civic affairs. These ideas also informed and shaped their espousal and practice of public theology. As AME clergy, the Careys did not separate the sacred and secular spheres in which they functioned. Each arena opened opportunities to defend the rights of blacks and to provide them with the same benefits of citizenship as all other Americans. In theologizing Allen and the emancipationist ethos that he exemplified through Wesleyan and black liberationist belief and practice, the Careys energized their public theology and aimed it at breaking barriers erected against African Americans.

A case study focused on the Careys will help scholars to address other issues relevant to understanding preacher/politicians in the African American context. That they have participated widely in civic affairs is not in dispute. Whether they have contributed a distinctive intellectual voice or a different analysis to public issues than have other advocates of black advancement deserves some exploration. Did their articulation of their theological perspectives simply attach religious nomenclature to existing rhetoric and ideas that condemned legalized racial discrimination and segregation, or did their sermons and speeches enrich, expand, and deepen discourse in the black freedom struggle? Did their biblically based ideas complement the political and constitutional arguments of other activists, or did black clergy in the public square redefine the intellectual context within which such ideas were advanced?

Despite their familiarity with the nomenclature of theology and their theologized understanding of their roles in the public square, the Careys did not bring added value to the rhetoric of civil rights. Their civic discourse drew on the same egalitarian language and constitutional vocabulary that shaped the speeches of their secular allies. Though they introduced biblical imagery and terminology and some scriptural references to their presentations on civil rights, the Careys generally did not say why their theological perspectives compelled their pursuit of equal and just treatment for African Americans. In a 1963 sermon, "A New Resource," Archibald J. Carey Jr. drew from Genesis 43:3, explicating, "Ye shall not see my face, except your brother be with you." In echoing his father, the younger Carey condemned racial discrimination and lauded the contributions of blacks to American society.

Yet it was important to recognize that black achievements in several fields made them "an untapped reservoir" for their nation's well-being. This sermon, like so many that both Careys delivered, did little to enhance civil rights rhetoric. The resources available in the emancipationist themes embedded in both Wesleyan and black liberationist theology did not inform Carey's pronouncements. Except for the biblical reference, Thurgood Marshall or Roy Wilkins could have delivered "A New Resource." The Careys did not fully integrate a compelling Wesleyan/black liberationist rhetoric into their sermons and speeches. Instead, these ideas became intrinsic to their public ministries and defined how they functioned in these roles.[16]

Also, did the roles of clergy/politicians change across the generations? When did strategies for social change move from elite leadership that emphasized brokerage roles to advocacy for grassroots mobilization and direct action protest? How did these changes affect clergy/politicians' behavior as political officeholders? Unlike other activists, clergy/politicians usually served two overlapping constituencies—their congregations and the larger communities that either elected or empowered them to hold political positions.[17]

Despite their denominational importance, the Careys could assist but could not completely deliver church constituencies to any individual politician or political machine. Professional black operatives, equipped with patronage and access to amenities for city residents, proved far more effective and influential than the Careys. In addition, political fissures among Chicago AMEs limited the political power of both Careys. Although their influence with some ministers and members provided them with high political standing, these alliances never supplanted the power of full-time black politicians who were prominent in GOP and Democratic Party machines.

Although African American operatives and officeholders wielded far more political control than the Careys, their ecclesiastical influence was hardly insignificant. Archibald Sr., a powerful AME official, was a dominant presence in Chicago church circles. Similarly, his son held two prominent pulpits and received several high-level solicitations to follow his father into the episcopacy. In their various ministerial offices, the Careys endorsed numerous candidates and commended them to voters both inside and outside their denomination. Precisely how many persons were persuaded by their political rhetoric cannot be determined. Nonetheless, white and black politicians viewed the Careys as valuable allies and believed that their support was indispensable. The question thus arises of just how effective the Careys were in translating their religious influence into political power and in becoming crucial players in public affairs. Did they attain either appointive or elected offices that realized their vision of public theology and delivered concrete benefits to their church and community constituents? Moreover, did the Careys ever permit personal ambition to undermine their altruism?

Though the term did not appear in scholars' vocabulary until after the Careys had spent decades as practiced exponents of public theology, they were serious and steadfast in their commitment to blending ministry and politics with the expectation that blacks would benefit. Only recently have African American scholars given a name to what both Careys embodied as Chicago clergy/politicians. Essentially, they were doing public theology. One scholar, Victor Anderson, has defined "public theology as the deliberate use of religious languages and commitments to influence substantive public discourse." In public theology, there is an articulation of "theological commitments to inform and influence substantive debate and policy." Moreover, public theology "emphasizes the use of religious resources for the advancement of moral and social discourse on public life." Anderson adds that a "viable public theology will not rest easy with any public/private distinction that might conceptually uncouple theological discourse from public discourse." For Anderson, there is no "private/public and world/church dualism."[18] The public theology that the Careys and other AME clergy espoused drew from an interpretation of Wesleyan theology that Allen transposed into a black liberationist praxis. His stand against slavery, colonization, and oppression of free blacks aimed to elevate African Americans' status. A century later, Allen's posture justified the civic involvements of both Careys. Though Allen's scattered writings never explicitly mentioned Wesleyan concepts, "practical divinity" surely shaped his ministry, and the "new creation" defined his goals as a Methodist preacher.

Though espousal of public theology served the Careys' personal aspirations for power and recognition, it also produced tangible social and economic advances for blacks. Ambition at times coalesced with the Careys' noble intentions with regard to their fellow African Americans. In other instances, however, both Careys focused solely on self-aggrandizement—for example, in 1928, when Bishop Carey put on a boastful display of his local influence at the AME's General Conference in Chicago, and in 1964, when his son was involved in seemingly duplicitous behavior toward Martin Luther King Jr. The Careys' shameless self-promotion showed how much they yearned for position and power even when it harmed their broader efforts to benefit the black population.

In addition, some contemporaries of the Careys did not endorse their political involvements and party affiliations. Though most African American clergy pursued civil rights advocacy as the essence of their public theology, the Careys believed that politics permitted them to better defend the black population. The Careys, notwithstanding their energetic protests and strong denunciations of racial discrimination and segregation, chose officeholding as their preferred public role. Scarcely any activist clergy were criticized for their presence in the public square as advocates for black civil rights. But the Careys, both of whom held various political positions, drew mixed assessments of their partisan affiliations. That they viewed public theology through the prism of politics won plaudits from some and condemnation from others.

For all of their assertions about their standing in municipal and national politics, just how significant were the Careys in the civic sphere? Despite his political versatility, the elder Carey was never more than a hired GOP spokesman and a minor official in Chicago politics. Other black loyalists in the city's various party organizations held major offices and wielded greater influence. In the 1910s, while he was a leading pastor and presiding elder, and in the 1920s as a bishop, Carey appeared more important in local politics than was actually the case. His presence in municipal affairs and his position on the local civil service commission, though important, did not mean that he was a major power broker in Big Bill Thompson's GOP machine. Like some other black politicos, Carey gained access to patronage positions that he dispensed to grateful blacks who may have had an exaggerated view of Carey's place within local government.

Archibald Jr., however, had broader political influence than his father. As an elected Chicago alderman and as a federal appointee, he had more authority and political autonomy than Bishop Carey ever achieved. In the late 1940s, the younger Carey sponsored an ill-fated ordinance to outlaw discrimination in public housing. As an appointee of President Dwight D. Eisenhower during the following decade, Carey had a substantive impact on black federal employment. Carey lacked the congressional power of his friendly rival, Adam Clayton Powell Jr., during the 1950s and 1960s, however, and could not overcome the ubiquitous presence of Democratic congressman William L. Dawson and his many minions on Chicago's South Side. They circumscribed Carey's political power and restricted what he could accomplish as a GOP loyalist.

As father and a son, the Careys were like few other clergy/politicians in the twentieth century. From their base in Chicago they exercised significant influence locally and at times nationally. Although their political involvements yielded successes that benefited blacks, their failures showed the limitations imposed on clergy/activists in the public square. Because Archibald J. Carey Sr. and Archibald J. Carey Jr. maintained a family ministerial tradition that stretched over four overlapping generations, their special contributions as clergy/politicians are crucial to understanding the American and African American religious experience. How their dual pursuits in ministry and politics mattered to the well-being of their congregational and community constituencies is the subject of this study.

CHAPTER I

Genesis in Georgia

THE CAREYS IN MINISTRY AND POLITICS

The blend of ministry and politics that defined the careers of Archibald J. Carey Sr. and Archibald J. Carey Jr. derived from earlier religious and political developments in the family's native state of Georgia. Aggressive ministers in the African Methodist Episcopal (AME) Church, especially in the late 1860s and 1870s, argued that newly freed slaves should join a black-controlled religious body. Because it recruited and evangelized thousands of Georgia's freed people, the AME Church became a major institutional presence in the state. Some of these same clergy believed that they should seek public office and use these positions to improve the condition of the African American population. Although their participation in Georgia politics declined after the 1870s, and only a few served in office after Reconstruction, the example of clergy/politicians in Georgia and in the South produced a paradigm that influenced the Careys.

The formal founding of the AME Church in Georgia derived from its initial affiliation with the South Carolina Annual Conference. In 1865, Bishop Daniel A. Payne arrived in Charleston with numerous northern and some southern ministers and launched the AME mission to former slaves. Although North Carolina, Georgia, and Florida started as jurisdictions within the South Carolina Annual Conference, blacks at several sites within these states already had withdrawn from the Methodist Episcopal Church, South and sought an AME affiliation. In Savannah, for example, blacks distanced themselves from white Wesleyan churches and presented themselves to a visiting AME missionary. William Gaines, a Georgian, traveled to South Carolina to receive ordination from Payne and then returned to Georgia and planted congregations in Macon, Atlanta, and Columbus. When

Gaines died in 1865, Henry M. Turner succeeded him as superintendent of the AME work in the state.[1]

Turner had been born free in South Carolina in 1834. He preached to slaves and free blacks as a Methodist Episcopal Church, South exhorter before entering the AME ministry in 1858. Pastorates in Baltimore and Washington, D.C., preceded his enlistment as the first black chaplain in the Union Army in 1863. His organization of AME congregations in Georgia after the war met with unusual success. The application of relaxed educational requirements allowed the appointment of pastors to a rapidly expanding number of churches, and having preachers in place further enhanced the recruitment of new members. Nationwide, the denomination had 50,000 members in the 1860s and six times as many by 1880. In Georgia, AMEs grew from no members in early 1865 to 29,071 in 1871. When Turner, who was elected to the episcopacy in 1880, returned to Georgia to preside as bishop from 1896 to 1908, he supervised 139,284 members in 919 congregations.[2]

Georgia separated from the South Carolina Annual Conference in 1868, when the first Georgia Annual Conference met at Macon. Rapid growth soon required the establishment of the North Georgia Annual Conference, which initially convened at Augusta in 1874. The Macon Georgia Annual Conference subsequently held its opening session in 1883 at Sandersville. The founding of these three jurisdictions testified to the efforts of Turner and other "Georgia Regulars," as the clergy were known, who developed their state as an AME bastion.[3]

Though Turner's reputation as an unusually effective evangelist reached legendary proportions, others played major roles in spreading the denomination statewide. In *African Methodism in the South* (1890), Turner's contemporary, Wesley J. Gaines, cited several ministers "who saw the rise of the AME Church in the South." Born during the antebellum period, most had been slaves; some, like Turner, had been exhorters in the Methodist Episcopal Church, South. Samuel Drayton, for example, had been a slave minister who "was regarded as one of the best preachers, white or colored, in the city of Augusta." Exhorter Andrew Brown joined the South Carolina Annual Conference before settling in Georgia. Although he was "not an educated man" and was "crude and unlettered," Brown "was filled with ripe judgment and the learning that comes from long experience and earnest endeavor."[4] Jefferson Alexander Carey Sr. and Jefferson Alexander Carey Jr. belonged to this first generation of Georgia AME preachers. Their important local and statewide involvements in the AME Church during the last three decades of the nineteenth century provided opportunities for Jefferson Alexander Carey Jr.'s son, Archibald J. Carey Sr., to develop ministries in religion and politics that affected black communities in the South and in the North.

The two Jefferson Careys had tilled the Georgia soil as slaves. They claimed to have seen General William Tecumseh Sherman and his Union soldiers "march[ing] through Georgia carrying news of Lincoln's Emancipation Proclamation." The Careys also claimed white ancestors with British origins, including Lord Fairfax, a protégé of George Washington, and Archibald Carey, a Briton.[5]

At the end of the Civil War, the Careys probably lived in the environs of Atlanta, where they appeared in the 1870 U.S. census. Jefferson A. Carey Sr.'s parents had been born in Maryland and probably had been sold south in the early nineteenth century, when Chesapeake slave masters found greater profit in slave trading than in farming in their region's exhausted soil. According to the 1870 census, Carey, age forty-five, was "black" and illiterate, and he operated a restaurant. His wife, Amanda, forty-two years old and also an ex-slave, was a housekeeper. Unlike her husband, she could read and write. Residing with them was a female relative, Rebecca Carey, age nine. Jefferson A. Carey Sr.'s two sons lived in the same neighborhood. Twenty-three-year-old Peter Carey worked as a cabinetmaker, while his brother, Jefferson A. Carey Jr., two years older, worked as a fireman station engineer and was recorded as black. His wife, Annie, was a twenty-one-year-old mulatto laundress. Their three children—Charlotte, age nine; Archibald, age three; and Emma, age six months—were classified as black. A decade later, the census listed Jefferson A. Carey Sr. as a driver. His household included his wife, Amanda; their son, Peter, now a grocer; Peter's wife, Ella; and five grandchildren.[6]

Neither of those censuses noted that Jefferson A. Carey Sr. had decided to be a preacher, but at some point he entered the AME ministry. He did not become an itinerant elder, a role that would have required pastoral assignments throughout the state. Instead, he was ordained as a local elder, attached to a specific congregation and subordinate to a local pastor. Although the name of Carey's congregation is unknown, he was listed on the 1886 roll of local elders in the North Georgia Annual Conference, a jurisdiction that covered Atlanta and adjacent areas stretching north to the Tennessee border. In the wake of his death on October 19, 1890, the North Georgia Annual Conference acknowledged his efforts.[7]

Jefferson A. Carey Jr. became more prominent in Georgia than his father. In 1890, Gaines included Jefferson Jr. on a long list of clergy "who have worked and fought the good fight for years." Carey's ministry started in 1873, when he was admitted on trial to the Georgia Annual Conference, and he was ordained as an itinerant deacon and elder in 1875. His election as a delegate from the North Georgia Annual Conference to the 1876 AME Church General Conference testified to his rapid rise through the ranks of Georgia clergy.[8]

For the rest of the decade, Carey, then in his twenties, was involved in an extensive itinerancy through various pastorates in Georgia. In 1878, Bishop Jabaz P. Campbell transferred Carey from the North Georgia Annual Conference to the Georgia Annual Conference, stationing him in Rome. Although his pastoral responsibilities took priority, Carey also participated in several denominational activities. During a pastoral assignment to the Marietta District in the North Georgia Conference, he served on the Sunday School Committee. While he was the pastor in Rome, he promoted the *Christian Recorder* and secured subscribers for the denomination's national newspaper.[9]

Carey thus became familiar among Georgia's AME congregations during the 1880s. His varying pastorates broadened his denominational interactions and put him in visible positions among his peers. At the 1882 Georgia Annual Conference in Thomasville, he was elected the post office messenger to handle various communications on behalf of Bishop William F. Dickerson and the delegates. In 1883, while Carey was serving as pastor of St. Thomas, in Thomasville, his Sunday school collected more money for missionary programs than any other Sunday school in the Georgia Annual Conference. Moreover, his presiding elder observed that the congregation "had been greatly built up by Elder Carey, both spiritually and financially"—including an impressive $1,265 in public offerings. Carey, three other ministers, and a layman also represented the Georgia Annual Conference at the 1883 commencement at the AME Church's Wilberforce University in Ohio. They spent a week on the campus and "decided that Wilberforce is the greatest enterprise owned by the colored people in the United States." They consequently urged Georgia's AMEs immediately to send money to the school.[10]

Before the end of the 1880s, Carey had attained first rank within the Georgia Regulars. At the 1886 North Georgia Annual Conference, the presiding elder of the Athens District praised Carey's pastorate at Washington, Georgia, as "a good work, spiritually and temporally." Moreover, "he has had quite a revival during the year and several persons have been added to the church." Carey's success with the 220 members at Washington led to a promotion to the First AME Church in Athens, a congregation with 350 members. He also played a major role at the 1886 North Georgia Annual Conference, participating in devotional services and accepting assignments on significant committees, including the Admissions Committee, which examined incoming ministerial candidates. Although the committee examined twenty-one persons in several subjects, including theology, history, and AME Church polity, only seven were recommended for admission to the annual conference. Bishop James A. Shorter appointed Carey and four other ministers to investigate sensitive allegations concerning the misconduct of a leading pastor. Carey also retained his position as a Georgia representative on Wilberforce's board of trustees. Moreover, his steadily rising stature assured his election as a delegate from the North Georgia Annual Conference to the 1888 General Conference, held in Indianapolis.[11]

At the 1889 North Georgia Annual Conference, Carey was transferred to the Macon Georgia Annual Conference. When Carey arrived at Milledgeville's Wesley Chapel AME Church, Gaines introduced Carey and provided him with an official seat. Gaines then appointed Carey to the congregation at Americus. In 1892, Bishop Abram Grant transferred J. A. Carey Jr. back to the North Georgia Annual Conference, assigning him to a pastorate on the Thomasville Circuit. Turner later moved Carey to the Alabama Annual Conference and stationed him at Mount Zion Church in Clio.[12]

Jefferson Carey Jr. may have had mixed feelings about his transfer out of the North Georgia Annual Conference. Just as he ended his service in this diocese, his son, Archibald J. Carey, was admitted as a ministerial candidate. Jefferson Sr. had greatly aided his son's ministry and his grandson's rearing. While Jefferson Jr. traveled, Jefferson Sr. oversaw Archibald's upbringing in Atlanta, and both father and grandfather were proud in 1888 when Archibald graduated from Atlanta University, a school with ties to the Freedmen's Bureau and the Congregational Church that had been founded in 1865 by the American Missionary Association. Jefferson Carey Jr. had already established his family's importance among AMEs statewide. On June 18, 1885, after the death of his first wife, Annie, Carey married Alice Dugged, a Michigan native and a Wilberforce graduate, who had been serving as assistant principal of a high school in Kansas City, Missouri. In 1886, she became the principal of Morris Brown College, the flagship school among Georgia AMEs, further increasing the family's prominence in church and educational circles. By the end of the 1880s, three generations of Careys—Jefferson Sr., a local elder; Jefferson Jr., an itinerant elder; and Archibald, a licentiate—appeared on the ministerial rosters of Georgia's annual conferences. Years later, Archibald "spoke tenderly" about his grandfather and father and their fifty years of ministry in their native state. The Careys and African Methodism in Georgia had become synonymous.[13]

Archibald J. Carey was one of a few educated ministers in the Sixth Episcopal District and hence rose rapidly, gaining a pastorate in 1890 and becoming his father's ministerial colleague in the North Georgia Annual Conference. Archibald Carey's growing importance in the North Georgia Annual Conference stemmed from his unusual success in developing Athens's Bethel AME Church into a thriving congregation. In November 1892, months before Carey made his annual conference report, presiding elder Joseph S. Flipper, also an Atlanta University graduate, lauded Carey's accomplishments: reports at the quarterly conference "were good and evinced the great work which had been done by the pastor and people." A few months later, Flipper noted that "all reports were better than [the] last [quarterly] conference": two members had joined, and one person had been licensed to preach. Flipper was similarly effusive in his praise of Carey at the June 1893 quarterly conference, when once again, "all reports were ahead of the [previous] conference"—Bethel had a further twenty new members and thirty-four probationers. "This church," Flipper said, "has been greatly revived and under Rev. Carey has doubled its members." By the

1893 North Georgia Annual Conference, Flipper declared that Bethel's membership had grown from eighteen to sixty-three over the preceding year.[14]

Carey's achievements at Athens led church leaders to accord him great visibility at the 1893 meeting. Bishop Grant called on Carey and another minister to respond to three speeches delivered by representatives of the Convention of Christian Workers. Carey also helped to draft a resolution that praised Bishop Thomas M. D. Ward for visiting the North Georgia Annual Conference and was also named a ministerial trustee for Morris Brown College and assigned to preach to the host congregation.[15]

Carey's steady rise in the ministry was confirmed when Bethel was chosen to host the 1894 North Georgia Annual Conference, earning the honor over the First Church, the city's older and larger AME congregation. This coup put Carey at the center of the conference proceedings and enhanced his stature among his pastoral peers. Carey's presiding elder reported that everything at Bethel "is in good condition [and that] several souls had been added," and Carey received further praise because he had "succeeded grandly" at the church. Moreover, "when he took charge of the work the membership was very small and they were worshipping in an old dilapidated dwelling house, but by hard work he, with his small band of noble workers, has given us this beautiful structure in which we are now holding the annual conference." Carey, the presiding elder said, "has the respect and love of his people."[16]

In addition to the hosting responsibilities, Carey performed several supportive but significant duties during the 1894 North Georgia Annual Conference. He assisted in the ordination of new clergy and examined candidates on their suitability for ministry. He also served on a committee that recommended support for Morris Brown College, for Ohio's Payne Theological Seminary, and for a ministerial student at Wilberforce University.[17]

In addition to his pastoral duties, Carey worked as a principal at Athens's Broad Street School. In this capacity, he saluted the "great work" the AME Church was doing "for God and for the race." Carey believed that his educational efforts complemented the denomination's attempts to train "youthful minds to grapple with the knotty problems of life."[18]

In 1894, pastoral term limits ended Carey's tenure at Bethel. As he prepared to transfer to the East Florida Annual Conference, the *Christian Recorder* declared that "Dr. Carey is a representative young man and he will be greatly missed [in Georgia]." He was described as "talented and scholarly, full of burning zeal for his Church, wrapped up in the Holy Ghost, ever on the alert to do what he can to push forward the cause in which he is engaged, Hence, he will hardly fail in having success wherever he goes." Moreover, Carey was known as "the best extempore speaker" in the North Georgia Annual Conference.[19]

All three generations of Carey clergy in Georgia believed that providing spiritual nurturance to their members was the purpose of their preaching and was central to their clerical leadership. Their ministries, however, developed in the context of Reconstruction and its aftermath, when politics affected how African American preachers envisaged and pursued their ministry. Blacks believed that Reconstruction reforms promoting African American political involvement would improve their social and economic condition. Both whites and blacks who sought the votes of the freed people promised land reform, publicly funded education, and protection of civil rights. Southern white Democrats, whether under the sympathetic policies of President Andrew Johnson or while subject to the punitive initiatives of Congress's Radical Republicans, nevertheless remained important players in state politics. In some states, their strategies brought them back to power before the end of the 1860s, but in the Carolinas, Florida, and Louisiana, Reconstruction lasted until 1876. Though blacks remained at least technically eligible to vote and hold office, violence, political chicanery, and fraud diminished their numbers until the disenfranchisement campaigns of the 1890s and early 1900s removed them from the body politic. Between 1865 and 1877, according to Eric Foner, "around 2,000 black men had held federal, state, and local public offices, ranging from members of Congress to justice of the peace."[20]

In 1871, the Redeemers (white Democrats) retook control of the Georgia government as a consequence of division and ineptitude within the state GOP. The fragile coalition between blacks and yeoman whites that held together the Georgia Republican Party depended on an electorate that included roughly the same number of whites and blacks. In 1867, Georgia had 95,214 whites and 93,457 blacks registered to vote. Although African Americans were numerically significant, they could not pursue any political objectives that whites opposed. Democrats exploited the Republican divisions and pushed through an initiative to expel blacks from both houses of the state legislature. The incompetence of GOP leaders and the questionable stance of Republican governor Rufus Bullock demonstrated whites' lack of support for Georgia's black population, laying the groundwork for the Democrats' 1871 political triumph. The state's Democratic Party subsequently developed as "a coalition tied together by determination to maintain white supremacy and never again to allow the state to fall prey to Republican rule." Ultimately, "the one issue on which all could agree was race solidarity."[21]

Among the 2,000 Reconstruction-era southern black officeholders were 237 clergymen, including 55 Baptists and 53 AMEs. In Georgia, 108 blacks held public office, many of them ministers and nearly a dozen of them AME clergy. Henry M. Turner, for example, helped to establish the Georgia Republican Party in 1867 and attended the state constitutional convention. He was elected to the state legislature in 1868 but was ultimately expelled along with 23 other black colleagues. He became

Macon's postmaster in 1869, before the U.S. Congress restored him to his seat, and he served again in 1871, initially winning reelection before a recount denied him the legislative post.[22]

Other Georgia AME ministers who embraced the preacher/politician role included Isaac Anderson and Thomas Crayton, who served as state senators in 1870. J. Brown sat in the Georgia House of Representatives in 1871. Among the state constitutional convention delegates during 1867–68 were Robert Crumley, Jesse Dinkins, William Noble, and John Whitaker. William Finch joined the Atlanta City Council in 1870, and T. G. Steward served from 1871 to 1873 on the state GOP central committee.[23]

After the disputed 1876 presidential election, in which Republican Rutherford B. Hayes gained the nation's highest office after agreeing to withdraw the remaining federal troops from the former Confederacy, Redeemers officially had regained control of southern state governments. Georgia's dormant GOP was not revived until 1880, when the Republican state convention in Atlanta included about a dozen African American participants. The presence of a Republican in the White House did not provide Georgia blacks with much in the way of federal appointments in the early 1880s, although African Americans did serve as collector of the Port of Savannah, in a few post office positions, and as deputy U.S. marshals. AME clergyman William H. Heard and a few other ministers continued as political players. In 1906, blacks were officially disenfranchised.[24]

But black preachers had established an important precedent. Ministry meant involvement in public affairs, and politics thus became a part of a preacher's pastoral portfolio. The social, political, and economic condition of newly emancipated African Americans compelled clergy to think of politics as a means to improve the material circumstances of their communicants and their communities. What would later become known as public theology defined such minister's activities. In addition, all AME clergy, including the three members of the Carey family, participated in celebrations of Richard Allen's birth and his founding of African Methodism, helping to provide them with an understanding of public theology that embraced the Wesleyan and black liberationist themes salient in Allen's life and ministry. These beliefs invigorated the holistic service that the Careys offered to both church and community.

Archibald Carey later dated his attraction to politics to his service as a ten-year-old as secretary of an Atlanta Republican group headed by his father. The examples of both his father and Turner provided the boy with a grounding in African Methodism as his denominational choice and in the GOP as his preferred political party. While still in Georgia, he honed his skills "in carrying the Negro vote to the republican party," gaining a reputation for fighting "with southern whites about the citizenship and voting rights" of African Americans.[25]

In addition to learning to negotiate the white political power structure, both Jefferson Carey Jr. and his son learned to wend their way through their church's infrastructure. Landing favorable pastoral assignments took a combination of merit, political savvy, and productive interactions with bishops, presiding elders, and other pastors. Hence, the Careys became adept at choosing the correct factions and forged the alliances that would enable them to succeed in the complicated AME system. These skills carried over to secular politics, which featured many of the same characteristics that existed in African Methodism. Hence, their experiences in church politics prepared them for the civic arena and aided their efforts to pursue their public theology objectives.

Archibald J. Carey later referred to Turner as a man whose leadership "was Gladstonian in character" and who was a "statesman in the largest, the broadest and highest conception of the term." Jefferson Carey Jr. and Madison Davis, Archibald's father-in-law, were similarly influential in Carey's growing commitment to public affairs. Born in 1833 in Athens, Georgia, Davis worked as a slave in a carriage factory. A mulatto, like Turner and the Careys, Davis was a delegate to a convention of blacks in 1866 and was elected to the Georgia House of Representatives in 1868. Although Turner and other African American legislators were expelled, the light-skinned Davis avoided this fate by claiming to be white. Despite denunciations of racial "treason," blacks strongly supported his reelection in 1870. President James A. Garfield appointed Davis to serve as U.S. surveyor of customs in Atlanta, and he chaired the executive committee of the Clarke County Republican Party. Although his 1882 support of a Democrat for Congress led to his dismissal from office, Davis bounced back, serving as Athens's postmaster from 1882 to 1886 and from 1890 to 1893. In 1890, Carey married Davis's daughter, Elizabeth, whom he had met at Atlanta University, and accepted an Athens pastorate. Given his political standing, Madison Davis was probably instrumental in Carey's appointment as principal at the city's Broad Street School.[26]

When he was transferred to Jacksonville, Florida, in 1894, twenty-six-year-old Archibald Carey had already established himself as a proficient pastor, principal, and political operative. His time at the East Florida Annual Conference's Mt. Zion AME Church further enhanced his preaching, pedagogical, and political abilities. Soon after taking over at his new pastorate, a report declared that he seemed "to have been called of God to this charge." Similar sentiments were expressed about his presence in the city. "Elder Carey," said one observer, "is now pressing the fight along all lines wherein the race in general, and African Methodism in particular are to be benefited."[27]

Carey's Jacksonville congregation was roughly ten times the size of his Athens church, and the Mt. Zion parishioners included some of the city's "most progressive and wealthiest" people—clerks, managers, merchants, government officials, artisans, and professionals in medicine, law, and education. They mingled with common laborers so that "a little of everything may be seen around [the Mt. Zion] communion table." By 1897, although the congregation still had significant debts, Carey had apparently added more than two hundred people to the church, and the congregation and the surrounding community seemed very pleased with him as pastor.[28]

When Bishop Wesley J. Gaines announced Carey's reappointment to Mt. Zion at the 1898 East Florida Annual Conference, "the house fairly shook with approval." A correspondent to the *Christian Recorder* described Carey as "a popular man," "of broad culture and . . . one of nature's noble men." He is a "most affable, polished and scholarly gentleman." Finally, Carey "would make a most excellent Presiding Officer for an annual conference."[29]

Carey's extensive involvement with other AME clergy and churches included an article he contributed to the *Christian Recorder* about the 1896 Jacksonville District Conference. He praised the presiding elder's annual address as "every way characteristic of the man—pointed, pithy, humorous and profound, abounding in metaphor and metonomy." His rulings were "fair and impartial." The district's future, therefore, remained "brighter than ever." At the 1897 Lake City District Conference, the presiding elder invited visiting clergy from other denominations to speak, with Carey and three other AME ministers offering "spirited responses." At the Lake City District Sunday School Convention, Carey preached an educational sermon on "The Faithful Utterance of the Divine Word," reserving most of his comments for an independent church movement that probably had started among dissident AMEs and dealing it "a blow that it [could] never outlive." He commended this religious body for its large congregation and headquarters in Lake City, but "hot and terrible thunderbolts of facts and truths let loose from his eloquent lips," and Carey "proved himself to be beyond a doubt a pulpit orator."[30]

In addition to his pastoral and district activities, Carey served as president of Jacksonville's Edward Waters College, the flagship school among Florida AMEs, in 1895. Since ministerial training was included in the school's educational mission, Carey's association with Edward Waters further increased his profile among the state's AME clergy, making the family name as well known in Florida as in Georgia.[31]

Nearing age thirty, Carey increasingly found himself associated with AME bishops and other persons of standing, marking him as a rising star in the national church. Hosting the East Florida Annual Conference or visiting dignitaries, Carey behaved as a "Chesterfield of Christian courtesy." T. W. Henderson, the business manager of the denomination's publication board in Philadelphia, visited Jacksonville and identified Carey as one of the ministers who had treated him well. Gaines and five general officers dined at Carey's residence and received "a most magnificent dinner at which all those present "felt like abiding around his hospitable home for a longer time than circumstances would admit." Carey assisted Bishop James C. Embry in promoting the *District Messenger*, a publication produced in Embry's South Carolina district.[32] These gestures cemented Carey's relationships with denominational dignitaries, who concluded that Carey's help and hospitality meant he wanted to be their peer and perhaps a prelate in the AME Church.

Politics, however, remained a significant part of Carey's ministry. He continued to campaign on behalf of the Republican Party in Florida. During the 1896 presidential election, Carey supported William McKinley, and they became friends. Carey's ability to mobilize black voters drew McKinley's attention and showed that the AME minister was a skilled political operative, and the two men continued their association until McKinley's assassination in 1901.[33]

During his time in Georgia and Florida, Carey always saw politics as secondary to his role as a minister to his congregants. Nonetheless, Carey's political involvements became integral to his ministry. Although parish and denominational duties claimed most of his time and energies, the mobilization of black voters and support for the GOP became intrinsic to his pastoral profile. Though the legal disenfranchisement of southern black voters did not culminate until after Carey left the region, his experiences as a preacher/politician prepared him for a broader role in Chicago politics.

Archibald Carey's son continued this family legacy of public theology pursued through politics and civil rights activism. Archibald Carey Jr. later traced his activities in Chicago not only to his father's example but also to the two Jefferson Careys in Georgia and their long ministerial service as preachers, pastors, and presiding elders. They were involved in "marrying the living, burying the dead, ministering to the sick and crying in the wilderness, like John the Baptist—'Repent ye for the kingdom of heaven is at hand. Prepare ye the way of the Lord, making His paths straight.'" Archibald Carey Jr. also recognized his grandfather's and great-grandfather's role as freedom fighters: "My grandfather was a boy in the fields of Georgia beside his father—both of them slaves and both of them plowing when [General] Sherman came thru on his march from Atlanta to the sea. And my great grandfather cried to my grandfather, [saying] 'Son, drop your plow and grab a gun. Let no one win your freedom for you. We'll win it for ourselves'—and together they marched with Sherman to the sea." Archibald Carey Jr. thus saw his participation in the 1965 voting rights march from Selma to Montgomery as completing the march the two Jefferson Careys had "started 100 years ago."[34]

CHAPTER 2

Pulpit and Politics
in Chicago

THE MINISTRY OF ARCHIBALD J. CAREY SR.

Thirty-year-old Archibald J. Carey arrived in Chicago in 1898 familiar with politics and power players in both church and state. In this dynamic Midwest metropolis, however, he learned that although clergy had long been active in public affairs, they had never possessed any "divine right" to leadership and influence among African Americans. Hence, Carey competed with a rising class of professional black politicians, rival ministers, female leaders, and others. These various African American leaders at times espoused different racial ideologies, while at other times they shared similar views but clashed on matters of temperament and style. Despite the diversity among Chicago's black leaders, ministers remained crucial spokespersons whose perspectives, programs, and political activities improved African Americans' lives.[1]

The city's black population grew as a consequence of a steady stream of migrants coming from the American South. In 1900, Chicago had 30,150 black residents (1.8 percent of the total); ten years later, that number had increased only slightly, to 44,103 (2 percent). The Great Migration during the World War I era, however, pushed the African American populace to 109,594 (4.1 percent) in 1920 and to 233,903 (6.9 percent) in 1930.[2] Leaders competed to serve and speak for this new class of industrial workers. Though public theology continued to shape his ministry and Carey remained committed to politics, he blended it with Social Gospel, self-help, and civil rights agitation.

Carey, ambitious and competitive, became one of Chicago's best-known pastors, and his public involvements and pastoral influence drew him into the thicket of city politics. Nevertheless, his political role relied on whatever powers white allies yielded to him. Carey received only minor and symbolic appointments as rewards for campaigning for white candidates, and these offices were less influential than those professional black politicians received.

Carey served as pastor at three congregations in the Iowa Annual Conference, of which Chicago was a part—the Quinn Chapel, Bethel, and Institutional Churches. All three grew substantially under Carey's stewardship, primarily because of the mushrooming of the city's black population, although Baptist and Pentecostal churches generally outdistanced the African Methodist Episcopal (AME) congregations in attracting southern black migrants. According to historian Wallace D. Best, the formality of AME Church worship and its stress on hymns and anthems proved less appealing than the emotional spontaneity and the singing of the gospel blues that occurred in Baptist and Pentecostal churches and storefronts. Carey, however, resisted this trend. Though he was identified with the city's light-skinned elite and Quinn Chapel had a reputation as a high-toned church that did not cater to the common people, Carey was an unapologetic southerner whose preaching style reflected his Georgia background. That hundreds flocked to the three churches that he served showed his effectiveness in reaching newly arrived migrants. These abilities enhanced his influence and visibility in AME Church circles and provided a foundation for his political activities on the city's South Side.[3]

Founded in 1847, the spacious and prestigious Quinn Chapel AME Church was Chicago's oldest black church. Its pulpit provided Carey with early opportunities to become a prominent denominational leader and an influential political spokesman. Two decades after his arrival, a contemporary observed that Carey had emerged as "a 'fighting parson,' not in military [affairs] but in civil life where his fight for the race in the pulpit and on the public rostrum is one grand chapter in Chicago life."[4]

Quinn Chapel stood with Bethel AME Church and Olivet Baptist Church as Chicago's leading African American congregations. In 1889, the Reverend John T. Jenifer had led Quinn Chapel to build a magnificent edifice at Twenty-fourth and Wabash. Finished in 1893 at a cost of fifty-five thousand dollars, the church added a pipe organ, stained glass windows, and other expensive fixtures over the rest of the decade. The resulting debts were so onerous that in 1898 the church faced foreclosure on its mortgage. Bishop Benjamin W. Arnett, a former Florida bishop and now the prelate in Chicago, drew Carey from his Jacksonville pastorate to rescue Quinn Chapel from financial ruin.[5]

Carey arrived to find his new congregation forty-eight thousand dollars in debt and quickly mobilized members to pay off that sum. He also attracted eighteen thousand dollars from Chicago's moneyed business and civic leaders, including

Philip D. Armour, Gustavus F. Swift, Cyrus McCormick, H. H. Kohlstaat, William Hale Thompson, and the Blackstone family. Carey also raised funds to renovate the sanctuary, install electricity, and make other purchases to enhance the structure.[6]

Carey "was a stormy preacher," according to one contemporary. When he preached, "his face became as red as a beet, the veins and arteries of his neck and throat seemed ready to burst, and the people often shouted uproariously." This pulpit style apparently helped Carey fill Quinn Chapel's sanctuary and balcony during both morning and evening services. One commentator said that Carey added 1,200 new members to the church rolls, while another put that number at 1,562. These members became intensely loyal to Carey. After he delivered his report and a sermon at the 1900 annual conference in Minneapolis, his "people came out to know if they would get their popular preacher back." Not surprisingly, Bishop Abram Grant reappointed Carey to the Chicago church, where he continued his successful financial and evangelical efforts.[7]

In 1904, Carey moved to Chicago's Bethel AME Church, remaining there through 1909. During his tenure, Carey led the congregation in retiring a fifteen-thousand-dollar mortgage, doing so "with such ease that some of the members characterized the doctor's efforts as a man with a modern touch of gold." When pastoral term limits mandated Carey's departure from Bethel, "great pressure [was] brought to bear to keep him in Chicago as the members of his congregation [thought] highly of him." His bishop subsequently sent him to the city's Institutional AME Church, where he stayed until 1918. Established in 1900 by Reverdy C. Ransom, this church emphasized social service rather than building a large membership—in the words of one contemporary, it tried to "help the community in practical daily living." The *New York Age*, a national black weekly, reported in 1909 that the parish had "peculiar promise" but had "never yet realized the high purposes of its origin. It has been handicapped from the beginning by lack of members." Too little support and encouragement from other AME clergy and congregations bore part of the blame. While committed to Institutional's original mission, Carey drew on his reputation as a popular preacher to build the membership. One 1915 Carey sermon, "God's New Year," provided so much comfort "to the storm beaten soul" that 5 people joined the church, raising the number of people that Carey had brought into the church to 503. One supporter declared that "never was there greater enthusiasm on the part of the members than now. The older members are coming to the front and the new ones are falling in line beautifully." In 1916, Carey delivered a series of sermons on "Vision and Power" that attracted a "large attendance" despite bad weather. It became conventional wisdom that "Dr. Carey's well known eloquence and earnestness will make the Institutional Church one of the most desirable places to worship in all Chicago." On one Sunday in 1918, "seating capacity was truly at a premium at both services," and 20 people joined, resulting in "universal rejoicing."

To supplement his sermons, Carey hired Marie Burton Hyrams, a talented vocalist, as music director. Her arrival "promise[d] to give Institutional one of the very best choirs Chicago ever had." Over time, these developments drew a thousand new members to the Institutional Church and solidified Carey's standing as the city's leading AME preacher.[8]

In 1918, the Chicago Annual Conference (formerly the Iowa Annual Conference) and the Institutional Church celebrated Carey's two decades in the city with a "magnificent banquet and testimonial" held during the annual meeting. Program participants recounted how Carey had "saved Quinn Chapel from sheriff's sale, rescued Bethel from mortgage foreclosure, brought the Institutional Church to one of the most substantial congregations in the city, and labored in every line for the improvement and betterment of the people."[9]

The honors coincided with Bishop Levi J. Coppin's decision to pull Carey out of the pastorate and to appoint him as presiding elder of the Chicago District in the Chicago Annual Conference, a position in which he would report to the bishop on the condition of several local churches. The Hyde Park AME Church, led by Pastor W. H. Griffin, had a "beautiful new church building" that was "crowded to overflowing" when Carey came to preside at the quarterly conference. Under the Reverend H. E. Stewart, Carey reported, Quinn Chapel hosted a quarterly conference that was "one of the greatest in all Quinn's glorious history." Carey, in turn, received glowing reports from those he supervised. In Stewart and Carey, according to one commentator, Coppin had "given the Chicago district and Quinn Chapel two of the most all around and strongest men in the connection—a team that cannot be beaten." Carey's superiors agreed. After a 1919 meeting cohosted by Carey, Coppin remarked that "the bishops are highly pleased over the work of Dr. Carey as presiding elder. His success is being heralded all over the connection." Moreover, "the Chicago district has taken on new life." During Carey's service as presiding elder, which lasted until 1920, the district purchased more than one hundred thousand dollars in church property. On one occasion, Carey and Coppin attended the dedication of Wayman Chapel AME Church's new building on the city's North Side, a stately former Swedish church with an attached three-story residence for the pastor.[10]

Walter Rauschenbusch and other Social Gospel advocates in the late nineteenth century challenged churches to address the effects of urbanization and industrialization on immigrants, the poor, and others in the working class. Their clarion call influenced numerous clergy and congregations throughout the nation, including Carey. His embrace of the Social Gospel enhanced his profile as a modern urban clergyman attuned to the needs of recent black migrants to Chicago.

Like other black ministers and their churches, especially those of the Episcopal, Presbyterian, and Congregational denominations, Carey helped to institute broad social service programs. Some churches built special facilities to serve the poor and neglected. In 1895, Hutchens Chew Bishop of New York City's St. Philip Episcopal Church initiated a broad range of athletic activities and located them in a newly constructed parish house. During the same decade, Philadelphia's Berean Presbyterian Church provided industrial training, an employment bureau, and a clinic for the city's growing black community. Just after the turn of the century, Hugh H. Proctor at the First Congregational Church in Atlanta developed an extensive outreach to disadvantaged blacks through a workingmen's club, a women's aid organization, and other groups.[11]

Reverdy C. Ransom introduced the Social Gospel to the AME Church in 1900, gaining permission to leave his pastorate at Bethel AME Church in Chicago to found the Institutional Church and Social Settlement. Bishop Benjamin W. Arnett authorized Ransom to solicit thirty-four thousand dollars from the denomination's financial secretary to purchase the spacious Railroad Chapel to house the new venture. There, according to Ransom, "men and women met for the betterment of humanity and the uplifting of their race." Along with a Sunday school, Ransom and his wife, Emma, started the Men's Forum, the Woman's Club, a nursery, and a kindergarten. Moreover, Jane Addams, Graham Taylor, and Mary McDowell, all prominent Chicagoans in the social settlement movement, became conspicuous supporters of the Institutional Church.[12]

Ransom and other black ministers committed themselves to Social Gospel ministries because black folk religion, while reflective of African American culture, did not address the concrete challenges of work, housing, health, and maintaining strong family structures. Though W. E. B. Du Bois had praised black religion for its spiritual depth and theological insights, he also acknowledged that blacks needed to understand the realities of the new industrial age.[13] Moreover, a Social Gospel emphasis could attract the working class because of the sundry services it offered and could satisfy the elite, who preferred to hear sermons about practical issues rather than the emotional and otherworldly preaching that emanated from many African American pulpits. Ransom developed this ministerial methodology among Chicago AMEs, and Carey emulated his rival in this pastoral pursuit.

Although Carey came to Chicago believing that political involvement could enhance his ministry, Ransom's Social Gospel initiatives pressured Carey to commit, at least in principle, to a new vision of his clerical role. In truth, political and Social Gospel activities complemented each other, since both sought to improve the condition of working-class blacks. Political involvement promised neighborhood improvements and other benefits from the municipal government, while the Social Gospel addressed specific concerns in employment, women's issues, and child care. Ransom, too, blended both approaches, working with Chicago politicians and later running for Congress from New York City in addition to developing Social Gospel programs in those two cities.[14]

Ransom and Carey were rivals, and their political and Social Gospel activities must be understood in that context. Ransom became prominent in Chicago before Carey's arrival. His pastorate at Bethel operated a much-admired kindergarten and "industrial school for children" and had a dozen deaconesses who canvassed the area "seeking strangers, visiting the sick and feeding, clothing and making warm the poor and needy." According to journalist Ida B. Wells-Barnett, Ransom "elevated the tone of the African Methodist pulpit, and a deeper, truer, more satisfactory spiritual life has resulted."[15]

In Ransom's view, Carey was jealous. "I was already established when he came to the city," Ransom recollected, and Carey "had not been there long before he sought to displace me in some of the honors and influence I had achieved." Ransom, who had come to the Windy City two years earlier, claimed that he had befriended his younger colleague and offered to tutor him in local political affairs. Carey, however, immediately entered politics and attempted to undermine Ransom's preaching popularity. Carey and A. L. Murray, the new Bethel pastor, convinced Bishop Grant to confine Institutional's worship services to Sunday evening, thereby preventing Ransom from drawing parishioners away from Murray's Sunday morning services. An outraged Henry M. Turner, the denomination's senior bishop, authorized Ransom to resume preaching at morning services and to ignore the petty opposition of Carey and Murray. On another occasion, according to Ransom, he yielded to Carey's tantrum and allowed President William McKinley to speak at Quinn Chapel rather than Institutional.[16]

In 1899, Carey and other AME Church ministers came to Bethel to commend Ransom at the conclusion of a successful financial drive, but a few months later, the two men became locked into a fiscal competition when the Iowa Annual Conference's financial secretary offered a prize to the church that brought in the most money. When Carey's Quinn Chapel won, the *Christian Recorder* reported, "shouts loud and long drawn out" erupted. After Carey accepted the victory, however, Ransom "quickly stepped forward . . . speaking words of fraternal feeling that did a great deal to soothe the intense strain that the contest had produced between the members of the two churches."[17]

Nevertheless, the competition between Bethel and Quinn Chapel and their pastors spilled over into their Social Gospel efforts. Ransom claimed that shortly after he launched his mission, Carey started "a program of activities which paralleled nearly everything we conducted at the Institutional Church." Though Carey had a kindergarten and a "Men's Sunday Club," Ransom contended that Quinn Chapel did not operate many of its announced programs. He either ignored or was unaware of other instances of Carey's outreach efforts—for example, his support of Richard R. Wright Jr., a divinity student at the University of Chicago. Although Wright had worked with Ransom at the Institutional Church, Carey appointed him a preacher in the Quinn Chapel Sunday School, and when Wright became the pastor at Chicago's Trinity Mission, he received assistance from Elizabeth Davis Carey and other members of Chicago's women's clubs. After Wright established the City Mission Society, Chicago's three leading pastors, including Carey, who had by that time moved to Bethel, supported him "with great enthusiasm." After taking over at the Institutional Church, Carey also continued the Social Gospel ministry that Ransom had begun, including such efforts as sponsoring lectures on timely topics. In 1914, for example, Mary E. McDowell, a University Settlement official, spoke on "Human Welfare and City Government." Jane Addams and Celia Parker Wooley, two Ransom supporters, also accepted Carey's invitation to return to the Institutional Church. He started a jobs bureau that helped church members find employment at the Pullman Company, in the stockyards, and in the homes of wealthy whites. Whatever difficulties existed between Ransom and Carey, they agreed that the Social Gospel was integral to modern ministry in urban churches.[18]

Both men sought political recognition and influence. Historian Allan Spear insightfully notes that Carey "participated in partisan politics more fully than Ransom and successfully used his congregation[s] as a base for personal political power." Ransom channeled greater energy into the Social Gospel as the best method to energize ministries to southern black migrants. Carey imitated Ransom's Social Gospel initiatives but believed that political power yielded greater gains for church members and community residents. Unlike the northern-born Ransom, Carey was an heir to the practice of politics as a conventional component of expansive ministries to an ex-slave and peasant people. The pursuit of political power, Carey thought, required a flamboyant and self-aggrandizing style that contrasted with the pious and selfless mien of a Social Gospel practitioner. Therefore, when Carey insisted that President McKinley speak at Quinn Chapel, Ransom may have been unaware that Carey had campaigned for McKinley in Florida; in this light, what Ransom perceived as petulance may have reflected an understandable desire to resume an existing political alliance.[19]

Ransom used political involvement to eliminate vice from the neighborhoods surrounding his church and to forge alliances with elected officials committed to black civil rights. Politics, however, remained ancillary to his primary focus on the Social Gospel. Carey, conversely, made politics intrinsic to his ministry, the praxis for his commitment to black advancement. Whereas Ransom saw public theology as an occasional means to invigorate the Social Gospel, Carey perceived it as the essence of his ministry.

Carey's public persona proved helpful in church circles and facilitated his rise within his denomination. As a pastor in Georgia and Florida, Carey had learned the complex AME hierarchal structure and how to advance within it, as his appointments to major pastorates in Jacksonville and Chicago demonstrated. The highly politicized denomination rewarded ministers who were skilled in their interactions with both colleagues and church members.[20] Carey's accomplishments at his Chicago congregations positioned him for leadership in the Fourth Episcopal District and convinced his peers to choose him as a delegate to every quadrennial general conference from 1904 to 1920.

Carey's travels within his episcopal district enabled him to forge friendships with fellow clergy and to aid their pastoral efforts, and in 1899, just a year after his arrival, his fellow Iowa Annual Conference ministers responded by electing him as an alternate to the 1900 General Conference in Columbus, Ohio. Two years later, the Reverend James Higgins, the AME Church pastor in Moline, Illinois, invited Carey to his church to help raise money to pay off the mortgage. In 1915, Bishop Benjamin F. Lee met with the four presiding elders for the Chicago area and invited Carey and another pastor to join the consultation. The presence of Bishop Henry B. Parks from the Far West showed the prestigious company that Carey kept.[21]

At the 1904 General Conference, held at Quinn Chapel, Carey served not only as a delegate but also as the host pastor to hundreds of officials—including the denomination's thirteen bishops and twelve general officers—representing the denomination's half million members. The program pamphlet featured a photograph of Quinn Chapel juxtaposed with a large likeness of Carey, making him recognizable to all of the delegates.[22]

At each of the next four quadrennial general conferences, Carey served on important committees, becoming a frequent speaker. In Norfolk, Virginia, in 1908, Carey served as secretary of the Episcopal Committee, the body that assigned bishops to jurisdictions. He also made a symbolic run for secretary of missions. Moreover, the host committee sent him to preach at Norfolk's Banks Street Baptist Church. At the 1912 General Conference, held in Kansas City, Carey, a member of the Financial Board, appealed to the delegates to approve five thousand dollars "for flood sufferers in the flooded Districts in Tennessee, Arkansas, Mississippi, and Louisiana." He also undertook a token run for the bishopric, throwing his name into the mix as a possible prelate, and launched an unsuccessful candidacy for the editorship of the *Western Christian Recorder*.[23]

Carey seriously contended for the episcopacy at the 1916 General Conference in Philadelphia. He traveled during the 1912–16 quadrennium to publicize his candidacy, especially in the South. He visited the 1915 Macon Georgia Annual Conference at Turner Tabernacle Church, where Bishop Joseph S. Flipper, Carey's former presiding elder, asked him to preside at an evening service and to speak on "The Development of Man," which Carey did "with great cleverness and ability." Flipper thus gave Carey a great opportunity to reconnect with Georgia and thereby lay claim to its votes at the forthcoming general conference.[24]

Carey arrived in Philadelphia as the endorsed candidate from the Fourth Episcopal District. Again, he represented his district on the powerful Episcopal

Committee, overseeing the choice of a bishop for the jurisdiction. With solid support as Illinois's favorite son, Carey declared, "I am going to be elected bishop." He claimed that "the South is for me and the West and East [are] lined up for me and when the conference is over Chicago and the West will have a bishop, which it so richly deserves." Several Chicago delegates affirmed Carey's prediction; said one, "The country needs Carey and we are going to make him bishop." An alliance between Illinois and the South seemed to validate Carey's optimism and moved him and his supporters to push for the election of four new bishops. The General Conference, however, decided that only two bishops would be chosen, and the first ballot showed Carey with 98 votes, trailing the 164 votes that Georgia's William A. Fountain received and the 159 votes cast for Maryland's Isaac N. Ross. On the second ballot, Carey received 93 votes, and he withdrew from the third ballot, on which Ross surged ahead and won the episcopacy.[25]

Carey further intensified his efforts to become a bishop. He maintained near unanimous support from the Chicago Annual Conference and solidified his standing in Georgia. He pressed the General Conference Commission to select Chicago to host the 1920 quadrennial meeting, although St. Louis was ultimately chosen. When the Bishops Council convened in 1918 at Quinn Chapel, Carey impressed the prelates with an address on the "Missing Element in Modern Preaching," generating "favorable comment and pledges" for his election to the episcopacy. By 1918, the *Chicago Defender* predicted that "sentiments from different parts of the nation indicate that the Rev. A. J. Carey [will] become a bishop at the next General Conference." Carey held the same duties in St. Louis as he had at earlier meeting, adding the honor of responding to two representatives from the Methodist Episcopal Church, South who came to deliver fraternal greetings to the delegates, a task he performed "to the satisfaction of the General Conference."[26]

However, Carey's alliance with Murray against Ransom seemed to set a pattern for his relations with other AME ministers in Chicago. When he clashed with another of the city's ministers, W. D. Cook, the popular pastor at Bethel, Carey faced renewed charges that he politicized relationships with other clergy. Although the two men had served together on the executive committee of Chicago's AME ministerial alliance, serious rivalries arose between the two pastors. In the run-up to the 1920 General Conference, Carey sought to bolster his campaign for the episcopacy with a unified and supportive delegation from the Chicago Annual Conference. Because Cook seemed unsympathetic to Carey's candidacy, Bishop Levi J. Coppin transferred Cook to St. Paul's AME Church in Des Moines, and appointed the Reverend S. L. Birt to Cook's congregation and promised him Carey's place on the Episcopal Committee at the St. Louis meeting. Carey had carefully cultivated Coppin's backing, presiding at the 1917 celebration of the bishop's fortieth anniversary in the ministry. Moreover, in early 1920, Carey had committed to help

Wilberforce University raise five thousand dollars, a pledge that combined with his honorary degree from the school to give Carey a crucial connectional credential.[27]

Carey appeared primed to become a bishop. The *Chicago Defender* declared in 1919 that Carey would be elected to the episcopacy "if merit counts," repeating this assessment just days before the 1920 General Conference opened: "The name of Dr. Carey is always the first one mentioned when talk of bishops get loose." The *Chicago Whip* concurred, exhorting the denomination to "awaken" and elect him to the episcopacy, since "there are few candidates riper for the bench than A. J. Carey of Illinois" and "none more fearless, scholarly, and practical."[28] Events proved such predictions correct. On the first ballot, Carey received 321 votes, trailing only Georgia's William D. Johnson with 372, and the two men won the episcopacy. When the presiding officer announced the results, "both Johnson and Carey were overcome with emotion and wept profusely." On the second ballot, William Sampson Brooks, a Baltimore pastor; William T. Vernon, a Republican politician from Memphis; and Fountain were also elected. The newly consecrated Bishop Carey was assigned to the Fourteenth Episcopal District, which covered Kentucky and Tennessee.[29]

African American clergy, especially those stationed at large, urban congregations, had traditionally served as point men, identifying and defining the issues of consequence to their communities and defending them from verbal, legal, and physical attacks. In an 1892 assessment of African American pastors, Francis J. Grimké, a black Presbyterian pastor in Washington, D.C., lauded some black clergy as "public-spirited men; men who love the race; who see what is needed; see just where we are weak; and are laboring unselfishly and earnestly to remedy these defects." Such "men of affairs" knew "how to put into motion the forces that are necessary to produce great results." Election as a bishop clearly demonstrated that Carey belonged in this category.[30]

Carey took sides in the ongoing debate within the black community about the best way to advance the race. Booker T. Washington, the principal of Alabama's Tuskegee Institute, emerged as the nation's preeminent black spokesman, arguing that African Americans should eschew political and civil rights activism in favor of landownership and business development. Moreover, Washington preached that industrial education better served the masses of poor and unlettered African Americans than did proficiency in the liberal arts. His accommodationism and refusal to take on the explosive issue of lynching angered W. E. B. Du Bois, William Monroe Trotter, and other educated blacks who believed that Washington's approach surrendered their suffrage and their right to civic equality to appease racist whites. Members of Chicago's black community, like others throughout the nation, divided between the two points of view. For example, Charles E. Bentley, a prominent dentist, identified unambiguously with Du Bois and joined the Niagara Movement, a forerunner to the National Association for the Advancement of Colored People.

George Cleveland Hall, an influential physician, conversely, became Washington's strongest backer in the Midwest, and pioneering heart surgeon Daniel Hale Williams remained friendly with Washington until they disagreed about staffing at the Freedmen's Hospital in Washington, D.C.[31]

Carey was strongly attracted to Washington's emphasis on economic development and became his staunch ally, although Carey also appreciated the importance that Du Bois attached to the ballot and the protection of black civil rights. Carey's business opportunities—including ownership of a black newspaper, the *Conservator*; a partnership in a haberdashery; and his interests as an officer in the Black Diamond Development Company, which participated in a natural gas venture in Kansas—placed him unambiguously in the Washington camp. Nevertheless, Carey never compromised on black civic equality: when one white disparaged black political involvement in favor of black economic pursuits, Carey declared that voting was "the only weapon of defense" for African Americans. Carey also embraced protest as a major tactic for defending black rights. Whereas Washington's location in the South required him to pursue these objectives surreptitiously, Carey, in a freer northern setting, was unrestrained in his public advocacy of black political activities. He thus chose Du Boisian methods without forsaking his admiration for and cooperation with Washington.[32]

Friendship with Carey gave Washington an AME Church ally who matched Ransom (an ally of Du Bois) in stature and influence in church circles, and Carey in turn became a trusted Washington supporter in the Midwest. In 1903, Carey pledged to defend Washington against "the relentless tirade which certain men are waging against yourself and your work in this city" and "to stand as firmly by you as ever." To show that his commitment was genuine, Carey declared from his Quinn Chapel pulpit and before audiences at the Iowa Annual Conference in Des Moines and at the Indiana Annual Conference in Richmond, "I am prepared to stand for Mr. Washington alone, if need be, against all Chicago; because of my implicit confidence in the man, in his methods and the ultimate triumph of the principles for which he contends." Carey told Washington that "the rank and file of our people believe sincerely that no man has the interests of the race at heart more than yourself." With the endorsement of Bishop Grant and a local white editor, Carey planned to have Washington come to Chicago and face down his critics with a public speech.[33]

Washington's influence in Chicago also extended with efforts to organize a local chapter of the National Negro Business League (NNBL). Through the NNBL, founded in 1900, Washington encouraged entrepreneurial activities. Chicagoans Alberta Moore Smith and Theodore W. Jones served as national NNBL officers and recommended their city as the organization's 1901 convention site, and in 1904, Carey allowed the group to meet at Quinn Chapel. But Carey's closeness to

Washington also annoyed Jones, who learned of Washington's impending visit only when "word reached me through Dr. A. J. Carey." Carey's preferred status with Washington, Jones complained, diminished the local NNBL, and the league's city officials had "to wait upon Dr. Carey and ascertain if he [would] permit the League to join with him in arranging for [Washington's] reception." Carey apparently chose not to accept the offer, believing that Bishop Grant's backing removed any need to appease Jones and the local NNBL.[34]

Although Washington's stature diminished between 1905 and 1910 after he took several stances that opponents perceived as overly accommodationist, Carey remained a firm Washington ally until his death in 1915. In 1908, Carey invited Washington to speak at Bethel. Although Washington could not accept, Carey opened the congregation's pulpit the following year to Charles H. Moore, the NNBL's national organizer. Moore discussed "the gospel of thrift and business" and drew questions from the audience of young people "concerning the progress of the league." In 1910, Washington returned to Chicago and gave a dozen speeches. Carey was among the dignitaries who attended Washington's address at the Negro Press Club, probably because he had been publisher of the *Conservator*, "the first Negro newspaper in Chicago." Though Carey was absent from his pulpit at the Institutional Church at the time of Washington's death, the assistant pastor spoke on "The Meaning of the Life of Booker T. Washington," and the church hosted an evening symposium that included several clergy and civic leaders.[35]

Carey's loyalty to Washington did not mean that he eschewed protest as a tactic to achieve African American advancement. In 1913, when the Illinois state legislature considered a Jim Crow bill, Carey offered the Institutional Church as host for a community meeting that featured Ida B. Wells-Barnett and prominent politicians who opposed the legislation. In 1917, Carey drew the Reverend George W. Slater, a fellow Fourth Episcopal District pastor and an avowed socialist, to Institutional during a tour to deliver his "message of emancipation for his people." Perhaps the most important gathering that Carey hosted at the Institutional Church occurred in 1917 to celebrate the *Buchanan v. Warley* decision, in which the U.S. Supreme Court invalidated residential segregation laws. Speakers at the meeting included Chief Justice Orrin N. Carter of the Illinois Supreme Court as well as Robert S. Abbott, publisher of the *Chicago Defender*; Edward Wright, assistant corporation counsel in Chicago; and Carey himself.[36]

U.S. involvement in World War I was another issue that especially stirred Carey. He and other black leaders strongly declared their patriotism—what Carey called "the Race's loyalty to the nation through all the country's trials and wars." In 1918, he chaired the Lincoln-Douglass celebration, which featured speeches about African American support of the war effort, a special message from the secretary of war, and music about the black struggle for freedom.[37] But Carey and other representatives of the African American community just as strongly protested the mistreatment black soldiers received in segregated army units. As chair of one of Chicago's selective service boards, evaluating "thousands of white and colored men alike," Carey denounced and worked to ameliorate such injustices. On one occasion Carey; his son, Archibald J. Carey Jr.; and another AME minister, N. J. McCracken, traveled to Camp Grant in Rockford, Illinois, to encourage "the men of the M.G. battalion and infantry." When the *Chicago Tribune* referred to a black soldier at Camp Grant as a "darkey," Carey castigated the newspaper for its general attitude toward African Americans and publicly criticized the *Tribune's* "antagonistic policy against the Race."[38] Carey traveled to Washington, D.C., to discuss the status of blacks in the military with a series of federal officials, including several members of Congress. When he returned to Chicago, a large crowd assembled at the Institutional Church despite "extremely disagreeable weather" to hear his report on his trip.[39]

Outbreaks of racial violence during the Red Summer of 1919 also moved Carey vigorously to defend African American interests. As black neighborhoods in northern cities expanded to accommodate the influx of black southerners, frictions arose with the surrounding white communities. Workplace competition and police misconduct further inflamed the situation, leading to rioting in dozens of cities, including Chicago. In July, a rock-throwing incident at a swimming pool led to days of interracial fighting in the city, during which almost fifty were killed and fires burned about 250 buildings. Carey believed that Chicago's blacks needed to push for full privileges as citizens and to refuse to submit to either segregation or discriminatory treatment. When whites blamed vice districts in the city's black neighborhoods for the rioting, Carey responded that such assertions only distracted attention from blacks' genuine grievances.[40]

Carey served on a committee of black leaders that worked with the mayor and governor to restore order. In persuading government officials to call in the state militia, Carey and his group told the mayor that "racial antipathy" had caused the riot and that police inaction had made matters worse, refusing to surrender to white explanations that ignored the role of racism in contributing to the violence. Although his light complexion at times made him the target of angry blacks who mistook him for a white person, Carey walked the streets of the "Black Belt and identified with the aggrieved African American population and defended them against those who dismissed their demands for their full rights."[41]

The following year, Carey visited the AME East Arkansas Annual Conference in Helena. The state had recently experienced racial violence, but only the blacks involved were slated to be punished. The Chicago minister did not shy away from expressing his views on the subject: "Justice and justice alone is all we are asking as a race," he said, adding, "No one can ever make the world believe that only the

Negroes are guilty and not a white man has been convicted or even arrested. It was not a one-sided affair."[42]

Carey's rivalries with other black spokespersons showed the complicated role that religion and politics played in the making of African American leadership. His conflicts with Ransom, for example, shaped his relationship with Wells-Barnett, a leading crusader against lynching and a major figure in the black women's club movement. Wells-Barnett had been Ransom's parishioner at Bethel and strongly disapproved of his successor, Murray, a well-known Carey ally. When a reputable female member accused Murray of sexual harassment, Wells-Barnett believed her, but Carey did not. When Bishop Grant, who usually sided with Carey and Murray, refused to intervene, Wells-Barnett withdrew her membership from Bethel. Another factor that contributed to the friction between Carey and Wells-Barnett was her belief that he had attempted to thwart her husband's ambitions. In 1906, when Ferdinand Barnett failed to win a judgeship, Wells-Barnett attributed the defeat to Carey and his influence within a minister's group. Moreover, Carey criticized her for cooperating with Robert Motts, a former tavern owner, in efforts to defeat an ineffective alderman. Carey was unconvinced by Wells-Barnett's attempt to cleanse the image of Motts, whom the pastor described as a "keeper of a low gambling dive."[43]

In 1915, Wells-Barnett was not appointed to help lead Illinois's celebration of the fiftieth anniversary of the end of slavery, although Carey was chosen to serve. Wells-Barnett responded by accusing Carey of having used money from Mayor William Hale Thompson to buy votes to win the episcopacy, a charge that may have contributed to Carey's defeat at the 1916 General Conference. She also criticized Carey for mixing politics and religion. W. D. Cook, Murray's successor at Bethel, agreed, barring politicians from campaigning at the church, and Wells-Barnett believed that Carey retaliated by plotting Cook's transfer to another church. When Cook established an independent community church, Wells-Barnett supported the effort.[44]

These uneasy interactions between Wells-Barnett and Carey revealed more about personal pique than about differences in social justice objectives. Hence, Wells-Barnett and Carey sometimes intentionally and at other times unwittingly allied on issues crucial to black civil rights. A protest rally over a lynching in Cairo, Illinois, involved Wells-Barnett at the Institutional Church while Carey was serving as pastor. Carey also joined Wells-Barnett in fighting the extradition of Steve Green, who escaped a lynching in Arkansas, and in helping Leroy Bundy, who had been arrested as a part of a mutiny of black soldiers during an East St. Louis race riot. Although Bundy's father had managed Carey's campaign for the bishopric, Wells-Barnett strongly defended Bundy.[45]

Carey engaged politicians, both black and white, as allies to advance the interests of African Americans and envisaged himself less as a potential officeholder than as a broker. Although he accepted appointments to perform special assignments, Carey thrived as a kingmaker, calling on politicians to deliver services to the black community in exchange for African Americans' votes. When Carey transferred from Florida to Illinois, he sought to build on the ties he had developed with national Republicans through Arnett, Carey's bishop in Jacksonville and later in Chicago. Arnett, a former Ohio legislator, had such a special rapport with President McKinley that the administration provided federal positions to various persons whom the bishop recommended. In 1899, Carey benefited from this relationship when Arnett persuaded McKinley to appear at Quinn Chapel "to meet our people." McKinley's appearance enabled Carey to create visibility for himself in the Chicago GOP. When the General Conference of 1900 moved Grant to Chicago as Arnett's replacement, Carey arranged with George Cortelyou, McKinley's secretary, for the president to meet Grant. However, McKinley's assassination thwarted Carey's plans for a stronger connection to the White House.[46]

Carey's zeal for African American advancement informed his political involvements. Despite his ambition and his desire for power and influence, the benefits of his political activities were not entirely personal. Carey and other members of Chicago's disproportionately mulatto elite believed that leadership of less fortunate African Americans was integral to their class identity and was an imperative pursuit in racially hostile circumstances. Politics became one of several strategies that satisfied personal aspirations and safeguarded the rights of the black population.

Carey's pastoral and political experiences in Georgia and Florida in the 1890s showed his ability to blend these commitments without shortchanging either his preaching or his public pursuits. When he arrived in Chicago, Carey discovered that blacks had been extensively involved in both local and state politics and that black clergy played public prominent roles. Since 1876, for example, African Americans had served in the state legislature. The 1918 legislature included three black representatives from Chicago.[47]

As Carey surveyed the important issues and influential individuals involved in municipal politics, he could not avoid a cadre of powerful officeholders who represented the political interests of black Chicagoans. Though most of these black politicians were Republicans, they at times cooperated with Democrats, compelling the two parties to compete for black votes. Carey's ties to black officeholders not only satisfied his personal ambition and his crude pursuit of recognition but also, he contended, served his church and community constituents.[48]

Edward H. Wright, Oscar De Priest, and Robert R. Jackson had far greater influence in Chicago than did Carey. In 1894, Wright had persuaded GOP officials to nominate an African American for county commissioner, and two years later, Wright was elected to that position. In 1910, he made an unsuccessful bid for the city council, and in 1920 he became a Second Ward committeeman. De Priest greatly benefited from Wright's sponsorship and the political alliances he forged in the Second Ward, winning election as an alderman in 1915. Wright also played a role in Jackson's successful 1912 campaign for the state legislature. All three men positioned themselves as Republican operatives and party loyalists and largely excluded black rights issues from their leadership profile. Carey, in contrast, maintained shifting alliances with Republicans and Democrats and frequently spoke on behalf of African American rights.[49]

Carey maintained occasional ties with a variety of white officials, but his main political ally was William Hale "Big Bill" Thompson. In 1900, when Thompson announced that he would run for alderman in Chicago's Second Ward, Carey was impressed that the candidate's father had been in the Union Navy during the Civil War. Though he never included political statements in his sermons, Carey allowed Thompson to attend various Quinn Chapel functions, providing him an entrée to the black community. When Thompson won the election, he remained indebted to Carey. The process was repeated in 1902, when Thompson ran for county commissioner, and in his subsequent election to the mayor's office, where he served from 1915 to 1923 and from 1927 to 1931. Thompson's closeness to Carey earned the politician a reputation as a "Second Lincoln": one publication noted that he had been "friendly to the Colored people" and attributed his reelection as mayor "largely . . . to the support of the Colored voters." Carey constantly delivered speeches on Thompson's behalf, often lauding his numerous black appointees. In 1915, Carey boasted to a cheering crowd, "I helped elect him alderman; I helped elect him county commissioner; I helped elect him mayor; and my work will not be completed until I have helped elect him president."[50]

Carey's ties to Thompson ultimately led to a lifelong friendship between the minister and William Lorimer, who represented Illinois in the U.S. House of Representatives for most of the years between 1895 and 1909 and in the U.S. Senate from 1909 to 1912. In the 1904 Republican gubernatorial primary, Carey backed Frank O. Lowden, the Lorimer machine candidate, over Charles S. Deneen, the eventual victor. Because Deneen had minimal influence in Chicago's municipal affairs, Carey's preference for the losing contender mattered very little in terms of his political clout. However, Deneen angered Carey by taking political stands inimical to the interests of African Americans. Deneen implemented a primary election system that identified candidates' racial identity, diminishing the number of blacks who won elective positions. The initiative, recall, and referendum process, which Deneen also supported, similarly harmed blacks, as in St. Louis, where voters approved a 1916 referendum that mandated residential segregation.[51]

Much to Carey's consternation, Deneen also endorsed the presidency of Theodore Roosevelt. Carey, an erstwhile Roosevelt supporter, had broken with the president after he dishonorably discharged African American troops in the wake of racial violence that broke out in 1906 in Brownsville, Texas. Some of the discharged soldiers came to Chicago, where Carey sought to clear their records. When U.S. Senator Ben Tillman of South Carolina came to Chicago to denounce the black soldiers, Carey held a protest meeting at his Bethel pastorate to criticize Roosevelt's actions. He also joined a committee that urged the mayor to stop the speech. In 1912, therefore, Carey supported Republican presidential candidate William Howard Taft and opposed Roosevelt's candidacy on the Progressive Party ticket. One pamphlet that circulated among Chicago's blacks featured not only Taft's declaration that he believed "in equal rights and equal privileges to all American citizens, black and white, north and south" but also a statement in which Carey expressed his anger at Roosevelt for "the discharge and disgrace of the colored soldiers."[52]

Thompson and other politicians recognized Carey's influence and paid homage to him at appearances at his churches or at district meetings where he served as presiding elder. During the 1915 election season, the Institutional Church hosted Congressman Martin B. Madden, Senator Samuel A. Ettleson, Thompson, and De Priest, among others. Moreover, a speech by Judge J. C. Pritchard, a former U.S. senator from North Carolina, at the Institutional Church showed that Carey's political standing extended beyond Illinois.[53]

Members of the black community understood Carey's role as a power broker. Jessie Thomas may well have joined the Institutional Church in 1916 in hopes that Carey's favor would help her obtain a political appointment as a Cook County probation officer. And when an insurgent group, the Municipal Voter's League, endorsed a saloonkeeper to unseat the incumbent Second Ward alderman, Carey stepped in and "quickly changed the minds of those who were about to follow" this course.[54]

When the Lorimer faction's influence in the Illinois Republican Party began to wane in 1911 and 1912, Carey turned to the Democrats. He supported victorious Democratic gubernatorial candidate Edward Dunne and the party's Carter Harrison, who was elected mayor of Chicago. The two Democrats provided Carey with tangible and public expressions of their gratitude, enhancing his importance as a political broker. In accordance with Carey's wishes, Dunne engineered a twenty-five-thousand-dollar appropriation for a celebration of the fiftieth anniversary of the Emancipation Proclamation and appointed Carey chair of the celebration committee. The Institutional Church then hosted the festivities on September 18, 1915. In 1914, Harrison appointed Carey to the Chicago Board of Moving Picture Censors, a position he used to denounce D. W. Griffith's *Birth of a Nation*. These appointments ratified Carey as among the most powerful preacher/politicians within Chicago's black population.[55]

Carey nevertheless maintained his ties to the GOP and to Thompson. After Thompson became Chicago's mayor, Carey added to the benefits he had received

from under the previous Democratic administration, receiving further appointments and favors that maintained his reputation as someone with access to City
Hall. When the city prepared to celebrate the centennial of Admiral Oliver Hazard
Perry's victory over the British at Put-in-Bay, Michigan, during the War of 1812,
Mayor Thompson insisted that an African American speaker appear on the program because Perry's crew had included black sailors. Thompson's fellow committee members preferred Booker T. Washington, but the mayor wanted "to reward
my friend Carey" and brought the group to Carey's residence, where the minister
"captivated them." At the celebration, Carey's speech drew the attention of former president Taft, and the two men talked for four hours.[56] The speech not only
extolled peace and justice but linked them to opposition to racial segregation, citing the "loyal[ty] to the flag" shown by Perry's African American sailors as well as
other blacks throughout the country's history. He excoriated the administration of
the new Democratic president, Woodrow Wilson, which "set apart" black federal
employees "as if they were lepers." Describing segregation as "unfair, unjust, un-
American, and un-Christian," Carey urged that the energies devoted to celebrating
the American victory over the British be "turned upon injustice and unrighteous-
ness as exhibited in every form of discrimination, disenfranchisement, segregation,
mob violence, and jim crowism," which he described as the real "enemies of our
nation."[57]

Thompson also acknowledged the importance of Carey's support by appointing African Americans to oversee Chicago's legal affairs, naming veteran politicians
Edward H. Wright and Louis B. Anderson to positions as assistant corporation
counsels. Carey, who was Wright's chief sponsor for his legal post, was appointed as
an investigator in the law department, and he served as a delegate to the 1920–22
Illinois Constitutional Convention. More concretely, Carey convinced the mayor
to support the construction of a playground on the city's South Side. The site chosen was located across from Quinn Chapel, Carey's former pastorate.[58]

Despite his unquestioned status as a leader, Carey was a member of the elite,
unlike and never a part of the black masses. His light skin and his prestigious address
signified his status, although Chicago's burgeoning black population increasingly
came to embrace darker-skinned leaders. At moments of community crisis, he and
other members of the talented tenth had to declare loudly and unambiguously that
they were African American. On at least one occasion, for example, Elizabeth Davis
Carey was accused of passing for white.[59] Carey's power derived from his class position and the esteem in which white politicians held him. These white officeholders,
in turn, treated Carey as a political insider because of the deference he inspired
among potential black voters. The result was a cycle in which all participants—
white politicians, black constituents, and Carey himself—benefited.

Not surprisingly, Carey downplayed the personal benefits he derived from this strategy. He claimed that when he came to Chicago, he became acquainted with Republican and Democratic politicians "who were disposed to give the Negro fair play." When these men lived up to their promises, "I became an ardent supporter, regardless of their political party creeds." He continued, "I have never voted for nor advocated any man whom I did not feel was interested in civic betterment, in the community uplift, and was disposed in his heart to give my people fair play." In his eyes, he was simply "a Negro minister, who loves his people and is interested in their securing their just and equal rights" and who consequently advocated "the claims of men whom he believes will deal fairly with the people of his race."[60]

Others saw the situation differently. In 1916, the *Chicago Defender* declared that "there is absolutely no logical reason for the active participation of a minister in politics, because religion and politics do not, in any manner harmonize. . . . It is difficult to understand how a man who aspires to be a good, honest and devout follower of the meek and lowly Christ, can also be a consistent political leader."[61] But such a position represented a very different vision of the minister's role than the one Carey possessed. And while Carey's achievements on behalf of his parishioners may seem minimal, he was clearly a significant player in Chicago's African American community.

CHAPTER 3

Immersed in Church and State

ARCHIBALD J. CAREY SR. AND RELIGION IN THE PUBLIC SQUARE

Election to the episcopacy of the African Methodist Episcopal (AME) Church provided Archibald J. Carey Sr. with broader opportunities to use public theology to benefit African Americans. Successfully doing so, however, required Carey to exert as much control as possible over the pastors and parishes in his districts as well as to curry favor with white politicians by persuading them that he could serve as a singularly important political ally. His attempts to forge these alliances and to exercise his episcopal authority pleased some members of the denomination and angered others. His old adversary, Reverdy C. Ransom, who became a fellow bishop in 1924, recognized what Carey was trying to accomplish but criticized his crude conduct in pursuing this objective. Though Carey's efforts ultimately served African Americans' interests, at least to some extent, his balance of civic and church affairs always remained uneasy and at times compelled Carey to treat harshly pastors who opposed his politicized ministry. He never gained enough political clout to change blacks' overall social and economic circumstances, and his use of episcopal authority did not always advance the morale of his ministerial subordinates.

For eight years after Carey was elected a bishop in 1920, he continued to reside in Chicago, but denominational assignments took him to other states, first in the South and then in the West. Carey maintained his relationship with William Hale "Big Bill" Thompson and accepted various appointments from the mayor of Chicago even as he developed ties with politicians elsewhere. Chicago's AMEs behaved as though the denomination had assigned him to preside in Illinois, and he frequently preached to his former parishioners. He delivered the Easter sermon at the Institutional Church in 1921, spoke there again in January and February 1922, and preached to the church's "newly elected officers" in 1923. Carey also held forth from his former pulpit at Quinn Chapel in July 1922 and returned to Bethel in 1923 and delivered "an inspiring sermon." Elizabeth Davis Carey was also a popular speaker at numerous events, among them Bethel's Allen Day celebration in February 1922. Two weeks later, she gave an address at an evening service at Institutional. The pastors of the three congregations welcomed the Careys to reaffirm their friendship, to curry favor with the bishop and his wife, or to please parishioners still loyal to the episcopal team. Whatever their motivations, Chicago AMEs claimed the Careys as their own, allowing the bishop to maintain a high profile in local religious and political affairs.[1]

Carey's bishopric brought him immediate dividends by increasing his national and international stature in denominational matters. His long support of Wilberforce University and his honorary degree from that institution drew him back to campus to deliver the baccalaureate address at the 1921 commencement. Moreover, he became chair of the denomination's financial board and president of the Allen Christian Endeavor League, which sponsored the AME Church's Young Peoples' Congress.[2]

Carey served as one of several respondents at a session on "Christ and the Social Order," at the Fifth Ecumenical Methodist Conference, held in London on September 6–21, 1921. There, he "recalled with pride some of the achievements of coloured peoples in the fights for freedom and liberty" and expressed his hope that white Wesleyans would "go forth re-christianized and re-baptized with power from on high" to deal justly with persons of other races.[3]

Carey's European experiences affirmed his belief in interracialism and his pride in what African Americans had done to safeguard democracy in the recent war. Carey told the 1920 Kentucky Annual Conference at Harrodsburg that the former slave "has suffered, sacrificed and died for this America he loves." Moreover, "the Negroes of Africa and America gave life not only for Great Britain and France, but to save the world and give the world a true democracy indeed." Also, at the 1921 Kentucky Annual Conference at Ashland, he recalled that while "upon the Alpine heights," he had stood "above race prejudice and injustice, realizing a common brotherhood." Since Acts 17:27 said that God "hath made of one blood all nations of men to dwell on all the face of the earth," Carey "pleaded for a contact of the best people of each race, that they may know each other and do more for the advancement" of all. He also hoped "that the world [would] not forget what the black man has done for freedom and justice." "The peaceful working together of the races in America," he noted, "must be continued to make her great. The bad must be worked out of each race for the good of all."[4]

He expressed these perspectives, however, at a time when the racial nationalism of Marcus Garvey was stirring millions of blacks in the Americas and Africa. On the one hand, his European travels revived his hopes for racial equality in the United States; on the other hand, his London experiences focused him on the special mission of the AME Church. Because "the needs of Africa" were especially important, Carey "urged that each man rise up and do the work assigned to the race and the AME Church in particular," because "Africa and India and all the world must be redeemed." Carey did not share Garvey's dream but appreciated the pan-African vision that invigorated his movement. Carey commended his Episcopal colleagues such as Bishops William S. Brooks and William T. Vernon, who served AME districts on the "mother" continent, and declared that as they "civilize[d] heathen," he would "remain here and civilize heathen America."[5]

Because the ecumenical conference represented a racial and religious watershed, Carey shared with other AME Church clergy tangible tokens from his sojourns at several sacred places. He gave coins from St. Peter's tomb to "deserving" ministers in the Kentucky Annual Conference. Such rewards demonstrated Carey's understanding of the service and sacrifice of dedicated clergy. At a deeper level, gifts from sacred shrines connected Carey to his ecclesiastical role and symbolically showed his acknowledgment of his apostolic antecedents. Carey thus joined St. Peter and John Wesley as church fathers.[6]

This blend of ecumenism and racial pride may explain Carey's later enthusiasm for organic union between the AME Church and the African Methodist Episcopal Zion Church. Carey was proud that they were religious bodies "controlled entirely by Negroes" and that "these Churches teach the Negro his worth as a man." At the 1924 General Conference, Carey discussed "the necessity of Organic Union with the AME Zion Church" as he introduced that denomination's bishop George C. Clement. In 1927, Carey, Clement, and other members of a joint commission produced a report that suggested an organizational structure for the new denomination, to be called the United Methodist Episcopal Church. At Pittsburgh's Avery AME Zion Church, Carey preached that God would be "the inspiration for union of the two great bodies." He also announced that his son, Archibald J. Carey Jr., had decided to enter the ministry and declared his desire that the newest member of the Carey ministerial dynasty would "be permitted to preach in a united Methodist church." At an annual conference in Ashland, Kentucky, Carey said that he hoped that the "union between the AME Church and the AME Zion Church [would] be accomplished by 1925." Such a union never materialized, however.[7]

The welfare of the numerous congregations in his Kentucky/Tennessee district, the placement of pastors and evangelists, the support of educational efforts, and the collection of funds for denominational programs claimed the lion's share of Bishop Carey's attention between 1920 and 1924. Despite his initial unfamiliarity with his district, Carey quickly learned about its geography and its pastoral requirements. At the 1921 Kentucky Annual Conference, for example, he assigned ministers to the seventy congregations and circuits in the Lexington, Danville, and Frankfort Districts and approved the realignment of several circuit congregations either for the convenience of pastors or in the interest of proximity. He transferred one minister to the Chicago Annual Conference and placed a Chicago pastor with a church in Kentucky. Moreover, Carey brought clergy from the East Tennessee, Tennessee, and West Kentucky Annual Conferences to fill pulpits in the bluegrass and coal mining areas of eastern Kentucky. He followed the same routine at the district's four other annual conferences.[8]

Carey also tackled the controversial issue of women in the ministry. Bishop Henry M. Turner had ordained the denomination's first female pastor in 1885, but the General Conference invalidated this action three years later. Most male ministers tolerated female evangelists who preached, pastored small churches, and conducted various missionary programs but opposed women's ordination. In 1924, however, Carey and other bishops proposed enfranchising women as voters for delegates to the General Conference. Speaking for his fellow bishops, William H. Heard acknowledged that "women have paid more dollar money, more educational money, and more missionary money, than the men who denied them the right to vote." Hence, Heard argued, they should "choose delegates to our law making body."[9]

Although Carey never supported full female ordination, he promoted women's roles in certain areas of the church. One member of his Institutional congregation, Emma Williams, received invitations to preach from as far away as Tennessee. Nora Taylor, a nationally known evangelist and missionary leader, was a Carey parishioner at Quinn Chapel who later spoke at Institutional while he occupied the pulpit there. When Carey became bishop of the Fourteenth Episcopal District, he met Martha Jayne Keys, a graduate of Payne Theological Seminary, a widely traveled preacher, and a member of the West Kentucky Annual Conference, and appointed her as pastor at Moore's Chapel AME Church in Clinton, Kentucky, where she had great success, vindicating Carey's daring appointment. Although Keys attended the General Conference in 1924 as a participant on a women's missionary society program, she returned to the conference four years later as a lay delegate, a direct consequence of the earlier proposal for female representation made by Carey and the other bishops.[10]

Three other female evangelists—Willie S. Wood, Rhoda Hynes, and Annie T. Foster—were prominent at the 1921 Kentucky Annual Conference. Wood had studied at Payne Theological Seminary beginning in 1919 and preached throughout central Ohio as well as in South Carolina and in Kentucky and Tennessee. She sang and prayed extensively at the conference, reporting on her ministry and appealing to Bishop Carey and the conference for scholarship assistance so that she could complete her seminary training. Two years later, two female preachers, A. J. Bradshaw of the Lexington District and Nettie Ingram of the Frankfort District, appeared on the conference roll.[11]

When Carey was elected a bishop, the denomination appropriated funds to support sixteen schools, with the episcopal districts in which the institutions were located providing supplemental operating monies. The Fourteenth Episcopal District bore responsibility for Turner College, a campus of two brick and frame buildings in Shelbyville, Tennessee. Founded in 1885, Turner had been a high school, a normal and industrial facility, and a Bible training institute. When Carey arrived, B. F. Allen was serving as president, but in June 1921, the new bishop brought back J. A. Jones, a previous president, as the school's head. Between 1920 and 1924, Turner graduated 385 students, mostly in the normal and English curricula but 8 on the theology track. During those four years, Turner's allocation totaled $32,102, with more than half of that money raised through educational rallies in Carey's episcopal district.[12]

At the 1921 Kentucky Annual Conference, Carey asked that pastors "go before the people and explain our general [fund-raising] days so we can be able to give more toward helping our Mission churches and fostering our educational interests." Toward that end, the bishop invited Jones to preach at a morning service at the conference. After delivering a "soul-stirring sermon," he remained at the church to appeal for help for Turner College. Donors responded, and the conference urged others in Kentucky and Tennessee to follow their lead and "thus enhance the great Educational System of the District."[13]

Each episcopal district also bore responsibility for raising money to finance pensions, missions, and the salaries of bishops and general officers. Districts charged each congregation an assessment of a dollar per member; during the 1920–24 quadrennium, Carey's small district collected $67,511 in such fees as part of an overall connectional budget of $1,371,098. When a congregation failed to raise its full assessment, as did the church at Parksville, Kentucky, for example, officials took up a collection to make up the difference.[14]

The AME Church's Five Million Dollar and Evangelical Campaign also drew Carey's enthusiastic endorsement. The 1920 General Conference "ordered the staging of a special campaign to increase our membership and raise Five Million Dollars outside of [the] regular Fund." Though the denomination paid some preachers to serve as zone and district directors to raise these monies, several bishops, including Carey, viewed the effort as falling within their sphere of responsibility. Moreover, although regular assessments fell under the control of treasurer John R. Hawkins, the bishops had discretion with regard this special effort. To highlight the importance of the Five Million Dollar campaign, Carey contributed an Italian coin purchased during his European travels to reward the support of the pastor at Monticello, Kentucky. At one session of the 1921 Kentucky Annual Conference, Carey collected $141.50 for the fund.[15]

Despite Carey's support of this denominational initiative, he refused to turn over all of the funds raised to Hawkins, who reported at the 1924 General Conference that the Fourteenth District owed $1,379 to the general treasury. Despite being new to the bishopric, Carey had learned quickly about the powers and prerogatives of his office and may have used the money to cover shortfalls in the regular annual assessment or to support Turner College.[16]

In 1924, Carey served as host to the General Conference when it met in Louisville, Kentucky. The choice of the city demonstrated that Carey's more experienced colleagues considered him an influential peer, as did Carey's selection as chair of the local commission. He and the Reverend Noah W. Williams of Louisville's Quinn Chapel spent nearly three years preparing for the thousands of delegates who would be arriving. As a border city in a state with Jim Crow laws, Louisville posed some special challenges for Carey and the other convention organizers, and he stood at the forefront of their efforts to obtain use of a federal military facility. After winning the needed access, committee members then had to arrange for postal, telegraph, telephone, and dining services.[17]

In addition to demonstrating his external influence, his efforts in staging the convention gave him power within the denomination. The host had control of many matters, both major and mundane. For example, as program chair, he provided visiting ministers with coveted assignments to preach at area churches. He also promoted Williams's candidacy for the post of secretary of missions and Jones's attempt to win election as editor of the *AME Church Review*. Although neither man won in 1924, Williams was elected a bishop in 1932, and Carey's efforts at least helped Williams start down the road toward episcopal leadership.[18]

Ransom, Carey's old Chicago nemesis, became a bishop in 1924 and succeeded Carey in Kentucky and Tennessee. According to Ransom, Carey's tenure in the Fourteenth Episcopal District had "left it in a storm." An "anti-Carey" faction, led by the head of the denomination's publishing house in Nashville, Ira T. Bryant, charged that several bishops had been irresponsible in handling "church finances," and Ransom contended that many of the district's ministers agreed.[19]

Carey, conversely, took the view that his altruistic intentions and his position as bishop entitled him to the trust and deference that the black community customarily offered to its church leaders. Support for Turner College and for the "establishment of Mission Churches" represented urgent efforts, and pointless queries about fiscal transparency should not interfere with satisfying such obvious educational and evangelical needs.[20] That Carey Chapel AME Church in Burlison, Tennessee, was named for the bishop demonstrates that the anti-Carey sentiment was not unanimous in the district.

Carey's religious and civic constituents accepted the selection procedures that made him a bishop and a public spokesman. Religious leadership then enabled him to become influential in secular spheres, and as in Chicago, politicians routinely appeared at Fourteenth Episcopal District conferences, and he continued to pursue political issues. In agreeing to appear at church ceremonies, political officeholders acknowledged church members as belonging to the body politic. Carey similarly saw AME Church gatherings as sites of both worship and political mobilization. Religion and politics reinforced each other, and African American advancement depended on ties between the two. Two white officials, a judge and a legislator, visited Carey's 1920 Kentucky Annual Conference. One noted that "men must be estimated by their true worth, regardless of race," and should expect the law to apply equally to all. The other declared that race relations would be improved through more interracial "contact" and "goodwill." Carey's chosen respondent asserted that "the new Negro knows his heritage and is proud of it" and only wants "a square deal" from whites. When the mayor of Ashland, Kentucky, addressed the AME's 1921 Kentucky Annual Conference in his city, he "paid high tribute to the sterling qualities of the colored citizens" and invoked "the spirit of Christ and its influence upon the various problems confronting the country and the world." He hoped that the AME proceedings would exhibit "peace and good will" and that "God's eternal truth" would be brought before the world. He declared that "brotherly love must be preached to help bring about peace and happiness." Carey chose the Reverend J. W. Hall, a visiting Memphis minister, to outline for the mayor "the history of the work done by the AME Church for humanity" and to remind the mayor that white officeholders had an obligation to treat blacks equitably. The AME Church thus worked to advance blacks' interests in civic affairs and to press their claims with white public officials, and politicians acknowledged the political importance of African Americans by paying their respects at the altars of black churches.[21]

At the 1924 General Conference, Carey and other bishops discussed at length the best way to safeguard African American interests in the civic arena. As part of his reelection campaign, President Calvin Coolidge sent greetings to the General Conference. Bishop Benjamin F. Lee motioned that Carey and the editor of the *AME Church Review* "formulate an answer expressing" the AME's attitudes on such pressing issues as lynching, black federal appointments, aid to Liberia, and staffing of the Tuskegee Veterans Hospital. The General Conference then directed Carey to lead a large delegation of bishops, ministers, and laypersons to testify at the platform committee meetings of the Republican and Democratic National Conventions.[22]

For the 1924–28 quadrennium, the General Conference assigned Carey to the Fifth Episcopal District, which included Missouri, Kansas, Nebraska, Colorado, and adjacent mountain states. As at his previous postings, Carey continued to work to maintain the church's visibility in public affairs. At a 1925 meeting of the Bishops Council in Los Angeles, participants denounced a general for saying that black soldiers in World War I had been cowards and protested to federal officials the Ku Klux Klan parade in the nation's capital. In 1925, Carey, A. L. Gaines, and Ransom visited the governor of Utah to press for the prosecution of whites accused of lynching an African American. In 1927, Carey addressed the Kansas legislature and praised the public schools that African Americans attended, earning Western University, an AME school near Kansas City, a $142,000 grant. Carey impressed on ministers and church members the importance of regular interactions with office-holders. At the 1927 Kansas Annual Conference, held in Topeka, for example, the bishop interrupted a morning session to introduce John W. Hamilton, the speaker of the Kansas House of Representatives. Hamilton then cited Carey's recent support of the appropriations for Western University as key to the measure's passage. Kansas's U.S. senator, Arthur Capper, "an associate member of St. John AME Church" in Topeka, later appeared at the annual conference to commend African American voters' "independent spirit" and to reiterate his backing of an antilynching bill that had failed to pass the legislature as well as his "cooperation in any measure pertaining to the interest of your race." Carey also drew on his Chicago political contacts to aid the preparations for the 1928 General Conference to be held there. Although his episcopal post took him far from his adopted home, Carey maintained his residence in the city and served as chair of the General Conference Commission.[23]

Ransom was outraged at Carey's ostentatious display of political clout, describing the unwanted attention of Chicago's city officials during the General Conference as "brazen, blatant, mercenary, [and] godless." At the welcoming ceremony, Chicago's police band "came blasting horns, trumpets, and drums" and leading a large group of policemen and city detectives. Moreover, when delegates arrived at the Eighth Regiment Armory, a facility for the black brigade of the Illinois National Guard, they were searched, and plainclothes detectives monitored the area "where the bishops presided." One policeman stopped Ransom, but the bishop "brushed him" away and took his seat. Ransom concluded that the parade, police, and security guards represented "a brazen attempt to overawe the General Conference and to impress it with the power and influence of our host." He added that "the politically controlled machine that had invaded us sought to hold us in its vice-like grip. It seemed to me, as it did to others, that Satan himself, had come in with a leering grin and derisive smile to preside over our deliberations."[24]

Carey thus strengthened his hold on Chicago's local church and public affairs despite his episcopal responsibilities in the South and the West, remaining a major player in some of Chicago's social and political institutions. Through his ecclesiastical involvements, his pronouncements and protests as an African American spokesman, and his activities as a political broker, Carey developed a ubiquitous presence among Chicago blacks. What Ransom observed and denounced at the General Conference represented but one aspect of Carey's prominence as a power in both ministerial and municipal affairs.

Although the 1924 General Conference assigned Bishop Abraham L. Gaines to the Fourth Episcopal District, Carey remained the city's most influential AME clergyman. Moreover, some leading ministers publicly showed their loyalty to Carey. One protégé, John M. Henderson, owed his assignment to the Institutional Church to Carey. Gaines later sent Henderson to Aurora and then to a smaller congregation in Elgin, a seeming demotion that caused Carey to transfer Henderson to the Missouri Annual Conference. When Henderson died in 1927, his funeral was held at Institutional Church, with Carey officiating, a break with the customary practice of having resident bishops oversee the obsequies of local clergy. Carey also presided at the 1927 funeral of another loyalist, N. J. McCracken, at Quinn Chapel. Carey thus ignored protocol and pushed Gaines to the periphery in his own diocese. Moreover, when Carey sent greetings from his Kansas-Nebraska Annual Conference to the Michigan Annual Conference, over which his ally, Bishop William T. Vernon, rather than Bishop Gaines, was presiding, the "enthusiastic" response showed Carey's continuing popularity and visibility in the Fourth Episcopal District.[25]

To his long-standing friendships with Henderson, McCracken, and other Fourth Episcopal District clergy, Carey added a relationship with W. W. Lucas, a recent migrant from the South who became pastor at the Institutional Church in the early 1920s. Lucas had attained some prominence in the predominantly white Methodist Episcopal Church, and he participated in a successful effort by the denomination's black members to elect two black bishops in 1920. Lucas was nevertheless disappointed by his failure to be chosen editor of the *Southwestern Christian Advocate*, and he transferred his membership to the AME Church, where he met Carey, who probably influenced Lucas's assignment to the Institutional Church. Carey and Lucas held similar sentiments about the need for greater church involvement with recently arrived migrants. In 1923, Lucas organized a "mass meeting of all newcomers to the city" at which "some of the Race's leading citizens" would examine the "mutual welfare and future interests" of the migrants. Carey applauded Lucas's efforts to maintain Institutional's Social Gospel programs. Despite Carey's support, however, Lucas, then serving at Ebenezer Church in Evanston, Illinois, found himself in hot water when he accused another minister of financial fraud and argued against his election as an officer in the AME ministerial alliance. The district's bishop, Gaines, then removed Lucas from Ebenezer. Historian Wallace D. Best believes that the behavior of Gaines and other AME clergy toward Lucas derived in part from their ineffectiveness in handling the challenges of the black migration and their indifference to Lucas's outreach to black newcomers. In any case, Carey's defense of Lucas became the subject of friction between him and Gaines. When Lucas jumped from a window on the third floor of Provident Hospital, Carey spoke at the funeral at Quinn Chapel, charging that some AME preachers had caused the suicide through deception, treachery, and backstabbing: "He is dead now and you are responsible." Carey publicly absolved Gaines of any guilt but clearly implied that the bishop had offered no help to the embattled pastor. The ministerial alliance subsequently denounced Carey's attitude, creating a split between the AME Church's Chicago bishop and the city's unofficial episcopal leader.[26]

Carey's aggressive intervention in Fourth District affairs extended to property dealings. In 1924, the Bethel building, purchased in 1922 for $91,000, burned to the ground. Whites and blacks immediately rallied, donating $18,461, including a $100 contribution from Mayor William Dever. However, Dever, a Reform Democrat, sent his regrets and his contribution to Carey rather than to Gaines, promising "to have a thorough investigation made by our fire commissioner as to the causes of the fire." In 1927, Bethel purchased a former Jewish synagogue for $450,000. The congregation's new home had a seating capacity of four thousand and an adjacent social service facility. The *Chicago Defender* gave credit to Bishop Gaines, general officer Ira T. Bryant, Pastor Henry Y. Tookes, and others who had "engineered the deal." Carey, however, told the *Chicago Daily Journal* that he was responsible for the successful negotiation between Bethel representatives and synagogue officials, a breach of ecclesiastical protocol that no doubt caused friction within the church hierarchy.[27]

As chair of the General Conference Commission for the 1928 quadrennial convention, Carey made additional inroads into Gaines's episcopal authority in Chicago. Carey invited several subcommission members to the city to finalize program plans and housing. After presiding at the meeting, Carey hosted three bishops, including Gaines, and several clergy and lay representatives for dinner at his spacious South Side residence. Carey invited some municipal dignitaries to attend the conference itself, and when Carey's political ally, Mayor Thompson, came into the hall, "America" was sung. Gaines introduced Carey, who in turn presented the mayor. Carey, a Thompson municipal appointee, presided at another conference session and received "a tremendous ovation." Delegates could not have failed to notice in Chicago, Carey exercised both church and civic authority.[28]

Perhaps in response to such demonstrations, a faction of bishops pushed for Carey's assignment to the Fourth District for the 1928–32 quadrennium. During the General Conference, Joseph Gomez and several other prominent pastors introduced a resolution to reassign all bishops. Though intended as a reform measure, this move benefited Carey, who wanted to leave his western diocese to preside at home in Chicago. He invited bishops who supported the idea to a dinner meeting at his Chicago residence, where they agreed among themselves about their appointments, usurping responsibilities that properly belonged to the episcopal committee. The group then compelled the General Conference to accept the arranged assignments. Ransom, however, rejected Carey's request for support for the idea and denounced the effort to circumvent the episcopal committee. In the end, Carey received the Fourth District assignment, while Ransom and the venerable Bishop J. Albert Johnson, another opponent, were punished with undesirable jurisdictions.[29]

The 1928 General Conference also approved a resolution that allowed the Institutional Church to sell its property and relocate. Though some observers criticized clergymen for costly expenditures and heavy mortgages for enlarged edifices, other church leaders, including Carey, argued that the black community benefited when its congregations had facilities that enabled them to address their communities' broader social and economic needs. Toward that end, Carey's ecclesiastical efforts in the Fourth District focused on the physical expansion of churches. Since the Social Gospel remained in vogue, the congregations he oversaw acquired buildings designed to deliver social service programs to southern black migrants and the disadvantaged. In 1923, for example, Bethel members planned to retire its indebtedness and "devote" the entire building "to social service and community work in connection with the religious services." Four bishops, including Carey, pledged to aid Bethel in achieving these objectives. Carey's appointment in 1929 of Anna T. Owens as general chair for social service in the Chicago Annual Conference signaled his continued commitment to community uplift ministries. Owens, a member of Bethel Church, had experience as a social worker in the city's boys court and had founded a fund for delinquent boys. Under Carey's stewardship, churches throughout his district acquired unprecedented amounts of property. The denomination helped Toronto's Grant Church buy a new debt-free building. St. Peter Church in Minneapolis planned a new structure worth two hundred thousand dollars that would "serve as a social center" for Minnesota's Twin Cities. Similarly, pastors at Chicago's Grant and Arnett Churches met with Carey to present blueprints for their new buildings.[30]

Carey's rising stature within the church increased his prominence in Chicago political circles. Within days of his election as a bishop, the Progressive Company invited him to speak at St. Mary's AME Church in support of a cooperative building program. When the Chicago school board proposed attaching a junior high school to the well-regarded Wendell Phillips High School, Carey, Robert S. Abbott, editor of the *Chicago Defender*, and S. E. White, president of the school's parent-teacher association, met face-to-face with the school superintendent to protest the plan on the grounds that Phillips had become a flagship institution among Chicago blacks: committee members feared that the merger would harm the school. School officials dropped the idea. AME pastor Robert E. Wilson of Chicago, like Carey, was active in politics and was "a forceful and vigilant defender of his race." He affirmed the bishop's activist credentials by praising "his unique usefulness in both church and state." Wilson argued that Carey was responsible for "the benefits our race group receive[s] from his influence . . . in Chicago."[31]

Carey did not limit his confrontations to local-level public officials. In 1927, for example, the Great Mississippi River Flood visited enormous "losses and hardships" across the South. Despite the devastation suffered by black farmers, however, relief officials were "notoriously discriminatory." Carey led a delegation of church and civic leaders to see President Calvin Coolidge about this urgent matter. That the president agreed to see the group testified to the bishop's growing importance as a black spokesman, although Coolidge offered only a dilatory response. Using his political savvy, Carey then turned to Mayor Thompson, who ordered Chicago's comptroller to disburse five thousand dollars to Carey for a Flood Sufferers' Fund, which would distribute the money to "the needy and suffering" through churches in Mississippi, Louisiana, Arkansas, Missouri, and southern Illinois. Thompson noted that Carey had "visited these states and [had] been in touch with the negroes who are suffering and are securing little or no relief from the Red Cross." Carey advised this combination of political contacts and agitation as the best response to similar threats to black's well-being. When attendees at the 1928 General Conference learned about inequalities faced by blacks in the military, Carey declared that "every delegate who knows a Congressman or one for whom he worked and voted" should send a letter to that politician demanding fair treatment.[32]

The Chicago allocation for Carey's flood victims fund solidified his brokerage relationship with Thompson. Though professional black politicians had largely displaced clergy as operatives and officeholders, Carey's activism and his view that politics was integral to ministry enabled him to resist this trend. Thompson's partnership with Carey proved a valuable factor in the mayor's political calculations. Carey brought Thompson reliable support from AME Church members and general backing from appreciative African Americans. While Carey validated to blacks that Thompson was a genuine ally in their fight for racial equality, the mayor's appointment of black officeholders and his support of initiatives beneficial to African Americans showed that the bishop's endorsement made sense.

Carey interacted with black public officials as a political peer. At the 1922 Illinois Republican Convention in Springfield, for example, he traveled with Edward H. Wright, Chicago's assistant corporation counsel and head of the Second Ward delegation; Louis B. Anderson, Thompson's floor leader in the city council; and Oscar De Priest, a former alderman and future congressman. When scandals and a failed lawsuit against the *Chicago Tribune* ended Thompson's 1923 reelection bid, Carey maintained communications with Thompson's Democratic successor, Dever, and others in government. When police randomly raided the South Side to intimidate potential Thompson supporters, Carey called on "certain judges of the Superior Court" to hold speedy trials to release "more than one thousand" blacks who had been "unjustly incarcerated." Carey's influence existed independently of Thompson's political career.[33]

Carey nevertheless remained loyal to Thompson and helped his 1927 campaign to regain Chicago's mayoralty. At the 1923 Chicago Annual Conference at Bethel Church, Carey introduced Thompson to the audience of AME ministers and members. The former mayor declared that "the colored people never asked for more than they were entitled to and no Negro appointment ever made by me has proved unworthy." Thompson clearly tied his political comeback to African American voters, and Carey's endorsement was key in keeping this constituency committed to the ex-mayor. During extensive campaigning in the South Side in February 1927, seven thousand supporters filled five churches to hear Thompson's reelection plans. De Priest presented the candidate at Ebenezer Baptist Church, where Thompson discussed federal legislation that would bring factories and employment to Chicago. According to the *Chicago Defender*, Thompson "promised jobs to hundreds of men and women of our Race" and pledged opposition to police who illegally invaded the homes of South Side residents. Carey, however, brought the rally to a climax. He praised Thompson for his appointment of Edward H. Wright to a high-ranking municipal position and for the help he had provided to "hundreds of men and women of our Race." Carey blamed Thompson's successor for cutting the number of African Americans working at city hall and urged African Americans "to use the ballot" to "settle our so-called race problem."[34]

Thompson's return to the mayor's office increased Carey's political influence. Thompson named Carey to the city's civil service commission, which had jurisdiction over law enforcement. Carey thus gained authority to investigate complaints of police misconduct, enabling him "to get at those persons who are protecting crime and criminals. We will insist that the police do not countenance any dives or other centers of law breaking and evil influence." The local black newspaper described Chicago as "the first city in the country to have a member of our Race as a member of a mayor's cabinet," and another observer wrote that "no Negro in the history of this country has ever been given so powerful a place." Carey's influence with Thompson also extended more broadly: said one contemporary, "There was no 'I' dotted and no 'T' crossed in the government of Mayor Thompson that did not have [Carey's] approval."[35]

The Reverend J. G. Robinson, editor of the *AME Church Review*, noted more specific benefits to African Americans from Carey's presence in city government: a group of young black men who had failed to move up the civil service ranks from junior to senior clerk "came into Bishop Carey's office with beaming faces to thank him for their promotions." In an instance where a white policeman had been harassing the owner of a black restaurant, who was afraid to testify against the officer, Carey compelled the police chief to pursue the charges, and the policeman, a twenty-year veteran of the force, "was discharged in disgrace." Carey also helped a black policeman win reinstatement after the previous commission had dismissed him for showing his revolver to a mob of whites threatening to attack him. Robinson also argued that Carey's authority as a commissioner extended beyond the agency: a supermarket hired three black women as cashiers because of Carey, and the bishop convinced the owner of an electrical facility "to put several hundred of our people to work in his plants."[36]

These gains came at a price, however. Dever was a supporter of Prohibition, and Thompson's apparent ties with such notorious organized crime figures as Johnny Torrio and Al Capone showed that he tacitly tolerated their business of bootlegging. After defeating Dever, Thompson turned a blind eye toward such criminal activities, and the mayor's critics again charged his administration with bribery and corruption. Carey refused to distance himself from his political ally. At the 1928 Michigan Annual Conference in Grand Rapids, he allowed the city's mayor to address the audience. Along with his praise for the denomination and exhortations for blacks to use the ballot to advance themselves, the mayor criticized Thompson, and Carey responded with "one of the greatest speeches" defending the Chicago mayor, declaring him "fair to our people."[37]

The accusations of corruption against Thompson eventually tainted Carey. In 1929, a Chicago grand jury indicted Carey for accepting bribes as a member of the civil service commission, resulting in wide publicity and considerable embarrassment. Though spared the humiliation of a trial, Carey was never either cleared or convicted. Chicago's AME ministerial alliance came to the bishop's aid, extending him "a vote of confidence." They were "pleased with Bishop Carey's conduct as a public officer" and promised that neither clergy nor laity in the Fourth Episcopal District would press any disciplinary action or censure against him.[38]

Nevertheless, Carey's blend of civic and church activities remained problematic. Carey removed the Reverend M. C. Wright as pastor of the St. Stephen AME Church on Chicago's West Side and transferred him to southern Illinois. The pastor refused the appointment, left the AME Church, and founded a nondenominational congregation, blaming his removal on "his independent stand in local politics." The bishop disputed Wright's version of events, claiming that "trouble" had arisen among members at St. Stephen. Whatever the true reasons for Wright's reassignment, the charge that Carey let his public involvements affect his denominational duties may have resonated with his critics and offered them ammunition with which to impugn his character.[39]

By 1931, Carey was presiding bishop of 250 churches in the Midwest and in Canada, and despite the damage from the bribery scandal, he had reached the zenith of his influence. When U.S. Representative Martin B. Madden died, Carey called home the vacationing Oscar De Priest and persuaded him immediately to announce his candidacy for the vacant seat. When De Priest won, becoming the first black to serve in the U.S. House from the North, he credited Carey.[40]

On March 23, 1931, Carey died of a heart attack. Mourners at his funeral filled the huge Quinn Chapel sanctuary to overflowing as a long, prestigious, and interracial roster of church and civic leaders paid tribute to him. Speakers focused on various facets of his involvements, but all agreed that his presence in the public arena had enhanced the lives of thousands of Chicago blacks. Carey's desire for influence and prestige seemed fully satisfied.[41]

In an insightful critique, the *Chicago Defender* declared that if Carey "had devoted himself [and] his powerful talents to the church, Carey would have been as dominant over it as [Daniel A.] Payne. If he had given himself, [with] zeal and unflagging industry, to the state, he would have been one of the great political leaders of the age." But because he divided his energies between the political and religious spheres, he never achieved dominance in either, failing to achieve the stature of either De Priest or Bishop Henry M. Turner.[42]

Richard R. Wright Jr., the editor of the *Christian Recorder* whom Carey had helped decades earlier, understood the tensions between the bishop's political and religious involvements. According to Wright, Carey was "the most hated of men in church and state," in large part because some people were simply "jealous of his power." Wright described Carey as "one of the few Negroes in America to prove the power of political organization," having mastered the "technique of practical politics which is ruthless, selfish and unrelenting." Although he was a minister who had a "kind-hearted, tender, sympathetic nature," he recognized that the political system "rewards its friends; it punishes its enemies, and will not brook even the semblance of disloyalty." Carey found it "difficult to keep" politics and the church apart, and "when Carey's political technique began to influence his church action, there was resentment."[43]

Carey's conduct, while hardly discrediting the practice of public theology, demonstrated the hazards of defining its core in purely political terms. The proximity between party politics and religious affairs carried with it the seeds of internal church divisiveness and elevated the importance of partisan preferences over ecclesiastical operations. Carey would have argued that the positive policy outcomes that these activities generated trumped the tensions between the bishop and some Fourth Episcopal District clergy. Fissures within AME ranks seemed an acceptable price for promoting the broader goals of black advancement.

Carey was not singularly sinful in inserting party politics into church affairs. Ransom, Carey's constant critic, was involved in a similar situation as the AME bishop in Ohio. As chair of the board of trustees of Wilberforce University, Ransom and the president navigated an uneasy partnership between the school's church- and state-controlled divisions. Since Republicans usually served as Ohio governors and dominated the state legislature, Ransom's affiliation with the Democrats became problematic for the institution. In 1936, D. Ormonde Walker, an AME pastor and a Democrat, became president of Wilberforce, "openly championing the cause of the democratic party from the pulpit, where he was a powerful and convincing speaker." The presence of Ransom and Walker "was represented as an invasion of vested, political power and control," as the Republicans who were trustees on the state side of Wilberforce opposed Walker, as did "the church board which was anxious to retain the state dole for the support of its own unit." Walker, who was ousted in 1941, declared that "his mixing politics with education was his greatest error in judgment even tho he was encouraged in this in the beginning by the chairman of the church board, Bishop R. C. Ransom."[44]

Carey's efforts on behalf of Chicago's black city employees and Ransom and Walker's work in higher education brought benefits to African Americans. The costs of these advancements were manifested in various stresses and intrusions into the regular operations of the AME denomination. Despite these results, Carey and his clerical colleagues stood proudly as politicized preachers, never convinced by their critics that that a public theology embedded in politics was anything but a blessing for black people.

CHAPTER 4

Leadership and Lineage

THE RISE OF ARCHIBALD J. CAREY JR.

Archibald Carey Sr.'s children surely knew that their father was an important man. Into their large Chicago residence came a perennial parade of bishops and high church officials, who dined at Bishop Carey's elegantly set table to settle denominational disputes and discuss church policies. Political dignitaries both black and white also knew the Carey address and made their way to 4744 South Parkway to plan strategies for electing municipal or state candidates or to arrange to have Carey speak on behalf of the GOP. Perhaps the sympathetic Carey children heard him say, "I have many duties that press me. I have no leisure. I seem not to have time for the enterprises in which I am engaged, but they are all important and I do the best I can."[1]

Three of Archibald Carey Sr.'s five children were daughters, for whom ordination to the ministry was forbidden. Eloise (1891–1971), Annabel (1894–1982), and Dorothy (1903–72) grew up under the watchful eye and stern supervision of Elizabeth Davis Carey and saw their mother active as the dutiful wife of an ambitious AME minister. Though educated like her husband, Elizabeth Carey drew praise for her superbly run household and her skill in hosting church dignitaries. At the 1899 Iowa Annual Conference, for example, she entertained at dinner a bishop, several general officers, a military chaplain, and various pastors and spouses. "Mrs. Carey, the cultured wife of the doctor," said one observer, "presided with dignity at the table and made us all feel at home." Raising funds for the Women's Parent Mite Missionary Society was another of Elizabeth Carey's responsibilities. At the same Iowa Annual Conference, she and Reverdy C. Ransom's wife, Emma Connor Ransom, raised $110 and $94, respectively, in a closely watched competition.[2]

Elizabeth Carey's full schedule of hosting, working with local and regional branches of AME missionary societies, and traveling with her busy husband meant that Eloise assumed an increasing number of domestic duties and helped at church. Though her brother, Madison (1896–1980), close in age to her and Annabel, needed no supervision, Archibald Jr., born in Chicago on February 29, 1908, became the responsibility of the older Carey children, especially Eloise; in fact, her maternal role seemed at times to supersede their sibling relationship. In 1916, during her father's pastorate at Institutional, Eloise also taught a "literary class": "quite a number of young people" were expected to benefit from her instruction. Eloise later received postsecondary education at Northwestern University and Chicago Normal College and earned a master's degree at Columbia University and went on to teach English both in Chicago and at Harlem's Harriet Beecher Stowe Junior High School. She thus belonged to what historian Evelyn Brooks Higginbotham has dubbed the "female talented tenth."[3]

Perhaps her mother's example influenced Eloise's decision to marry a minister. Shelton Hale Bishop (1889–1962), a New York City native and curate at St. Thomas Episcopal Church in Chicago, was also a child of the parsonage. His father, Hutchens Chew Bishop (1858–1937), was the longtime rector of New York's St. Philip Episcopal Church, a prominent parish that he relocated to Harlem in 1910. Eloise and Shelton's 1919 wedding, with her father officiating, received widespread coverage in the black press. Shelton Bishop was serving as rector at Pittsburgh's fledgling Holy Cross Episcopal Church, and Eloise assumed duties at her husband's parish that resembled those she had performed at her father's churches. When Shelton left for New York to assist at St. Philip, Eloise resisted the move. Now the mother of three children, she resented her sister-in-law, who presided at the Bishop household as Eloise had done for her busy parents. An ugly divorce and an acrimonious custody battle ended what had appeared to be an ideal union between two elite families.[4]

Eloise's sisters followed her into the teaching profession. Annabel studied at the University of Chicago and earned a doctorate at Columbia University. She returned to Chicago and taught at Wendell Phillips High School, served as a vice principal, and became director of human relations for the Chicago public schools. Dorothy, an alumna of Northwestern University who received a master's degree at Columbia, also taught English in the Chicago schools before earning a degree in social work and finding employment with the Cook County Department of Public Health. Annabel married Patrick Prescott (1890–1945), a lawyer and later a judge, while Dorothy married a fellow teacher, Dewey Patton (1898–1967).[5]

Although Madison Carey sometimes performed political chores for his father, the streets seemed to hold greater attraction for him than did the churches, and the behavior of Madison, better known as Dave, proved increasingly embarrassing for the Careys. He was called "'a black sheep' as a result of having been spoiled by his parents." Contemporaries described him as a "professional gambler" and "a man about town." When a "gambling house" opened near his brother's Woodlawn AME Church and Dave allegedly was offered the manager's position, Archibald "opposed this and carried on a vigorous campaign against the gambling interests." Dave reportedly brought his brother a thousand-dollar bribe from "the Chicago gambling syndicate" to stop the effort to close the activity, though the reverend refused the money. On March 6, 1944, Dave was arrested for embezzlement but was released when the plaintiff dropped the charge. Two and a half years later, he was taken into custody again on the same charge, but again it was dismissed "for want of prosecution." He was charged with embezzlement for the third time on January 20, 1947. This time, the case proceeded, and he was found guilty and sentenced to between one and ten years at the Illinois State Penitentiary at Joliet. He was paroled on April 30, 1948, and discharged from parole on May 8, 1951. One observer characterized his "criminal activities [as] more of the manner of irresponsibility than maliciousness," and he became "a harmless and likeable person" who worked for Chicago's sanitary department.[6]

The role of ecclesiastical and civic heir thus fell to Archibald J. Carey Jr. The focus on Archie seemed natural and divinely determined. When he was young, a serious illness threatened his life. Elizabeth Davis Carey, fearful that she might lose her youngest child, promised God that if he lived she would give him back to the Lord. This apocryphal story, reminiscent of the Old Testament account of Hannah and her son, Samuel, may have been the prelude to the father's careful cultivation of Archie for leadership in the pulpit and on the public platform. Not everyone in the Carey family believed that the combination of preaching and politics was desirable. Though always supportive of her brother, Annabel Carey Prescott developed "theoretical reservations" about his dual roles as pastor and politician, perhaps as a consequence of some of their father's unhappy experiences in pursuing these bivocational commitments.[7]

Studies on African American leaders, especially those in the ministry, often overlook the fact that clerical involvement in the public square often was intergenerational and fundamentally familial. Public theology envisaged as civic engagement and political activity, though pursued by a minority of preachers, drew practitioners whose impact exceeded their small numbers, and their actions often shaped their heirs vocational decisions.

George C. Clement (1871–1934), Carey's ecumenical partner in the merger negotiations between the African Methodist Episcopal (AME) and AME Zion Churches, was a successful pastor in North Carolina and Kentucky and editor of the *Star of Zion*. After his election to the episcopacy in 1916, Clement developed expertise in race relations as an official in the Federal Council of Churches and in the Commission on Interracial Cooperation, two moderate organizations that valued dialogue and interaction between educated blacks and whites as the best strategy to ameliorate racial tensions. Clement's maverick political views, however, positioned him as a potential Woodrow Wilson appointee and as an advocate for black support of the Democratic Party.[8] His son, Rufus E. Clement (1900–1967), who followed his father in the AME Zion ministry, earned both a divinity degree and a Ph.D. in history at Northwestern University. Although he served as pastor to two North Carolina congregations and was constantly lobbied to run for the bishopric, he focused his energies in higher education. As a professor at Livingstone College, a dean at Louisville Municipal College, and president of Atlanta University, Clement emulated his father's patient and painstaking efforts to promote black advancement through interracial, religious, and philanthropic organizations. Clement departed from this pattern, however, as he thrust himself into the public square as a successful 1953 candidate for the Atlanta Board of Education.[9]

Like Carey and Clement, Adam Clayton Powell Sr. (1865–1953), another peer of Archibald Carey Sr., became a paradigmatic preacher whose civic engagements benefited the black population and influenced the career of his son and namesake. During his long pastorate at New York City's Abyssinian Baptist Church, Powell developed a public theology that marked his congregation as a social and political nerve center for Manhattan's black population. His popular evangelical preaching and the church's 1923 move to Harlem helped Abyssinian grow from sixteen hundred members in 1908 to ten thousand members in 1937, requiring the full-time services of three clergy and nineteen other staff. During the depression, the church administered a free soup kitchen, an unemployment relief fund, and a relief bureau. Abyssinian also offered a teacher-training program and an adult education curriculum that included physical education, English, political science, dressmaking, nursing, and typewriting. Civil rights activism and politics comprised the other components of Powell's public theology. He played leading roles in the National Association for the Advancement of Colored People (NAACP), the National Urban League, and various initiatives to safeguard the rights of African Americans. Though he was deeply involved in the Republican Party, he believed that better possibilities for blacks lay in Franklin D. Roosevelt's Democratic Party and its New Deal. Unlike Reverdy C. Ransom, who joined the Democrats in 1928 and supported FDR in 1932, Powell did not shift his party affiliation until 1936. His presence among the Democrats, however, was short-lived, as the American Labor Party attracted his participation. This group supported both Republicans and Democrats who were friendly to legislation that aided the working class.[10]

Adam Clayton Powell Jr. (1908–72) succeeded his father as Abyssinian's pastor in 1937. He followed the same public theology paradigm and broadened his impact beyond what the elder Powell had achieved. The younger Powell's protest activities, pickets, and boycotts won him constituencies both within his congregation and in the larger Harlem community, and in 1941, he won election to the New York City Council. Three years later, he gained a seat in the U.S. House of Representatives. As chair of the House Education and Labor Committee, he crafted legislation that benefited the nation's black population. During his more than two decades in Congress, he retained his pastorate.[11]

While exposing his children to appreciative church and civic crowds, the senior Carey paid special attention to grooming his son as his successor in religious and political leadership. In 1918, when the Institutional Church celebrated Carey's two decades as a Chicago pastor, Eloise, Annabel, Dorothy, and Archibald Jr. shared recognition with their parents. Archibald Jr., his fiancée, and Dorothy were present at the 1930 Michigan Annual Conference, drawing applause. Archibald Jr. was also honored in 1924, when the *Chicago Daily News* sponsored an oratorical contest and he was one of two students selected to represent three area high schools. The assigned topic on the U.S. Constitution seemed an easy one for the senior at Wendell Phillips High School, who won a bronze medal at the district competition and moved on to the semifinals to contend for a silver medal and the chance to speak before President Calvin Coolidge. At the regional level, he defeated contestants from adjacent midwestern states and won a thousand dollars. Although the top prize eluded him, the bishop's friend and successor at Institutional, the Reverend W. W. Lucas, invited Archie to "present his famous oration on the 'The Constitution—A Safeguard of Human Liberties.'" At the 1924 AME Church General Conference in Louisville, Kentucky, Bishop William A. Fountain also recognized young Carey's oratorical achievement.[12]

The senior Carey licensed his son to preach at Institutional Church in 1928 and ordained him as an itinerant deacon at the Chicago Annual Conference a year later. Bishop Henry B. Parks, Bishop Carey's eulogist and successor in the Fourth District, fully ordained the junior Carey as an itinerant elder in 1931. Hence, right after his father's death, Archibald J. Carey Jr. became a fully credentialed AME Church minister. Bishop Carey also exposed his son to the possibilities that political service offered. When Archie was twenty, he accompanied his father to the U.S. Capitol in Washington, D.C., where he "stood in the House gallery" and dreamed of election to Congress. He later told his sister, Eloise, "I think Mom and Pop both wanted me to go." Moreover, he said, a political career would help him "break out of the psychological shackles that segregate and isolate a minister."[13]

Bishop Carey aided these aspirations by obtaining a first-rate higher education for his son. None of the Carey children attended their parents' alma mater, perhaps because segregated Atlanta was less inviting than the comparative openness of Chicago-area institutions. The junior Carey enrolled at Lewis Institute, established in 1895 and named for Allen Cleveland Lewis, the school's benefactor. The institute initially offered evening classes in mechanical engineering for adult males and practical training for women in art, science, and design. During the second decade of the twentieth century, President William Rainey Harper of the University of Chicago suggested that Lewis develop a liberal arts curriculum and become a full-fledged college, and in 1917 the school won approval to grant bachelor of science degrees. Archie Carey entered Lewis Institute in 1925; because it was affiliated with the University of Chicago, he also matriculated there but was "dismissed 'without dishonor' for poor scholarship" in March 1926. Though he returned in October 1927, Carey was again dismissed from the College of Literature in March 1928. He tried once more the following October but was found guilty yet again of "poor scholarship" and dismissed on August 3, 1929. That Carey was repeatedly permitted to return, observed the university registrar, "indicated that he was highly regarded at the school." He managed enough credits at Lewis to receive a baccalaureate degree in 1929 with a C+ average.[14]

Pampered and doted on by both parents and siblings, Archie Carey, an affable and easygoing youth, apparently was a lazy pupil. Though he demonstrated his intelligence and ability in various oratorical contests, Carey revealed few of these attributes in his academic work and seems to have chosen to do the minimum necessary to prepare for the career his father had selected for him. Perhaps he believed he did not have to work hard because his future seemed set. When he entered the seminary, however, he took his studies more seriously.

Bishop Carey had supplemented his bachelor's degree from Atlanta University with divinity courses at the University of Chicago and at the Chicago Theological Seminary but determined that his son should matriculate fully at the Methodist-sponsored Garrett Biblical Institute at Northwestern University. At Garrett, Carey enrolled in standard courses in theology, church history, ethics, homiletics, Old Testament, the life of Jesus, world religions, and religious education. His father's emphasis on the Social Gospel, however, was reflected in such courses as "The Economic Order in the Light of Christianity" and "Current Social Applications of Christianity." "The Economic Order" was taught by Murray Howard Leiffer, assistant professor of sociology and home missions and director of city field work. The instructor analyzed capitalism and "the problems arising out of it, such as standard of living, protection of the worker, and class conflict." Albert Z. Mann, professor of the Rural Community Extension Service, taught Carey "Current Social Applications." Students in both classes surveyed "current social problems and the evaluation of current social movements and events in the light of Christian principles with a view of discovering the social objectives of the Christian Church in America and the world." Carey's bachelor of divinity degree, awarded in 1932, thus provided him with both intellectual and practical skills needed for urban ministry.[15]

In 1935, Carey received a bachelor of laws degree from Kent College of Law, a school attended by Robert S. Abbott, the founder and publisher of the *Chicago*

Defender, and by the attorneys who headed some of the city's top firms. This credential would expand his ministry into areas that few pastors could enter and would enhance his political prospects, qualifying him for positions open to few other clergy. Carey continued his lackluster academic performance, graduating fiftieth in a class of sixty-four; however, he won the Burke debate prize in recognition of his forensic abilities. One observer later noted that Carey was a "more capable attorney than his poor grades" would have predicted.[16]

In 1930, Bishop Carey assigned his son to Woodlawn AME Church, a small congregation near the University of Chicago. The sons of bishops usually received choice appointments, but Carey, still in the seminary, accepted a church that had just forty-nine members; other novice pastors received missions with far fewer members. Moreover, the location spared young Carey the rigors of travel to either Iowa or Wisconsin, both of which lay within the Chicago Conference's boundaries.[17]

Both Careys believed that their anchoring in the AME Church provided them with broad reputational credibility and a base of supporters that they could parlay into political influence. Both also contended that loyalty to the GOP best served the interests of African Americans. But they pursued the objectives of public theology in strikingly different circumstances. Although he decried the power that southern segregationists wielded in the Democratic Party, Archibald Jr. bolted the Republicans when Barry Goldwater, an opponent of the 1964 Civil Rights Act, received the party's presidential nomination. And although the younger man inherited his father's brokerage role, as African Americans began to resist Jim Crow more aggressively, especially during the 1940s, his brokerage posture became more audacious and his commitment to direct action tactics increased. He recognized that the pace of positive change for African Americans depended less on white generosity and more on black militancy and insurgency. Carey's leadership shifted in concert with these developing strategies in the civil rights struggle.

Through the 1930s and 1940s, Carey developed extensive Social Gospel ministries at Woodlawn. A gifted preacher who emphasized spiritually moving worship services, Carey had a vision of Woodlawn as a community-oriented congregation and accordingly involved it in numerous political, social, and economic projects. Moreover, his fund-raising skills became legend among Chicago clergy, and his evangelistic successes marked him as a "rising young giant of a new day." By 1938, the congregation numbered four hundred and had "outgrown the size of the present church building," according to the Reverend Robert Thomas Sr., a family loyalist and the presiding elder to the district that included Woodlawn. Under the thirty-year-old Carey's stewardship, Woodlawn purchased a building lot and raised a building fund of forty thousand dollars despite the depression. Woodlawn continued to grow through the 1940s, with membership expanding to fifteen hundred. In addition to its spacious new edifice, the church acquired three additional properties and employed a full-time staff of seven. "Got over $20,000 in [the] Building Fund," he boasted to a ministerial friend in 1945, "maybe $25,000" in a few months. Wood-lawn developed such a reputation as a leading AME congregation and a center for various community services that George W. Baber, the pastor at Ebenezer in Detroit, told Carey that a female congregant and evangelist who was headed for Chicago was "anxious to serve in your church." In the mid-1940s, another minister advised Jesse W. Cotton to attend Woodlawn because of Carey's "dynamic" preaching. Similarly, Glen Johnson, a Wilberforce graduate, arrived in Chicago in 1946 to study at John Marshall Law School and joined Woodlawn. Celebrities, too, came through the church's doors. Congressman Adam Clayton Powell Jr. preached there, and heavyweight boxing champion Joe Louis married a congregant. Before becoming a football star at University of Illinois, Buddy Young was a Woodlawn altar boy. Another parishioner, Kenneth Childers, appeared on the radio on the popular Quiz Kids broadcast. Although some Chicagoans believed that Woodlawn catered to the elite, the congregation was also attractive to working-class blacks. Timuel Black Sr. and his family migrated to Chicago from Birmingham, Alabama, in 1919 and joined a succession of AME churches, including Quinn Chapel, Bethel, Coppin, and, in 1941, Woodlawn. They remembered the senior Carey as presiding elder in a district that included Quinn Chapel and were happy to be his son's parishioners.[18]

During the early 1940s, the church's community activities included the West Woodlawn Club for Service Men, which sponsored entertainment for draftees and others in the military. Carey organized a chapter of the American Veterans Committee and provided legal counsel to those in court-martial proceedings. As Wood-lawn's visibility increased both locally and nationally, so did Carey's prominence. Although his father had given him a boost up the ecclesiastical ladder, he soon climbed higher on his own, forging his own persona as a successful Chicago pastor, and Woodlawn joined the circuit of important pulpits for denominational dignitaries. In 1943, he received an honorary doctorate from Wilberforce University. He responded by inviting the school's president, Charles H. Wesley, to preach to his congregation so that Wesley and Woodlawn would "know each other," thereby increasing the church's support for the school. Carey also became a sought-after preacher on special occasions. President William A. Fountain Jr. invited him to speak at a seminar at Morris Brown College in Georgia. Carlyle F. Stewart, himself a pastor of prominence and pedigree, arranged for Carey to preach at St. Peter's in Minneapolis and to give "a brief talk from any subject" at an evening forum.[19]

Carey's ministerial and legal talents convinced others that his leadership should extend beyond the Chicago Annual Conference, and his peers elected him a delegate to the 1944 General Conference, where he was named chair of a special committee that would assess the condition of blacks just before the presidential election. Carey observed that the denomination should "scrutinize the platforms and nominees advanced by all political parties" and influence "those men and measures which offer the greatest hope of democracy." The Carey group also gained an audience with the GOP resolutions committee, and Bishop David H. Sims tried to get a hearing for them with the platform committee. Carey hoped for a similar response from the Democratic Party. Moreover, the committee, which sat for the entire 1944–48 quadrennium, was charged with preparing a report to be sent to the president of the United States and Congress. In 1945, a Dayton, Ohio, pastor and others urged Carey to run for the presidency of the Connectional Council, a ministerial body that recommended policies to the General Conference and the bishops. Bishop Noah W. Williams backed Carey because he "had such a wonderful father that I loved so much." Similarly, Bishop Sherman L. Greene "was more than happy to do anything that might bless the memory of your distinguished father and evidence my personal gratitude for the many wonderful things he did for me." However, Bishop John A. Gregg, Carey's prelate in Chicago, warned that Williams, Greene, and the other five bishops who endorsed Carey were "small potatoes" with respect to council activities. Carey lost the election but nonetheless remained popular with other pastors, who relied on his advice and perspectives when legal interpretations of church law and procedures seemed unclear.[20]

When a citizens committee in the Lilydale area organized a mass meeting to press for a new school in 1936, Carey was chosen to speak. Carey, "one of the city's most militant young clergymen," called on the audience to demand a decent facility for black children instead of the portables with which they had been provided and urged residents to "organize, publicize and persevere if they would realize their goal." Carey's activism drew the attention of a local education professor, who recommended him to serve on the city school board. "I have known Mr. Carey for almost ten years," he said, "and have had opportunity to become fairly well acquainted with him during that time. I have always found him a man of integrity, strictly honest and straightforward. He is independent in his thinking and broadly social in his outlook." Carey has "an unusually keen mind and knows how to use it." The president of the West Woodlawn Community Council had similar views, which he expressed to Mayor Edward J. Kelly. Although an appointment to the board of education did not materialize, word of Carey's forthright defense of Chicago blacks spread to the Detroit Civil Rights Committee. This group, which included two leading AME pastors and the widow of an AME bishop, asked Carey to speak in 1939. According to the organization's chair, Snow F. Grigsby, Carey "really started the ball rolling in this town," arousing citizens and community groups, who were "now asking what they might do to help this situation."[21]

Carey's activism intensified during the 1940s as a consequence of the changed racial atmosphere of the World War II period. As large numbers of blacks entered the armed forces to fight for the United States, they began to question why they lacked full rights at home, a sentiment captured by the "Double V" campaign—victory against Nazism and fascism abroad and victory against rampant racism in the United States. Blacks, particularly those in the military, began to defend themselves increasingly vigorously against physical assaults. Moreover, A. Philip Randolph and the National Negro Congress, which he had founded in 1935, argued that the consolidated efforts of various black organizations and religious bodies could aid campaigns to unionize black workers and advocated the mass mobilization of African Americans to pressure the federal government to protect black civil rights and promote employment opportunities. These developments signaled a new militancy that was reflected in Carey's civic engagements and civil rights activities. He claimed, for example, that a columnist wrongly blamed the "colored press" for causing a 1943 Detroit race riot. Instead, according to Carey, the unrest had resulted from a host of "undemocratic practices in America." He cited the city's substandard housing for African Americans and employment discrimination as well as such national issues as the discriminatory treatment of blacks by the Red Cross and the War Department. Carey's concern for blacks in the military had a personal component as well: after undergoing training at Camp Blanding, Florida, in 1943, his nephew, Madison D. Carey Jr., was shipped to Burma to fight the Japanese in the Pacific theater.[22]

In Randolph, Carey found a kindred social activist. Both were sons of AME ministers, and both believed in strong protests against racial discrimination. In his persistent fight to force the Pullman Company to recognize the Brotherhood of Sleeping Car Porters, Randolph found few black clergy courageous enough to support him or to allow him to speak in their churches. Although Archibald Carey Sr. had actively opposed Randolph's efforts to unionize the porters, the younger Carey embraced the view that direct action tactics were needed to advance the black struggle. After President Franklin Delano Roosevelt, in response to Randolph's threatened march, established the Fair Employment Practices Commission (FEPC) to fight discrimination in industries holding federal contracts, the labor leader worked to ensure that the committee would live up to expectations. Carey supported Randolph's efforts, speaking at a March on Washington Movement (MOWM) rally in Chicago on January 26, 1942. The following year, Randolph addressed Woodlawn's current issues forum, where he delivered "the best speech of his career to an overflowing crowd," Carey wrote.[23]

On black military matters, Carey interacted with Truman K. Gibson Jr., an African American lawyer from Chicago who in 1940 became an assistant to William H. Hastie, who was on leave from his position as dean of the law school at Howard University to serve as a civilian aide to Secretary of War Henry L. Stimson. Gibson and Hastie knew of Carey's civic involvements in Chicago and of his discussions with selective service officials about racial issues. Gibson and Hastie also wanted Carey to tell them about "the general community attitude towards the Army."[24]

An uncompromising proponent of integration in the military, Hastie resigned as Stimson's aide in 1942 to protest separate training facilities for ground personnel in the U.S. Army Air Force. Gibson remained in Stimson's office and immediately developed conflicts with Carey. Some black Chicago entrepreneurs agreed to sponsor a recreational center for black soldiers at Fort Huachuca in Arizona. After learning that Gibson had approved the scheme to bring gambling and vice to the base, an outraged Carey announced, "The whole plan is a vicious and iniquitous enterprise which I chose to protest." He preached about it at Woodlawn and denounced it at an AME meeting.[25]

Gibson contended that Carey had received false information and expressed surprise that he would act on unfounded rumors. Moreover, some of Carey's comments were published in the *Chicago Bee*, leading Gibson to charge that the minister had infringed on "the war time censorship code" and promoted "the spread of a rumor detrimental to the conduct of the war effort." Gibson added that no one in the army would support a "project deleterious to United States soldiers." The recreational effort envisaged for black servicemen at Fort Huachuca had been "initiated by the army, sponsored by the Governor and one of the senior Senators from Arizona and [was] currently pending before the War Production Board as being necessary for the war effort." Moreover, "it was never contemplated that there be any of the vice and gambling as alleged in the *Chicago Bee*." Carey's concerns, according to Gibson, were therefore totally unfounded.[26]

Carey remained unmoved by Gibson's defense. He knew the identity of the investors and trusted the people who had given him the information about the project. He asked Gibson, "Why doesn't the army provide recreation centers for the soldiers at Fort Huachuca?" and "Why is it only Chicago men who are financing this recreation center [and] do the investors make an outright contribution to this center or do they expect it to be returned and when and how?" Moreover, Carey wondered, would any profits the investors realized "come from the pockets of the soldiers?" Carey vowed to continue his criticism of the Arizona project: "When I become convinced that the proposed recreation center is a purely service enterprise and was planned so from the beginning, I will, from the pulpit and through the press, withdraw my statements concerning the whole affair." In later years, Gibson conceded that his father, Truman Gibson Sr., and some associates had tried to establish a beer joint at Fort Huachuca with seed money from Chicago numbers racketeers, thereby confirming Carey's accusation. Gibson, however, maintained his belief that the tavern would have improved the black soldiers' morale. Conversely, Carey's loud and public objections echoed Hastie's opposition to segregation and its exploitation of African Americans by both whites and blacks.[27]

Carey's wartime activities gained him a reputation as a civil rights activist, and he maintained that position after hostilities ended. In 1946, the Conference on Civic Unity invited him to Portland, Oregon, to address "Democracy's Unfinished

Business." Edwin C. Berry, an Urban League official and chair of the civic group, asked Carey to talk about how the Chicago mayor's committee handled civic and diversity issues and why a national FEPC and other civil rights measures could "establish the Darker Brother as a full citizen." Carey came because Portland whites "need to see, hear and meet more Negroes of ability" and African Americans "need encouragement and inspiration" from accomplished blacks.[28]

Other black ministers shared Carey's perception that clergy had a large role in the public square. Another Chicagoan, the influential and versatile Reverend J. C. Austin, pastor of the populous Pilgrim Baptist Church, won 4,850 votes to become a delegate to the 1936 Republican National Convention. Marshall L. Shepard, pastor at Philadelphia's Mt. Olivet Tabernacle Baptist Church, served three terms in the Pennsylvania legislature in the late 1930s and early 1940s and served as chaplain to the Democratic National Convention in 1936. W. H. Peck and George W. Baber, pastors at Detroit's largest AME congregations, were leaders of the city's Civil Rights Committee. Dwight V. Kyle, pastor of Avery Chapel AME Church in Memphis, fought vigorously for the FEPC.[29]

Adam Clayton Powell Jr., like Archibald Carey Jr., was the light-skinned son of a publicly involved clergyman and had educational and social advantages that most African Americans lacked. Like the younger Carey, the younger Powell had trained at a bulwark of liberal Protestantism—in his case, Union Theological Seminary in New York City—where what he learned fitted the praxis that his father had pursued in his ministry. And both men used sustained protest tactics and militant direct action techniques to extend their father's attempts to press influential whites to support initiatives that would improve the condition of blacks.

How Carey became acquainted with Adam Clayton Powell Sr. and his son is unknown. However they met, Adam Clayton Powell Jr. invited Carey to stay at his home during a 1937 visit to New York, and Carey came to know both of the Powells well. In October 1939, the younger Powell preached at Woodlawn. Barely two months later, his father followed, including in his talk plaudits for Carey's pastoral achievements. By 1943, when he was coming to Chicago for the National Baptist Convention, the elder Powell requested a preaching invitation: "If you can use me to an advantage, I will be glad to speak for you."[30]

When he was in New York, Carey not only tried to make time to preach at Abyssinian but also sought to arrange social gatherings with Powell, on one occasion suggesting that both men and their wives "run up to Martha's Vineyard for a while." Despite the comfortable middle-class status enjoyed by both Carey and Powell, the Chicagoan firmly believed that all "Negro Americans must resist the divisive influences which play upon us": "We are all Negroes together. Whether light or dark, or rich or poor, whether you came from the First Families of Virginia or the other side of the tracks makes no difference to Old Jim Crow." He added, "Negroes will not gain complete emancipation until all Negroes get it. Freedom does not belong to the rich or to the educated or to the light skinned. Emancipation says to us all—'You shall not see my face except your brother be with you.'" Whenever Carey's racial identity was questioned, he vehemently declared that he was a Negro. Such sentiments meant that Powell's misbehavior and utterances about race, class, and color at times strained Carey's patience. By the 1960s, when Powell spoke at a "big dinner" at Chicago's Ebenezer Baptist Church, Carey described him as "at his bombastic worst." The congressman talked in derogatory terms about staring down a white man, making Carey "quite uncomfortable" because several whites were present. Moreover, Powell "made bold to say, 'I am the only Negro leader who has lived all of his life in the slums of Harlem and in the slums of Washington,'" leaving Carey itching to point out that he had been to Powell's "home up on the Hudson in New York," the congressman's "smart apartment" in Washington, D.C., and his island getaway in Puerto Rico. "I love the guy," Carey declared, "but I'd wash his mouth with soap."[31]

Another trait that Carey and Powell shared was the recognition that whatever the persuasive potential of sermons and speeches, moral suasion was not enough to challenge ongoing discrimination. In the early 1940s, Carey spoke to the board of the Chicago Urban League regarding "Unenforceable Obligations." He declared, "Every man has certain unenforceable obligations." For example, "the law requires that you live peaceably with your neighbor, but there is nothing in the law which requires that you shall be a neighbor to him or that you shall practice democracy or initiate the spirit of brotherhood." The nation's war effort, he continued, had unenforceable obligations pertaining to race. The United States needed "to integrate and utilize ALL Americans in the effort to win the war." In the "titanic struggle with the forces of enslavement . . . America needs everything she can get to win this war." Above all, victory would require "not guns, nor ships, nor planes, nor tanks—but manpower. And yet there is a great reservoir of manpower among the Negroes of America that remains thus far untapped." The main culprits, "color prejudice and race discrimination," allowed "unenlightened employers [to] say 'Whites only'" even though African Americans had vital skills that could aid in defeating the Axis powers. Mere exhortations about unenforceable obligations that valued "the spirit of brotherhood to all peoples" were not sufficient to compel the observance of black inclusion and racial equality. Something more was needed.[32]

Carey had already begun that something more. In 1938, he launched a crusade against the discriminatory hiring practices of local milk companies, endorsing a boycott of firms that would not employ African American drivers and organizing a "Milkless Day" to press for the acceptance of blacks into the Milk Wagon Drivers Union. In New York City, Carey confronted the president of the International Union of Motion Picture Operators and condemned him and his organization for racial exclusion. He was part of a delegation that approached the Surface Lines Rapid Transit and Motor Coach companies to demand the hiring of African Americans as motormen, conductors, and bus drivers. Another Carey delegation went to a local telephone company to seek the employment of black women as operators and black men as collectors and mechanics.[33]

Carey's growing commitment to direct action protest never dampened his support for the NAACP's patient and painstaking efforts to challenge Jim Crow in the courts. The organization had officially chartered a Chicago branch in 1912, and it had successfully challenged discrimination in Chicago schools, at University of Chicago dining halls, and in municipal employment. Although members of the Chicago branch had denied Archibald Carey Sr. a leadership role because of his connections to the Republican Party, he supported the organization's efforts and spoke at the group's 1926 national meeting, which was held in Chicago. The event returned to the Windy City in 1932, spurring the younger Carey's development as a NAACP activist. He, in turn, inspired his congregation to become a leading supporter of the Chicago branch. In 1945, for example, twenty-six churches were involved in the group's membership campaign, which resulted in 5,041 new members, 559 of them from Woodlawn. Nevertheless, his political involvements initially prevented him from assuming a leadership role in the local chapter.[34]

In 1937, Carey became involved in the Scottsboro Case, in which nine African American men were falsely accused and wrongly convicted of rape by an all-white Alabama jury. The case became a cause célèbre in the black community and resulted in a heated rivalry between the NAACP and the communist-affiliated International Labor Defense, both of which sought to defend the men. Carey sided with the NAACP and joined other prominent Chicagoans who sponsored a December 8 rally at which two of the Scottsboro defendants appeared. The same year, Carey chaired a Chicago branch committee that organized a rally in support of the Gavagan Anti-Lynching Bill, which sought to make lynching a federal crime. The measure's sponsor, U.S. Representative Joseph A. Gavagan of New York, and the national head of the NAACP, Walter White, spoke at the rally, with White thanking Carey "for the tremendously effective work which you did in making the meeting such a success." He added that "the Chicago and Los Angeles meetings particularly are going to play a big part in forcing action on the bill." Carey also joined the Chicago Free Herndon Committee, which sought to obtain the release of Angelo Herndon, a black communist imprisoned in Georgia as a consequence of his efforts to organize the unemployed.[35]

By 1942, officials in the Chicago NAACP realized that Carey was a tremendous resource, and they invited him to join the group's executive board. He spoke at the branch's Town Hall and became involved in efforts to pressure the state legislature to provide housing for victims of a recent catastrophe. Word of Carey's oratorical abilities spread rapidly, and he soon became a popular speaker at NAACP branches nationwide. Attorney T. G. Nutter invited him to address the Charleston, West Virginia, NAACP, and reminded the Chicago pastor that his bishop, John A. Gregg, had spoken the previous year. A branch official in Maryland who wanted Carey to kick off a membership drive worked to fit an appearance into Carey's schedule because Baltimore "never gets tired of the future Bishop Archibald J. Carey, Jr." In 1942, the Springfield branch drew him to Illinois's capital city to deliver the Lincoln-Douglass Day Banquet address about African American attitudes toward World War II. In 1946 he spoke to the Beloit, Wisconsin, and St. Louis branches as well as to the Virginia State Conference of Branches. Carey also became a much-sought-after speaker at non-NAACP events. In May 1946 alone, Carey delivered baccalaureate addresses at Tuskegee Institute in Alabama, Allen University in South Carolina, and Kentucky State College before firing up an audience for the NAACP's Pittsburgh membership campaign. He gave many of his speeches extemporaneously, without prepared texts.[36]

Carey thus gave himself national visibility and marked himself as an important spokesman on civil rights matters. Carey, like other black clergy, employed universalist language to bolster claims for racial equality. Casting the black struggle in the global context, Carey compared the condition of African Americans to colonized populations in Asia, Africa, and South America and to Jews recently victimized by Hitler's Holocaust. He thus argued that alliances between blacks and other oppressed peoples were possible and that politicians who ignored racism in American society imperiled the nation's international credibility. By stressing these themes to NAACP audiences, Carey reinforced the organization's emphasis on interracial partnerships with white and Jewish supporters and echoed the rhetoric of Benjamin E. Mays, Howard Thurman, George D. Kelsey, William Stuart Nelson, and Mordecai Johnson, leading religious intellectuals who discussed the black struggle in universalist terms. In his 1946 Tuskegee address, Carey contended that "the little people all over the world are rising and the underprivileged and the oppressed propose to be underprivileged and oppressed no more. . . . [I]f the rulers and their classes recognize this and welcome their brethren to the full estate of freedom there can be peace. But whenever they do not, there will be explosion. We are living in a new day and the oppressors will find a very different victim. American fascists are attempting to revive the Ku Klux Klan but in Mobile, Alabama and in Beaumont, Texas and in Columbia, Tennessee, Negro Americans wrote an answer in blood: 'There'll be no more of that.'"[37]

The planners of the national NAACP's 1946 annual meeting compiled an all-star roster of speakers in an effort to attract widespread attention since no gathering had been held the preceding year. Those slated to appear in Cincinnati included Franklin D. Roosevelt Jr., the son and namesake of the recently deceased president;

NAACP lawyers Charles H. Houston and Thurgood Marshall; and Walter Reuther, the progressive president of the United Auto Workers. Archibald J. Carey Jr. was the planning committee's unanimous choice to give the keynote address, even though that honor was usually reserved for members of the NAACP's "inner family"—"a staff member or a Board member." In this instance, however, organizers sought someone who not only was "familiar with the general philosophy of the Association and . . . in harmony with its aims and purposes" but also was "capable of arousing the audience and the delegates and pushing the conference off to an inspirational start." A speech by Carey would surely be "a highlight of our conference."[38]

White worked closely with Carey on the Cincinnati speech, especially with regard to "some things we face in the days immediately ahead." The NAACP faced a possible rivalry with the leftist National Negro Congress (NNC). Though Randolph had launched the group in 1936, he resigned from the presidency in 1940 because he suspected communist infiltration. Carey had been active in the NNC, serving as a leader of the Chicago chapter and as a member of a coordinating committee and delivering the benediction at the group's second annual convention in Philadelphia in 1937. However, he apparently resigned from the organization shortly after Randolph did so. The NNC survived and met in Detroit in 1946 with strong endorsements from several activists, including Paul Robeson and Harlem's Communist city councilman, Benjamin Davis. Gloster B. Current, the executive director of the Detroit NAACP, characterized their rhetoric as "leftist" and noted that they planted "in the public mind a gargantuan movement which we know to exist on paper only." Current feared that by casting the black struggle in an "international" context, the NNC had "captured the imagination of the masses in Detroit and elsewhere, and no doubt will succeed throughout the country in arousing renewed [attention] in the Congress." Hence, Current believed that much was at stake at the Cincinnati convention. Carey had to demonstrate that the NAACP as more worthy of black support than was the NNC.[39]

In his keynote address, Carey explained that the NAACP viewed the status of African Americans as both an international concern and a pressing national issue. He emphasized the NAACP's recent court victories and avoided "any awareness" or acknowledgment of the NNC. Touching on topics as diverse as the labor movement, anticolonialism in India, and the new Philippine republic, he included "a specific urging that Negroes be citizens of the world." He tried "to walk a tight rope" between acknowledging the special predicament of African Americans and a recognition of "the problems of all the people" across the globe. Carey's Cincinnati presentation was so successful that Current offered him a position as a member of "the Speakers Bureau for the NAACP nationwide membership drive."[40]

The Cincinnati speech also ended whatever impartiality that Carey attempted between the integrationist NAACP and the leftist NNC. Shortly before the Ohio meeting, Robeson was the main speaker at an International Workers' Organization dinner in Chicago. Carey, a Robeson friend, had a prior commitment to speak at another banquet and consequently made only a ceremonial appearance at the dinner before departing. Robeson then made a disparaging remark about Carey's early exit. Hurt by Robeson's comment, Carey wrote to the multitalented entertainer to issue a stern rebuke: "It was not a little disappointing to learn that when I had put myself out in order to make a gracious gesture, that I had been held up as an example of sham." Though he admired Robeson's "loyalty" to friends and his "service to worthy causes," Carey felt that their relationship had been adversely affected, even though "the fact that we may not always see eye to eye [has] not impaired my esteem of you." With Carey headed to Cincinnati to defend the NAACP against challenges from the left-leaning NNC, this seemingly petty incident sparked an ideological polarization between Carey, the liberal reformer, and Robeson, the left-leaning radical, and Carey grew increasingly disenchanted with Robeson's "adherence to the Communist Party line."[41]

To go along with his deepening commitments to the NAACP and its legal strategy for African American advancement, Carey became one of the founding fathers of another interracial civil rights organization, the Committee on Racial Equality (CORE, later renamed the Congress of Racial Equality). A small group of pacifists and divinity students at the University of Chicago spearheaded the creation of CORE in 1942. Though A. J. Muste of the Fellowship of Reconciliation (FOR) had been their mentor and model in the pacifist cause, their interest in race relations drew them to two African American activists, Carey and physician Arthur C. Falls, whom the pacifists perceived as effective opponents of racial discrimination. In the 1930s, Falls, the scion of a Roman Catholic family and the brother of a nun, became "one of the best known race Catholics" in Chicago as a consequence of his service as chair of the Catholic Interracial Commission.[42]

James Robinson may have made the initial contact with Falls and his wife, Lillian, who gave FOR a tour of Chicago's South Side. The couple familiarized Robinson and his colleagues with Chicago blacks and offered strategies to attract their support. Bernice Fisher, a "rock ribbed Baptist," was impressed with Carey's social activism and his oratorical skills, and she and her friend Jane Douglas, the wife of a labor education professor, became Woodlawn's first white members. Fisher brought Carey to CORE.[43]

Fisher, a pacifist and a civil rights advocate, often sought Carey's guidance on both matters, and her pastor cooperated when she and her CORE colleagues targeted discriminatory public and private facilities. For example, Carey and Fisher debated whether the inequitable treatment of blacks at Northwestern University could best be remedied by a lawsuit or by some other means of public pressure. In 1943, as a result of their friendship, CORE held its first national conference at

Woodlawn Church. Carey also allowed CORE to use his office as the headquarters. When the organization launched its 1947 Journey of Reconciliation, which sought to assert the principle of nonsegregated interstate travel in the South, Carey gave his support. Carey's connections broadened to include other CORE activists: he helped Homer Jack, head of the Chicago Council against Racial and Religious Discrimination, by joining the council's advisory board and allowed George Houser to solicit Woodlawn's congregants for funding for scholarships and for an interracial workshop.[44]

As committed practitioners of nonviolent direct action, Fisher, Robinson, Houser, and Jack viewed Carey as the exemplar of what they wanted to achieve. Carey thus helped to nurture a new civil rights organization that later played a major role in bringing about the end of legalized racial segregation. Moreover, these CORE contacts brought Carey into contact with James Farmer and Bayard Rustin, who later became major civil rights crusaders. During this period, Carey became more cognizant of Gandhian nonviolence and precisely how it shaped CORE's tactics in achieving social change. At a 1949 Chicago Council on Foreign Relations dinner, Carey heard India's prime minister, Jawaharlal Nehru, laud his nation's "achievement of freedom" via nonviolent "techniques." Carey later observed that "the Negro-American has comprehended and embraced this truth" and showed American society "a new determination" and "a new courage" in peaceably ending African Americans' second-class citizenship.[45]

The Chicago Urban League also commanded Carey's attention. The Urban League, established in 1911, addressed the housing, health, employment, and recreational needs of rural blacks newly settled in the cities. The Chicago affiliate, founded in 1915, became a major social agency, and Carey served on its board for a time and used his oratorical skills to the league's benefit.[46]

Carey's affiliations with the NAACP, CORE, the Urban League, and other organizations blended with his GOP activities and allowed him to press party and public officials to address the needs of Chicago blacks. In 1937, when a federal official urged Carey to run for Congress as a Democrat, he refused, even though Chicago blacks were moving en masse into FDR's party, as Democrat Arthur W. Mitchell's 1934 victory over incumbent Republican congressman Oscar De Priest illustrated. Buoyed by New Deal legislation and its seeming racial inclusivity, Chicago blacks, like their counterparts elsewhere across the United States, embraced the Democrats, becoming an indispensable part of Roosevelt's winning coalition of labor unions, southern whites, and urban ethnics.[47]

Carey, however, remained convinced that blacks would fare better with the GOP. He distrusted the Democratic dependence on southern segregationist politicians, who fought civil rights and prevented FDR from taking stronger actions that would benefit blacks. Carey also told Republican officials that the inclusion of

African Americans guaranteed the party's electoral success. In 1946, when Carey's friend, William Waugh, was elected a judge in the Probate Court of Cook County, the pastor suggested, "Name a Negro as one of your assistants, and if you don't do the naming, urge it strongly on whoever does. I do not believe we have ever had one and this trailblazing on your part would go far to establish you as a man of real stature and courage." Carey argued that such a gesture would have more than local importance: "In the upward push of Negro-Americans to gain full stature and complete emancipation from the limitations of race prejudice, a thing like this would be of tremendous significance . . . and widely heralded, not only by the more than four hundred thousand Negroes of Chicago and the more than thirteen million Negroes of America, but among the numberless ranks of the little people who feel that their cause has been identified with Negro-Americans." He added, "The Republican Party will consolidate its recent gains if it can recapture the imagination and the support of Negro-Americans."[48]

Carey made such appeals as both a political operative and a religious leader. This dual role led Dwight H. Green, a Chicago attorney and a gubernatorial candidate, to accept Carey's offer to help Green's campaign for the state's highest office. In July 1939, Carey went to Green and "pledged" support. When the candidacy was formally announced two months later, Carey "lobbied friends and constituents" on Green's behalf. He campaigned throughout Illinois and became "one of the most used speakers from [Green] headquarters, making from two to five meetings almost every night." Although Carey received some criticism "for introducing 'politics' in [religious] meetings," he did so because of his "concern for" Green. At the time of the November 1940 election, Carey mobilized fifty-one campaign workers, many of them leading AME pastors, to promote Green's candidacy. The efforts paid off when Green was elected.[49]

Carey also experienced the vicissitudes of political participation and sacrifice, however. In addition to the time and effort he put into Green's campaign, Carey spent his own money for travel and other expenses and paid for a luncheon where Green met both ministers and executives (and potential campaign contributors) from two black insurance companies. Carey believed that his efforts entitled him to some special consideration from the governor; instead, people who had opposed his candidacy had gotten "good salaries" in state government, while Carey had been mistreated. "I asked for a place," Carey wrote, "in connection with the Industrial Commission. Nothing ever happened. I asked for a place in the Finance Department. Nothing ever happened." Other requests also were not honored: a position on the parole board for a police officer who was a Woodlawn member and a transfer for a friend who worked in the office of unemployment compensation. Though Carey served as chair of the Committee to Investigate Segregation of Negroes in Industries Having Defense Contracts and he and others examined the employment record of a Great Lakes, Illinois, company, the Green administration refused to pay the committee's executive director and secretary, and the Illinois attorney general "would not let it function." Some Green subordinates believed that favors for Carey's brother-in-law, Patrick Prescott, represented Carey's payback, but he disagreed: "I made my own contribution, separate and distinct." Carey's letter to Green made a deep impression on the governor, who responded by naming Carey to the staff of the Department of Revenue at a monthly salary of $250. Those responsible for arranging the details on the Carey appointment quickly paid close attention to the task because "the Governor wants it done." Carey immediately thanked Green and repeated his "pledge of loyalty."[50]

By 1946, Carey's visibility led Republican officials to appoint him to the party's Speakers Bureau, whose members traveled around the state speaking on behalf of candidates. Though Carey consented, he insisted that his duties for the party could not interfere with his obligations to Woodlawn Church: "I am the minister of a congregation and rather active in the community," he noted.[51]

Carey's activities with the Illinois GOP paralleled his national political involvements. In 1940, the RNC chose him to deliver a radio address on behalf of presidential nominee Wendell Willkie. Four years later, Carey again campaigned for the Republican candidate, Thomas E. Dewey. He told a friend who supported FDR that "the trouble with you Roosevelt lovers is the fact that you live in the past. The young progressives of the group to which I belong are looking to a future in which southern reactionaries won't be able to filibuster to death every liberal measure." Carey offered praise to the president "for what he has done and to Negroes for their support and loyalty" but insisted, "We are looking to a better day." He also traveled to Baltimore, New York, Detroit, St. Paul, and Toledo on behalf of the national GOP. And in 1946, Carey took to the road once more to help Republican congressional candidates. In California, he appeared at Los Angeles's First AME Church before a crowd of nearly thirteen hundred and at Hamilton Methodist Church, where about three hundred people gathered, and "both messages were enthusiastically received." Carey also "activated" ministerial groups and several of his business and professional acquaintances on behalf of GOP candidate Fred Roberts. When Roberts lost to the popular Democratic candidate, Helen Gahagan Douglas, a friend told Carey that blacks had helped to defeat the Republican. But Carey's reputation did not suffer: a black insurance executive wrote that his "expressions will long be remembered in the community and that he was "one of the ablest speakers we have had."[52]

Carey also cultivated relationships with national Republican officeholders. In 1943, Carey traveled to Toledo and joined Ohio governor John Bricker in a "statewide broadcast" on behalf of the Republican Party. In 1946, when President Harry S. Truman proposed a bill that would make the FEPC permanent, opposition, mainly from southern Democrats, threatened to cripple the measure. Carey looked to another powerful Ohio Republican, Senator Robert A. Taft, to keep the proposal alive. In response to Carey's request, Taft backed cloture on filibusters against the bill, taking what Carey commended as an important "stand." When Taft's efforts failed, Carey blamed Democrats for the FEPC's demise and remained hopeful that blacks would acknowledge that Republicans protected their rights with greater zeal than a Democratic Party beholden to its antiblack southern wing.[53]

Carey's leadership, though anchored in his pastoral and political activities, was enhanced by his legal and business involvements. His position as an established attorney practicing with his brother-in-law, Patrick Prescott, and three other lawyers added to his network of associates. Earl B. Dickerson, a leading black Chicago lawyer, had known Carey since the 1920s and endorsed his application to practice law before the U.S. Supreme Court. Carey reciprocated by assisting Belford V. Lawson, a black Washington, D.C., attorney, in becoming a municipal judge. Carey's recommendation could "get word through [his] senators to President Roosevelt and Attorney General [Francis] Biddle" to push Lawson's candidacy. Carey also joined Dickerson and other attorneys in challenging their racial exclusion from the Chicago Bar Association (CBA). In 1943, members of the group applied to join the CBA and were denied. Two years later, while the black lawyers were attempting to get the courts to force the CBA to admit them, a new CBA president eliminated the racial restrictions. Carey became a member of the leftist National Lawyers' Guild in 1937 and served on the board of directors of the insurgent Chicago Civil Liberties Committee in 1943. Though thoroughly mainstream in his civic sentiments, Carey was willing to forge alliances with organizations across the political spectrum to fight for civil rights, although if he learned that an organization was communist-dominated, as in the case of the NNC, he quickly ended his involvement. He paid dues to the National Lawyers' Guild only once before severing his affiliation, and communist influences within the Chicago Civil Liberties Committee compelled Carey to resign and to advise a friend to follow his example.[54]

Precisely because Carey was a frontline attorney tied to civil rights causes, fellow lawyers believed he had much to share with students aspiring to enter the legal profession. Hence, Scovel Richardson, dean of the all-black law school at Lincoln University in Jefferson City, Missouri, invited Carey to address the student body in 1947, an offer Carey found "flattering."[55]

Carey's legal expertise also aided his friends in the South Side Chicago business world, most prominently Albert Williams. Williams appointed Carey general counsel for the Unity Mutual Life Insurance Company, and in 1935 Robert Taylor, an adviser to philanthropist Julius Rosenwald of Sears Roebuck, invited Williams, Carey, and Sydney P. Brown to join him in starting the Illinois Federal Savings and Loan Association. Carey's legal talents provided these black entrepreneurial ventures with a valued resource.[56]

Carey also blended his legal and business activities with his membership in Alpha Phi Alpha Fraternity. Carey, the onetime president of Chicago's Theta Chapter, aided Theodore M. Berry, the general counsel for the national office, in clarifying issues surrounding a loan for a facility to house another chapter. Berry paid Carey's way to Champaign, Illinois, to discuss the matter and asked Carey for advice about a private housing project. To that end, Berry asked Carey to introduce him to Taylor, a member of Chicago's Metropolitan Housing Authority, and inquired about the Illinois Federal Savings and Loan Association.[57]

Carey thus wove together his ministry, his civil rights involvement, his political work, and his legal and business activities to create a seamless persona as a clergyman concerned with every aspect of the African American condition. In keeping with the ideas of public theology he had learned from his father, Carey concluded that politics offered the best means by which he could serve both his congregation and his community.

CHAPTER 5

Doing Public Theology

ARCHIBALD J. CAREY JR.
AND THE MINISTRY OF POLITICS

After a decade of community and civil rights involvement, Archibald J. Carey Jr. plunged into the political arena as a candidate for public office, as a party operative, and as a federal appointee. At the same time, he maintained his ministry and served in several denominational roles. Carey saw all of these activities as intrinsic parts of a public ministry designed to lift African Americans and reform their religious institutions—that is, as part of a public theology.

Carey believed that his legal training and practice enabled him to be engaged "vitally in the government under which I and my people live." Since government affected "every important phase of our lives," Carey wanted to influence "what kind of government it shall be." At the same time, however, he was "first and foremost an African Methodist preacher and the African Methodist Episcopal Church is at once my home and my first love." He cited Richard Allen, the church's founder, "as a fighter against segregation" as well as "a workman in the building of the Kingdom of God." Hence, members of the African Methodist Episcopal Church (AME), he believed, should emulate their first bishop and become "dedicated not only to the calling of God but to the service of man" and to "making a kingdom of men [into] a kingdom of heaven." AME preachers should serve as officers in local chapters of the National Association for the Advancement of Colored People (NAACP), Urban League affiliates, "and all other movements for civic improvement or human freedom." Ministerial involvements with government were also desirable, as in the case of Bishop Decatur Ward Nichols, who "sat and counseled" with President Dwight D. Eisenhower. Carey hoped that "every leader of African Methodism" would follow Nichols's example.[1]

Both Archibald J. Carey Jr. and his father learned that the practice of public theology drew not only commendations but also criticism from contemporaries. The *Star of Zion*, the organ of the AME Zion Church, for example, praised the senior Carey as having done "good service" for blacks as a political officeholder. Despite "the feeling of impropriety of a bishop identifying himself with a political machine," said the newspaper, some people saw the benefits of Carey's partisan involvements. According to Howard University professor Kelly Miller, however, Carey, though "a man of intelligence, energy and resourcefulness" and "loyal to his race and church," was guilty of poor judgment, having engaged in an "unfortunate involvement . . . in crooked politics" that was "pernicious not only to his denomination, but upon the religious and moral life of the colored race." Miller doubted whether "any member of the great African Methodist [Episcopal] Church [could] come forth and declare that [Carey's] meddling in politics has resulted in any good to the church or to the race." Miller therefore warned ministers "to let politics alone."[2]

Archibald J. Carey Jr. received similar criticism. One Chicagoan charged that while at seminary, Carey had stated that he was studying theology because it was "as good a racket as any." She thus "could not respect" him "as fit to preach God's word" and believed that he would fail in his "various appointments" in government. Carey vehemently denied the statement and declared that he "could not have had any such feeling" but also wrote, "I have long been interested in many activities outside of the church and perhaps I do not conform to your idea of a typical minister." He affirmed "without qualification, my own reverence for God and my sincerity of purpose, both as a minister and in any other activity in which I may engage." Another observer, certain that Carey's congregation had suffered because of his political aspirations, asked, "Who will bury the dead . . . ?, who will visit the sick . . . ?, who will baptize our children . . . ?, who will say the prayers and give comfort when we need them most . . . ?" Therefore, Carey needed to decide whether "to be a Minister of the Gospel or a Politician." If Carey continued to "dabble in politics," he would become contaminated and his usefulness would become compromised. A political opponent accused Carey of trying to serve both God and Mammon. Though such comments stunned and hurt Carey, he never wavered in his faith that preachers belonged in the public and political arenas.[3]

Despite their detractors, both Careys contended that holding public office enhanced their advocacy for their church and community constituents. In fact, several bishops and leading clergy believed the younger Carey's civic activities qualified him for election as a bishop. Bishop Richard R. Wright Jr. admired Carey's "magnificent work . . . for the people and for humanity" and argued that "if there ever was a time that needed a man of [Carey's] qualifications on the bench of Bishops, it is now." Wright affirmed the compatibility of Carey's civic activities and his ministerial responsibilities: "The best men we have had for the church are men who gave a lot of their time to public affairs with no hurt to the people." Wright cited Bishop Benjamin W. Arnett, who served in the Ohio legislature and had a close relationship with President William McKinley. Arnett convinced AME officials to relocate the church's finance department from Wilberforce, Ohio, to Washington, D.C., "to bring the church in closer touch with the government." Regrettably, according to Wright, the AME Church had relinquished its government contacts "because we failed to elect men of the kind of experience and training that Bishop Arnett had." Bishop Greene agreed and became an "ardent" supporter of Carey's candidacy for the episcopacy at the 1956 General Conference. When Carey declined to run, Greene advanced his name for the "Episcopal line-up for 1960."[4]

Several pastors concurred that Carey's blend of ministerial and political involvements prepared him for the episcopacy. An Atlanta clergyman, Lutrelle Long, commended Carey's "superb guidance" of his congregation and "magnificent" televised speech on behalf of the Republican Party. He assured Carey that if he ran for the bishopric, he already had votes from Georgia as well as other episcopal districts. A California candidate acknowledged Carey's popularity and proposed "a combination" with Carey at the 1956 General Conference. Edward S. Foust, a Missouri minister, sent several black newspapers an assessment of Carey and Kentucky pastor Ernest L. Hickman as a perfect pair for the bishopric: "Great men can save us. Dr. Archibald Carey stands alone. He is our most direct contact with the White House," and he speaks "with those who we need to help our purposes in both church and state alike." Moreover, Carey "doesn't necessarily need Us, we Need him." "Progressive Bishops, ministers, and laymen are looking his way." A North Carolina pastor agreed that the church needed Carey "on the bench of bishops," telling Carey, "God bless you for the great service you are rendering our Country and our God." A Texas minister thought that Carey had given "unqualified service to the race and the nation at large" and that the episcopacy stood to gain from his presence.[5]

Prominent laypersons also supported Carey for the episcopacy. The venerable Mary McLeod Bethune, a former adviser to President Franklin D. Roosevelt, told Carey that she liked "the idea of [his] entry into the bishopric of our great AME Church. I think your leadership in that field will mean more to Peace, Freedom, and Brotherhood of the world than any position you could hold in Government. We need you on the bench." An Illinois Elks official recalled the senior Carey's advice to episcopal candidates that money and the votes of southern delegates were necessities. Bailey believed the younger Carey could get southern votes and offered one hundred dollars to help with a campaign.[6]

High-level interest in Carey as a bishop drew in part from his success as a pastor and community leader. Stirring sermons and serious social outreach marked him as a progressive preacher. Moreover, his presidency of the Connectional Council provided him with opportunities to recommend reforms to the AME Church's structure and governance.

Bishop George W. Baber announced at the 1948 Chicago Annual Conference that Carey would be serving his final year as the pastor of Woodlawn. In 1931, Woodlawn had had four dozen members, four hymnals, a Sunday school bell, and no property; at the time of Carey's departure, the congregation had grown to 836 members (including 27 conversions and 84 accessions during the previous year), ranking Woodlawn ninth among the Chicago Annual Conference's seventy-five congregations. During Carey's tenure, the church had purchased a new sanctuary as well as a separate building for the congregation's extensive "community activities," and no indebtedness remained on either structure; the treasury held more than ten thousand dollars. Carey had proven himself as a pastor, preacher, and administrator.[7]

In 1949, at Baber's special request, Carey moved to historic Quinn Chapel. Carey confided to a friend that it "is at once one of our hardest churches to pastor, because it is a downtown church with a very large budget and a considerably reduced membership; but it is also one of the easiest to pastor because of the loyalty and generosity of the members." The congregants included many people of high professional and political standing, among them Reverend Corneal A. Davis, a veteran member of the Illinois state legislature; Kit Baldwin, the owner of Baldwin Ice Cream Company; Margaret W. Batteast, a well-known educator; and John Chamberlin, an official in a large detective agency.[8]

On December 8, 1951, a fire caused five thousand dollars in damage to Quinn Chapel. Though the fire affected only sections of the sanctuary, the memorial windows, and the Sunday school room, Carey identified other areas of the building that needed attention, using the calamity as a catalyst for a broader fifty-thousand-dollar renovation project. Ten thousand dollars came from the insurance settlement. Illinois Federal Savings and Loan Association, of which Carey was vice president, provided a twenty-thousand-dollar loan. Members contributed seventeen thousand dollars, and six thousand dollars was disbursed from the Quinn Chapel treasury. Carey also raised another thirty thousand dollars for other physical improvements. By 1959, Carey's "splendid leadership" had enabled the church to retire the debts incurred to fund the repairs and improvements.[9]

Carey also focused on attracting new members and instituting new programs, although he insisted that Woodlawn's parishioners should not follow him to Quinn Chapel. Carey's predecessor had reported Quinn Chapel's membership at 1,201; Carey soon adjusted that figure to a more believable 655 and set to work attracting new members, including residents of nearby public housing projects. Carey planned "a real program of recreational activities" to spearhead growth.[10]

Carey served as a valuable resource for bishops in the Fourth Episcopal District and for fellow pastors. At the 1947 Chicago Annual Conference, Carey clarified balloting procedures for electing General Conference delegates. And at the 1949 Chicago Annual Conference, he read a report about salaries for presiding elders and forwarded a recommendation to create a fourth presiding district. In 1956, Bishop Joseph Gomez asked Carey to chair a committee "to deal with legal matters" at the AME congregation in Robbins, Illinois, and "to assist the churches in the Chicago Conference with such problems." His comments on handling reports from the Episcopal Committee, the Revisions Committee, and legislation to establish a Judicial Council clarified issues for presiding officers and delegates at the 1948 General Conference.[11]

These introductions and presentations enhanced Carey's position in both denominational and civic affairs. Hence, at the 1947 Chicago Conference session, he initiated a resolution asking the 1948 General Conference to reassign Bishop John A. Gregg to the Fourth Episcopal District. At the 1950 session, he presented Bishop Carey A. Gibbs, the prelate of West Africa, and Baber and acknowledged the Reverend Arthur Gray, a local black Congregational pastor.[12]

Despite such gestures of deference, Carey was not uniformly popular among his pastoral peers. Although he could depend on the friendship of one presiding elder, Robert Thomas Sr., his relationship with another, A. Wayman Ward, was filled with friction. In the election for delegates for the 1948 General Conference in Kansas City, for example, Ward and Carey presented competing motions about balloting procedures. Carey's proposal prevailed, but he only barely won a seat as a delegate, and his Chicago colleagues did not elect him to the 1952 and 1956 General Conferences.[13]

He nevertheless made himself noticed at the 1952 assembly, taking the floor to praise J. Waties Waring, a federal judge who had called segregation unconstitutional, and to introduce Illinois senator Everett M. Dirksen. Similarly, Bishop Greene invited Carey to address the 1956 General Conference about the NAACP Legal Defense and Educational Fund as a prelude to a speech by the group's lead attorney, Thurgood Marshall. The same year, the General Conference appointed Carey to its newly created General Board.[14]

Both bishops and pastors beyond the Chicago Annual Conference recognized Carey's importance in church and civic arenas. Whether attending to hotel requests for visiting bishops at the 1952 General Conference in Chicago or to major denominational issues, Carey emerged as an influential voice in AME affairs. Although a special housing committee had charge of General Conference hotel arrangements, some bishops preferred that Carey handle their accommodations. Bishop Baber, the host, allowed Carey to bypass housing committee members, using his influence to secure suites and upgraded rooms for the visitors. Knowing that some ministers envied Carey, however, Baber said that he would "keep these matters to myself."[15]

In 1949, Carey assumed the presidency of the Connectional Council, a church-wide clergy/lay organization that provided forums for developing initiatives for denominational reform. Carey's election buoyed numerous members eager to improve the church's governance and to encourage the church to take progressive stands on civic and ecumenical issues. Reformist clergy and lay leaders had already tied Carey to their cause. In 1947, Frank R. Veal, a Cincinnati pastor, had invited Carey to a meeting at which like-minded ministers and laypersons considered proposals regarding election procedures, fiscal accountability, and efficiency in school operations that would be put forth at the 1948 General Conference. "You are invited to be a part of this group," said Veal, because "of our confidence in your integrity." Such sentiments led to Carey's election as president of the Connectional Council. Bishop Gregg told Carey, "It was justly your time."[16]

As Carey prepared for his first national meeting as president of the Connectional Council, AME clergy raised pressing issues with him. The council, unlike other denominational venues, applied "no restriction whatsoever on bishops, [general] officers, ministers or the humblest members of our Church in [their] right to speak," and many contacted Carey in hopes of doing so. John H. Lewis, the Yale-educated dean of Payne Theological Seminary, asked permission to make a financial appeal for constructing a new building at the Ohio campus. Dean Daniel G. Hill of the School of Religion at Howard University wanted to discuss a merger with the AME Zion and Colored Methodist Episcopal churches and an eventual union with the white Methodists. Carey liked Hill's idea and asked Frederick D. Jordan, a Los Angeles pastor and future bishop, to lead these discussions. Ward, Carey's presiding elder, raised several legal, insurance, educational, evangelical, and fiscal matters. On a less lofty level, a Birmingham minister who was a candidate for editor of the *AME Church Review* asked for a preaching spot to help his campaign.[17]

At the Connectional Council's 1950 meeting in Jacksonville, Florida, Carey communicated a broad vision focused primarily on expanding democracy in AME Church affairs. According to Carey, the arduous process of balloting and counting votes at the General Conference required urgent reform. He also proposed that the denomination elect a general officer to serve as "general counsel" for the AME Church, "advis[ing] and protect[ing] many of our preachers and church officers who have a zeal of God, but are laymen in the knowledge of the law." Similarly, an AME architect was needed to guide congregations as they erected and remodeled buildings, thereby saving congregations unwise and unnecessary expenditures. Moreover, Carey restated his belief that clergy should be socially active. "We must never abandon the problems of the people," he said. Involvement "for better housing, for fair employment practices, for the Civil Rights that will give a first class citizenship to all Americans" demanded ministerial engagement. Jesse E. Beard, the secretary-treasurer of the denomination's Pension Department, described Carey's address as "splendid" and offered a contribution to print the speech as a pamphlet.[18]

Despite Carey's ambitious goals for the council, he realized that they would have to be tempered by the exigencies of church politics. The 1951 Los Angeles meeting, for example, featured a special forum for candidates for bishop and general officer. Although candidates had demonstrated their pulpit skills by delivering sermons at previous conventions, Carey recommended "that preaching in the Connectional Council should be reduced to a minimum if not eliminated altogether" so that the council could devote itself exclusively to the "free interchange of ideas." In his 1951 annual address, he again pushed for a general counsel and an architect and recommended a judicial council to handle internal disputes. In addition, he suggested ongoing discussions about the wisdom of pastoral term limits and whether the 1948 General Conference and the Bishops Council had ruled clearly on the matter. Carey asked both bishops and pastors to reflect on how needless reassignments created "upheaval in so many well-organized churches." With backing from Bishop Baber, Carey also suggested the use of voting machines for General Conference elections and convinced the Chicago Board of Election Commissioners to allow the church to use its machines in exchange for a nominal fee. This innovation and the creation of a church election commission would bring order and fairness in the electoral contests for bishop and general officer.[19]

In another address, Carey proposed a "Master Plan for African Methodism" to achieve uniformity in worship and outreach programs. He declared that the denominational assessments should be "reasonable" and that a better pension system was needed. Equally important would be subsidies for pastors in small congregations, who should be "guaranteed an annual minimum."[20] These issues, especially the proposal on clergy compensation, continued to occupy Carey into the 1960s. Though Carey refused reelection to the council presidency, he became active in another reform organization, the Brotherhood of the AME Church, led by H. Ralph Jackson, a Tennessee pastor. Carey was initially wary of Jackson, who succeeded the Chicagoan as president of the Connectional Council, but the two men eventually cooperated to plan changes to the denomination's financial structure. Under the dollar money system, each AME member paid at least a dollar a year to support denominational departments and programs and contributed funds to other connectional projects. The brotherhood proposed a new budget system in which each member paid four dollars annually and each episcopal district contributed a specific sum. This approach provided a rationale for fund-raising and accountability in the disbursement of money. At the 1956 General Conference, Carey supported Jackson and other maverick ministers' efforts to implement budget reform and to establish a General Board to oversee denominational departments and their annual expenditures. He was elected as an at-large member of this new denominational body. At a 1957 General Board meeting in Nashville convened to clarify the new budget law, Carey drew commendations from a future general officer, Henderson S. Davis, who admired Carey's church and civic contributions and praised him for his leadership in the budget fight and "for giving us a start on a denominational statement about African Methodism, racism, and brotherhood."[21]

Carey believed in the new budget system and defended it even when doing so brought him into disagreement with close friends. When Bishop Greene sought Carey's opinion on a 1958 "Churchwide Appeal" to supplement budget shortfalls, he answered that it would be "better to suffer the hardships" than to undermine the new fiscal structure. Carey also opposed possible "plans for a large fund raising program" because he wanted to protect the "principles" of the budget system, which was designed "to protect pastors against excessive and indiscriminate assessments." Even when Bishop Nichols, whom Carey had previously held up as an example for his fellow pastors, was accused of flouting the new budget law, Carey remained committed to it. Denominational reform trumped all of Carey's other allegiances. Carey became so closely associated with these reforms that one Washington, D.C., pastor mistook him for the president of the brotherhood.[22]

Carey's backing of Jackson continued through the 1956–60 quadrennium. In 1957, Carey invited the Tennessean to preach at Quinn Chapel, praising him as "the author of the new Budget Law which has sort of revolutionized operations in the AME Church." Carey also supported Jackson's idea, which reached fruition at the 1960 General Conference, for a minimum salary department to enhance the income of underpaid preachers. When Jackson was selected to head the new department, he demonstrated his gratitude to Carey by depositing seventy thousand dollars in department funds in the Illinois Federal Savings and Loan, of which Carey was now president, and by promising to open additional accounts. Jackson also affirmed his appreciation by declaring that the denomination "owes Archibald J. Carey a debt that it may never attempt to pay" and that Carey should be elected a bishop so that he could assume his "rightful place" in the church hierarchy. Carey demurred—he would forgo the episcopacy because it would preclude his involvement in the other facets of public theology that he so valued—but promised to think about taking the brotherhood presidency and agreed to host its conference at Quinn Chapel. He also promised "to safeguard the gains" of the organization.[23]

Carey maintained his connections to other clergy and educators by accepting numerous speaking invitations, especially at AME colleges. While his pastoral prominence partially explains his popularity, Carey's municipal and federal activities also contributed to the demand for his presence. In 1952, Sherman L. Greene Jr., then serving as president of Paul Quinn College in Texas, wanted to celebrate the construction of four buildings worth $250,000 before a mixed audience of white and black benefactors and sought the high-profile Carey to speak. Similarly, President Charles Leander Hill of Wilberforce University desired Carey to speak at commencement because he would deliver "a great message," and Bishop William R. Wilkes, chair of the board of trustees at Arkansas's Shorter College, believed that in getting Carey to address the 1954 graduating class, "we will have one of the top leaders in this nation." Also in 1954, his alma mater, Garrett Biblical Institute, asked him to be its convocation speaker to commemorate the newly established Archibald J. Carey Jr. Scholarship. The benefactor who contributed to the fund wanted to validate Carey's varied ministries and his "outstanding services to both city and country."[24]

Bishops and other denominational leaders also turned to Carey to be the public face of the AME Church. Bishop Greene, who served on the executive committee of the Fraternal Council of Negro Churches, informed Carey that the AME Council of Bishops had selected him to head the Fraternal Council and had pledged funds to underwrite his salary and allow him to continue his legal practice. Greene also recommended Carey to address the 1961 World Methodist Council in Oslo, Norway, on "the work of Negro Methodists during the last five years."[25]

Balancing his ironclad commitment to ministry with his involvements in politics, banking, and social justice often proved a challenge for Carey, as his dealings with Bishop Alexander J. Allen illustrate. When the bishop invited Carey to the Third Episcopal District convocation in Columbus, Ohio, Carey agreed to come though he was unsure if competing obligations with the Chicago City Council and sessions of the United Nations would interfere. In 1956, Carey could not attend the AME district convocation because his responsibilities for the President's Committee on Government Employment Policy required him to be in Washington, D.C.; he wrote to explain to Allen, who had been assigned to preside in the Fourth Episcopal District, "I am a little disturbed because I am not able to be present [though] I wish to do whatever my Bishop asks of me."[26]

Unfriendly colleagues in the Chicago Annual Conference used such instances to question Carey's loyalty to the AME Church. Carey responded by defining his public theology and how it shaped his ministry. At a denominational meeting in Hot Springs, Arkansas, friends urged him to counter the charge that he was indifferent to the church by writing to all General Conference delegates and others about his activities and their relationship to his AME obligations. Carey, they believed, needed to explain why the Chicago Annual Conference had not chosen him as a delegate and to answer the charge that he was indifferent "to the Church since he "did not attend the preachers' meetings in Chicago." Carey agreed.[27]

Carey offered two observations regarding his defeat as a General Conference delegate: "First," he said, "there is nothing in the books that said I had to be elected. Other men with longer service and more deserving than I were not elected." He believed that the seventy-five votes he had received—ten fewer than he needed on the first ballot—constituted an impressive showing. The lack of alliances to sustain him on subsequent ballots explained his loss. "Everybody could not be elected," he noted, "and there was no obligation to see that I should be." Since the successful candidates "are able and representative delegates," the Chicago Annual Conference would have a first-rate delegation to the 1956 General Conference.[28]

Carey used the opportunity to argue that his nondenominational activities were at least as important as his attendance at local "preachers' meetings." Carey reminded his audience that his service on the Chicago City Council "was important to our race group in Chicago." The same held true, on a larger scale, for his membership in the U.S. delegation to the United Nations, as a consequence of which Carey had spent "three months solid" in New York. Although his involvement with the President's Committee on Government Employment Policy indeed caused him to miss some of those "preachers' meetings," he argued that the drawbacks were outweighed by the importance of working "to prevent discrimination in the hiring, firing, and promotion of persons employed by the Federal Government." Carey also attributed his failure to be elected as a delegate to the 1956 General Conference to his absence on the day of the election; however, he noted, he had not attended because he was "in a committee meeting planning action following the lynching of the [Emmett] Till boy in Mississippi." Carey declared that "these activities were important to the people of our race group and the Church of Allen and warranted my being present to do what I could." Carey believed that such involvements constituted a more important part of his ministerial vocation than did the "preachers' meetings."[29]

Carey also contended that he never neglected his pastoral responsibilities: in his "twenty-sixth consecutive year as a pastor in the AME Church," he cited various concrete achievements both at Woodlawn and at his current pastorate. Furthermore, Quinn Chapel disbursed more funds to the denomination "than any other church in the Chicago Conference except one." He repeatedly reminded listeners about his grounding among local AMEs. When Carey Temple AME Church was established in Chicago, he became its "first member." "Although it was named for my father," he said, "and is now one of Chicago's flourishing churches, I started with it when there were no members and nothing but an organization a-borning." This was another indication of his denominational loyalty. In addition, Carey contended, in 1953 he had "declined to be considered for a very significant appointment from the President because it would have required my giving up my Church." And before running for the Chicago City Council and accepting presidential appointments, Carey had received approval from both Bishop Gregg and Bishop Baber.[30]

In conclusion, Carey strongly reiterated his commitment to public theology: "I do not regret using my energies as I have because I have tried to render the sort of service that I felt was in keeping with the spirit of Richard Allen in responding to the needs of our people." Involvement in civic affairs took precedence over insular clergy meetings. If Carey's absence from such events cost him election as a General Conference delegate, he believed that the sacrifice was worthwhile.[31]

Many church leaders believed that Carey would make an excellent bishop. In 1954, Bishop John H. Clayborn wrote to Carey, "I have wanted for sometime to see you, along with other fine young men, to seek this office, for we need men so very badly of your character, to say nothing of your qualifications, to be on the Bench." The bishop offered his assistance and reminded Carey that his father "was a very true friend of mine." He urged the younger Carey to campaign "and walk in the footsteps of your noted father, for on the Bench is where you can best serve our great church."[32]

But Carey did not want to be a bishop as much as others wanted it for him. He believed that the episcopacy should not be pursued like positions in secular politics. Though experienced in municipal, state, and national campaigns, Carey refused to apply their tactics to a church setting. He constantly told supporters that "any man would be honored to serve as a Bishop in the great Church of Allen and this is particularly true of one who is [a] fourth generation . . . African Methodist minister as I am." Though he would be "honored to be bishop," Carey did not think "that it is dignifying to the Church to launch the kind of political endeavor which we do in secular political campaigns." He added, "I am thoroughly familiar with these because I have run for public office seven times (including primaries) and have won five times, but I would not like to see our episcopal leaders chosen on the basis of political skill." One contemporary believed that Carey wanted to be a bishop but did not want to "hit the circuit" to attain the office. Moreover, election to the episcopacy would have required him to leave Chicago, and that price was too high for Carey.[33]

Harrison J. Bryant, a Baltimore pastor and episcopal candidate, saw no conflict in the dual spheres in which Carey operated. In 1952, Carey appeared at Bryant's Bethel Church in support of the Republican Party, offering "one of the greatest [speeches] ever delivered in behalf of a political party." Bryant hoped that Carey would be elected to Congress and later become "one of the bishops of our church." But both men believed that high church offices should not go to "the highest financial bidder," thus corrupting the church's electoral process. Bryant, a future bishop, admired Carey "as a Churchman and Statesman" but agreed that the methods of secular politics should not invade the religious arena.[34]

Carey contemporary Rufus E. Clement, also a bishop's son and an alumnus of Garrett Biblical Institute, faced the same dilemma as did Carey. Clement held a doctorate, making him, like Carey, one of the best prepared preachers in his denomination. Clement's seminary training, stature as president of Atlanta University, and involvements in the AME Zion Church both as a pastor and as an ecumenical representative convinced Bishop James Clair Taylor to press him to run for the bishopric. Despite Clement's indecision, Taylor floated his name among church leaders, receiving a "favorable response" "in nearly every instance." Despite the urgings of Taylor and others, Clement ultimately declared, "I am not now a candidate for the Bishopric in our Church nor do I expect to be. I am honest in my conviction that I can be more service to the Church off the bench than I can be on it." When another church leader brought up the matter again a few years later, telling Clement that "realizing that the episcopacy should represent our best, we are hereby seeking your prayerful consideration of permitting Zion to do you this honor," Clement replied firmly, "I have many times given this matter most serious attention. Reluctantly, I have had to decide that I should continue in education as my major field of work. I continue to be intensely interested in the church and I assure you that except for accepting an office therein I shall do all in my power to advance the work." Clement, like Carey, was committed to public theology, serving with the National Public Housing Conference and the Southern Regional Council. In 1953, when Clement won election to Atlanta's board of education, Carey offered his congratulations. Clement responded that he on hoped he would "measure up to all that is expected of me."[35]

According to AME Bishop Richard R. Wright Jr., himself a Ph.D., Carey and Clement may have eschewed the episcopacy because "the men elected to the Bishopric have for the most part been average men": "no theologian or outstanding scholar has ever been elected." Both Charles H. Wesley, a Harvard Ph.D. and prolific historian, and Charles Leander Hill, another Ph.D. and a Reformation scholar, "missed the Bishopric by very narrow margins." Wright also observed that "with the growth of the large city pastorate, and the improvement of ministerial education in the AME Church, many younger men are not so clamorous for the bishopric as their forefathers were, so that those elected in this generation do not stand as far above their fellows as was the case in former generations."[36]

Carey, as a high-level appointee of President Dwight D. Eisenhower, and Clement, as president of a leading black university, may also have thought that they had already attained positions on par with the bishopric. Moreover, since they were sons of bishops in two African Methodist denominations, the episcopacy might have lacked some of the mystique it held for others. Carey may also have bypassed the bishopric because of the high tension/low stakes issues that would consume his time and energy or because he had been sobered by his Chicago colleagues' behavior in refusing to elect him a delegate to the 1956 General Conference. For some combination of these reasons as well as perhaps others, Carey and Clement contended that public theology was better served off the bench than on it.

Some of Carey's supporters nevertheless persisted in pushing him toward the episcopacy. Ulysses S. Robinson, the pastor at Ebenezer AME Church in Evanston, Illinois, was among those who kept alive rumors that Carey "may run for bishop in 1960." Homer A. Jack, a Unitarian pastor in Evanston, received this message from Robinson and later told his friend Carey, "If a Unitarian can help you in any way, please let me know!"[37]

Carey always conceived his primary role as that of pastor. He declined when asked to serve on a National Council of Churches commission, pleading his busy schedule as a lawyer and bank president as well as the fact that "basically I am a churchman, the fourth consecutive generation of Methodist preacher." Carey presented his pastoral service as the basis for doing public theology. At Woodlawn and Quinn Chapel, he engaged issues that affected his members and their environs. Though protest and agitation were in his arsenal of tactics, he turned primarily to electoral politics as the most effective means to bring benefits to his church and community constituents.[38]

Archibald Carey Jr.'s path into politics had been partly paved by his father; the younger Carey inherited the GOP network that had sustained Bishop Carey in public life. Dwight H. Green, who served as Illinois governor from 1941 to 1949, reminded Carey of his father's friendship with another leading Illinois Republican politician, enabling the junior Carey to receive the same favor from white party elders that they had extended to his father. Veteran black Republican state legislators William E. King, William Haynes, and Charles Jenkins mistakenly perceived Arch Carey as a political neophyte and underestimated the strength of his ties to local and state GOP officials. As a consequence, Carey circumvented these lower-echelon gatekeepers and drew favor from another set of influential Republican politicians of both races who viewed him as a promising standard-bearer. His most important ally, Val J. Washington, was an Indiana native who worked for the *Chicago Defender*. In 1941, Green appointed Washington to the Illinois Commerce Commission, and he held the post until 1949, when he joined the staff of the Republican National Committee (RNC) as its liaison to African Americans. Washington's political relationship with Carey intensified as they interacted with numerous black GOP operatives and supporters and advanced their political aspirations within Chicago's party organization. Washington also became a major political mentor for Carey.[39]

Although Republican Oscar De Priest had won election to the U.S. Congress in 1928 from Chicago's South Side, becoming as the first black U.S. representative from a northern congressional district, the Democrats had subsequently eclipsed the GOP among the city's African Americans. In 1934, Arthur Mitchell, a little-known black Democrat, defeated De Priest for the seat, riding the wave of approbation for Franklin D. Roosevelt's New Deal. Mitchell's victory signaled that Chicago's black votes were now up for grabs.[40]

De Priest subsequently won election on the GOP ticket as an alderman and forged a friendship with Mayor Edward Kelley, a Democrat. De Priest's bipartisanship may explain why Green, already in political debt to Carey, persuaded him to challenge De Priest in 1947. Moreover, Democratic nominee Roy Washington, like Carey a lawyer and an AME minister, had poor relationships with fellow Democrats. Carey had been wanting to run for alderman since 1942, and he believed that under such favorable circumstances, the time was right.[41]

Before he decided to run, however, he informed Bishop Gregg, his prelate, that he was considering the idea. Carey reminded the bishop that he had "sort of endorsed the idea" four years earlier, and Carey hoped that Gregg's "attitude is the same." He assured the bishop that he did "not intend to leave Woodlawn as long as you and the people want me to stay." Gregg gave his blessing and said that he was sure the congregation wished to retain Carey as pastor, but the bishop also cautioned, "I do not want anything to divorce you from the Church Work, where I believe that there is a bigger future than even law can offer." Gregg probably viewed politics as a mere interlude between the pastorate and the bishopric for Carey.[42]

In the February 25 election, Carey, who had been assured of the governor's "financial help, and . . . unqualified backing," was "the only candidate endorsed by the Regular Republican Organization." He faced eight other candidates, including De Priest and Washington; if no candidate won a majority of the votes cast, a runoff would take place. Carey expected "a tough fight, in which I will be called a lot of names, but if I wage a good campaign, I will probably be in the run-off."[43]

As part of his "good campaign," Carey released a long roster of his accomplishments over the preceding sixteen years, describing himself as "an able, intelligent and vigorous leader in community affairs." He reminded voters that "as Minister of Woodlawn AME Church, lawyer and public-spirited citizen, he has been in daily demand by individuals and organizations where the rights and privileges of Negroes were at stake." He had gone to the Illinois capital to speak out for a state Fair Employment Practices Commission (FEPC) and lobbied members of Congress on behalf of a permanent federal agency to fight job bias. Governor Green had appointed him "to investigate discrimination against Negroes in War industries," and he had cochaired the Mid-West Conference on the Negro and the War. He had attended city council hearings to advocate improvements in public education. And he was a founder and "first commencement chaplain" of the innovative Roosevelt College. In summary, Carey asked, "Can Negroes afford not to send this man to City Council?"[44]

Carey received an impressive array of endorsements, including those of the Independent Voters of Illinois, the People's Progressive Civic League, and the Chicago Neighborhood Improvement and Protective Association. In addition, although such efforts brought churches into the realm of partisan politics, the AME Ministers' Alliance and Woodlawn AME Church publicly promoted their favorite son. But the backing was not universal: one layman said that he did not "think it becoming for a Minister of the Gospel to enter the political field or hold a political office." Carey responded, "Why should not a preacher be in politics or even hold political office—because the business is dirty? Then it's up to people like you and me to clean it up." Moreover, "preachers have business everywhere, except in those things that are devilish and ungodly." He observed that "while Christ never ran for public office, he certainly went wherever people were and tried to improve their conditions." Carey sought "to use all of my energy and influence to gain for Negroes of the Third Ward, [the] respect and service to which they are entitled. I do not think this program is displeasing in the sight of God." After learning of Carey's candidacy, Adam Clayton Powell Jr., a Democrat, wrote, "Off the record, I certainly wish you well and hope you make it." Such sentiments from his close friend, who was also a pastor and a congressman, could only have reinforced Carey's belief that he was doing the right thing.[45]

As Carey had hoped, he survived the primary election and reached the runoff, to be held on April 1. Washington, his opponent, was the assistant pastor of Institutional AME Church, rendering moot the question of whether clergy should be in politics, at least as far as voters in the Third Ward were concerned.[46]

Woodlawn's parishioners drafted an open letter in support of their pastor's political aspirations: "Of the two ministers [Carey and Washington], we believe Carey is the better one." The document continued, "Dr. Carey will work hard to get better housing, better schools, more police protection and better services for the Third Ward." One Woodlawn member, Willard S. Townsend, president of the United Transport Service Employees of America, said, "I became a member of this Church because I appreciate the leadership Archibald Carey has given the Negro people and the cause of labor." Other labor support came from the South Side Motion Picture Operators, who credited Carey with "gaining us full union membership status." He received endorsements from several newspapers, including the *Chicago Beacon*, which said that Carey was "widely known throughout the city and nation and brings to the office a wealth of first hand knowledge of the needs of the people of the Ward as well as a fine background of religious activities." With Washington's weak support from Democrats and Carey's solid GOP backing, his victory surprised very few observers.[47]

Carey's win was nonetheless not without controversy. Some members of Bethel AME Church who supported De Priest in the primary had remarked that if "Bishop Carey had been living, he would not have permitted his son to run against Oscar." On the contrary, Carey replied: De Priest had been hostile to some members of the bishop's family, and he "might have nominated me to run against Oscar." With victory in hand, however, Carey was in a mood to be magnanimous: while he found Bethel's lack of support "discouraging," it was "all past," and he wanted to "forget it." The expression of these raw sentiments showed the institutional costs of ministerial involvements in secular politics. Factional tensions, politicized preachers, and partisan parishes sometimes occurred. Carey believed that the benefits his election would bring to the ninety thousand residents of Chicago's Third Ward—including its AME Church members—outweighed any drawbacks.[48]

These political battles signified the development of politicized congregations—what political scientist Eric L. McDaniel describes as churches that hold "political awareness and activity as salient pieces of [their] identity." Such religious institutions, McDaniel continues, "decide that politics is an important means of achieving their overall goals." The attributes of these churches include pastors "interested in involving [their churches] in politics," members who agree to pursue this objective, and a setting that "both necessitates and allows political action." McDaniel also observes that "clergy facilitate the connection between religion and politics" and that pastors and parishioners must agree about constructing "a political church." Congregations develop in this direction, according to McDaniel, "because of their pastors."[49] These characteristics precisely fit the congregations that Carey served. Moreover, his bishops and congregants acquiesced to his partisan political activities and allowed him broad latitude in conflating these involvements with his pastoral duties.

Carey believed that his election to the Chicago City Council did more than satisfy personal ambition. Rather, it enabled him to advance Social Gospel objectives by improving the condition of African Americans in the Third Ward. Carey obtained committee assignments with that goal in mind: he served on the Committees on Consolidation, Reorganization, and Taxation; Health; Housing; Judiciary and State Legislation; Planning; and Traffic and Public Safety. He also fixed or directed public relief payments for senior citizens, children, the blind, and others in need. He secured a $425,000 appropriation to pave Forty-seventh Street, arranged to have new traffic signals installed and playgrounds built, and brokered a "90% improvement in street cleaning and garbage collection," in part by getting the city to use mechanical street sweepers in the Third Ward for the first time. At Christmastime, he sponsored a "giant movie party" for young people. Most importantly, Carey addressed the poor relationships that existed between African Americans and the police. He proposed a course "to teach police to protect minorities" and introduced an ordinance to create a Division of Human Relations in the police department. He also took on the matter of back vacation pay that had been denied to twenty-nine temporary policemen, most of them black, who had been hired as emergency employees during World War II, served for more than two years, and then abruptly been dismissed. In obtaining $4,000 for the policemen, Carey showed himself attentive to crucial issues affecting African Americans.[50]

A belief in black solidarity motivated Carey to push Second Ward alderman William Harvey for membership on the influential Finance Committee. The Committee on Rules had appointed neither Carey nor Harvey, meaning that the Finance Committee would have no black representation. Carey protested and sought support for Harvey's assignment to the committee. Carey also obtained the cooperation of other colleagues for initiatives pertaining to African Americans. For example, Carey and alderman Benjamin Becker of the Fortieth Ward cosponsored an antihate ordinance that required either a fine or imprisonment for persons convicted of denigrating or causing disorder based on racial, color, or creedal condemnations. Alderman John S. Duffy of the Nineteenth Ward aided Carey in getting the policemen's vacation pay. Carey also forged a long-term alliance with Democrat Robert Merriam, who was a "vigorous supporter" of the antihate ordinance and offered his "earnest support" for the measure to provide the police with training in race relations. Carey also credited Merriam with forcing Commonwealth Edison to insert an FEPC clause into its franchise agreement to supply electricity to Chicago. This proviso, which mandated unbiased hiring and promotion practices, resulted in the employment of "one colored person for every nine white persons." Carey later wrote, "Bob Merriam and Arch Carey have voted the same about 98% of the time and on every issue affecting the rights of minorities have voted exactly the same, without exception."[51]

The fight against discrimination became the defining feature of Carey's public theology. When a critic denounced the Mayor's Commission on Human Relations and recommended its dissolution, Carey strongly opposed the idea. Because Chicago was "a cosmopolitan community" of "many races, creeds, and nationalities," an agency was needed to restrict "the human disposition to look for difference[s] and exploit them." The commission's program of education "urges and insists upon equal treatment for all people regardless of color or creed." He added, "There are those who would exclude Negro-persons, Japanese-Americans, Mexican-Americans, Americans of Jewish Faith and other minorities from certain areas of living, whether in the matter of homes or jobs or opportunities." Such behavior contradicted "the American way." At the urging of Homer Jack, a former colleague of Carey's at the Congress of Racial Equality (CORE) and head of the Chicago Council against Racial and Religious Discrimination, Carey proposed an ordinance that would prevent police from arresting people for disorderly conduct and then jailing them for failure to appear in court, a tactic used most frequently against blacks and other vulnerable populations.[52]

Carey's most important legislative effort, however, focused on the elimination of racial discrimination in Chicago housing. In a 1940 case, *Hansberry v. Berry*, black Chicago attorneys had won a ruling against race-restrictive covenants. While the suit benefited some home buyers, it established no precedent to prevent discriminatory housing in other covenant cases. The national NAACP chose to hold a 1945 conference on race-restrictive covenants in Chicago, and the group's local chapter took this cue and identified this issue as an urgent matter for African Americans. Chicago branch president Oscar C. Brown observed that the city's four hundred thousand blacks lived "in an area that was built for about half that number," and whites were circumventing the 1940 ruling by putting "into effect more and better restrictive covenants." In 1945, the Chicago NAACP spent nearly five thousand dollars to deal with legal challenges to these covenants, but it needed five times that amount. Carey not only volunteered to help the group raise the money but lobbied for a law to ban restrictive covenants and joined a citizens' committee that sought to expand public housing for blacks. Carey also opposed "rent gougers and absentee landlords" who exploited African Americans.[53]

Carey's attempt to calm racial tensions in the Fernwood area validated his ongoing work in behalf of fair housing. In 1947, seven black veterans and their families joined forty-three white veterans and their families in residing in a Chicago housing project, stirring opposition from Fernwood residents. Carey engaged in talks with community leaders, including the local alderman, but his efforts could not prevent a mob from hurling "bricks at automobiles passing with Negroes, and beating up any Negro upon whom it could lay its hands." Carey worked to restrain the violence by "speaking in different communities and to the Washington Park crowds" and by negotiating with the mayor to deploy twelve hundred policemen in Fernwood. The Reverend Clarence Cobbs of the First Church of Deliverance allowed Carey to use his church's weekly radio broadcast to advise blacks "to exercise restraint" and to admonish whites "that Negroes were prepared and intended to defend themselves and their homes."[54]

After the situation calmed down, Carey sponsored a resolution stating that "the City of Chicago was disturbed by the acts of individuals and mobs" and that "personal injuries and property damages" had occurred. He proposed an investigation of the "influences which instigated and incited" the violence and called on the mayor to appoint a committee from the city council to conduct an inquiry. In a letter to his sister, he compared his actions to those of their father nearly thirty years earlier: "I have been in '47 what Papa was in '19," when the city endured its infamous race riot.[55]

The NAACP's legal campaign against restrictive covenants reached fruition with the Supreme Court's 1948 ruling in *Shelley v. Kraemer*. The decision pertained to private agreements, however, and Carey wanted a statute that outlawed discrimination in public housing. To that end, on September 15, 1948, he introduced a bill "which declares that where public aid is provided for housing units, there shall be no discrimination on account of color or religion or ancestry, even though such housing units are built with private funds." The Non-Discrimination Ordinance for Publicly Aided Housing, Carey contended, "simply spells out and implements" *Shelley v. Kraemer*. "By forbidding discrimination in the housing which the City will provide (whether in whole or in part) this ordinance guarantees our City Government will not lend itself to discrimination of that sort."[56]

The *Chicago Daily News* called the proposal "Alderman Carey's Ordinance," a designation that Carey protested, noting that "thirteen Aldermen signed it and many of Chicago's outstanding individuals and organizations are sponsoring and urging this legislation." Nonetheless, the name stuck. Public support for the law was impressive, as nearly ninety groups from all across Chicago's economic and social spectrum endorsed it—Jewish, Mexican, and Japanese organizations; black and white women's clubs; religious, business, and labor organizations; and veterans and civic groups as well as the Chicago Urban League, CORE, and the Chicago Council against Racial and Religious Discrimination. Jack's group distributed flyers urging citizens and community organizations to pressure thirty-two undecided aldermen, send telegrams and letters to the mayor, and attend a public hearing.[57]

In addition to generating political and public support for the bill, Carey contacted experts involved in similar housing efforts in New York, which had enacted a law against discrimination in government-aided housing. Carey sought information that would strengthen his arguments on behalf of the ordinance and counter criticisms aimed at discrediting his proposal. Although he affirmed the principle of fair housing and applauded Carey's proposed ordinance, the president of one integrated housing development declared that in New York City, "racial and color groups naturally gravitate into certain neighborhoods and are happiest in their own surroundings." Compelling "non-segregation," he believed, "may discourage rather than encourage housing promoters, private or group sponsored." Similarly, an associate of retail magnate and educational benefactor Julius Rosenwald who was involved with integrated housing in New York City could offer only tepid endorsement for Carey's bill. Modest integration had occurred, but builders and bankers had become reluctant to construct new housing, blaming the state antidiscrimination law. Both of the men Carey contacted agreed, however, that high costs were the real reason for the decline in new construction.[58]

This lukewarm support presaged more overt opposition in Chicago. Attacks on the proposal ranged from fears of forced "admixture of white and colored people in every apartment building" to warnings that investors would refuse to finance integrated housing to admonitions that the impact of the legislation was "too uncertain and immeasurable to warrant the risk of disaster." More reasonable opponents simply argued that existing legislation and the recent Supreme Court decision made the ordinance unnecessary. Carey was prepared to counter the barrage of criticism, however. His bill would not mandate integration, he constantly said, but "forbid discrimination." Moreover, the ordinance would not apply to builders who developed projects without public funds. Although Carey conceded that African Americans had access to new housing, he warned that dwellings exclusively for particular ethnic and racial groups would "extend and crystallize the ghetto pattern, which the great city of Chicago should not countenance."[59]

Carey insisted that "no evidence" supported the charge that the ordinance would hinder "the rebuilding of blighted areas." As in New York, investors, especially insurance companies, would shun black Chicago only because of "high building costs," and these firms were not the only available investors. The municipal government could secure federal funds for housing construction. Moreover, insurance companies were already involved in building homes for blacks and had unrealized opportunities to serve "the better paying tenant market among Negroes." Most of all, Carey declared, African Americans wanted "to live in any housing in a truly free society rather than to enjoy the luxury under a 'jim-crow' or ghetto arrangement."[60]

Carey was astonished at the depth and persistence of the opposition to his ordinance. But, he believed, the bill's opponents were merely using "technical and devious arguments" to raise a smokescreen that obscured the true issue at hand, which was "the basic American question: Shall we discriminate against people where public investment is present?" Critics made contradictory statements about the legislation: "On the one hand they say the ordinance is a tight unreasonable restriction and in the same breath say all of its provisions are included in the Constitution. . . . [I]t is condemned at one and at the same time for being too narrow and too broad, for emanating from high ideals and base chauvinism."[61]

As Carey recalled, debate on the proposed ordinance "kept the City in a dither for about four months." On March 2, 1949, the aldermen finally voted on the bill. The result was a resounding defeat, as just thirteen of the council's fifty members voted in favor. Not only did just six of the council's thirty Democrats back Carey's proposal, but his fellow Republicans abandoned him. Carey blamed Mayor Martin Kennelly for the bill's defeat. Although the council's Housing Committee held four public hearings and endorsed the Carey bill, Kennelly asked aldermen "to defeat it," making the dubious argument "that the Ordinance would retard the [city's] housing program."[62]

Despite the bill's failure, Bishop William J. Walls of the AME Zion Church commended Carey "on the great fight" to end "racial inequality for housing in our city." Jack asserted that Kennelly "will not soon forget what he did the other day" while Carey deserved praise for standing "against the most powerful combine of prejudice and cash in this city." Jack's alderman, Frank Keenan, had voted against the ordinance, and when he ran for reelection, Jack said, "I believe many of our constituents will remember this vote of yours for segregation and against the concepts of high religion." A real estate agent appreciated Carey's "battle against injustice and discrimination in Chicago." One Carey supporter declared that the "fight brought clearly into the open the pitiful duplicity of Democratic Party leadership on civil rights." Perhaps blacks would learn not to help Chicago Democrats again. Val Washington was most disappointed in U.S. Senator Paul Douglas, a progressive

Illinois Democrat. Washington was "preparing some facts which I think illustrate in which Party the interests of the Negro lie." Carey agreed that Kennelly and Douglas "have turned out into the streets people who thought they were welcome in their houses. Now, what the Republicans must do is to open their doors and announce to these people 'you are welcome here.'"[63]

Despite the lopsided city council vote, the proposal generated intense interest outside Chicago. A federal housing official solicited copies of the Carey measure, writing that its defeat was a "miscarriage of democratic practice" but might help "Cleveland and Ohio" move "in the right direction." In 1951, the mayor of St. Louis invited Carey to a National Housing Policy Conference to emphasize the importance of decent housing for all. A banker associated with the group echoed the mayor's sentiments and said that he was dismayed at efforts to hinder equal housing initiatives "in other cities, in state legislatures, and in the National Congress." He believed that Carey's presence was "necessary to the success" of the conference. Social scientists Edward Banfield and Martin Meyerson, who were writing a book on public planning in Chicago, asked Carey to review the relevant chapters for accuracy. The vice president of New York Life Insurance Company endorsed Carey's approach and adopted his principle that nondiscrimination had no place in housing. Even after the Carey measure was defeated, the insurance executive invested funds in Chicago's Lake Meadows development and voluntarily added a proviso opening occupancy to all eligible applicants.[64]

Carey remained vigilant in monitoring racial patterns in Chicago housing. A few months after the ordinance vote, Gerald Bullock, CORE's executive director, contacted Carey about white hostility toward blacks seeking to move to the Park Manor area. Bullock proposed a plan that CORE and NAACP activists hoped would head off possible violence and suggested that Carey present the plan to his fellow aldermen. Carey was heartened by the antidiscrimination policy of the city's housing authority but was disappointed that new housing for blacks was located "where Negroes are now living or where it will be 'acceptable' for Negroes to live." "Maintaining such ghettos will never banish blight," Carey declared.[65]

Thus, even though the Carey Ordinance went down to defeat, the measure enhanced Carey's political reputation as a forthright fighter for black and minority civil rights. This development, he believed, brightened the prospects that the GOP would attract black voters and elect black Republicans to office. The Democrats, he argued, did not deserve African American loyalty: the Chicago council's burial of the Carey bill offered an egregious example of the party's indifference toward nondiscrimination. Though Carey knew that the Chicago/Cook County Democratic Party machine kept numerous black officeholders—including Congressman William L. Dawson—in elective and patronage positions, Carey remained convinced that the GOP offered better alternatives for Chicago blacks. In 1950, therefore, Carey announced that he would challenge Dawson for the First Congressional District seat that he had held since 1943.

Carey had always envisioned the city council as a stepping-stone to higher office: in 1947, he confessed to his sister, Eloise, "The reason I am running is because I want to go to Congress." Since his visit to the U.S. Capitol with his father, he had dreamed of serving there.[66]

Carey bore no personal animus against Dawson. While still contemplating his congressional candidacy, Carey contacted Dawson's office on behalf of a member of Woodlawn AME Church who wanted a federal position. Dawson was happy to help, especially in light of the congregant's education at Howard University and her intention to take the civil service exam. However, Dawson was a Democrat, and Carey had numerous problems with the party. He thought that the Korean War was "a tangled international situation" that resulted from "bungling by the Democratic leaders" and shared the "resentment of others" who denounced "sending Colored Americans to shoot other Colored peoples of the world." He criticized Congress for failing to enact serious measures to "give all Americans equal opportunity in the matter of housing, employment, education, the right to vote and the full enjoyment of every other American liberty." Voters needed to choose politicians who presented "the greatest hope of realizing full first-class citizenship" for African Americans. Moreover, he believed that members of different parties should be elected to "maintain that balance which is the foundation of America's freedom." He recognized the weaknesses of his own party, which he thought was no longer "the party of progress," although not all Republicans "are opposed to the ideals that made it once the strong and dominant party in America." And his loyalty to the GOP was not absolute: he would not "remain in the Republican Party and accede to the wishes or corrupt purposes of men who may dominate it for selfish purposes." Speaking to an audience of Progressive Party members, he declared, "I as a Republican and you as Progressives stand on common ground" with respect to civil rights, but in the contest for Chicago's First Congressional District, the GOP was the best vehicle to oust the Democratic standard-bearer.[67]

Republican Party leaders chose Carey as their candidate over another African American, Roscoe C. Simmons, a veteran Republican operative and a contemporary of Archibald Carey Sr. Despite Simmons's experience under Mayor William Hale Thompson, the GOP power brokers believed that the younger Carey was a fresh face who had a better chance of defeating Dawson. Washington, from his influential position at the RNC, seconded Carey's nomination, arguing that he could "give Dawson the fight of [his] life."[68]

Washington saw the contest as one of four elections with particular national implications for African Americans. In addition to Carey, the Republicans fielded black candidates in three other urban districts with large pools of potential sup-porters: Elmer A. Carter in New York City, Theodore Spaulding in Philadelphia, and William Hodge, an AME minister, in Cleveland. Because, according to Wash-ington, "the Dems are beginning to pussyfoot on civil rights," the GOP issued a campaign flyer that criticized President Harry S. Truman for failing to establish a permanent FEPC and for neglecting federal protection against lynching. Unlike their Democratic opponents, the four black Republican candidates could be trusted "to carry an all-out fight for civil rights." Washington also promised to devote "at least six weeks to [Carey's] effort plus occasional trips for conferences." Moreover, a political insider reported that Joe Martin, the House minority leader, was "most anxious to get a colored Republican elected to the House" and was willing to pro-vide Carey with campaign funds.[69]

Carey solicited technical assistance from high-level GOP officials. Early on, Carey chastised the chair of the RNC for overlooking Carey's campaign, insisting on "a team for the First District." Carey also convinced the party's state vice chair to commit "a team to work" in the First District and offer Carey "every possible assistance."[70]

Carey, for his part, advised the GOP on strengthening its profile among black voters. The RNC's Illinois vice chair acknowledged Carey as an expert on "the racial question" and solicited his "suggestions as to the wording of a plank or paragraph that would be effective." Historically, replied Carey, the Republicans had abolished slavery, championed black voting rights, and opposed monopolies. As advocates of "individual enterprise," the GOP became "the party of progress," a characteristic it had lost during the New Deal. To become competitive again, the Republican Party "must re-dedicate itself to serving human rights." Specifically, it had to push civil rights "to protect the people from exploitation" from both business and organized labor and support fiscal discipline in public spending. Carey also declared that "the way to beat Communism is make democracy better and the way to win and hold any government is to give the people more and better service." In summary, "the Republican Party must be a better thing." For this reason, Carey chastised GOP senator William Langer of North Dakota when he attached a civil rights rider to an unpopular bill to ensure its defeat. Carey reminded Langer that he was running for Congress and that the behavior of GOP senators on civil rights issues drew the attention of black voters. "To millions of Negro-Americans and non-Negroes, who believe in equal opportunity for all Americans, it appears that you are making a joke of a matter which is of vital concern to many of us."[71]

Carey's comments implicitly acknowledged that the Democratic Party had become a champion of civil rights issues and that the GOP needed to recapture its reputation as the Party of Lincoln. The inclusiveness of Franklin D. Roosevelt's New Deal programs, the visibility of his "Black Cabinet," and the establishment of a wartime FEPC reaped for Democrats a harvest of new black voters. The rise of innumerable black Democrats in local, state, and federal positions helped to consolidate these political gains.[72] Moreover, Truman had campaigned in Harlem in 1948, ordered the desegregation of the military, and commissioned a hard-hitting report, *To Secure These Rights*, that chronicled in graphic detail the violence of American racism and the injustices of discrimination. Carey, however, believed that Truman and the Democrats received too much credit for black progress and argued that Republicans could improve on Fair Deal policies.[73]

Carey pursued a two-pronged strategy against Dawson. Like the other black Republican candidates, Carey emphasized national Democrats' poor record on civil rights. Second, he contrasted his strong stand in favor of civil rights to Dawson's complicity in his party's tepid support of African American interests. A Republican Party pamphlet used by Carey and the party's other black candidates charged that Truman could have used executive orders to ban racial discrimination in federal employment, extended the Department of Justice's civil rights jurisdiction, established a Civil Rights Commission, appointed integrationist commissioners for the District of Columbia, and recommended that a federal official be assigned to focus on "Negro problems." But the president did none of those things. The pamphlet also highlighted the views of southern Democrats, such as the one who proudly proclaimed, "States' Rights Democrat[s] . . . made possible the defeat of [the] F.E.P.C. and the other so-called civil rights bills." Another was quoted as boasting, "We Southern Democratic Senators—21 of us—are banded together and pledged to use every parliamentary device possible to defeat Civil Rights legislation." The pamphlet also cited newspaper columnists' assessments, including one that said, "The South is already assured that Harry Truman is a hypocrite on civil rights." Finally, the pamphlet used southern Democrats' own words to boost Republican candidates: the southerners claimed that Republicans were responsible for the civil rights bills brought up in Congress and were prominent in the "fight over the anti-lynching bill."[74]

Under the editorship of J. S. Brookens, the *AME Church Review* enthusiastically backed the candidacies of Carey and Hodge. In a strongly partisan article, "Negro Candidates of the Republican Party," Brookens endorsed the "unusually representative group of Negro candidates" and admonished Democrats that black voters were wise to their duplicity on civil rights. An admirer of Ohio senator Robert A. Taft and his antilabor Taft-Hartley Act, Brookens called Carey, Hodge, and an AME minister running for the Pennsylvania legislature "three of the ablest American Negroes" seeking public office. Brookens extolled Carey's church and civic credentials and said that he would "prove a most worthy addition to the Congressional ranks" and would "not sell our interests short on Capitol Hill."[75]

Brookens's preference for Republicans and his suspicions about Democrats drew from an antidiscrimination battle he had fought in the South. President

Franklin D. Roosevelt had established the Warm Springs Foundation in Georgia to treat patients with polio, but the facility refused to treat blacks. Brookens protested, persuading the foundation to provide African Americans with a separate facility at Alabama's Tuskegee Veterans Hospital. In addition, the only two black Democratic congressmen, Dawson and Powell, seemed powerless to push their party to support desegregation of the military and establish a permanent FEPC. If black Republicans were elected to Congress, they could work with an influential cadre of Republican civil rights backers to advance African American interests and safeguard "American Democracy from Communistic infiltrations."[76]

At the same time Washington and Brookens were providing national publicity for the Carey candidacy, GOP officials were putting party resources into the campaign. In February 1950, Washington sent Carey sixteen hundred dollars to help pay for a mass mailing to potential supporters and promised to "go over the details for financing the whole thing." In March, Carey forwarded to Congress's GOP election committee a fifteen-thousand-dollar budget for a Carey for Congress headquarters, billboards, an advertising truck, and campaign letters. Carey paid for amenities for members of Carey for Congress clubs and precinct captains and hoped that the local Republican organization would pay Election Day expenses for precinct captains.[77]

Later in the campaign, Carey appealed to the RNC for another $5,000 to fund his headquarters. He had already received $1,500, but he needed "$3500 as soon as convenient" for a mailing to the First District's 199,891 voters and for newspapers ads. Another request to the RNC soon followed: $6,230 for campaign letters, billboards, and posters. In the final month of the campaign, Carey asked Washington to come to Chicago because "we are raising 'cain' in a sort of a way and for the first time, I am of the opinion that your skill in the precincts could clinch this darn thing. This is the candidate, not the Reverend talking." Moreover, Carey said, Washington should "bring $2500 since the RNC dropped me $3500 short of what they promised."[78]

Perry W. Howard, a veteran black politician from Mississippi and an RNC member, planned a conference in Washington, D.C., for black GOP candidates, with a special focus on those running for Congress. He invited Carey to address the meeting regarding how "we can best help the election of our Candidates for office in the Fall Campaign." After consulting with Washington, Carey declined to attend the meeting, citing his pastoral and denominational duties, but thanked Howard for the offer of a "place of prominence in the program." After Howard sent Carey twenty-five dollars and a note that said, "We really want you to come to the Conference," Carey changed his mind, telling Howard, "Twenty-five bucks make a lot of difference." Howard also selected Carey to serve on a committee to write an "address to the Country" regarding "why the Colored voters should vote

for a Republican Congress." Further help came to Carey from Illinois's GOP senator, Everett M. Dirksen. Dirksen provided "tremendous material assistance," which,
Carey said, "in some instances has been the difference between doing or not doing
a vital thing."[79]

Carey drew heavily on Washington's advice and support. Washington was especially helpful in mining the Dawson record for missteps in defending African American interests. In January 1950, Washington told Carey that Dawson had harmed
himself when he missed the "fight for the F.E.P.C. bill." Speaker of the House Sam
Rayburn, "with help from the White House," called for a discussion of an unrelated
bill. Dawson "knew the deal [but] stayed away and was not present for any of the
five roll call votes." Washington hoped that Carey would "develop these facts where
they will make you some votes." An AME pastor, Frank Veal, wrote from South
Carolina that a local newspaper had criticized Dawson for setting "a record of being
absent from Congress." He and Bishop Frank Madison Reid hoped that the article
would provide Carey with "good campaign material." Carey also learned that Dawson had visited President Truman and told him about his "tough fight" for reelection. Dawson was "alarmed enough" to urge action by Democrats on pending civil
rights legislation. Continuing his attack on Dawson's civil rights credentials, Carey
later asked Washington whether the congressman had "introduced any Civil Rights
measure." Washington replied that although Dawson had submitted bills barring
discrimination in employment and in public facilities and seeking to eliminate poll
taxes and mob violence, "at no time . . . does the record show any effort was made
to get these bills passed." Even more disturbing, said Washington, was Dawson's
vote against an antidiscrimination housing bill and his support of white rather than
African American candidates in Illinois.[80]

Carey's campaign rhetoric overlooked not only the favor Dawson had done
for the Woodlawn parishioner but also the congressman's courageous defense of
black federal employees wrongly accused by the anticommunist Dies Committee.
Carey also made no mention of Dawson's efforts to persuade the Democratic Party
to retain a civil rights plank in its 1944 platform or of Dawson's support for Truman and the party's strong language against racial injustice in the wake of the Dixiecrat split at the 1948 Democratic National Convention. Carey was also unaware
of or chose not to mention a voter registration campaign Dawson had initiated in
the South and the congressman's efforts to forge alliances with party liberals to promote progressive positions on domestic issues. Instead, Carey accepted what the
Chicago Sun-Times said about Dawson: He "has built up a nationwide reputation
as a champion of Negro rights in Congress. But he spends about half of his time
in Chicago running his political machine, which, he admits, is oiled in part from
numbers of racketeers." Such gambling associations offended Carey's religious sen-
sibilities, and he thought Dawson viewed civil rights as secondary to his quest for

political control of Chicago's South Side. This theme became the centerpiece of Carey's congressional campaign.[81]

In contrast, the Carey for Congress committee trumpeted all of Carey's achievements on the city council: the Carey Ordinance, the antidiscrimination requirement in the Commonwealth Edison franchise, and the Chicago Police Department's human relations office. In short, the minister received credit for "an unceasing fight to break down jim-crow, [creating] jobs, [protecting] civil rights and [working] in every other field to make his people first class citizens." In addition, his achievements during his 3½ years as an alderman included major street and traffic improvements in the Third Ward, new playgrounds, and a weekly radio broadcast to update his constituents on pressing municipal issues. Addressing the National Progressive Party Convention, Carey charged that Dawson "believes the way to get ahead is to be a good cog in a political machine," but that was not how "to represent people." Carey declared that Dawson was "selling out the things" that were in the best interests of his constituents, trading "their demands for first class citizenship for three dozen political jobs." Several periodicals agreed that Carey, unlike Dawson, fought hard for black civil rights. According to the *Crusader*, "Carey's entrance into the national cause will give our people in America the first real Race Leader we have had in quite some time in Congress." The *Baltimore Afro-American* described Carey as "a man who . . . can create a political sensation out in Chicago this November and become the talk of Washington." The influential *Chicago Tribune* and *Chicago Sun-Times* also came out in support of Carey.[82]

For Powell, his longtime friendship with Carey and their shared commitment to forthright advocacy of black causes trumped party loyalty, moving the congressman to surreptitiously support Carey rather than Dawson. Moreover, bad blood existed between the two Democrats since Dawson had helped Truman pursue a grudge against Powell by shifting Harlem patronage to Dawson's congressional office. When Carey asked Powell whether Dawson had been absent during a FEPC vote, Powell suggested that he and Carey "get together in person" to discuss the matter. During that conversation, Powell apparently agreed to help Carey unseat Dawson.[83]

Carey also drew endorsements from ecclesiastical officials who supported the idea that preachers should hold public office, a sentiment that spread to Wilberforce University and Payne Theological Seminary, both of which were AME campuses. One Wilberforce undergraduate, H. Hartford Brookins, who went on to become a Los Angeles political broker during the 1960s and a bishop in 1972, "was very happy" to learn of Carey's candidacy and noted "most favorable publicity" about him in the Wilberforce community. Payne's dean, John H. Lewis, told Carey that "the Church and country would be happy to see you elected." After Carey delivered his pastoral report at the 1950 Chicago Annual Conference, his denominational rival, A. Wayman Ward, put aside his conflicts with Carey to solicit support for his election. The Reverend Granville W. Reed, pastor of St. Stephen AME Church on Chicago's West Side, who had been a delegate to the 1948 Democratic National Convention, was willing to breach party loyalty on Carey's behalf because of his "outstanding record of public service." Bishop Baber declared his support for Carey, as did Chicago's AME Ministerial Alliance and the denomination's Connectional Council. At the local, regional, and national levels, therefore, Carey's denomination not only approved of ministerial involvement in politics but believed that Carey was the right person to uphold this principle.[84]

Historian Wallace D. Best has noted that despite their long history in Chicago, AME churches were eclipsed by "the growing number of Holiness, Pentecostal, and Spiritualist churches after 1915, as well as the growing number of autonomous black ministers and independent black churches." Carey acknowledged these changes in Chicago's religious landscape and sought support from pastors of these socially insurgent religious bodies, including Clarence H. Cobbs, founder and pastor of the First Church of Deliverance. Starting in 1929, Cobbs's congregation pioneered the development of religious radio and popularized gospel music. Cobbs used his radio broadcast to endorse political candidates, leading his program to be taken off the air. Carey however, approved of such political activity and registered his "protest" at the censorship: "If any minister wants to express a political opinion, that is his privilege as an American citizen."[85]

Carey knew that he needed the votes of members of dozens of other rank-and-file political, religious, and community groups. Early in the campaign, he reported that the Oscar De Priest Charity Club had embraced his candidacy and wanted to sponsor a testimonial banquet for him. He also planned an appearance at a birthday celebration for the former congressman. Ministers at several churches, including Woodlawn AME, where Carey had served as pastor, welcomed campaign stops. The Greater St. John Baptist Church, the Pentecostal Church of God, the Blackwell AME Zion Church, and the AME Zion Ministerial Alliance all declared their support for Carey's candidacy. He requested that his clerical colleagues "ask their congregations to be sure and register" to vote. Carey's campaign also received a boost when he got the backing of several labor unions, most notably the Farm Equipment Workers and the Packinghouse Workers, while other unions considered endorsing Carey despite their Democratic leanings. Appearances at Poro College, the Central Y, the National GOP Women's Council luncheon, the Rust College Alumni, the Negro Chamber of Commerce, and the predominantly white Interprofessional Committee of Physicians, Dentists, and Pharmacists filled Carey's schedule from January to November 1950. He believed he was his "own best salesman" and that he needed to speak to these various groups "personally."[86]

Despite the endorsements and his tireless grassroots campaigning, Carey still had a "steep hill to climb." The countywide Democratic Party organization, which included Dawson's political machine, posed formidable difficulties. In a majority Democratic city, the congressman had an edge in precinct workers and funds. Moreover, incumbency provided Dawson with an advantage that any Republican, even one as popular as Carey, would have had trouble surmounting. Endorsing Dawson, the *Chicago Defender* noted, "With due respect to the abilities and character of Archibald Carey, we firmly believe the reelection of Congressman Dawson . . . will serve the best interests of the citizenry." Dawson's seniority and his status as the first African American vice chair of the Democratic National Committee and chair of the influential House Committee on Executive Expenditures gave him political clout, which the *Defender* believed outweighed Carey's reputation as a civil rights champion.[87]

On November 7, Dawson tallied 69,506 votes to Carey's 41,944, a margin far smaller than Dawson had garnered in 1948 but a decisive victory nonetheless. Carey explained to an RNC official that Dawson had won because of his "psychological advantage" as a DNC official and a House committee chair, his money and organization, and "the general affection of Negro Americans for the Democratic Party." Moreover, Dawson had benefited from a well-financed "National Dawson Day" celebration and an ample supply of cars to transport supporters to the polls. Carey also blamed malfunctioning voting machines for robbing him of votes: on one machine, "the selector over my name was stuck all day, with a final tally of 301 for Dawson and 19 for Carey." He called it "the greatest ineptitude, but probably, money was a factor."[88]

After the congressional election, he told Bernice Fisher, a CORE founder, that he would "rest and not even think about big decisions." His repose, however, was short-lived; he was up for reelection to the city council in 1951. The Dawson machine was determined to unseat him and the other remaining Republican officeholders as part of the effort to consolidate control of Chicago's South Side. The *Chicago Defender*, which had supported Dawson for Congress, backed Carey for alderman, describing him as "deservedly seeking reelection on his record to the Council. His capable service, highlighted by strong fights against discrimination in housing, has brought citywide recognition to his efforts."[89]

Carey retained his seat by what he and others described as a "slim margin." According to Carey, "Dawson's machine 'threw the book' at me," forcing him to overcome "terrific odds" to win. The Democrats went on to score impressive victories in the 1954 city elections, and Carey recognized that defeating the Democratic machine belonging to Mayor Richard J. Daley and Congressman Dawson would be even more difficult in 1955.[90]

Carey, already a favorite of national and state Republicans, asked an aide to President Eisenhower whether to seek reelection as alderman. The ward was "heavily Democratic." Since 1932, he reported, it had only "gone Republican the two times I ran." Moreover, "the Democrats are counting on me not to run, expecting that I would be somewhere in the Eisenhower Administration before the election came on." The reasons for staying in the race included supporters who argued Carey that was the "only Republican who could win" and the fact that the Illinois governor and others wanted him "in some official position." If Carey retired from the city council, he would be acknowledging that he would eventually lose his majority Democratic district. Conversely, if Carey stood aside early enough, another GOP candidate would have a chance to attract support. After weighing these pros and cons, Carey decided to stand for reelection.[91]

In announcing that he would run, Carey noted that because the office was nonpartisan, "many friends, Democrats, Republicans and Independents alike, have urged me to continue the fight for better housing, better government, a better city and the full enjoyment by our people of all their rights as first class citizens." Taking a swipe at Daley and Dawson, Carey invited "all those who do not belong to any selfish political machine" to help him safeguard the rights of all.[92]

His opponent was Ralph Metcalfe, an Olympic track and field medalist in 1932 and 1936. Since 1952, Metcalfe had held several political appointments, among them the post of Third Ward Democratic committeeman. To defeat Metcalfe, Carey mobilized support from attorney Bindley C. Cyrus and Olympic champion Jesse Owens, who had taken the gold ahead of Metcalfe in the 100 meter race at the 1936 Olympics. Cyrus and Owens sponsored a fund-raiser, the "Citizens' Salute to Alderman Archibald James Carey Jr.," at which they announced, "From early manhood [Carey] has been in the forefront of the battle for civil rights" and especially for "progress which involve[s] the colored citizen." Cyrus and Owens emphasized that the banquet was nonpartisan, like the election itself, perhaps in hopes of peeling wary Democrats away from the Dawson machine. The program included several of Carey's ministerial colleagues, among them Bishop Baber and Cobbs. Famed gospel singer Mahalia Jackson, another Chicagoan, sang two selections, while several federal, state, and local officeholders offered words of tribute. Illinois's Republican governor, William G. Stratton, said, "I honestly believe that Carey's reelection is more important to the Republican Party than to Carey as an individual. His win would keep Democrats from getting everything." Carey also appealed to Dirksen for an endorsement; the senator responded that Carey was "a friend, a patriot, and an unselfish and useful public servant." Charles F. Carpentier, Illinois's secretary of state, also supported Carey.[93]

As in other campaigns, Carey produced literature that addressed his numerous achievements as an alderman. He divided the brochure into issues he had already championed and those for which he vowed "to continue to fight." He opposed a taxicab ordinance because insurance rates increased fares for South Side residents. He also denounced another ordinance that imposed a levy on moviegoing, calling it a "poor man's tax." Moreover, he promised "more and better housing, street lighting, ward services, [and] recreational facilities" as well as improved police and fire protection so that the Third Ward would be "a cleaner, safer, and better community." Carey again solicited Washington's help: the testimonial dinner would "pay for all expenses except the workers," so he asked for forty-five hundred dollars to compensate precinct workers and other monies for the Third Ward organization, "which [was] pitifully weak," and for volunteers. Fisher volunteered to help, and Carey eagerly accepted her offer since he needed people "to canvass and carry my story." He promised to pay them "the going rate for Election Day," and Fisher provided the names of four women and offered herself "to stuff envelopes . . . or scrub floors . . . . to get you back in office."[94]

Metcalfe, however, had Dawson's backing, and this time Carey could not overcome the machine, receiving just 5,311 votes, less than half Metcalfe's tally of 10,913. Carey commended Metcalfe, saying he "has made a fine record as an athlete and now has the opportunity to make an even finer record in public office." Four other black aldermen, all Democrats, joined Metcalfe on the new city council, and the *Chicago Defender* featured them in a photo taken with Mayor Daley. The Democrats now controlled Chicago's South Side.[95]

Friends rallied to Carey. Homer Jack told Carey that despite the defeat, "Chicago was with you—even if the people in the third ward weren't." Moreover, Jack declared, "You will be Mayor of Chicago, yet!" Bishop Walls called Carey's loss "a little reverse" and predicted that it would not prevent him from rising "to larger usefulness to the people" since Carey still had "high esteem" from "throughout the country." He had already begun to rise through the national Republican ranks and had received appointments from President Dwight D. Eisenhower, involvements that Walls believed were beneficial "for the race and nation." Carey responded that he was "very grateful for the experiences I gained during my eight years of service in the City Council" and now wanted to devote his "energies to other fields."[96] Carey would turn to developing his public theology in newer areas and broader spheres.

Archibald J. Carey Sr., ca. 1920. Used with permission of the Department of Research and Scholarship, African Methodist Episcopal Church.

Elizabeth Davis Carey, ca. 1920. Used with permission of the Department of Research and Scholarship, African Methodist Episcopal Church.

Archibald J. Carey Sr., ca. 1910. Used with permission of the Chicago History Museum; ICHi-31007.

Elizabeth Davis Carey, ca. 1890. Courtesy of
Dorothy E. Patton.

Eloise Carey Bishop, late 1940s. Courtesy of
Dorothy E. Patton.

Wedding of Shelton Hale Bishop and Eloise Carey (center), 1919. Next to Eloise is
Annabel Carey Prescott. At right (left to right): Hutchens Chew Bishop, Elizabeth Davis
Carey, Archibald J. Carey Sr., Archibald J. Carey Jr. Courtesy of Dorothy E. Patton.

Archibald J. Carey Jr., ca. 1924. Courtesy of
Dorothy E. Patton.

Archibald J. Carey Jr., ca. 1960. Used with
permission of the Chicago History Museum;
ICHi-31010.

Hazel Harper Carey, ca. 1960s. Used with
permission of the Department of Research
and Scholarship, African Methodist Episcopal
Church.

Wedding of Hazel Harper and Archibald J. Carey Jr. (center), ca. 1930. Next to Carey are Elizabeth Davis Carey and Archibald J. Carey Sr. Courtesy of Dorothy E. Patton.

(left to right) Annabel Carey Prescott, Archibald J. Carey Jr., Hazel Harper Carey, Carolyn Carey, ca. 1950s. Used with permission of the Chicago History Museum; ICHi-31009; photograph by N. M. Lofton.

AME Bishops Council, Detroit, 1926. Archibald J. Carey Sr. is third from right. Used with permission of the Department of Research and Scholarship, African Methodist Episcopal Church.

Archibald J. Carey Sr. (sixth from the left) with President Calvin Coolidge, June 9, 1927. Bishop William T. Vernon is standing to Carey's right; Bishop William D. Johnson and Bishop William H. Heard are standing to Coolidge's right. Used with permission of the Chicago History Museum; ICHi-31006.

Archibald J. Carey Jr. (seated, front) at the Sherman Hotel, Chicago, mid-1950s. (left to right): Fannie Mae Taylor, Carey's secretary at Quinn Chapel; Dorothy E. Patton, Carey's niece; Demetrios Maktos, friend from the United Nations; Dorothy Carey Patton; Annabel Carey Prescott; Geraldine Tillison, Carey's secretary at his law firm. Courtesy of Dorothy E. Patton.

(left to right) Archibald J. Carey Jr., Dorothy Patton, Martin Luther King Jr., July 22, 1957. Used with permission of the Chicago History Museum; ICHi-31012.

Children of Archibald J. Carey Sr. and Elizabeth Davis Carey, September 1966. (standing, left to right): Archibald J. Carey Jr., Madison Carey Sr.; (seated, left to right): Dorothy Carey Patton, Eloise Carey Bishop, Annabel Carey Prescott. Courtesy of Dorothy E. Patton.

Archibald J. Carey Jr. (third from the left) with President Dwight D. Eisenhower, ca. 1960. Used with permission of the Chicago History Museum; ICHi-31008.

Archibald J. Carey Jr. in his judge's chambers at the Chicago Civic Center, 1970s. Courtesy of Dorothy E. Patton.

(left to right) Russell DeBow, Archibald J. Carey Jr., Jesse W. Cotton, ca. 1970s. Courtesy of Jesse W. Cotton.

CHAPTER 6

Plant My Feet on Higher Ground

ARCHIBALD J. CAREY JR. AND THE NATIONAL GOP

Archibald J. Carey Jr. was undeterred by the rough-and-tumble of Chicago politics. His strong commitment to public theology and his belief in the Republican Party as an effective vehicle for advancing African American civil rights remained a primary focus in his civic career. He never wavered in his conviction that clergy should be involved in electoral politics to push policies and initiatives that would benefit the disadvantaged. To a Spiritualist pastor active in political advocacy, he said, "I am aware of the prejudice many people have against preachers in politics." Nevertheless, he believed, clergy, "charged with the solemn responsibilities of a pastoral shepherd," should express their political views in the pulpit and in public. Moreover, the "freedom of speech should not be denied any American citizen, least of all a responsible community leader" who happened to be a minister. Carey reiterated these perspectives when advising his friend, Adam Clayton Powell Jr., who was considering a run for the New York mayor's office. Carey urged, "Don't give up the church" but "go ahead and run." Powell believed that his candidacy would "force people to think, both Negroes and whites," that African Americans could attain high political office. Though Powell doubted that he would receive the Democratic nomination, the attempt would "plant the seed and some day someone [an African American] might get it." Carey agreed. Carey also acknowledged his ups and downs in politics but remained firm in his conviction that political office was a proper place to do public theology and enlarge his ministry to benefit the church and community that he served.[1]

To achieve this objective, Carey thought that the Republican Party was a better ally for African Americans than the Democrats. As a successful candidate in two aldermanic elections, Carey had become a valued Republican officeholder and a vigorous GOP advocate. During his campaigns for the Chicago City Council and for Congress, his name became increasingly familiar to officials at all levels of the party hierarchy. Hence, he forged a close alliance with Illinois senator Everett M. Dirksen, who described Carey as among the "greatest guys" he knew and as someone with a "'top flight' reputation."[2] Carey also became an enthusiastic supporter of Dwight D. Eisenhower's 1952 and 1956 presidential campaigns. Dirksen, Eisenhower, and other high-ranking Republicans rewarded Carey with political favors and appointments, which satisfied his political aspirations and helped him advance black civil rights.

A member of the U.S. House of Representatives from 1935 to 1949, Dirksen had become an influential GOP figure in Downstate Illinois. In 1950, he was elected to the U.S. Senate, where he served until his death in 1969. Carey became acquainted with Dirksen during the 1950 election, when both were candidates for Congress and when Dirksen aided Carey's challenge to William Dawson. Although Carey lost, he thanked the senator for "the fellowship of campaigning" and hoped someday to join him "in some good cause to help the people." Not long thereafter, Carey moved to solidify the relationship. In 1951, he invited Dirksen to address the thousands of participants at the 1952 African Methodist Episcopal (AME) General Conference meeting in Chicago, an appearance that would benefit not only Dirksen and the AME but also the Republican Party. Because of the presidential election year and because the denomination had to appear nonpartisan, "a big Republican as well as a big Democrat" would be invited to speak to the delegates, but Carey offered to use his influence to arrange Dirksen's appearance during the welcome program, when the convention's "biggest crowd" would be gathered.[3]

Dirksen accepted Carey's invitation but came during General Conference balloting for new bishops and general officers. The presiding officer, Bishop George W. Baber, interrupted the election and presented Carey to introduce Dirksen. Dirksen focused his remarks on the meaning of the AME Church motto, "God Our Father, Christ Our Redeemer, Man Our Brother." That he brought with him a fellow GOP senator from Missouri must have gratified Carey. Baber reminded the senators that the AME Church stood for civil rights without compromise and wanted "the leaders of our Nation to help make wrong things right." Carey hoped that delegates' applause meant that they understood that the Republicans offered an alternative to the Democrats' weak civil rights record.[4]

In 1954, as the political friendship between Carey and Dirksen deepened, the minister volunteered to aid the senator in his role as a congressional campaign chair. Moreover, Carey kept Dirksen informed about federal appointees assigned to Illinois. On one occasion, for example, Carey reported on a luncheon for Robert Tieken, the newly designated U.S. attorney for the Northern District of Illinois, whom Carey had known since 1936: Tieken "made a fine impression and you would have been quite pleased." Knowing that senatorial courtesy required President Eisenhower to get Dirksen's endorsement for federal nominees who would serve in Illinois, Carey predicted that the senator would be "proud" of Tieken's future record. Other political information passed back and forth and cemented Carey and Dirksen's alliance.[5]

Carey and Dirksen performed significant favors for each other. In 1954, at the request of Clarence Mitchell of the National Association for the Advancement of Colored People (NAACP), Carey asked Dirksen to check the status of pending federal legislation banning discrimination in interstate travel. Harold Rainville, Dirksen's senatorial assistant, solicited Carey's help in landing a taxicab operator's license for a Chicago friend. Since Rainville did not know in what ward the petitioner lived, he asked Carey to relay the request to an alderman who could endorse the man's application. Carey also invited the man to a meeting. An army chaplain and the son of an AME minister in Downstate Illinois contacted Rainville about securing a state prison chaplaincy; Carey knew the family and promised to help. In a more complicated case, Carey and Dirksen tried to assist an Illinois constituent and company owner in obtaining overdue payments from the U.S. Navy and the Department of Defense. On other occasions, Carey and Dirksen exchanged social invitations and gifts that demonstrated their close connection. In 1954, Dirksen invited Carey to a reception for Illinois's members of Congress, and Carey reciprocated by inviting either the Dirksens or the Rainvilles to dine at his home with journalists from the *Chicago Daily News* and the *Chicago Sun-Times*.[6]

While benefiting from his friendship with Dirksen, Carey thrust himself into the 1952 presidential election. Senator Robert A. Taft was a front-runner for the GOP nomination. Val Washington had already stated that he preferred Eisenhower because of "Taft's unpopularity among Negroes." Despite these sentiments from his valued ally, Carey remained publicly noncommittal and told the *Chicago Tribune* in January 1952 that he had not issued "any official statement about any candidate for President." His posture changed within a few weeks, however, and Carey began expressing doubts about Taft—in particular, about his views on civil rights. *Jet*, the popular black weekly, reported that Carey said that if Taft won the nomination, the minister would do all he could to oppose the senator. Carey claimed, however, that *Jet* quoted him inaccurately and missed some nuances in his remarks. His perspective was anchored, at least in part, in his belief that Democrats would not choose President Harry S. Truman to run for another term because he would certainly go down to defeat in the general election. Since the GOP would have a clear shot at the White House, it was in the interests of African Americans that the Republican nominee should be friendly to their civil rights concerns. Though he was "the best informed man in Government," Taft was unpopular among blacks. Moreover, "their balance of power in many key states" could deny Taft the presidency. Carey was especially disturbed that Taft, while speaking in North Carolina, said that he opposed the use of federal power "to break down segregation." Carey responded that he "would do everything in my power to prevent him from getting the nomination." According to Dirksen, however, Taft denied making such a statement, and Carey subsequently moderated his public statements and said that if Taft became the GOP standard-bearer, he would "exert every influence to get Taft's position in line with the aspirations of Negro-Americans to be treated like all other Americans."[7]

One party member chastised Carey because she believed that Democrats benefited from his comments and it was "tragic to have Republicans aid" the other party in maligning the Ohio conservative. Carey's critic understood his "desire for equality for your people and I am sure Senator Taft does too." Nonetheless, it is "more important to work for good schools and hospitals for your people—something that can and should be accomplished quickly." She also believed "that all of us will get the fairest treatment from Taft," so Carey should reconsider his "unfair criticism of the senator." Carey, however, remained doubtful, especially in light of such condescending statements from one of his conservative supporters.[8]

Carey's opposition to Taft's candidacy did not harm his high standing with GOP officials. The 1952 Republican National Convention met in Chicago, and Carey, as one of the few local GOP aldermen, won a prominent place on the program. Carey credited Werner W. Schroeder, a local party official, for this large favor. "I am keenly aware," he recalled, "that it was you who first proposed me and even stood up for my integrity and good judgment when some persons wondered if my sympathies for the General would hurt their interest in behalf of Senator Taft."[9]

At the convention, Carey delivered an address that was broadcast on radio and television and that became one of the most important speeches of his career. In addition to declaring his support for Eisenhower, Carey challenged Republicans to take advantage of their opportunities to attract African American voters. Carey credited Republicans with ending slavery, releasing "the grip of monopolies," and crushing trusts. In the twentieth century, the GOP had matured into the party of peace and the party of industrial and urban development, while the Democrats, he declared, had become "the party of promises." They had vowed to keep America out of World Wars I and II, yet "we entered both those wars as soon as we had elected Democrat Presidents either because they wouldn't or couldn't keep their word." He added, "As a taxpayer, I have heard them promise to reduce the cost of government, but under the Democrats taxes have multiplied." These broken promises, Carey declared, were especially harmful to African Americans. In particular, he cited promises of antilynching laws, a federal Fair Employment Practices Commission (FEPC), legislation to abolish the poll tax, and military desegregation. When Democrats blamed such failures on the Dixiecrats, Carey responded, "There is no Dixiecrat Party—only the Democrat." He declared, "The string of promises dangled before my people like a glittering necklace has been fashioned into a tight-fitting noose strangling their freedom [and] sometimes, even their hope." One scholar has termed some passages in the Carey address "more daring" than Martin Luther King Jr.'s landmark "I Have a Dream" oration at the 1963 March on Washington, which drew on Carey's speech.[10]

Carey complimented Democrats for providing "some help" to the "little people" in taking "from the favored" and giving "to the less favored." Standing on his own scriptural exegesis, he declared, "I do not quarrel with this for I believe in the spirit of the gentle Nazarene and the words of Paul that 'we who are strong ought bear the infirmities of the weak.'" At the same time, he admonished listeners about the "unseen tragedy" of giving someone a "pittance" and robbing from that person "his initiative, his industry, [and] his incentive to high endeavor and even the reward of his enterprise." In these respects, the Republicans differed from the Democrats, who had deprived the poor of both self-reliance and pride despite the party's pursuit of charity. Moreover, the GOP should demonstrate its commitment to civil rights and recognize that black voters in strategic northern cities and certain important states could swing the presidential election in Republican's favor. The Party of Lincoln, therefore, should identify with the "complete emancipation" of African Americans and "millions of non-Negroes too—Jews, Catholics, Mexicans, Orientals and immigrants from the corners of the earth, whose major love is freedom, too." Furthermore, the nation's global leadership required the Republicans to acknowledge the world's majority "colored" population and the need to "proclaim and practice complete freedom for all Americans." This task, he said, demanded forthright action, not gradualist solutions for the nation's "disfranchised."[11]

In answer to the question, "What does the Negro-American want?" Carey declared, "Just what everybody else wants—nothing less." He added "We don't want any special cars to ride in or rooms to wait in. We don't want any special houses and blocks to live in or schools to go to. We don't want any special favors to put us ahead or special arrangements to hold us back." Instead, African Americans demanded "the right to live and work and play, to vote and be promoted, to fight for our country and hope to be President, like everyone else. More than that we do not ask, but with less than that we shall never be content." Standing fully in his clerical and civic roles, Carey reminded the GOP audience that blacks sang "with all other Americans" the familiar patriotic song,

My country, 'tis of thee,
Sweet land of liberty
Of thee I sing.
Land where my fathers died
Land of the pilgrim's pride
From every mountain side
Let freedom ring.

In a rhythmic refrain, Carey rose up rhetorically like the effective preacher that he was, declaring,

> That's exactly what we mean—from every mountain side, let freedom ring. Not only from the Green Mountains and the White Mountains of Vermont and New Hampshire; not only from the Catskills of New York; but from the Ozarks in Arkansas, from the Stone Mountain in Georgia, from the Great Smokies of Tennessee and from the Blue Ridge Mountains of Virginia—Not only for the minorities of the United States, but for the persecuted of Europe, for the rejected of Asia, for the disfranchised of South Africa and for the disinherited of all the earth—may the Republican Party, under God, from every mountain side, LET FREEDOM RING![12]

Carey was uncharacteristically astonished when his speech generated five hundred communications from religious and political leaders. His audacious address had touched a chord, becoming a *kairos* moment in which Carey's ministry in sacred and secular spheres reached fruition. Clergy affirmed him as the embodiment of a public theologian who connected the pulpit and the public square to facilitate black advancement. He served as a committed moral exemplar for whom politics provided opportunities to bring equality and fuller freedoms to the disadvantaged. His father's denominational nemesis, Bishop Reverdy C. Ransom, commended the speech and told the younger Carey that he had honored his race, church, and country.[13]

Patrick Henry's famous declaration, "Give me liberty or give me death," was "never more meaningful" than the sentiments echoed in Carey's address, said an influential AME pastor. Judge Perry B. Jackson, a Cleveland jurist and a member of the AME Judicial Council, lamented that "more delegates" were not present to hear the speech. These AME leaders validated Carey's blend of religious and civic involvement and the belief that blacks were better off because of it. The head of the El Paso, Texas, NAACP summed up the sentiments of most African Americans, noting that Carey's speech had "left no doubt in the minds of the Republicans, the Democrats, the Americans, [and] the nations of the World as to what the American

Negro wants." A black Chicago physician and fraternity brother of Carey's insight-fully noted the intergenerational significance of his address, commenting that Bishop Carey would have been "as proud as we were." Similarly, an AME official in Canada heard the speech on the radio and told Carey that "the unseen spirit of your dad was blazed in glory as you spoke."[14]

White clergy who listened to the speech may not have known that Carey was a fellow pastor, since he was identified only as a member of the Chicago City Coun-cil. Such listeners, therefore, might have missed his clear articulation of a public theology and instead emphasized Carey's call for civic equality and justice. One New York preacher described the speech as "the greatest public utterance since the Gettysburg address" and asked Carey, "What can be done to place your name in nomination for the vice presidency?" A Methodist minister praised the speech for its emphasis on "civil rights and universal franchise of all peoples." "From every mountainside—let freedom ring," he repeated.[15]

Politicians and party supporters embraced Carey's powerful presentation of black civil rights claims and their convergence with the nation's constitutional and egalitarian principles. Barry Goldwater, at the time a Phoenix city councilman and the leader of an incipient conservative movement, described the speech as "one of the most forceful" he had heard from the convention: "You as a negro did a lot for your people today in being forthright in your presentation of your problems." The future U.S. senator was looking forward to meeting Carey, perhaps to satisfy his curiosity about this unusual Republican. One GOP supporter was glad that Carey's "splendid speech" rose above the "political harangues" that usually characterized convention rhetoric. She especially liked his reference to "the colored peoples of the world look[ing] to the United States for better treatment of minority groups before they can believe what we say." Another commentator had not heard "a more profound statement of American Democratic principles." The address established Carey as a national leader among both African Americans and Republicans. One admirer suggested that Carey should succeed the late J. Finley Wilson as grand exalted ruler of the half million members of the Improved, Benevolent, and Protec-tive Order of Elks of the World, while a Chicago Republican commended his "high integrity and caliber on the city council" and hoped that he would pursue a "suc-cessful political career."[16]

Nevertheless, Carey's speech had only minimal impact on the GOP platform. Some well-wishers reminded him of this unpleasant truth and were disappointed that the Republicans, including Eisenhower, opposed the use of federal power to protect black civil rights. Though states were obligated to safeguard African Ameri-can interests, the platform allowed for the "supplemental" and constitutional exer-cise of federal authority in civil rights matters. Government action against lynching, poll taxes, and segregation in the District of Columbia were the only areas where the GOP pledged direct intervention. Black Republicans wanted more from the platform and the nominee. They were especially annoyed that Eisenhower opposed FEPC proposals and courted southern white voters. AME bishop Joseph Gomez shared other blacks' disappointment with the GOP's tepid support of civil rights and accused the party of failing to heed Carey's "sound advice" to support "a worthy civil rights plank." One exception, in Carey's view, was California senator Richard M. Nixon, the vice presidential nominee: Carey had been told that Nixon believed that the party platform should have been stronger "on civil rights." Carey added that "as a Republican, I am anxious for our party to win." Since blacks would be a "decisive factor, the position taken by the respective Parties and standard bearers will determine how the Negro-American votes in this election." Therefore, Nixon deserved commendation for his "discernment" and his opinion that a "positive, aggressive position for human freedom will be the means of waging a successful campaign." To Carey's dismay, however, most black newspapers endorsed Democrat Adlai Stevenson for the presidency.[17]

Carey kept an open mind about Eisenhower and his attitudes about civil rights, traveling to Denver in August 1952 at the candidate's request to discuss issues of interest to African Americans. Carey later reported that the general was "an excellent listener" and allowed Carey ten to twelve minutes to outline his views on antilynching legislation, poll taxes, military desegregation, Senate filibusters, discriminatory election laws, the need for an FEPC, and bias in public and publicly aided housing. "At some points," noted Carey, Eisenhower "asked for more details." Carey was also surprised by the general's detailed knowledge of some of these issues. He knew, for example, the latest statistics on lynching. Moreover, he announced he was "more than one hundred percent" for the desegregation of the armed forces. He recalled that while on active duty, he had encountered resistance to desegregation from within his staff. Eisenhower "was immensely sorry that the pressures of a war kept him from pursuing his own objective" and pledged that as president, he would abolish military segregation "entirely." After some persuading, Eisenhower also backed the abolition of the Senate filibuster, and he reversed himself and promised to support legislation to revive the FEPC. Overall, Carey was thoroughly impressed with the general. When an aide wanted to summon others who had appointments with Eisenhower, Carey prepared to leave but was beckoned back to his seat; those next in line would wait because Carey's counsel was too important to rush. Moreover, just before Carey left, Eisenhower strongly asserted, "Alderman Carey, I believe in the Declaration of Independence, every detail of it and I want to see every promise of it made real for all our people." His embrace of "first class citizenship" convinced Carey that Eisenhower was "committed to the full freedom for . . . minorities." The meeting seemed proof positive that the general would be a friend and advocate for African Americans.[18]

The session affirmed Carey's confidence in Eisenhower's presidential candidacy, and he agreed to serve as a consultant on civil rights and engaged in discussions about speaking on behalf of Eisenhower's civil rights positions. The leader of Chicago's Democrats for Eisenhower, a white man who was principal of an elementary school, urged the general to use Carey in the campaign: "I know of no Negro in America who can and will present to Negro voters your stand on civil rights and related matters as eloquently, as intelligently and as persuasively as Alderman Carey. He is your kind of man. His integrity and sincerity are unquestioned. He has the confidence of the Negro group. He is highly respected by white people." Moreover, maintaining "our standing in international affairs" made it "critically important" to "clean up 'the mess' as far as our treatment of minorities is concerned." Carey thus became an operative in the Eisenhower election effort and a public face for the national GOP.[19]

Within days of the Eisenhower-Carey meeting, the National Republican Speakers Bureau, based in Washington, D.C., developed plans to put the alderman on the campaign trail. Carey was fully prepared to promote the GOP cause and the interests of its presidential standard-bearer. When the Christ Church Forum in New York City asked him to speak on "Malice toward None, Charity for All," Carey refused "to make a partisan, political speech under the pretense of discussing civic or social matters." He was an advocate for Eisenhower and wanted to pursue that objective without subterfuge. He also preferred that national Republicans and others should understand that he was in a purely political role and had no problem functioning as a party regular. Nevertheless, he was unwilling to make unlimited sacrifices on behalf of the Republican ticket. During the planning for a speaking tour in the Far West, for example, Carey insisted that his hosts respect his pastoral obligations and pay him appropriate honoraria. On another occasion, he firmly refused to attend a reception for two GOP officials, citing his pastoral obligations at Quinn Chapel: "I wish very much that it were possible for me to be in Washington, but because it comes during Holy Week, the schedule of my church will require my being here." Despite his willingness to wade into Republican Party politics, GOP leaders needed to understand that his ministerial pursuits took precedence.[20]

Beginning in late September 1952, Carey spoke to dozens of audiences nationwide. He addressed 1,200 teachers in Daytona Beach, Florida, and 400 people at a mass meeting at Bethel AME Church in Baltimore. Between September 27 and October 2, Carey appeared in Oakland, San Francisco, Vallejo, Los Angeles, and Pasadena, California, and in Las Vegas, Nevada. In San Francisco, Carey spoke to "a large enthusiastic crowd" at "a leading Negro night club." On a return trip to the city, Zeke Griffin, a "popular Negro disc jockey" at radio station KSAN, gave Carey five minutes of airtime to deliver a pitch for Eisenhower to between 75,000 and 100,000 listeners. On another radio station, KNBC, Carey appealed to an audience of 250,000 to 300,000 potential supporters for the GOP ticket. The *San Francisco Examiner* trumpeted his visit to the Bay area with a headline, "Dr. Carey Urges Negroes to Vote for Eisenhower."[21]

Carey also logged thousands of miles in other sections of the Far West; through the Northeast in Rhode Island, New York, and Pennsylvania; across the Southeast in Atlanta and in various cities in Florida; and in the Midwest in Ohio, Michigan, Indiana, and Illinois. Whether in churches or synagogues, Elks' halls, public school auditoriums, community centers, or radio stations, Carey praised the Eisenhower candidacy. In Denver, he appeared at a "torchlight parade" prior to his arrival at radio station KOA. On the air, Colorado's governor provided an introduction before Carey spoke to 150,000 listeners. The city's *Rocky Mountain News* covered the visit with "a good story and pictures." He later solicited support from seven Jewish leaders. In Chicago, he made several speeches and participated in a debate with Edith Sampson, a black lawyer and Truman's appointee to the United Nations and North Atlantic Treaty Organization. In the closing days of the campaign, Carey went to New York City to meet with Eisenhower and returned with him to Chicago, where the two men "rode in an open car" from downtown to the South Side so that Eisenhower could place a wreath at a monument to African American soldiers. Carey's final campaign stop occurred on November 2 in Joliet, Illinois, where he addressed 200 people at a Baptist church.[22]

Throughout his extensive travels, Carey adhered to a set of basic themes. The Democrats, despite their pro-civil-rights rhetoric, had produced little legislation on behalf of African Americans. Conversely, on both the federal and state levels, the Republicans had tangible civil rights achievements that made them worthy of black support. The Democrats were cursed with a Dixiecrat wing hostile to African American advancement, while the GOP was freer to embrace policies favorable to the same black voters the other party too often took for granted. African Americans should abandon their expected support of the Stevenson/Sparkman ticket and shift to Eisenhower/Nixon. The same applied to candidates for Congress. Whereas Democrats had squandered opportunities to pass substantive legislation that would benefit blacks, Republicans could be counted on to safeguard civil rights.

While campaigning in California, Carey blasted the Democratic vice presidential nominee, declaring, "I don't want John J. Sparkman of Alabama to be the co-pilot of my government." He described the nomination of Sparkman, a consistent opponent of black civil rights, as "an insult to the people of my race group." Moreover, the presence of the Alabaman on a major party ticket signaled American indifference to the world's majority colored populations. Civil rights legislation had enjoyed solid support from GOP-dominated Congresses, and seven of the eleven states that had passed FEPC laws had Republican governors and legislative majorities. "As long as the Democrats are in control," Carey asserted, "civil rights laws never will be enacted because most principal Committees of both Houses have Southern Democrats as Chairmen." Sparkman had told an Alabama audience in 1950, "I am against the Civil Rights proposals, always have been and always will be." Hence, Carey argued, only with the election of Eisenhower and Nixon and a GOP Congress would civil rights bills become law.[23]

Carey's political commitment to the Republican victory seemed total. In the midst of a campaign tour in the Midwest and West, he wrote talking points on civil rights for Eisenhower to articulate. Because some Democrats had criticized the general for making conflicting statements on civil rights in the North and in the South, Carey advised that the candidate present ideas that are "the same wherever he is." He needed to denounce second-class citizenship imposed on African Americans and other minorities because of "the color of their skins rather than the quality of their skill." Carey urged Eisenhower to "make a bold statement" about "equal opportunity for everybody." Moreover, Carey outlined issues that the general should champion, including support of an FEPC, abolition of segregated schools, ending segregation in the District of Columbia, "readjustment" of the filibuster to stop its use against civil rights legislation, elimination of the poll tax, and an end to discrimination against Jews, Asians, Mexicans, and others. Carey also emphasized the need to abolish segregation in the military "because many Negro-Americans say that Eisenhower did not do what he could to break up segregation in the army when he was in charge."[24]

The highest levels of the Eisenhower organization acknowledged Carey's efforts. Nixon extended thanks for Carey's support during the campaign's "hectic days." New Hampshire governor Sherman Adams, an Eisenhower assistant, noted Carey's value to the election effort and tried to get Carey on a train with Ike, although missed communications scuttled the effort. Eisenhower's national campaign headquarters and the Republican National Committee (RNC) sponsored the majority of Carey's numerous engagements. Carey and about forty other African Americans, including former Pennsylvania legislator Hobson R. Reynolds, Cleveland judge Perry B. Jackson, Memphis politico George W. Lee, and Baptist leader Nannie H. Burroughs, belonged to a special national organization affiliated with the RNC. Of this group, Carey had the highest profile in the Eisenhower campaign. His visibility owed much to Val Washington and other black Republicans. Washington, still an RNC official, played an important role in arranging Carey's itinerary and paying his expenses. Several black Republicans concluded that Carey was a comer in national politics.[25]

Throughout the 1952 campaign, the GOP remained concerned with attracting black support. W. B. Banta of the Michigan Young Republican National Federation invited Carey to Muskegon because the GOP "has neglected" African American voters, thus leaving them to become "predominantly Democrat." To address the situation, Banta formed an alliance "with three Republican negro ministers" and requested the use of a black church for a GOP rally. They planned for "an outstanding Negro speaker" and asked for sponsorship from "negro professional men and two church brotherhoods." John R. Williams, a black Republican in Los Angeles, shared the Michigan Republicans' hopes, but much to his regret, although Carey gave a "marvelous address" for the national GOP ticket, only a "handful of people" came to the "small church" to hear him, and the attendees were "already on [the Republican] side." According to Williams, this poorly organized meeting reflected how the GOP was "missing the boat" with respect to recruiting black voters: "I have done everything humanly possible to encourage the Republican Party both nationally and locally to go after the Negro vote. . . . Friend Carey, in my thinking, you can do the Republican Party the most good by endeavoring to influence the powers-that-be to wake up at once and go after the Negro vote in some organized fashion."[26]

Despite Carey's efforts, blacks nationwide voted for the Democrats by a margin of three to one. The reason, "right or wrong," he noted, was that "Negro-Americans felt that their interests had been most advanced by the Democrats." Nonetheless, he believed that the Republicans could "capture and hold this same kind of loyalty" if they treated the "issues and symbols" of African Americans seriously and if African Americans were appointed "to places of significance and dignity." Carey rejoiced at Eisenhower's comfortable victory. Because Carey had spoken on behalf of Eisenhower in twenty-five cities and logged twenty-one thousand miles, the minister asked for two inauguration tickets: receiving them would signify to all Chicagoans that his services to the campaign had been highly valued.[27]

Not long after the election, Carey reminded Adams, who would become Ike's chief of staff, that Chicago newspapers had informed their readers about Carey's closeness to the Eisenhower organization. The *Chicago Sun-Times*, for example, identified Carey as a "Top Negro in Ike's official family" and said that he would be considered for an "undersecretary" position in the administration. Chicago's mayor announced that Carey would join the new cabinet and believed that he deserved such a position. Carey also had learned that two New York newspapers were seeking information about him from *Ebony*, the *Chicago Defender*, and local white dailies and asked Adams to verify this rumor. Finally, Carey requested a meeting to discuss "the place of Negro-Americans in the new administration."[28]

While Carey awaited word about whether he would receive a federal position, he continued his exhortations to the GOP about racial equality. At the Lincoln Day Banquet of the Republican Central Committee of Multnomah County, Oregon, Carey gave attendees "a spiritual shot in the arm," reminding them of their responsibility to stand for a color-blind society. He was assured that a pending civil rights bill in the Oregon legislature had near-unanimous support from GOP members of both houses. On other occasions, Carey honed his reputation as champion of African American rights. From speaking to the "big annual Emancipation occasion" in Windsor, Ontario, to addressing the Urban League of Minneapolis, Carey carried the mantle of black advocacy to numerous venues. AMEs seemed particularly proud of Carey, as evidenced by invitations to speak at the literary forum of St. Paul Church in Canton, Ohio, and to preach at Howard University's chapel, whose dean was a fellow AME.[29]

Carey's balancing act between church and state remained difficult, however. He wanted to reap the rewards of his service to the 1952 presidential campaign, so when a local headline declared, "Carey Announces for Bishop," he told Washington, "Don't believe everything you read in the newspaper." Moreover, when Rainville stated that Carey had no desire to serve as an Eisenhower appointee, Carey wanted Washington to know that Rainville had been wrong: "I am still interested in talking about federal work." To further solidify his relationship with Washington, Carey thanked him for funding some Eisenhower campaign activities and repaid him "fifty bucks," adding, "It ain't much but it's a starter." The money represented a symbolic down payment for additional assistance in getting Carey a job in the Eisenhower administration. Carey reiterated his position to Dirksen: although some newspapers had reported that Carey planned to "abandon" his political involvements and restrict himself "to the affairs of the Church," Carey believed that he could "be a useful public servant in government and in the Church without transgressing the rights of either."[30]

At least one AME admirer disagreed, writing that Carey should "receive the very best that Ike can give"—a position such as "Under-Secretary or something as outstanding." Although an appointment would require a "severance with the ministry of our church," it could "make . . . history" for African Americans. Carey's supporter had heard "whispers" that he "might not accept a large political appointment" because of his commitment to Quinn Chapel, but he believed that Carey was "young and can always return to the Church ministry." Moreover, "America needs you now."[31] Carey's public theology, however, meant that he saw no such contradiction and could function simultaneously in both church and civic activities.

The Eisenhower administration developed a narrow approach to civil rights policy that focused on action exclusively within the federal sphere—the military, the District of Columbia, the appointment of persons based on merit rather than race, and fairness in federal employment and contracting. In this arena, the president and the federal government had uncontested constitutional and statutory authority and did not encounter the possibility of vetoes by state and local officials. According to one scholar, emphasis on these issues allowed Eisenhower to restrict "his subordinates' activities to areas of clear federal jurisdiction, greatest international propaganda, and minimum risk of political fallout or domestic unrest." Carey's advice to Eisenhower generally followed these lines, albeit with some modifications. Right after Ike's first State of the Union address, Carey commended the president's appointments and described himself as "immensely gratified" by Eisenhower's "forthright position and commitment against segregation in the nation's Capital and in the Armed Forces." Such actions were "exactly the guarantee" Eisenhower had given Carey when they met in Denver prior to the election. Carey believed that his enthusiastic support for the general had been justified.[32]

Carey also offered some ideas to Washington, asking him to communicate these proposals to his "White House Man." Carey argued for a program that reflected "the viewpoint of Negro-Americans," seeking to "satisfy them" and address their priorities. Given the competing demands of "Labor, Industry and Korea," Carey asserted, Eisenhower might neglect issues important to African Americans, and Washington's White House contact therefore had to aggressively advocate black interests. He should persistently but tactfully "create and exert a respectful and friendly pressure on race affairs." Moreover, Eisenhower should be persuaded to "speak on civil rights issues" and propose "committees . . . and laws affecting Negroes." To White House aide Charles F. Willis Jr., Carey argued that Eisenhower needed an "Advisor on Negro Affairs" and that Washington was not adequate for the job: though he was "sound," he was "concerned primarily with matters of patronage." Other crucial subjects required the attention of a special official assigned to monitor the desegregation of "army schools, the Howard University budget and other affairs important to Negro communities." Carey made such suggestions through private channels because he was loathe to publicize his differences with the administration's restrained posture on civil rights.[33]

Publicly, however, Carey defended the Eisenhower administration against critics, including Congressman Powell. Prior to his presidency, Powell pointed out, Eisenhower had opposed military "desegregation below [the] platoon level." After his election, he maintained an "unobtrusive, gradual implementation of desegregation orders" that the Truman administration had initiated. Eisenhower had forbidden segregation in schools on military bases, but twenty-one post schools remained segregated. Powell sent several public telegrams to the president to protest cabinet and agency officials' failure to comply with military desegregation orders, resulting in a promise that these matters would be investigated.[34]

Carey, too, was greatly disturbed by Ike's hesitation in combating segregation in military base schools and in public education and by the challenge of Powell's public "blast at the Administration." To help Carey prepare for an upcoming speech to the NAACP's 1953 national meeting in St. Louis, Willis arranged a high-level briefing for the alderman. The meeting gave Carey access to various Eisenhower officials and documents, one of which said that the administration sought "to end segregation in the army schools as quickly as possible." Eisenhower also said in

Carey's presence that he expected the Supreme Court to outlaw school segregation in its forthcoming decision in *Brown v. Board of Education*. Nevertheless, Carey found this briefing inadequate and appealed for additional guidance from Bernard M. Shanley, special counsel to the president. Carey was pleased to hear that Eisenhower hoped for a favorable ruling in *Brown* but was disappointed that he could not "quote the President" to the NAACP. To defend the administration, Carey asked permission from Shanley "to say that the President indicated to me that he hoped that we could win the segregated schools case pending before the Supreme Court," or "if that is too strong, could I say that the President reiterated the sentiments favoring abolishing discrimination, which first won me to his support?" Carey left "no stone unturned" in trying to present the best spin on Eisenhower policies on civil rights, asking Shanley for permission to discuss some of the administration documents that opposed army school segregation and sought to minimize damage to students, teachers, buildings, and accreditation if southern states withdrew funds from public schools attended by children of military personnel. Or, Carey suggested, he could indicate that the administration would soon institute fully integrated schools at Fort Benning, Georgia, and that other schools on various bases would follow. Carey also sought instructions about what he could say "in answer to Powell." He noted, "This is the price we have to pay for being useful to our esteemed friend, the General." With such seemingly obsequious queries, Carey was attempting to push the administration to abandon restraint and boldly to declare its full and unambiguous commitment to black civil rights.[35]

Shanley shifted Carey's inquiry to Maxwell M. Raab, an Eisenhower adviser on black issues. Robert F. Burk, a historian of the Eisenhower presidency, has written that the appointment of Raab, a Jewish lawyer, allowed the administration to avoid appearing "too fervent" in its pursuit of black civil rights. Raab also had a reputation in the White House as a racial "liberal" and "as the sole staffer who took racial problems seriously." Moreover, Burk observes, Raab's principal role lay in "containing politically embarrassing racial incidents, providing the administration's response to minority complaints, and promoting Republican interests in the black community."[36] Raab responded to Carey's letter by conceding that the NAACP address offered the "opportunity to make an effective presentation of the remarkable progress which is now beginning to manifest itself under the leadership of President Eisenhower in the field of segregation and discrimination." Nonetheless, Raab advised Carey to forgo any comments about the internal documents he had seen or about Powell's criticisms. In fact, Raab declared, "Congressman Powell was very much satisfied with what the President told him and he, in his note, called the President's letter 'The Magna Carta of Minorities' and a 'second Emancipation Proclamation.'" Raab asked that Carey "let it rest that way for the time being." Carey disagreed with Powell's assessment but promised "to let good sense and good taste govern" his remarks. However, he insisted that it would be safe to tell his audience about an exchange in which Eisenhower had "reiterated the positions which he set forth on the subject of first-class citizenship for everyone when we first talked about the matter during the campaign."[37]

After the NAACP speech, Carey reported to Raab, "I was sorry I did not have authority to discuss what I knew" concerning the administration's desegregation efforts. Because he was muzzled, Channing Tobias, an NAACP leader who spoke prior to Carey, had free rein to highlight Powell's attacks on the Eisenhower administration and the president's inadequate response. Because they went unchallenged, Tobias's comments became the prevailing view of the White House on matters of civil rights. Though agitated, Carey "followed orders and stayed off the specifics." A skilled speaker with "experience with audiences," Carey believed that his listeners had offered less-than-enthusiastic applause whenever he mentioned Eisenhower's civil rights record and that he could have made "a better case if I could have cited the specifics and adduced the evidence of my own experiences in the White House." The NAACP meeting, Carey contended, represented a lost opportunity to win over blacks who still doubted Eisenhower's sincerity on African American issues. Raab regretted "the straight jacket imposed by us here" but commended Carey on his presentation, which three sources had described as "a magnificent job." Raab invited Carey back to the White House to learn about the administration's planned civil rights programs.[38]

Carey was also involved in black patronage recommendations for various federal appointments. In some instances, he attempted to find new jobs for people who already had government positions; in other cases, he worked to get consideration for other able or deserving prospects. Carey again directed his suggestions to Washington, who was vetting names of potential appointees for attorney general Herbert Brownell. Carey suggested that Washington consult a roster of black federal officials that the *Pittsburgh Courier* had compiled and named Dirksen as someone who could "help carry our ball." Carey was particularly concerned with getting Ralph J. Bunche, the 1950 Nobel Peace Prize recipient and the nation's most prominent African American, into the Eisenhower administration. However, Bunche's wife, Ruth, had angered some within the GOP because of her "vigorous criticism" of Eisenhower, and Bunche remained at the United Nations. Carey also urged Washington to sponsor Sam Shepard, the owner of the *Akron Informer*, for a position in the Department of Commerce, and sought job protection for his uncle, James Perry Davis, an administrative officer at the Department of Agriculture. Similarly, Frank Horne, who had been an adviser to Franklin Roosevelt, needed help in staying at the Home and Housing Finance Agency, and John Parker Prescott, the half-brother of Carey's brother-in-law, wanted to keep his position with the New York office of the Public Housing Administration.[39]

Carey's efforts on behalf of Horne and Prescott annoyed Washington, who ignored two letters from Carey on the subject. Carey then sought to go directly to Eisenhower, requesting an appointment with the president. Washington suspected that Carey would try such an end around and wrote to an Eisenhower aide regarding Horne and Prescott: Washington understood that Carey's family connection to Prescott but saw "no reason in the world . . . why [Carey] would want to save Frank Horne, who has been one of the most vicious partisans since the beginning of the New Deal." Moreover, Horne, "an optometrist, learned all he knows about housing at the expense of the taxpayers—not from experience before he entered Government." Washington argued that the time had come to reward the "many qualified persons in the Republican party who not only have ability but are loyal." Eisenhower and his aides, therefore, should ignore "the mournful tones of these payrollers as to their indispensability." Partisan patronage carried the day.[40]

The incident highlighted the developing friction between Washington and Carey. The alderman had previously seemed content to respect Washington's role as the GOP gatekeeper for high-level black appointments. Now, however, although Carey consulted with Washington, he also felt free to take his requests directly to the White House. In another instance, Carey wrote to Eisenhower regarding E. Frederic Morrow, Genoa S. Washington, and Lou Swee. Morrow, a campaign aide, had been told at the inauguration "to go home and pack up and get ready to come to Washington." Morrow relayed this message to CBS, his employer, "and gave them notice." The broadcaster hired Morrow's replacement, leaving him with only a part-time job when no offer from the administration was forthcoming. Several persons wrote to Eisenhower in support of Morrow, but not until 1955 was he hired as an administrative assistant to the president. Carey also brought up Genoa S. Washington, a Chicagoan and an Eisenhower alternate delegate to the GOP national convention who had not been rewarded for supporting Ike against an Illinois majority in favor of Taft, and Swee, a policeman friend who had served as a bodyguard for the Eisenhower campaign. Carey believed that his standing with the administration was sufficiently strong that he did not need to channel his requests through Val Washington.[41]

By the middle of 1953, although Carey remained involved with the Eisenhower administration, he had not received an official appointment. He seemed patient, but the Chicago press did not. When the *Chicago Sun-Times* ran a June 11 column referring to discussions about possible jobs for Carey, the alderman dissociated himself from the report, telling Adams that he was "not seeking a political job" because "those responsible for the overall administration of the government [can] best determine where I might be useful." In midsummer, the *Chicago Daily News* speculated on a diplomatic post for the alderman, an appointment that would have been in keeping with what Burk has described as the president's "conscious[ness] of the importance of international opinion" and consequent propensity to make black appointments in this area, as in the case of Howard University professor Frank Snowden, who became a cultural attaché in Rome, and Clifton R. Wharton Sr., who was appointed minister to Romania. According to the *Daily News*, "Reports here are that [Carey] may be nominated to be ambassador to Liberia or put into sub-cabinet rank as an assistant secretary of state." Though Carey had Senator Dirksen's endorsement "for any office the administration cares to offer him," an upcoming congressional adjournment made an early confirmation unlikely. Carey probably found such positive coverage flattering but nonetheless told a White House aide that he "had nothing to do with this" article and "promised to keep" the administration informed about any other unauthorized publicity. In return, Eisenhower's special assistant assured Carey, "We are seriously trying to find the right spot where you can best assist the Administration and hope to be in touch with you very soon with some definite information." Carey may have turned down Eisenhower's initial offer of an appointment because the job would have required his presence in Washington, D.C., and kept him away from his Quinn Chapel congregation. Despite his ambition, Carey would not countenance any serious encroachments on his pastoral obligations.[42]

Nevertheless, Carey lobbied subtly but aggressively for a presidential appointment. During a May 1953 trip to Washington, D.C., to speak at Howard University, he offered to meet with Adams and the president to talk about his prospects. He also asked to have his daughter, Carolyn, greet the president, shake his hand, and tour the White House. All of Carey's requests were granted. In July, he returned to the capital to attend a housing conference and asked Willis and Raab if he could come to the White House and learn "what thinking is going on concerning me."[43]

By that time, the administration had already decided to offer Carey the position of alternate delegate to the United Nations, and Secretary of State John Foster Dulles had asked FBI director J. Edgar Hoover to initiate a confidential security investigation of the Chicago clergyman. Numerous interviewees praised his record as a pastor. A Cincinnati commentator "could furnish no derogatory information" and described him as "a capable, well-educated person of good character and reputation and a loyal American." The only criticism another informant could muster was that Carey "has sometimes sacrificed his principle for political expediency." Yet another interviewee noted Carey's "reputation of being a good and honest alderman, . . . a rare thing in Chicago politics." One report described Carey as "very aggressive in matters involving public housing and racial discrimination but not . . . allied with [any] Communist clique." Another person recalled, "Carey has been critical of the Communists and has particularly criticized Paul Robeson for adherence to the Communist party line," while still another source did "not know Carey as a member of the Communist Party or any other Communist organization, nor does he know that Carey had any sympathetic views toward Communism." Such observations were crucial during this era of McCarthyite communist witch-hunting. Although Carey had never hesitated to cooperate with or to address meetings of alleged radical groups such as the National Negro Congress as part of his efforts on behalf of black civil rights, one commentator explained that Carey's speeches to such organizations "were in the field of social life and politics." His association with the Progressive Party, for example, focused on its "aims for democratic action." The informant was willing to "stake his life" that Carey was "very definitely not a Communist."[44]

These investigations, however, were perfunctory. Many of the reports were filed after Carey's appointment had been announced. In July 1953, Dulles met with Carey and offered him the United Nations post. Carey accepted, embracing "the opportunity with high anticipation." Before Carey could share the news with local supporters, he learned from a *Chicago Tribune* reporter that the newspaper's Washington Bureau had broken the story. Henry Cabot Lodge Jr. would serve as U.S. ambassador to the United Nations, with Carey as his first deputy. Though pleased with Carey's appointment, one Chicago Democrat expressed disappointment that the alderman "didn't land a cabinet post"; such an assignment would have been "a master stroke by the President" and "would have attracted large groups to the Republican Party." He told Carey, "If Mr. Eisenhower is as smart as I think he is, he will put you on the Supreme [Court]—which would really give us something to talk about!" Whether Carey had expected more from Eisenhower is unclear. The United Nations position enabled him to remain a Chicago alderman and pastor, and he would serve only from September 12 to December 9, 1953. Despite his short tenure, Carey took the opportunity to hone his skills and experience in foreign affairs, an area in which he had no previous experience.[45]

Carey's time at the United Nations brought him into contact with an expanded stratum of the nation's political and economic leadership. Among those whom he came to know in greater depth were the patrician Lodge and delegates Henry Ford II, heir to the automobile fortune; Mary Lord, heiress to the wealth of the Pillsbury Flour Company; and segregationist South Carolina governor James F. Byrnes. Carey was most impressed with other diplomatic corps, particularly those from the United Kingdom, Israel, and the Soviet Union. Moreover, he became a believer in the United Nations and its aims of banishing war and securing "the peace and dignity of every individual on the face of the earth," which he contended, "are such objectives as honorable men and women can never abandon" and "are dreams in the heart of God Himself." The United States needed to pursue "worldwide peace and freedom" lest other nations embrace those goals and "leave us behind." Carey ultimately believed that the "moral judgments" of the United Nations were important to all and justified not only the body's existence but American contributions to its budget.[46]

Carey served on various United Nations committees and as a spokesman for American foreign policy. As a member of the Legal Committee (Committee VI), he dealt with "the study and development of arbitral procedure to settle international disputes." Also, he stood for immediate approval of a "Genocide Convention." American abstentions on this issue ended because of "Carey's interest" and the importance he attached to this moral matter. On the Political Committee, he worked to ameliorate tensions in Burma and to facilitate the removal of Communist Chinese troops.[47]

On other occasions Carey, like other members of the delegation, articulated Eisenhower foreign policy. Carey was especially pleased with his participation on the Commission on Human Rights and with presenting his government's endorsement of reports coming from member nations on their efforts in this field. On one occasion, he asserted that "the record of the United States in the United Nations on questions of racial discrimination is good," referring to resolutions addressing "the treatment of persons of Indian descent in South Africa" and attacking that nation's pernicious apartheid policy. Carey, however, failed to compare South African segregation with similar practices in the United States itself. Carey also commended the United States for its concurrence with a 1946 United Nations statement that "it is in the higher interests of humanity to put an end to religious and so-called racial persecutions." Carey later protested when a committee chair failed to "accord proper recognition to the Representative of China," subjecting him to a "unique and discriminatory practice." "I am against discrimination," Carey declared, "whether it is based on a man's race or color, his religion or the part of the world from which he comes, or the fact that the chairman of a committee may not like his government."[48]

Byrnes's presence in the United Nations delegation proved problematic for Carey, who could not avoid collegial contact with the segregationist politician. Carey cautioned the press to remember that his "friendly pose" should not be construed as a sanction of Byrnes's racism. At the end of his United Nations term, Carey told one confidante that Lodge had commended Carey's "sober and balanced method of dealing with Governor Byrnes." The delegation had been "a little tense about possible eruptions between him and me," but Lodge "felt well pleased with my own manner of stating my position, 'forcefully, but with a calmness that was very mature.'" Lodge also told Carey that "the position of the United States in the world is definitely better for your having served." Eisenhower, too, was satisfied with Carey's performance, describing him as having "reflected great credit on the United States."[49]

The United Nations experience affected Carey. When the National Council of Churches invited Carey to deliver a radio sermon, he discussed "One World or None" and considered the desirability of healthy international relations. The existence of "a highly explosive age" with "the discovery and release of atomic power" required methods to address "this new terror." Humankind needed to embrace "Cooperation" and to "make the spirit of our times, 'Fellowship.' These things we must do or we shall surely die." Moreover, the earth's resources would have to be shared, lest the world's oppressed and exploited "colored peoples" continue their revolts. "Peace, prosperity [and] progress," he said, "are the result of working together." These sentiments reflected an enlarged vision of global affairs derived from his United Nations experiences.[50]

Carey's extensive campaigning and service as a United Nations appointee increased his visibility, and both black and white supporters urged the president to elevate him to increasingly lofty positions. Right after his United Nations term ended, Brigadier Fritz W. Nelson of the Salvation Army's Chicago headquarters appealed to the White House to reappoint Carey. Though consideration of this request was promised, nothing materialized. In 1953, another Chicagoan urged Eisenhower to appoint Carey as the replacement for recently deceased Chief Justice Fred Vinson, describing Carey as "a man of exemplary character, a loyal American. . . . [H]is appointment would be a masterpiece throughout the world." When Justice Robert Jackson died the following year, the same supporter suggested that Carey fill that vacancy since "every nationality is represented on the bench except the American Negro."[51] In April 1955, a member of the Board of Commissioners of Cook County, Illinois, Charles F. Chaplin, nominated Carey as governor of the U.S. Virgin Islands. A property owner on one of the islands, Chaplin said that he and others there believed that the new governor should be an African American: "Any racial difficulties there are at an absolute minimum, and the whites I know feel that a colored Governor is best equipped to maintain the status quo." Maxwell Raab apparently agreed, and Carey became a serious candidate for the position. Later that year, Carey wrote to the president and his chief of staff to request an appointment as judge of the Federal District Court of the Virgin Islands. Throughout the Eisenhower presidency, Carey continued to receive consideration for various influential offices, including the post of assistant secretary of state. None of these possibilities materialized, however.[52]

On January 18, 1955, Eisenhower established the President's Committee on Government Employment Policy to fight racial and religious discrimination in federal departments and agencies. Carey became the committee's vice chair and ultimately its chair, holding that post for the remainder of Ike's presidency. The committee offered Carey's most substantial opportunity to actualize the public theology that had defined his more than two decades of pastoral ministry. Through the committee, Carey had oversight over thousands of federal professional and service positions. The committee worked to develop policies against job discrimination in hiring and promotion and investigated complaints that federal agencies and officials engaged in unfair employment practices. Thus, Carey had both the authority and the opportunity to implement government policies and practices to enhance the economic condition of innumerable African Americans.

In creating the committee, Eisenhower displaced a similar agency President Harry S. Truman had established within the Civil Service Commission. A principal difference was that Ike's new entity reported directly to him. The committee would "make inquiries and investigations and advise the President concerning the conformity of department and agency personnel practices with the non-discrimination policy of the order." There was to be no "discrimination in civilian Federal employment because of race, color, creed, or national origin." To implement the order, each federal department and agency head designated an employment policy officer to work with the committee to insure compliance. In addition, the committee could review cases and issue "advisory opinions" about how agencies could bring their policies and practices into harmony with the order. The committee could recommend "corrective measures" to stop discriminatory behavior. The committee's effectiveness was limited, however, because it lacked enforcement power: it could only appeal to the president and use the threat of public exposure of discrimination. Carey seemed to care little about these constraints. Rather, he possessed a zeal for exposing misconduct and subjecting perpetrators to the scrutiny of his committee and the sanction of public condemnation.[53]

Carey initially served as the committee's vice chair under Maxwell Abbell, a wealthy Chicago attorney and businessman. The committee also included three other Eisenhower administration officials: J. Ernest Wilkins, a black Chicagoan who was assistant secretary of labor, and two alternates. Abbell suggested a delay in starting committee business until Carey resolved "matters" from his recent reelection campaign for alderman. Raab agreed with Abbell and set March 7, 1955, as the date of the committee's first meeting. Congressman Powell was impressed with Carey's new position and sent him a congratulatory note. For his part, Carey planned to seek Powell's counsel and "ideas" about how to attain the committee's objectives.[54]

Abbell, "an eminent philanthropist of the Jewish community," was often absent from committee meetings and frequently relied on Carey's assistance. Committee member W. Arthur McCoy, chair of the defunct Fair Employment Board, described Carey as doing "an excellent job of presiding, having always taken a completely objective approach to the many troublesome problems coming before the Committee." In late 1956, Abbell became seriously ill, and the White House began considering who should replace him at the committee's helm. McCoy strongly recommended Carey: "In the delicate type of work in which we are engaged," the committee would certainly benefit from Carey's "near amazing ability to lead discussions with large groups of top government officials." Carey "did such an outstanding job in putting that Committee's policies over, and in breaking down the obvious reserve noticeable in many of the conferees" at the first area conference with federal field staff, that McCoy "concluded then and there that [Carey's] presence at future such conferences was practically a must. We have had about ten subsequent similar conferences, and the success of this phase of the program must be attributed in large measure to his splendid leadership." Raab concurred, telling Adams that although appointing Carey "would place a Negro in this post, he merits it because he is next in line and has done a remarkable job as a moderate, understanding member of the Administration." He added that Carey "is an outstanding speaker and we can use more people with stature" to represent the administration's perspective on equal employment opportunity. When Abbell died in 1957, Carey joined the select ranks of Eisenhower's high-level African American appointees.[55]

Under Carey, the committee conducted a survey of "personnel practices" and held additional area conferences to examine particular settings where biased employment policies allegedly occurred. "Enlightened self-interest" dictated that the federal government should use the full "reservoir of manpower and talent" available regardless of race, religion, or national origin. Carey noted that in addition to African Americans, Jews and Catholics faced employment discrimination and was "startled as the list lengthened to a total of 23 different kinds of American[s] who received special treatment or mistreatment because of their identification." He commended Ike for acknowledging that "God has hidden his treasures of talent and capacity in surprising places—yea, earthen vessels . . . in different colors and creeds and national backgrounds."[56]

Carey's leadership role on the committee became well known to African Americans, who began to send employment grievances directly to him. Black leaders with whom Carey was friendly often interceded on behalf of aggrieved employees. Bishop E. C. Hatcher, for example, communicated with Carey through the committee's executive director concerning an acquaintance, and Carey promised to give "careful attention" to and "keep in mind" this matter. When Powell pressed Abbell to investigate a charge of discrimination by a black U.S. Air Force employee stationed at the Pentagon, Carey, serving as acting chair while Abbell was overseas, responded, noting that no complaint had been filed and that the supervisor involved in the incident was also African American. When the NAACP retained Austin Norris, a prominent black Philadelphia attorney, and his law firm to handle a case involving an African American woman, Carey told the lawyer that "because we are old friends," he would look into why additional information on the matter had not been forthcoming. Even persons unknown to Carey contacted him directly: an African American woman from Toledo, Ohio, sought Carey's help in winning reinstatement as a clerk-typist at the Rossford Ordnance Depot. Carey was personally getting information about so many cases that his legal secretary, Geraldine F. Tillison, asked "where to direct these complaints." Between May 1, 1956, and January 18, 1958, Carey and his colleagues received 271 reports of discrimination, with 243 of those allegations coming from blacks. In nearly half of the cases, the committee's investigation found no discrimination. In other circumstances, corrective action or explanations were offered or the grievances were withdrawn. The committee offered advisory opinions in 70 cases and recommended corrective action in 16.[57]

Carey and other committee members also took the initiative, investigating federal employment policies even when complaints had not been filed. Carey and others traveled to hold meetings with agency supervisors and with employees. In 1959, Carey reported that over the three years of the committee's existence, area conferences had taken place in thirty-three cities, and discussions had occurred with thirty-three hundred federal workers. In St. Louis, Houston, and San Antonio, the committee had examined various cases and heard a "southern administrator" urge Carey and his colleagues to "go for broke" in uprooting job discrimination. An elated Carey told Powell that "the Lord was with us." In 1959, Ike agreed to make a public show of his support for the committee, taping "an inspired message" for use at area conferences. The president stressed that Executive Order 10590 barred discriminatory practices, authorized federal departments to institute "merit fitness as the only criter[ion] for government employment," and charged the committee with achieving these objectives. Carey noted that Eisenhower's presidential state-ments drew the serious attention of federal officials and showed his commitment to this issue.[58]

At conferences in Atlanta, New Orleans, and Dallas, the committee learned that while African Americans and Latinos "were being employed on more than the laborer level," there were too few blacks and Latinos in supervisory positions, and in some agencies, blacks and Hispanics did not appear on lists of candidates for promotion, with that absence frequently blamed on a "shortage of qualified appli-cants." Better recruitment at "Negro schools and colleges in the local areas" was a suggested remedy. Many supervisors also stated that "supposed fears" about whites working with blacks "just did not materialize" when antidiscrimination policies were implemented. Only one incident was recorded in which a white worker had left because an African American was hired. A survey of New Orleans released in 1959 showed that the number of blacks in clerical, stenographic, and typing jobs had grown "sevenfold since 1951" despite an overall decrease of two thousand in area federal employment. Whereas 17 blacks held had held federal jobs in the city at the beginning of the decade, that number had increased to 115, demonstrating what Carey termed "increased opportunities for white-collar office employment" in the Crescent City.[59]

Before the Dallas meeting, Carey gave a speech covered by a local newspaper. During an interview with a reporter, he appealed for "any information disclosing techniques of discrimination." At the meeting itself, Carey explained "that for 350 years the United States had indulged itself in a double standard of morality in human relations." By eliminating federal employment discrimination, the United States would be able to face other nations and honestly declare that the American "promise of freedom" was real. Carey also said the high or low number of complaints gave no "indication" of whether "proper policy was being followed." The committee bore responsibility for investigating even where the situation seemed benign. There should be no "favoritism for any particular group" and no "quota system"; rather, the committee sought equity for all workers. Carey further noted that minority group organizations could "be of considerable help in providing background concerning the complainant; they are thoroughly informed on the problems of their people in their own local areas. More important, these organizations are not subversive in any sense. They are staffed by able and intelligent people who are sincerely interested in the objective of equal rights for all citizens." This statement may have constituted a response to unfounded charges that the Fort Worth Urban League was a communist organization and to efforts to stop the founding of an Urban League chapter in Dallas.[60]

Carey at times corrected misstatements by Abbell and smoothed over other committee blunders. In Atlanta, for example, Abbell seemed to rationalize the lack of progress for blacks by saying that recently hired employees had too little seniority to expect advancement. An Atlanta NAACP official disagreed: "We do not agree with the statement that it is normal for Negroes to be at the 'bottom of the ladder,' because Negroes are still new to the Federal Service here and have not worked up to responsible positions." Blacks had been in the Atlanta postal system since the late nineteenth century, he noted, and had been relegated to lower-echelon jobs because "the white people in control have confused 'lack of ability' for 'Lack of Opportunity.'" This problem may have been exacerbated because local NAACP officials knew that the committee had been in Atlanta but had failed to consult with them. When the committee's executive director, Ross Clinchy, defended Abbell and declared that he had been misinterpreted, Carey stepped in.[61]

Another conference was planned for Atlanta in 1959, and Carey informed President Rufus E. Clement of Atlanta University that he would be coming. Carey wanted to meet with Clement and the other presidents in the Atlanta University consortium to discuss black federal employment in the region. The main purpose of the Atlanta visit was to consult with National Urban League (NUL) officials about "problems of mutual concern." Clinchy advised Carey "to give some background material on the policy and the work of Committee" to league leaders; Clinchy would discuss "the practical problem of employment situations and the handling of complaints." Carey and Clinchy would also inquire about the plans of the league's "southern field people" with regard to black employment. The meeting yielded information about relationships between African Americans and the civil service and about league efforts to assess the impact of fair employment legislation across the region, and participants planned another meeting about the "southern situation." The committee benefited because Carey was invited to address a league conference in Washington, D.C. Carey also proposed consultations with Roy Wilkins, the NAACP's executive director, and Herman Edelsberg, the head of the Anti-Defamation League.[62]

Carey was fully aware that he was pursuing employment equality for blacks within a federal structure in which blacks had limited influence, and he often tried to maximize the African American presence in behind-the-scenes committee operations. While still the committee's vice chair, Carey tried to engineer the appointment of a black person as the committee's executive director. "Since the Chairman was a white person," Carey believed, "a Negro should be in the position of Executive Director." Moreover, "he thought a colored person could do the job as well as a white person." Carey particularly thought that James C. Evans, an African American who held degrees in electrical engineering from the Massachusetts Institute of Technology and served as a civilian assistant in the Department of Defense, would be a good choice. The two men respected each other, with Evans describing Carey as a deft and skillful administrator. Evans was particularly impressed by Carey's "ability for cutting through" bureaucratic red tape to achieve committee goals. Carey asked Evans if he was "at all interested" in serving as the committee's executive director and urged him either "to submit a written application" or to discuss the matter in person. Abbell, however, believed that "no member of a minority group, such as a Negro or a Jew . . . should be selected [as executive director] since he believed that such persons would not be as effective in selling the program" as would a Caucasian. The other black on the committee, J. Ernest Wilkins, sided with Carey, arguing that either Evans or another black person would be preferable because "a Negro would feel the problem more than a white person who had never been discriminated against." Though Clinchy was appointed to the job, Carey soon succeeded Abbell, thus bringing black leadership to the agency.[63]

Though the committee's interactions with the African American press, the NUL, and the NAACP were sometimes uneasy, Carey believed that these relationships were crucial to building credibility with African Americans. These organizations had perspectives, programs, and initiatives that Carey thought should be aligned with committee objectives. Despite criticism from black newspapers, the league, and the NAACP, Carey viewed these institutions as necessary partners for improving black federal employment. While whites were wont either to ignore or devalue these groups, Carey perceived their input, even if critical, as ensuring significant black participation in committee activities.

The interracial National Association of Intergroup Relations Officials understood the duties and the limitations of Carey's committee. Alexander J. Allen, also the son and namesake of Carey's new bishop, served as executive director of the

Pittsburgh Urban League and chair of the association's Commission on Manpower Utilization. In 1956, Allen asked Carey to address the group, focusing on how it "can best cooperate [with the] work of the Committee" and which of its "techniques" could be adopted by these agencies. Although Allen recognized that Carey's committee "is limited to the Executive branch of the Federal government only," he believed "its influence goes much beyond this."[64]

Carey also had strong relationships with W. Beverly Carter, the publisher of the *Pittsburgh Courier*, and with the widow of Robert L. Vann, the paper's founder. In 1955, Carter lodged a complaint about racial practices at the Tennessee Valley Authority (TVA). The agency's job applications asked for "racial identification"— "for 'statistical purposes,'" according to TVA officials. Carter had evidence that this data "was being misused in the hiring of Negroes in Knoxville," and he wanted the practice stopped. Though the TVA promised to do so, Carter was skeptical and contacted Carey. Carey agreed to have the committee investigate and invited Carter to send "other suggestions" to help him and his colleagues "to do a worthy job." The queries of the *Courier's* Washington, D.C., correspondent apparently moved the federal government to end the practice on its own, before the committee became involved, but Carter had trusted Carey to be a forceful opponent of employment discrimination and was pleased with his speedy response. Carey realized that the black press could help to explain committee objectives, and he educated his colleagues about the medium's importance. Clinchy was elated that a committee press release had been shared with "over 100 minority group papers" and that Carey had been featured prominently, concluding, "We have gotten more publicity from the Negro newspapers than we would have had through a general release." Carey also drew on his friendship with John Johnson, the publisher of *Ebony* magazine, for help in covering committee activities.[65]

In 1959, another journalist, Simeon Booker of *Jet*, which Johnson also published, characterized Carey's committee as a "G.O.P. dominated" body that "slants data to make it appear that Negroes are gaining much under the party." To the contrary, Booker argued, "discrimination is rampant in Federal employment," with no enforcement of antibias regulations. Carey denied all of Booker's charges, pointing out that the committee included "an avowed and articulate Democrat." Moreover, the committee reported facts that highlighted persistent federal discriminatory practices. Carey also invited Booker to interview Evans for an "objective" opinion of the committee. Booker renewed his scrutiny two years later, accusing the panel of being "used for political purposes" in presenting an updated survey of black federal employment that showed progress in upper-level positions. Carey rebutted the charges by pointing out that the 1956 survey showed a marked disparity between the number of Negroes in the lower echelon and those in higher grades, while a 1960 survey revealed that the number African Americans in the higher job levels "had increased from 4,979 to 9,295." These facts, Carey noted, had not been "planned for political purposes." Moreover, despite Booker's skeptical perspective, President Eisenhower had in no way been "reserved in his approval of our work."[66]

Booker's negative comments, though biting, reflected what had been the buoyed expectations of some African American leaders, who thought the Chicago minister could deliver on their hopes for equitable employment practice. NUL and NAACP officials similarly insisted that Carey should do all he could to establish model job procedures in the federal government. League observers in particular valued Carey's position as a civil rights advocate within the Eisenhower administration. In 1953, Carey had addressed the annual meeting of the Minneapolis Urban League, delivering a speech that the local executive director described as having done "much for our membership." Later that year, when the head of the Urban League of Greater Cincinnati questioned whether Carey would be an effective communicator at the annual meeting of his affiliate, a national NUL official responded in the affirmative and urged his colleague to remember Carey's new appointment to the United Nations. Carey subsequently received an invitation to come to Cincinnati and discuss domestic civil rights and "its impact on our world position." In return, during the early months of the committee's operations, Carey defended the league's leader, Lester B. Granger, when skeptics accused him of disparaging the agency's importance. Carey demonstrated that Granger's comments had been taken out of context, illustrating to committee members that the NUL official had "great respect" for them. Furthermore, to ensure cooperation between the committee and the league, Carey urged "complete fellowship" and consultation with Granger and suggested that he meet with the committee on his next visit to Washington. Abbell concurred: more interaction with Granger "would be worthwhile."[67]

Granger later invited Carey to be the principal speaker at an important banquet at the NUL's 1959 convention. Despite his pastoral commitments, Carey attended, formalizing a partnership between the league and the committee. The league's long experience in employment training and placement provided Carey's group with much-needed information and expertise.[68]

League officials found the committee receptive to their reports on discrimination and their assessments of the status of African Americans in federal employment. Carey and his colleagues also wanted the league's strategic advice. When Granger, drawing from an inaccurate report from a league affiliate, told Carey and his colleagues that the number of blacks in federal positions had been decreasing since 1950, Carey chose to overlook the mistake: it was, he said, a single occurrence, and "it might be harmful to our relations with the National Urban League" if the committee faulted the organization. Early in 1956, Abbell invited Granger and Lisle C. Carter Jr., executive director of the NUL's Washington, D.C., affiliate, to address the committee. Granger had already endorsed the committee's work and told Abbell, "You are charged with a most important assignment—one of the most important assignments by the President of the United States."⁶⁹

Granger and other league officials tried hard to share their expertise with the committee and to endorse its initiatives. Granger, for example, told Carey and the committee that relying on complaints from aggrieved employees was an unreliable method of uncovering discrimination. "Sly tricks" from federal officials could thwart the hiring and promotion of African Americans, Granger said, and new procedures were needed. He recommended the use of some racial markers to monitor whether blacks were moving to higher positions and pushed for a black consultant to the Civil Service Commission. He also suggested that sample investigations be conducted in two agencies to determine how black employees were treated. Moreover, information about job rights should be disseminated, and a committee of "technicians, composed not entirely of Negroes, who know their way around the Federal Government" should aid efforts in fighting employment bias. When Carter advised Carey and his colleagues to consult with officials of local black organizations, Granger promised to provide a roster and a suggested agenda for the meeting. Moreover, R. Maurice Moss, the NUL's associate executive director, appeared before the committee to warn that the increased presence of blacks in federal employment did not mean that their rates of promotion were acceptable. "Some agencies," he said, "have a far less percentage than others," and African Americans had difficulty transferring "from one agency to another at the same grade level." Since the committee had much work to do in this area, Moss presented the NUL as a key partner in improving prospects for black federal workers. Granger, Carter, and Moss demonstrated that the League's know-how, experience, and perspective could help the committee. The head of the Seattle Urban League, Lewis G. Watts, responded to committee requests for examples of federal employment discrimination in the Northwest. Watts preferred that information be provided confidentially to Carey and possibly Clinchy because blacks were afraid "of losing they jobs" if superiors learned about their complaints. At both the national and local levels, the league fought in the trenches with Carey's committee.⁷⁰

Cooperation with the NAACP supplemented the committee's involvements with the league. Perhaps the earliest NAACP complaint filed with Carey arrived in 1955 from Willard L. Brown, the head of the Charleston, West Virginia, chapter, who accused the state's employment agency "of discriminating against Negroes in placement" and in hiring. In addition, several local firms held federal contracts but were guilty of biased behavior toward African Americans. Brown was confident that Carey would conduct a vigorous investigation. Carey would have accepted Brown's invitation to address the Charleston chapter if his denomination's annual conference had not been meeting in Chicago, and he promised to appear on another occasion. By 1959, however, Carey had become disappointed in other NAACP officials' failure to take advantage of the antidiscrimination agency.⁷¹

Though Eisenhower had drawn black support in his presidential bids in both 1952 and 1956, some leaders of black organizations never had full confidence in his advocacy of civil rights. The NAACP's Wilkins was not convinced that Ike used the full weight of his presidential office on behalf of black advancement. Granger, however, was friendlier to the Eisenhower administration and expected that blacks would benefit. One historian has noted that both Granger and Eisenhower were "out of touch with urban and urbane Negroes' hopes and dreams." Eisenhower preferred "moderation or only hesitantly addressed the issue of civil rights," and Granger, despite the doubts of some local league executives, was comfortable defending the president.[72] Carey shared Granger's optimism but believed that the skepticism of Wilkins and other prominent blacks should be acknowledged. Carey recognized that African American leaders and black Eisenhower appointees needed to prod the administration to act resolutely in favor of black civil rights. Though Carey assumed Ike's goodwill, he never relied on the administration to act on its own.

In 1958, Carey chaired the Committee on the State of the Country at the AME Church's Chicago Annual Conference. In a lengthy report, Carey conceded that Ike had said "something about going slower on integration" and that the president's statement had "caused anger and dismay to many people." Carey contended, however, that the comment was not Eisenhower's "official position." Blacks should pay greater attention to presidential appointees, who actually articulated where the administration stood on civil rights matters. The solicitor general, for example, had appeared before the Supreme Court and supported the NAACP in opposing delays in southern school desegregation. All of Ike's cabinet and agency heads, Carey declared, were "positive and unequivocal" in their commitment to black equality. Bishop Gomez, who was proud of Carey's role in the Eisenhower administration, directed him and two others to write a resolution stressing the Chicago Annual Conference's firm backing for the fight for African American advancement. Carey was probably happy to use this resolution as another nudge to the president to remain a civil rights ally and to answer legitimate criticism of his apparent vacillation on this crucial issue.[73]

Because Eisenhower appeared chronically ambiguous about his stands on civil rights, Carey was constantly challenged and at times frustrated in trying to defend the president. In 1959, Carey and Clinchy were disappointed when the president failed to consult with the committee in crafting his civil rights message to Congress. The absence of Vice President Nixon and the secretary of labor from the committee was a weakness and may explain why Carey and Clinchy were "ignored."[74]

Carey was determined to address his committee's bureaucratic isolation. When the secretary of labor replaced his representative to the agency, Carey was disheartened that the new member ranked below his predecessor, an assistant secretary: "The stature of the men in government who were part of our Committee has been an impressive and invaluable factor." High-ranking committee members bestowed credibility at area conferences and reassured reluctant complainants that significant Eisenhower officials were involved in fighting employment discrimination: "The stature of an Assistant Secretary is of immeasurable value in lending dignity and authority to the representations which we make and to the opinions which we render."[75]

Carey recognized that he needed to remind others within the Eisenhower administration that his committee's work formed the core of the president's credibility on civil rights and consequently pressed two aides to grant the committee a special audience with Eisenhower. Twice in 1959, attempts were made "to get Carey's group" in to see the president. On March 25, 1960, Carey alone finally received an appointment to meet with the president and cabinet. Carey discussed cooperation with "Departments and Agencies to prevent cases of discrimination" and how to "handle them short of referral to the Committee." Although "measurable progress is being made in relieving discrimination" and "Federal employment does provide many opportunities for minority groups," racial prejudice in particular locales could wreck "the anti-discrimination program." Moreover, Carey reminded cabinet members that problems of bias persisted throughout the bureaucracy, from entry-level positions to the top employment grades. Eisenhower was concerned about how much publicity the committee was generating. Lodge, Carey's former boss, commended the committee and said its efforts were important "in the eyes of the delegates of the new nations entering the United Nations" and would "be of great moment to our own foreign relations."[76]

Carey recommended an "acceleration" in the cabinet's cooperation with attaining his agency's objectives. He suggested broader dissemination of committee reports within federal departments, better in-service training about ending employment bias, a designated fair employment officer in each department, and proactive advocacy for equal employment opportunities by members of the cabinet. Eisenhower "approved in substance" the Carey recommendations and promised "final approval" after reviewing the written report.[77]

Carey followed up on Eisenhower's suggestion about publicizing the committee's "work and accomplishments," telling the president that a press release from the White House or inclusion of such information in a presidential message to Congress would be desirable. Carey advised Ike to emphasize "that a Negro-American made [a] report to the President and the Cabinet for the first time in the history of the Nation, as head of a federal agency or Chairman of a White House Committee." He reminded Eisenhower that "at the very time when there is such pulling and tugging on civil rights matters, it would graphically demonstrate your own position and attitude." Such a declaration would dramatize the president's "deep interest" in civil rights. Carey also insisted that the president meet with the Committee to boost morale among its members. "Just a word of greeting and, perhaps, your commendation," Carey said, "could afford an excellent opportunity to publicize the policy, the Committee and its efforts and achievements."[78]

Carey had long sought to have the entire committee meet with the president, making requests to that effect in 1958, 1959, and 1960 and promising that "the presentation would only take two or three minutes and we would not burden the President with a discussion of the subject matter." His efforts finally reached fruition on June 2, 1960, with a meeting Carey called "an exhilarating experience." White House press secretary James C. Hagerty was especially cooperative in developing a press release about the committee's activities and checking with Carey regarding its accuracy. The session provided Carey with substantive evidence of the administration's serious support of civil rights, thereby strengthening his resolve to defend Eisenhower's performance.[79]

Carey frequently functioned as a cheerleader for Ike's administration. At a 1959 NUL meeting, Carey ranked Ike as better on civil rights than any other president since Abraham Lincoln. Because of Eisenhower's antidiscrimination committee, a "new wind is blowing through the whole federal structure." Carey also claimed 100 percent cooperation from federal departments and agencies in fighting job bias. The audience applauded when Carey noted Eisenhower's role in the passage of the 1957 Civil Rights Act and in the desegregation of Little Rock's Central High School. Carey's favorable assessment of Ike apparently resonated among African Americans.[80]

Carey, however, misread the NUL's response to the Eisenhower administration, perceiving his relationships with league officials as close and cordial. In 1958, for example, H. Hartford Brookins, the pastor of St. Paul AME Church in Wichita, Kansas, invited Carey "to enlighten officials of the city on the Urban League." Granger was delighted that Carey was going to Wichita since there was no "more effective person to preach the Urban League gospel." The following year, Granger invited Carey to become an NUL member at large, in which capacity he would belong to "the Delegate body which elects the League's Board of Trustees and advises on other important matters affecting the League movement." Granger praised Carey's "interest" in the league and his "demonstrated willingness to assist" the group. Later in 1959, the director of the league's Southern Field Division, M. T. Puryear, asked Carey to speak in Atlanta at an Equal Opportunity Day event. Carey did so. On December 29, 1960, therefore, Carey was stunned to learn of a United Press International report that the league had criticized his committee's reluctance "to carry out its mission of opening all facets of the Federal government to qualified Negro applicants." This story, Carey declared, was "completely untrue and unfair"; anyone who would make such an assessment was "woefully ignorant of the facts." He cited a recent report showing that the number of black employees in five cities "in upper level jobs had nearly doubled in four years" and that "corrective action [had been taken] in 16% of all the cases" that the committee reviewed. Segregated offices had been abolished in Atlanta. Although Carey conceded that some federal departments remained all-white, he said that was "the reason President Eisenhower created this Committee in 1955." Moreover, according to Julius Thomas, the NUL's industrial relations director, Carey's speech to the league had energized its partnerships with southern black colleges and high schools to introduce students to civil service examinations. As a result, the committee's efforts had resulted in "abundant examples of Negroes in responsible positions."[81]

Granger subsequently admitted to Carey that the report had come from league president Henry Steeger but stressed that the comment "was in no way questioning the integrity or the intelligence or dedication of the Committee's members." Nevertheless, Granger stood behind the criticism, noting the "placid rate at which such Committee programs as your Committee directed have moved during the past eighteen years. There has been no sign of Presidential interest in these efforts—neither from President Eisenhower nor Presidents Truman and Roosevelt." Carey received Granger's letter in a spirit of "personal friendship and helpful association in common cause" but disputed this assessment: "If somebody from the Urban League wanted to say that the high officials of government have maintained a 'placid rate'" of elimination of job discrimination, further elaboration should be provided. To say that "the committee has been 'reluctant to carry out its mission,'" Carey declared, was totally unfounded.[82] Carey remained grateful that Ike had empowered him to improve the job status of thousands of black federal employees and continued to believe that the President's Committee on Government Employment Policy had been a success. Though such naysayers as Granger and Steeger assessed the Eisenhower administration as deficient in serious civil rights advocacy, Carey contended that the Republican Party deserved the continued support of African Americans.

Despite his other involvements, Carey never lost sight of the interests of the AME Church, and his denomination's bishops and clergy remained conscious of him. Church leaders wanted him to leverage his diplomatic position to elicit favors from the Eisenhower administration, and Carey hoped that the overall thrust of his political activities would redound to the advantage of his church constituents. In the late summer of 1953, Bishop E. C. Hatcher, an African American whose jurisdiction covered four West African countries, requested Carey's assistance in getting "official recognition, reception, and attention that is given any other head of state" when Liberian president William V. S. Tubman of Liberia visited the United States. Hatcher asked Carey to persuade administration officials to send a "battleship here to Monrovia to bring the President and his coterie to America" and suggested that the bishop and his wife be included on the passenger list. Moreover, the bishop wanted "very much for you and Bishop [Decatur Ward] Nichols to use your political influence and your personal interest with President Eisenhower to see that every courtesy and all of the fanfare that goes with a state visit is accorded to President

Tubman." In return, Bishop Hatcher promised to assist Carey's potential candidacy for the episcopacy: "I will talk with you and give you some of the keys that I used to unlock the doors that were closed against me." Carey "communicated" Hatcher's grandiose desires, almost verbatim, to Raab but declared that he was "in no position to evaluate the merit of these requests." He told Raab to respond to Hatcher in whatever way the White House deemed appropriate.[83]

Carey made only limited attempts to intervene on Hatcher's behalf but played a role in "initiating" Tubman's 1954 visit. Tubman came to Chicago, where Carey arranged meetings with various black and white political dignitaries, a press conference, and interactions with Liberians living in the city. Carey and Morrow subsequently cooperated (without Hatcher's involvement) in matters concerning Liberian affairs. At a 1955 event sponsored by the National Conference of Christians and Jews, the Liberian ambassador awarded Carey and another official the Knight Commander of the Humane Order for African Redemption. Morrow spoke at the ceremony, with his presence adding what Carey termed "tremendous dignity to the occasion." The occasion also offered Morrow the opportunity to present the Eisenhower administration's accomplishments and outlook.[84]

In another instance, an AME minister in Ohio urged Carey to push the nomination of Charles Leander Hill, the president of Wilberforce University, as governor of the U.S. Virgin Islands. The clergyman believed that Carey's letters to Eisenhower and other high federal officials "would mean much toward having the appointment offered" to Hill, the "best qualified individual." It was important to Carey that AME interests be advanced, at least symbolically, during the Eisenhower years. Carey attempted to have the president speak at Quinn Chapel, but scheduling conflicts prevented Eisenhower from appearing; however, the president later sent a letter of greeting to the denomination on the two hundredth anniversary of the birth of AME founder Richard Allen. Overall, AMEs benefited from Carey's role as a federal official, though those benefits mostly took the form of symbolic public gestures.[85]

The patronage and presidential recognition that AME leaders sought illustrate that Carey and some AME officials had different visions for his political involvement. Carey ultimately viewed his ties with the Eisenhower administration as opportunities to do great good for black Chicagoans and African Americans in general, a perspective that his former colleagues in the Congress of Racial Equality (CORE) understood much better than did his fellow AMEs. Homer A. Jack, a Unitarian pastor, and George M. Houser of the pacifist Fellowship of Reconciliation (FOR) perceived Carey's presence in the United Nations in policy rather than patronage terms. Hence, Jack informed Carey about Michael Scott, a South African who was supportive of black liberation struggles and "had tremendous experience with native Africans." Jack believed that Scott could provide Carey with "the kind of information about Africa" that he would need in his United Nations role. Carey met Scott and agreed. Jack also praised Carey's strong stand against genocide. Houser was "anxious" to discuss with Carey FOR's activities "on the African question." Carey maintained a serious interest in the moral commitments of Jack, Houser, and Bernice Fisher, another CORE founder. A year after hearing from Houser, Carey invited him to preach at Quinn Chapel. Whereas Bishop Hatcher focused on amenities for an African president, Jack and Houser emphasized the promotion of Africa's collective welfare and other liberationist concerns.[86]

By 1954, Chicagoans were fully aware of Carey's national and international reputation. The University of Chicago, which merged with his alma mater, Lewis Institute, conferred on Carey the Worthy Alumnus Award, and Tabernacle Baptist Church gave him and a Roman Catholic archbishop plaques "for outstanding service to human relations." Perhaps most important for Carey was his selection as the first recipient of the Abraham Schwartz Award, in recognition of his "effective human relations leadership in community and government." Carey was particularly pleased that Lodge agreed to speak at the occasion and reciprocated by delivering a Boston address on Lodge's behalf. The two men had solidified their political relationship and friendship. When the Israeli government invited Carey to visit, he kept Lodge, who was still Eisenhower's United Nations ambassador, informed about his findings. An Egyptian colleague at the United Nations extended special passport courtesies to Carey; his wife, Hazel; his daughter, Carolyn; and his sister, Annabel Carey Prescott, and helped to arrange various amenities during their Middle East travels. Carey's party visited Egypt and Jordan as well as Israel, where Carey met Prime Minister David Ben-Gurion. Carey subsequently relayed to Lodge information about his conversation and about "the need for ameliorating the differences that prevail in the Middle East." Carey was impressed with both "the accomplishments in Israel" and "the determination of the Arabs to be a free people."[87]

Carey also continued his efforts to build the GOP among African Americans. A. T. Spaulding, vice president of the North Carolina Mutual Life Insurance Company, pressed Carey to intervene with President Eisenhower to address either in person or on the radio the convention of the National Negro Insurance Association, a group that likely leaned Republican. Carey also traveled to New Orleans to speak to the People's Republican Club of Louisiana. The meeting was held at Union Bethel AME Church, whose pastor, George N. Collins, seemed friendly to the GOP. As a consequence of the influence of Collins (later an AME bishop) and club president A. F. Laneuville, the church's "large auditorium and the main floor," noted Carey, were "darn near full and a few people sat in the balcony." A white GOP committeeman and a Republican mayoralty candidate were among the speakers. Carey's hour-long speech was well received and secured favorable coverage in the *New Orleans Times-Picayune*. Carey then wrote to Val Washington to urge that a black Louisiana Republican receive a patronage appointment, an action that "would have tremendous psychological impact." Similarly, the Baptist Minister's and Laymen's Conference in Houston, Texas, shared Carey's goal of stopping "the inroads that the Democrats have made among the Negro voters." To "redeem our racial segment and bring them back to the fold," the group urged Carey to come and speak.[88]

Carey was confident that Eisenhower deserved blacks' support for reelection in 1956. His "promotion of civil rights and the improvement of the status of minority groups," Carey and other supporters contended, made Eisenhower a much better candidate than the renominated Democrat, Stevenson, citing progress in integrating the military, in fighting Jim Crow in the District of Columbia, and in ending racial bias in employment in companies doing business with the federal government. The president's critics, however, cited his equivocation on desegregation and his preference for local solutions to civil rights issues.[89]

Carey, who served as cochair of Friends for Ike, wrote a persuasive pamphlet, *Why Negro-Americans Should Vote Republican in 1956*, in which he argued that support for Eisenhower would "keep and consolidate the tremendous gains in the fields of human rights." Carey believed that "more has been done by President Eisenhower to widen the borders of freedom for Negroes in America than by any president since Abraham Lincoln struck off the chains of slavery." These concrete achievements included the abolition of segregation "in army schools, naval installations, veterans hospitals, and many federal agencies." Moreover, Washington, D.C., "has been changed from a city of southern tradition to a city where Negroes enjoy the restaurants, theatres and hotels like all other Americans," and Ike had fulfilled his pledge to appoint African Americans to responsible positions "that in some instances had not even been urged by Negroes, much less expected." Carey cited blacks who served as chairs of the Federal Parole Board and the Public Utilities Commission in Washington, D.C., and Morrow's White House assignment. Carey also noted that one presidential committee had inserted an antidiscrimination proviso "in every contract the government lets to private contractors." In a replay of his rhetoric during Eisenhower's earlier presidential campaign, Carey admonished voters that if Democrats won, crucial congressional committees would have segregationist southerners as their chairs. Mississippi's notorious James O. Eastland, for example, would head the Judiciary Committee, while Alabama's Lister Hill would head Labor, and Georgia's Richard B. Russell would supervise Armed Services. These and other federal legislators had signed the Southern Manifesto, which recommended resistance to the Supreme Court's *Brown* decision. Carey did not mention that Stevenson's vice presidential running mate, Senator Estes Kefauver of Tennessee (along with two other southern senators), had refused to sign the document. Carey contended that although "many Negro-Americans are in the ranks of labor and the leadership of labor has endorsed the Democratic ticket, . . .

Eastland of Mississippi and his fellow Southern Democrats [would] run the government" if Eisenhower lost. Therefore, "the choice we must make at this time is between material things and manhood." Crucial to Carey's promotion of the president was the backing of "thousands of Democrats who believe in equal rights [who] have switched to Eisenhower and are supporting him vigorously." He mentioned three clergymen in particular: J. C. Austin and A. Lincoln James, both in Chicago, and Adam Clayton Powell Jr. They and various "business leaders and laboring people will make up the army leading this new crusade for freedom."⁹⁰

Despite Powell's complicated reasons for establishing Independent Democrats for Eisenhower, Carey must have been incredibly pleased that his friend and ally joined him in the president's reelection campaign. Powell previously had charged Ike with being "'hypocritical' in his approach to the Civil Rights question," and Carey had responded unequivocally, "for the record," that his experience with Eisenhower did "not justify such an opinion at all." Burk has suggested that after a meeting with the president, Powell endorsed Ike's reelection in return for help in squelching a potential investigation into charges that Powell had evaded taxes. Powell attributed his backing of Eisenhower to the Democratic Party's tepid support for black civil rights. Carey, not surprisingly, approved of Powell's about-face, telling him, "You have rendered another outstanding service to civil rights and the status of Negroes by your announcement for Eisenhower." Carey continued, "You and I both know what a significant stand the President has taken. The position you hold as Congressman, as minister of Abyssinian and by the weight of your own personality makes your articulation especially symbolic for all of us who are concerned in equal rights." Carey pressed Powell to speak on Eisenhower's behalf in Chicago.⁹¹

Carey also continued to argue that African Americans had an ally in Vice President Nixon. Carey believed that he personally knew Nixon and could count on him to broaden the GOP's appeal to blacks. Though a schedule conflict had prevented Nixon from joining Carey at a 1955 United Negro College Fund event, the vice president assured Carey that they would meet eventually to discuss "plans" for a Chicago visit and to cement their relationship. When Nixon came to Chicago to speak at a 1956 "Eisenhower Salute" dinner, however, Carey was addressing a similar event in Jackson, Mississippi. Hazel Carey attended Nixon's speech and told her husband that she was "tremendously impressed." Not a "generous critic," Hazel Carey commended the vice president's talk for "its substance, its sincerity and its vigor."⁹²

The Carey's favorable sentiments about Nixon may have helped in some small way to keep him on Ike's reelection ticket. Morrow noted the "terrific anti-Nixon feeling in this country—even among Republicans," ascribing such perspectives to residual hostility regarding illicit funds collected for Nixon's 1952 senatorial campaign. Morrow nonetheless liked Nixon, describing him as "a very capable, qualified, dedicated young man" possessed of "maturity of mind, purpose and vision to do a good job." Carey agreed, deploring the "blind prejudice . . . directed against" Nixon and characterizing him as "completely worthy, most conscientious and capable, diligent and resourceful" and deserving of renomination as vice president. Carey told Nixon, "I know better than you may realize the stout part which you have played in this Administration in the cause of human rights." Moreover, Carey pledged his "personal support, whether that should take the form of quiet conversation or coast-to-coast campaigning."[93]

In 1956, Carey repeated his earlier pattern of national campaigning for Eisenhower. With Val Washington's assistance, George W. Lee, a veteran Republican operative in Memphis and district manager of the Atlanta Life Insurance company, planned a mass meeting at Clayborn Temple AME Church with Carey as the featured speaker. Lee promised "an outpouring of people" to hear reasons to support the Eisenhower/Nixon reelection. Carey's cross-country itinerary also took him back to Los Angeles, where 125 people, most of them Republicans and GOP candidates, attended a Women's Political Club event. The 250 attendees at a "mass meeting at [a] big Baptist Church" in Pasadena included "a number of previous[ly] strong Democrats." One of them, a physician, hosted another gathering at his home, where 30 people came and debated and all but 2 committed to Ike. But Carey's efforts only achieved what he described as "fair to middlin'" success. Despite what he predicted would be "a good increase in the Negro vote," he told Washington that "California really needs Republican leadership "to galvanize supporters."[94]

Carey's appearances in Tennessee and California were funded by the RNC, and party officials also paid for him to travel to Oklahoma, Kansas, and Indiana as well as throughout Illinois. At Oklahoma's all-black Langston University, he addressed more than 700 people, but his experiences in Topeka and Hutchinson, Kansas, were "poor." His accommodations in Topeka were "ragged," and local GOP officials' treatment of him bordered on rude. Only 125 people, mainly "candidates and their families," came to the downtown auditorium to hear him speak. The high point was seeing a fellow AME, attorney P. A. Townsend, "who made a fine Em Cee and gracious host." In Hutchinson, just 72 people—again, mostly candidates and their families—were present. Instead of going to Parsons, Carey insisted on returning to Chicago for a Friends of Ike gathering and to speak to an audience of 1,000 in nearby Gary, Indiana. Whenever Carey could not assume an assignment, he recommended other black clergy that the RNC could send to promote the Eisenhower/Nixon ticket. They included not only James and Austin but Ulysses S. Robinson, pastor of Evanston's Ebenezer AME Church, and a partner in Carey's law firm, James T. Horton.[95]

Eisenhower won a decisive victory in 1956, in part, Burk contends, because the president made "modest inroads among middle class blacks in border South and Northern urban districts." Between 1952 and 1956, Eisenhower increased his vote totals in the black areas of Memphis by 25 percent; in Carey's Chicago, that figure was 11 percent. Though Powell's support of the Eisenhower/Nixon ticket drew denunciations from New York's black Democrats, 16.5 percent more voters in Powell's Harlem district voted for the Republicans than had done so four years earlier. Although Stevenson again won the majority of black voters nationwide in 1956, Ike increased his overall share by 5 percent. Morrow cheered because "thousands of Negroes across the country broke their ties to the Democratic Party for the first time in twenty years and voted for the President." He continued, "The fact that a great many prominent ministers came out for Ike reassured Negroes" and gave Eisenhower a big boost. Carey was similarly satisfied. On Election Day he congratulated the president on "the high quality of the campaign" and told him that Friends of Ike had worked "to organize voters outside of the regular political channels . . . especially among Negro-Americans." The president thanked Carey for his coast-to-coast campaigning and for "the results of the vote in Chicago."[96]

During his second term, Eisenhower justified Carey's generous claims about his civil rights record. In 1956, at the urging of attorney general Herbert Brownell, the president proposed the first civil rights bill since Reconstruction. Despite its flaws, the law, which Ike signed on September 9, 1957, created the Civil Rights Commission and established the position of assistant attorney general for civil rights. At the AME's 1959 Chicago Annual Conference, Carey urged his colleagues "to memorialize the Senate and the House through their majority and minority leaders to extend the life of the Civil Rights Commission," which "has reported findings of appalling violations of the civil rights of Negro-Americans in the areas of education, housing and voting." Under the name of Bishop Joseph Gomez, a telegram supporting the commission was sent to Vice President Nixon, Speaker of the House Sam Rayburn, and other congressional leaders of both parties. The Civil Rights Act of 1960, which Eisenhower approved, further refined provisions for the protection of black suffrage.[97]

However reluctantly, Eisenhower was pulled into another situation that drew Carey's praise in September 1957. In defiance of a federal court order mandating the desegregation of Little Rock's public schools, Arkansas governor Orval Faubus dispatched the National Guard to stop nine African American students from entering Central High School. When Faubus persisted in his obstructionism, Eisenhower sent in the U.S. Army to enforce the court order, escort the black students into the school, and protect them. Not since Reconstruction had federal troops been stationed in the American South to safeguard black civil rights. Though Ike resented Faubus for putting him in this unwelcome predicament, the president became a hero to African Americans. Carey believed that these progressive civil rights actions provided a strong foundation on which Eisenhower's successors could build. Hence,

he challenged Republicans and Nixon, their 1960 presidential candidate, to maintain this momentum and bring to fruition the GOP's historic mission as the Party
of Lincoln.[98]

Carey was determined to remind Republicans about his positive view of Eisenhower's contributions to the civil rights cause and their obligation to maintain
them. His role as chair of the President's Committee on Government Employment
Policy gave him standing to address the 1960 Republican Platform Committee. He
commended Ike's "bold steps to combat discrimination in employment" and contended that the platform should mention Executive Order 10479, which had established the President's Committee on Government Contracts to ensure equal treatment for "minority groups," as well as Executive Order 10590, which had created
the committee Carey headed, the "first committee in this field established at [the]
White House level." Both agencies took "significant steps toward the elimination of
second class citizenship in the field of employment." Finally, Carey proposed that
the Republican Party pledge "to sustain and strengthen the work of these Committees in the effort to assure that every American, without regard to race, religion, or
national origin, may secure employment in accordance with his qualifications."[99]

Carey's was not the only civil rights proposal, and he offered suggestions for
supporters of these measures if a floor fight occurred. "It is profitable to adopt a Civil
Rights plank," he said. Since Ike's support from blacks had grown between 1952 and
1956, the GOP could gain in future contests "another measurable increase which
might be the margin of victory." He added, "It is consistent with the Republican
record to adopt a strong Civil Rights Plank" because the GOP had a "traditional
role of leadership in civil rights matters." Finally, Carey argued, "It is morally right
to support principles of equality of opportunity and the Party of Lincoln ought to
take a stand for that which is morally right in human affairs."[100]

Nixon, Carey believed, had proven himself a friend and advocate of black civil
rights and was the appropriate candidate to continue the president's progressive
policies in this area. Carey cited his firsthand experience with the vice president. In
1955, when Carey was appointed to head the Committee on Government Policy and
Nixon was named chair of the Committee on Government Contracts, Nixon had
asked Carey to meet with him, probably to discuss the racial issues that they would
confront. In 1956 and 1957, Nixon had invited Carey to attend two committee-
sponsored conferences, and the vice president's efforts had ultimately compelled
companies with federal contracts to write into these agreements provisos against
discrimination. "There are approximately six million of these contracts," Carey said,
"and they total nearly forty billion dollars." In 1959, Carey reported to the AME's
Chicago Annual Conference that seven of the denomination's bishops had recently
attended a Washington, D.C., conference of religious leaders and been briefed by
Nixon and his staff about "methods of advancing the national policy of equal job

opportunities." He called on the ministers "to mobilize the country in the struggle to achieve the unrestricted access to employment and training." These accomplishments, according to Carey, demonstrated Nixon's genuine commitment to civil rights. When the *Chicago Daily News* ran an article charging that Ike's failure "to take a strong position on civil rights would rub off on Mr. Nixon," Carey wrote a vigorous rebuttal, arguing forcefully that Nixon's "image among Negro voters has improved considerably—and I believe it will improve even more." Moreover, he disagreed that Eisenhower's civil rights record was weak: "I think he might have articulated more the kind of program he was carrying forward, but in terms of performance I think it has been the best to date." For that, Carey said, "Thank you, Mr. President."[101]

When the Reverend Ezra M. Johnson, an AME denominational official, asked Carey about exactly what Nixon believed and what he wanted in the 1960 GOP platform, Carey explained that while Nixon opposed a "so-called federal FEPC," he favored "the establishment of an equal Job Opportunities Commission." The difference was mainly semantic: references to the FEPC, which had originated under Democrat Franklin D. Roosevelt, "may be expected to antagonize" Republicans who were less friendly to the civil rights cause than their presidential nominee. Nixon, however, had several affirmative stands that Carey thought would impress Johnson: the vice president did not object to the sit-ins launched by African American students in Greensboro, North Carolina, and elsewhere in 1960. Nixon agreed that the attorney general should have authority "to go to court in behalf of a person denied his rights by economic pressure or physical threat." He deplored the use of filibusters in the U.S. Senate to stop the passage of civil rights legislation and advocated "non-discrimination in voting, housing and education." Moreover, the GOP had proposed a weak civil rights plank until "the attitude and influence of Richard M. Nixon" compelled the party to strengthen it. Carey had no hesitation in vouching for Nixon's "heartening performance in the field of civil rights," and he thought that blacks could "trust their future with him far better than with" Democrat John F. Kennedy, "whose maneuverings for political advantage cause many people great concern." Nixon's choice of Lodge as his vice presidential running mate also pleased Carey, who believed that African Americans could enthusiastically embrace the GOP's national ticket.[102]

Nixon was much aware of Carey's strong support of his presidential candidacy and acknowledged his "very special insight into and knowledge of some of the problems we will have to face." Hence, GOP senator Hugh Scott of Pennsylvania would notify Carey about "some specific and important responsibilities." Carey was happy to join the campaign and offered Quinn Chapel "as the place for the making of [Nixon's] major statement on Civil Rights." He further described Nixon's support for civil rights as having been uniformly "applauded" and as having won "many new friends . . . to your cause."[103]

But Carey and other black Republicans were profoundly disappointed by the Nixon campaign, which, Carey believed, "ignor[ed] the Negro vote." Morrow agreed. Though Morrow took a leave of absence from his White House duties to promote the Nixon candidacy, he was marginalized, with no funds, "no literature, no work, [and] no assistants." Val Washington was similarly situated, "trying to direct a nationwide campaign with a staff of about five people." Most troubling for all of these black GOP leaders was Nixon's missed opportunity to show empathy and understanding of the plight of Martin Luther King Jr., who had been incarcerated on some minor charge and sent to a remote and dangerous Georgia jail. Kennedy called King's wife, Coretta Scott King, and worked to obtain the civil rights leader's release, while the Nixon team did nothing. Kennedy's actions, Morrow argued, "won the election" for the Democrats, "electrif[ying] the entire Negro community and result[ing] in tens of thousands of Negro voters going over to the Democrats' banner." Carey expressed "great sympathy for the situation in which [Nixon] found himself." He believed that Nixon's major miscalculation had been caused by "reports rolling in that the Negro community was trending heavily democratic." Nonetheless, Carey was "irked" because Nixon "failed" to capitalize on existing "Negro sympathies" in favor of his candidacy, whereas "Kennedy went after them—and got them. We had a much better story but did nothing with it."[104]

In 1960, during the final few months of the Eisenhower administration, Chicago Republicans nominated Carey for an elected position as judge on the Cook County Superior Court. Carey noted that he had not sought "this spot, but was chosen by my party" to run. Since, as one newspaper observed, the Democratic Party "had almost a monopoly" on the area's municipal, circuit, and superior courts, a Carey win could bring some partisan balance to the judicial system. His service in the Eisenhower administration and his long career as a local attorney drew Carey the endorsement of the *Chicago Daily News*, and the local bar association rated Carey higher than his Democratic opponent, James B. Parsons, an African American and an assistant U.S. district attorney. However, as Carey correctly observed, "The Democratic organization is still the biggest thing in Chicago and it ain't for me." Parsons won.[105]

Although Dwight D. Eisenhower's political retirement and Richard M. Nixon's loss in the 1960 presidential election displaced Carey as an officeholder, he remained active in Republican Party politics. In 1962, he received the GOP nomination for a position as a probate judge. His opponent would be incumbent Robert Jerome "Duke" Dunne, the son of a former Illinois governor, an athletic star at the University of Michigan, and a Carey acquaintance. Although Dunne was backed by the power of Chicago mayor Richard J. Daley's Democratic machine, Carey, too, had some impressive weapons in his arsenal. Robert E. Merriam, a former deputy assistant to President Eisenhower and the GOP nominee to run against Daley, chaired Carey's finance committee. Their former Republican colleagues on the Chicago

City Council also signed on to the Carey campaign. Branch Rickey, who brought Jackie Robinson to Major League Baseball and who had served on the President's Committee with Carey, contributed one hundred dollars. Moreover, the AME's 1962 Chicago Annual Conference passed a resolution to "endorse, work for and pray for the election" of the Quinn Chapel pastor.[106]

Carey staged his run for the judgeship as part of his ongoing campaign for civil rights. He surely wanted to show that the Daley machine was not all-powerful and could not control every political office in Cook County, but he was less concerned with winning than with "helping to widen the frontiers of opportunity." Neither the Democrats nor the GOP had ever "selected a Negro-American for a position of stature in the County." Since most black Chicagoans voted straight Democratic tickets, Carey hoped to attract significant African American support for his candidacy. He could carry whites in Evanston and Oak Park, remarked experienced observers, but his standing in the "Negro wards" would be decisive. He believed "political opportunities for other Negroes in the immediate future are going to be determined, to some extent, by the vote I get." Whereas it had previously been "unthinkable to put a Negro up for this post," his candidacy showed the realms of what was now possible. "There is a great measure of race pride at stake," Carey told his bishop, and the outcome would matter much to Chicago blacks.[107]

Changes in the civil rights movement in the early 1960s, however, pushed Carey toward a moral and political crossroads. For Carey, the welfare of blacks was a moral matter, and his attachment to the GOP depended on its commitment to this critical issue. Carey had always aligned himself with liberal Republicans from the Northeast and Midwest who were sympathetic to African American interests and solicitous of their votes. His political relationship with Illinois senator Everett M. Dirksen, for example, went back more than decade, and Carey believed that Dirksen had served as Eisenhower's "quarterback" in the push to enact the Civil Rights Act of 1957. By the early 1960s, however, Dirksen was wavering on the section of President John F. Kennedy's proposed civil rights bill that would have prevented proprietors of public facilities from excluding patrons on the basis of race.[108]

In September 1963, Carey admonished Dirksen that "support of the public accommodations section is regarded as support of civil rights, and opposition to that section, in the public image, is opposition to equality of opportunity." To counter the argument that civil rights "should be left to the states," Carey told Dirksen that the southern states had already shown that blacks could expect no fairness from them. In contrast, Illinois and several other states had civil rights statutes with public accommodations sections, and the inclusion of this proviso in the Kennedy bill "would only be an extension to make it national policy." Carey also rebutted the argument that a public accommodations mandate "would infringe upon the private rights of persons engaged in business" by arguing that business owners should "abide by the principle of service to any orderly person of the consuming public." Finally, Carey disputed the assertion that judicial history favored the rights of property owners, noting that court decisions have always been revised "as conditions and ideas of the general public have changed." Civil rights for blacks had become a "burning issue" as a consequence of "national events and international implications." Hence, public accommodations for blacks superseded declarations of "property rights" as a basis for denial of services to African Americans. Carey further attempted to pressure Dirksen by submitting a resolution to his church's 1963 Chicago Annual Conference that urged the senator "to support the public accommodations section of the Civil Rights bill": "To eliminate this provision is to deprive many citizens who might be discriminated against of basic rights and also personal dignity." Dirksen responded that he continued to "struggle with this rights issue" and pledged his support for all other provisions of the bill.[109]

Carey also found his long-standing relationship with Illinois's Republicans tested by the party's 1964 gubernatorial nomination of Charles H. Percy, the president of Bell and Howell and a rising GOP star. When Carey convened a group of black clergy to hear Percy's views on civil rights, the candidate stated that he favored "Fair Employment legislation" and supported the "principle of open occupancy" in housing but had doubts about particular housing proposals. Carey accepted Percy's professed steadfast commitment to the idea of nondiscrimination, endorsing the candidate and defending him when others questioned his commitment to black civil rights.[110]

President Kennedy's assassination on November 22, 1963, and new president Lyndon B. Johnson's determination to enact his predecessor's landmark legislation put Dirksen and others in Congress on the defensive. At the 1964 AME General Conference in Cincinnati, Carey delivered a major civil rights address. Also present was Randolph, a member of Bethel AME Church in Harlem, who encouraged Carey to solicit a strongly worded resolution concerning the bill. The result was a telegram from the General Conference to the U.S. Senate "urging the immediate enactment of the Civil Rights Bill, without crippling amendment." Faced with these and other pressures and intense lobbying, Dirksen and a majority of his Republican and Democratic colleagues passed the Civil Rights Act of 1964, which Johnson signed into law on July 2. Carey thanked Dirksen "for the stalwart part which you played in effecting the passage" of this major legislation.[111]

But the political winds were changing. The dominant bloc of liberal northeastern and midwestern Republicans saw their party power eclipsed at the 1964 GOP National Convention. Senator Barry M. Goldwater of Arizona led a vanguard of conservatives who opposed the New Deal welfare state and were unsympathetic to African American civil rights. Carey vehemently opposed the presidential nomination of Goldwater, who had voted against the Civil Rights Act, preferring his former colleague at the United Nations, Henry Cabot Lodge, who was a member of the Republican establishment that Goldwater disdained. Carey and Goldwater appeared together on a television program during which Goldwater belittled Lodge's primary victory in New Hampshire because the ambassador "never took a position on anything." Carey responded, "Senator, how can you say that when Senator Lodge was our nominee for vice president in 1960 and as a candidate took a position on every issue all over the country?" Goldwater backed off from his comment, but a "disillusioned" Carey wondered how Goldwater, who was not a lawyer, could declare "that the civil rights proposals were unconstitutional."[112]

Carey thus backed Lodge, in part out of friendship but largely because his wing of the Republican Party remained supportive of black civil rights. In the event that Lodge's candidacy failed, Carey pledged to throw his support to Pennsylvania governor William W. Scranton and to recruit others to stop a Goldwater nomination. Carey also extended his "good will" to a campaign to nominate New York chief executive Nelson A. Rockefeller.[113]

Dirksen found himself caught in the intraparty crossfire. Carey unequivocally told the senator that he opposed the conservative movement and would "not invest my money or my energy in the cause of one Barry Goldwater." But when the Arizona senator received the Republican presidential nomination, Rickey told Carey that Dirksen, "a smart fellow—politically," "pretty nearly had to do what Goldwater asked him to do." Dirksen, Rickey added, "could miss the right door to Heaven trying to make the result justify the means."[114]

Unlike Dirksen, Carey refused to acquiesce to the new GOP realities. Goldwater's record made it "impossible" for Carey to back "the Republican team." Though he "highly esteemed" his friends in the party, Carey felt "that a larger issue than personal consideration is involved." Soon after writing that Goldwater's rise had "just about driven me to the brink of becoming a Democrat," Carey made that leap.[115]

Carey considered supporting "the State ticket of Republicans" while shunning Goldwater and his running mate, conservative William Miller, but concluded that "this would result in my strengthening the effort of those who would be obligated to promote the Goldwater ticket." Rickey tried to persuade Carey to remain a Republican: Rickey disagreed with Goldwater's opposition to civil rights but thought him "forthright and honest but basically deluded." If Goldwater lost, then the old GOP establishment could return to power; if he won, civil rights laws would still be enforced because Goldwater "has personal integrity [and] plenty of it, enough to conform with his oath of office." Rickey wanted Carey to remain a Republican "for the future of the party and the future of the country." Nevertheless, Rickey confessed, he was "sick about everything," especially the party's national committee, which "is a machine controlled by Goldwater lieutenants." Rickey cautioned Carey against "a radical jump" and urged him to discuss his dilemma with Lodge; however, Carey remained adamant. Rickey understood his friend's decision: "If I believed that the election of Goldwater would mean the slowing down of progress in the field of Civil Rights, I would not vote for him. In that case, I would probably do exactly as you have done."[116]

Chicago commentator Len O'Connor admonished Republicans to take Carey's defection to the Democrats very seriously. He had been a GOP officeholder and a popular vote-getter in an overwhelmingly Democratic city and county. "Carey, in a word," he said, "is a man who has a following." Moreover, "when he says it is unthinkable to remain neutral, his followers will make note of it." The *Chicago Daily News* highlighted Carey's decision, quoting him as saying that he had "reached this conclusion only after measured and agonizing deliberation." Because of the Goldwater candidacy, "the image of the Republican Party . . . is not that of the party of freedom which once commanded the respect and affection of a majority of the American people."[117]

Carey had always maintained amicable ties with Mayor Daley. At a 1958 anniversary program for Quinn Chapel, Carey honored Rickey but invited Daley to the celebration. This gesture and Carey's established relationships with Democrats eased his entry into the party. In addition, Carey developed a favorable opinion of President Kennedy. In 1963, JFK addressed the nation in the wake of violent police repression of civil rights demonstrators in Birmingham, Alabama, defining African Americans' efforts to attain equal rights as a moral moment in American history and proposing the measure that became the Civil Rights Act of 1964. Carey told John M. Johnston, the editor of the *Chicago Daily News*, that Kennedy deserved "commendation" for his civil rights speech and predicted that "from a political standpoint, it will diminish even further the ranks of Negro Republicans unless Republican leadership does something very dramatic to match it." Carey insisted, however, that the Kennedy address represented the "culmination" of the Truman and Eisenhower administrations' efforts to elevate African Americans' status. Nonetheless, Carey gave full credit to the president and his brother, attorney general Robert F. Kennedy, for their efforts to advance black civil rights.[118]

Carey was much impressed with the elaborate preparations and the dignitaries who came to a May 1964 Chicago regional meeting of the President's Committee on Equal Employment Opportunity. Hobart Taylor Jr., the son and namesake of a black Houston millionaire and the committee's executive vice chair, recognized Carey and commended his contributions to antidiscrimination efforts in federal employment. Taylor observed that the current committee was "deeply indebted" to Carey and his colleagues for their work in this field during Ike's presidency and for the advice Carey had extended to his successors. Carey was also cheered because Taylor had been appointed special counsel to the president, making him "the closest Negro to Lyndon Johnson." The presence of Taylor and other high-level blacks in the Johnson administration showed Carey national Democrats' openness to talented African Americans. Though Rickey disliked LBJ, he shared Carey's enthusiasm about the President's Committee on Equal Employment Opportunity. Moreover, Johnson's "position on the Civil Rights bill has been forthright and positive." Even Rickey, both a staunch Republican and a staunch supporter of civil rights, was open to voting for a "reputable" Democrat other than LBJ.[119]

Carey formally endorsed Johnson's election on July 14, 1964. "To me," Carey said, "the great issue is the support of civil rights, in law and in spirit." While Goldwater had opposed the Civil Rights Act, Johnson "gave his enormous influence to the measure." Carey sent an official letter in which he informed LBJ that both Daley and Congressman William Dawson knew about Carey's decision to join the Democrats. Chicago's newspapers and television stations publicized his "disavowal of the Republican ticket" and his willingness to do the same sort of "vigorous" campaigning for the Democratic ticket that he had previously done for Eisenhower.[120]

Carey was welcomed into the Democratic fold and commenced promoting the party ticket. LBJ chose as his running mate a civil rights champion, Senator Hubert H. Humphrey of Minnesota, whom Carey had met in 1947, when both were involved in Americans for Democratic Action. At a breakfast that Mayor Daley hosted in Chicago, Carey told Humphrey "that a principal factor in clinching" his decision to support the Democratic ticket "was your selection for Vice President," and he described Humphrey as "one of the most eminent and courageous liberals the country has ever seen." Carey asked Humphrey "to alert those sources that can arrange to use my platform energies to advantage." The Democratic National Committee subsequently dispatched Carey to campaign in Gary and East Chicago, Indiana; Louisville and Anchorage, Kentucky; and Columbia, South Carolina. Carey also organized the Non-Partisan Ministers for Johnson-Humphrey, a "biracial" and "interdenominational" group of fifty-six "pastors of substantial congregations" who were asked to aid "get out the vote" efforts.[121]

Rivalry between two black Democratic groups threatened to complicate Carey's visit to South Carolina. Carey was invited to address the Progressive Democrats, a group that veteran civil rights activist Modjeska Simpkins described as a "paper organization" that seemed to be aligned with the GOP and to have designs to misuse "the Negro vote." Her group, the Richland County Citizens Committee, was loyal to LBJ. Carey did not see Simpkins's letter before he left Chicago but found that the Progressive Democrats were authentic and had the approval of the Democratic National Committee. The five hundred members of the audience approved of Carey's laudatory speech on behalf of the Johnson-Humphrey ticket, and the Chicagoan described his campaign stop as "worthwhile." While in South Carolina, Carey also addressed a mass meeting at Columbia's AME-affiliated Allen University, where he exhorted another five hundred listeners to vote and to urge their families to do the same. His next stop was scheduled to be Michigan, where he would speak to Young Democrats groups in Detroit and Ann Arbor, but these appearances were canceled as a consequence of poor organization by local campaign staff. Carey was nevertheless "glad to have been of service to the cause."[122]

Carey's switch to the Democrats also put an end to his rivalry with party members in Chicago. Now that he and Dawson were on the same political team, for example, Carey reported to the congressman on his activities in support of the Johnson/Humphrey ticket. And when Johnson came to Chicago in 1965, Dawson included Carey at "the big dinner" where the president spoke, earning the minister's gratitude for this and other courtesies. Moreover, Carey spoke to a Democratic group in the Third Ward at the request of alderman Ralph Metcalfe, who had defeated Carey in 1955, as well as to audiences of between 125 and 500 people at other Chicago-area meetings.[123]

Days before the presidential election, Carey told Humphrey, "It is safe to congratulate you upon your certain election as Vice President of the United States."[124] Carey had calculated correctly: the Johnson-Humphrey ticket swept forty-four of the fifty states. President Johnson followed up his electoral victory by signing the landmark Voting Rights Act of 1965. Thus, Johnson oversaw the realization of many of the dreams for which Carey had worked since the 1940s, thereby validating Carey's calculation that the Democrats were now the party that best served the interests of African Americans.

Carey remained friendly with his former GOP associates. He apologized for missing a 1966 testimonial for Dirksen, sending a contribution and adding, "I appreciate to the utmost, the warm personal friendship which we have enjoyed for more than sixteen years and I am ever mindful of the kind things that you have done to help and boost me."[125]

Though high-level federal appointments in the Eisenhower administration and a Cook County judgeship eluded Carey, he, Powell, and a few other black clergy colleagues occupied positions of federal influence and power that were unprecedented for African Americans. But Carey, Powell, and other politically activist ministers did not believe that theirs was the only way: they agreed with A. Philip Randolph and other advocates of grassroots mobilization that demonstrations and various protest activities were effective strategies that could supplement the achievements of black officeholders. For their part, James Farmer, James M. Lawson Jr., Martin Luther King Jr., and other militant ministers respected Carey and Powell's approach but preferred nonviolent direct action as a means of compelling social change and pressuring authorities to end oppressive practices. As the civil rights movement developed momentum in the 1950s and 1960s, Carey and Powell supported nonviolent direct action protests, essentially becoming background benefactors to the civil rights movement and using their political and religious connections to aid the fight for racial equality.

CHAPTER 7

Background Benefactor

ARCHIBALD J. CAREY JR. AND
THE CIVIL RIGHTS MOVEMENT

As early as the 1940s, both Archibald J. Carey Jr. and Adam Clayton Powell Jr. had supported A. Philip Randolph's March on Washington Movement, which built on their earlier leadership of community-based protests against substandard schools in Chicago and biased hiring policies in New York City. Though Carey and Powell preferred political office and the give-and-take of city council and congressional sessions, they neither eschewed nor denied the effectiveness of grassroots protest against Jim Crow violence and discrimination.

Starting in the 1930s and 1940s, Randolph's influence and the impact of Gandhian satyagraha (passive resistance) made disciples of a small but significant cadre of African American religious intellectuals, including Mordecai W. Johnson, Benjamin E. Mays, Howard Thurman, Sue Bailey Thurman, William Stuart Nelson, Blanche Wright Nelson, and George D. Kelsey. These preachers, lecturers, and professors produced sermons, speeches, and texts that circulated in various black religious venues and familiarized African American seminary students with how Gandhian nonviolence and grassroots mobilization harnessed to black prophetic Christianity could challenge and morally undermine idolatrous and legally sanctioned segregationist structures and practices. With a reinvigorated emancipationist theology and a Gandhian praxis, James L. Farmer, James M. Lawson Jr., Martin Luther King Jr., and others sidestepped Carey and Powell's brokerage leadership model and focused on organizing grassroots activists to become frontline participants and leaders in the civil rights struggle.[1]

Carey and Powell agreed that this new model for religious activism could be an especially effective way of envisaging and pursuing public theology, complementing their political activities and reviving earlier methodologies. Therefore, they and other black preachers of their generation signed on to the grassroots mobilization tactics that a younger group of ministers used to advance black civil rights. Carey, for example, wrote to commend King's leadership in Alabama: "I have watched with intense interest and admiration the performance of Negro-Americans in the Montgomery bus strike. I certainly want to salute your own magnificent leadership in it. Be comforted by knowing that there are tens of thousands who are giving you their support and their prayers. May God bless and keep you through these trying hours." Powell similarly praised King's "technique," adding, "We shall go from here with massive unity based on passive resistance. Both locally and nationally, wherever the need arises we shall use boycotts, pickets, work stoppages, slowdown strike[s]—until we bring American bigotry to its knees. Through these techniques we can turn the tide of hypocrisy to honesty." In 1956, Powell and Carey agreed to spearhead an All National Deliverance Day of Prayer movement that highlighted mobilization through a nonviolent methodology. Carey preferred an emphasis on adult participation and an avoidance of disruptive activities. He doubted whether schoolchildren should be involved and questioned the wisdom of any work stoppage. Powell told Carey that the rallies should be "led only by the clergy . . . headquarters to be only the churches [and] methods only to be only prayer." The prayers would have a twofold purpose: "deliverance of our brothers in Montgomery and all Americans who are the victims of prejudice" and "praying for salvation for all those whose souls are afflicted with the sin and disease of hatred." In New York, Powell proposed "prayer mass meetings" in various churches, an idea that won enthusiastic endorsement from the city's Protestant Council. Carey's former brother-in-law, Shelton Hale Bishop, rector of St. Philip's Episcopal Church in Harlem, urged the bishops in his denomination to participate, describing himself as "deeply concerned that the Episcopal Church shall bear some manifest share of Christ's Wounds in the suffering of his people at this critical time." Bishop added that parishioners should wear insignia that read, "Good Lord, deliver us from Prejudice, Injustice, [and] Segregation—Make America Truly Free." Moreover, monies from individuals and institutions would be disbursed to the Montgomery movement and any other "crisis in the life of oppressed people."[2]

Carey had similar success in Chicago. Jews and black and white Christians promised cooperation, and Ralph Abernathy, King's Montgomery lieutenant, and Roy Wilkins, the new head of the National Association for the Advancement of Colored People (NAACP), were slated to speak. The program was presented as "a 'massive mobilization of Chicago's resources, both spiritual and temporal' to aid the oppressed people of the South." The mobilization "would take the form of a Prayer-Report meeting and would include a one hour Service of Prayer followed by a mass meeting." Most importantly, "the meeting will follow the pattern of non-violent meetings of prayer which began in Montgomery and have been held throughout the country." Carey convinced A. Lincoln James, the pastor of Bethesda Baptist Church, to serve as the event's cochair and urged local ministers and their choirs to attend. In his appeal, Carey reminded the Baptist pastors "how the ministry has led the fight for freedom in the South." He said Chicago clergy, too, should "play a part worthy of our own ministerial leadership." In addition, Carey solicited the support of the Church Federation of Greater Chicago. The group's Department of Citizenship Education and Action issued a hard-hitting "Message to the Churches Regarding Racial Tensions" that endorsed the Montgomery Bus Boycott and "the use of Christian nonviolence." The federation commended the boycott as "led by intelligent, well-trained Christian pastors, who are counseling the boycotters to refuse to hate" and exhorted churches to fight "discrimination and injustice" and to pray that "Jesus Christ may open the hearts of all people everywhere[,] implanting both the will and the power to love our fellowman sincerely." The federation joined others in urging prayer protesters to meet at Carey's Quinn Chapel African Methodist Episcopal (AME) Church for a citywide service of prayer "to assert the power of love through prayer and fellowship in Christ, as over against the evil of hate and violence." Powell expected forty-five hundred attendees in New York City; in Chicago, Carey reported that seven thousand people gathered and that fifty-three hundred dollars was received. Carey declared the event "a magnificent idea," showing how "a massive influence" can be exerted through "non-violent performance following religious leadership." In Chicago, John W. Harms of the church federation had offered a "Prayer for the Oppressed," while a "Prayer for Brotherhood" was led by Rabbi Eric Friedland. Clarence Cobbs, a popular black Pentecostal preacher, gave the "Prayer for the Oppressors."[3]

Carey and Powell again partnered in 1957 in Detroit. At a mass meeting at Bethel AME Church, they were the featured speakers, focusing on the election of a black member of the city council, denouncing discrimination in some unions within the AFL-CIO, and supporting better bus service for an area where twenty-five black churches were located. In these and other activities, the two ministers remained committed to protest tactics. Nonetheless, they also insisted that their insider positions within the federal government safeguarded recent gains in black civil rights and enabled them to push vigorously for enforcement of antidiscrimination measures.[4]

Carey's preference for working within the governmental system never caused him to eschew the tactics of agitation, protest, and insurgency that characterized the major civil rights organizations. In addition to the NAACP and National Urban League (NUL), Carey gave his endorsement to and remained engaged with the Congress of Racial Equality (CORE) and the Southern Christian Leadership Conference (SCLC). As one of CORE's earliest backers, Carey, worked closely with

Bernice Fisher, a white woman who was involved with a series of civil rights and labor groups and who stayed in contact with Carey, enlisting his help in various causes. In 1953, in her role as a board member of the Housing Conference of Chicago, she solicited his guidance in pushing public housing bills in both the Illinois legislature and Congress. Although Fisher and other CORE colleagues had often teased Carey about being a Republican, his connections "on the inside" were now needed to aid these legislative efforts, and she wanted "very much to sit down with you to plan the best approach." Later, when Carey learned about Fisher's application to work at the New York State Commission against Discrimination and her job with the administration of Democratic Mayor Robert Wagner of New York City, he lauded her "rare vision and indomitable courage." At her death in 1966, Carey described her as a forerunner to the "present generation" of civil rights activists.[5]

Carey and Homer A. Jack, another CORE founder, cooperated extensively on issues involving civil rights and international affairs. When Jack attended graduate school at the University of Chicago, he was a "sometime member" of Carey's Woodlawn AME Church. After he became a Unitarian pastor in Evanston, Illinois, he and Carey occasionally exchanged pulpits. Carey greatly admired Jack's courage in fighting housing discrimination in tough Chicago neighborhoods, describing him as "an unqualified equalitarian." They joined in backing King and the Montgomery Bus Boycott, with Jack traveling to Montgomery and keeping Carey informed about attempts to arrest and imprison King. Jack also became a student of Gandhi and nonviolence and shared his thoughts on these matters with Carey as he prepared for Chicago's National Deliverance Day of Prayer. Jack noted that CORE employed "Gandhian methods in American race relations" and commended the Montgomery protesters for "studying Gandhi" and applying "his universal techniques to their situation." He was cheered that King "repeatedly emphasized love and nonviolence" and that the boycott developed as both a "Gandhian and Christian" movement. In 1965, both Carey and Jack participated in events surrounding the Selma to Montgomery march for black voting rights.[6]

Jack was among the happiest of Carey's friends when he received the appointment to the United Nations, where the two men would have enhanced opportunities to collaborate on international racial and anticolonial issues. In 1955, Jack became excited about the Bandung conference in Indonesia, which would bring together representatives from twenty-nine Asian and African nations to celebrate their recent release from colonial rule and to discuss how to interact with both the western democracies and communist countries. He urged Carey to attend, in part because Powell planned to go and in part because doing so would "enhance your reputation as an international figure." When Jack learned that Carey could not join him in Indonesia, he promised "a confidential report" on the proceedings. He convinced Carey to intercede with John Sherman Cooper, the U.S. ambassador to

India, to receive Jack while he was in Asia. When Eisenhower invited the Indian prime minister Jawaharlal Nehru to the White House in 1956, Jack asked Carey to give the president his "manuscript" about Nehru, and Carey passed the writings to Eisenhower aide Maxwell Raab with the advice that "if you ever have occasion to name a citizen in the field of civil rights," Jack should be appointed.[7]

Jack pushed Carey to identify more openly with emergent nations in the Third World and especially in Africa. Powell's flamboyant behavior at the Bandung conference convinced Jack that Carey was a better representative for African Americans at such international venues. Jack wanted Carey to be a part of the American delegation to the Ghanaian independence ceremonies in 1957: Powell would surely would be chosen, Jack reasoned, and Carey too "should put in a bid," since "this will be one of the historic moments in Africa and you should be there." Carey agreed and told Raab that he wanted this assignment but was passed over in favor of Powell, King, and others.[8]

Unlike Fisher and Jack, who moved on to other organizations, George M. Houser remained intimately involved with CORE and its former sponsoring group, the Fellowship of Reconciliation (FOR). Nonviolence and Africa became Houser's principal foci, and he continued to work with Jack, especially on issues related to the continent. In 1954, Jack informed Carey that Houser would be in the Chicago area speaking to CORE about his meetings "with some African leaders." Houser developed lectures about "Non-Violent Resistance toward African Freedom," South Africa, and American policy toward Africa. Jack suggested that Houser ask Carey for an invitation to preach at Quinn Chapel and later discuss his "terrific" trip to Africa. In 1955, Houser and others planned a permanent American Committee on Africa and solicited Carey's help for a school in South Africa and an agricultural project for youth in the Gold Coast.[9]

Houser believed that Carey's civil rights reputation could be channeled into FOR and CORE's organizational activities. On one occasion, he asked Carey to speak at a FOR workshop in collaboration with the NAACP in Fort Wayne, Indiana. Though AME commitments prevented him from going, he promised to write letters and make phone calls to assist the effort. Houser subsequently tried to get Carey to support CORE's summer interracial workshop in Washington, D.C., hoping that Quinn Chapel would underwrite scholarships to bring participants, especially "several African students," to the conference.[10]

Though Carey had less frequent interactions with James Farmer than with other CORE founders, the minister was aware and proud that Farmer headed the national organization during the height of the civil rights movement. "I have seen you a great deal in the news columns and on the T.V. screen," Carey wrote to Farmer in 1963, adding, "I have sustained the sense of spiritual alliance which you and I established years ago." Carey invited Farmer to speak at Quinn Chapel, and Farmer agreed to do so during a 1964 trip to Chicago.[11]

Carey engaged in extensive NAACP activity, especially on the organization's speaking circuit starting in the late 1940s. However, he and Wilkins, at the time second in command to NAACP executive director Walter White, sparred in 1952 about Democrats' and Republicans' civil rights positions. Whereas Carey was a strong GOP partisan, Wilkins pointed out the flaws in both parties' policies. Carey respected the NAACP's nonpartisan posture and agreed that both the Democrats and the Republicans had underperformed on civil rights issues. Nonetheless, Carey criticized Wilkins for being "horribly biased and prejudiced" against the GOP and for his mistaken beliefs that "Democratic talk for civil rights is genuine" and that Republican attitudes were "sinister and venal." Carey was most annoyed that the NAACP saw no difference between the civil rights records of Republican vice presidential candidate Richard M. Nixon and his Democratic counterpart, John Sparkman. "I do not justify all of Nixon's record," Carey declared, "but when Nixon voted six times for civil rights and Sparkman voted all twenty-three times against, it is gross deception to leave the unsuspecting thinking that their records are just alike." Though Carey would not predict whether Eisenhower would "lead a crusade for civil rights" as president, he was a safer bet than the disappointing efforts of the Democrats.[12]

Wilkins wanted the last word on this matter: "We really are not far apart," he replied to Carey; "I have never been convinced that ALL the talk about civil rights by either the Democrats or Republicans is genuine." Despite the presence of racial progressives in both parties, they were "never a majority." The Roosevelt and Truman administrations and the Supreme Court deserved credit for creating a favorable "climate" that allowed for "enunciating and reiterating government policy" beneficial to blacks. Though the GOP had some reason for pride, Wilkins cited instances when the lack of Republican support had caused civil rights proposals to fail. Wilkins hoped that racial liberals in both parties would remain committed to "the civil rights front" and agreed with Carey that it was "not a good thing for all Negroes to be concentrated in one political party." He hoped that Eisenhower would "be wise enough to heed the counsel of persons like yourself."[13]

Whatever their disagreements about strategy, Carey and NAACP leaders agreed on the goal of advancing racial equality, and Wilkins viewed Carey as a reliable ally within the GOP and never questioned his commitment to black civil rights. White affirmed the group's alliance with Carey by scheduling him to deliver a major address at the NAACP's 1953 meeting in St. Louis. There, Carey acknowledged the NAACP's role in eliciting favorable Supreme Court rulings. Moreover, he confided in Henry Lee Moon, the NAACP's public relations director, that he had spoken with Ike and other administration officials about some message of support for civil rights. Carey also remained a strong financial backer of the NAACP.[14]

On one occasion, however, George D. Cannon, a prominent Harlem physician and cochair of the NAACP's National Life Membership Committee, attempted to merge NAACP concerns with GOP politics, drawing a rebuff from Carey. To enhance Nixon's 1960 presidential candidacy, thirty influential African Americans, including Cannon and Carey, were brought to Washington, D.C., to hear the Californian solicit black support. According to Cannon, Nixon noted that his competitors also wanted black votes, and he could say nothing to show that he would be the better choice for African Americans, who "would just have to have faith" in him. This statement annoyed Cannon, who challenged Nixon to buy a life membership in the NAACP to demonstrate his seriousness. To Cannon's surprise, Carey interjected, "No! No! Not now. Not this year," while Nixon remained "absolutely silent."[15] Carey intervened because he felt that a formal affiliation with the NAACP might prevent Nixon from winning the White House, and the value of having a true friend in the presidency trumped that of any symbolic gesture of solidarity.

Carey was also involved with the NAACP's regional and local chapters. In 1953, an official with the Tennessee State Conference of NAACP Branches asked Carey for advice regarding the poor state housing provided for blind African Americans and the discriminatory practices in state vocational education programs. Shortly thereafter, John W. Lee, the pastor of Bethel AME Church in Greenwich, Connecticut, asked Carey to speak at a "Freedom Rally" to raise funds for the NAACP attorneys arguing the public school segregation cases pending before the Supreme Court. Lee believed that Carey's GOP affiliation "would be of great value" in this "solid Republican community."[16]

Closer to home, Carey served as the Chicago NAACP's third vice president in 1948, though he was hardly a policymaker within the organization. He denounced local employment discrimination at a 1949 rally and served as cochair (with a black Democratic alderman) of the group's 1952 membership campaign. In 1957, while away from the city, Carey sent a message to Quinn Chapel to remind parishioners to join or rejoin the NAACP and to attend a meeting to reelect the president of the Chicago chapter, Willoughby Abner, who had overseen substantive increases in membership and fund-raising during his two years at the helm.[17]

Carey also threw his weight behind Carl Fuqua, who became the executive director of the Chicago NAACP in late 1959. Fuqua, a fellow Garrett graduate, had served as Carey's assistant minister at Quinn Chapel since 1956. Fuqua advocated the creation of an Illinois Fair Employment Practices Commission and attacked the Chicago Board of Education for sustaining racial inequality in the public schools. In 1963, Fuqua and Carey joined others in paying tribute to the NAACP's martyred Mississippi field secretary, Medgar Evers. In 1965, when Fuqua relinquished his position, Carey commended him for building the Chicago NAACP into one of the organization's largest chapters.[18]

Carey's interactions with the NAACP brought him into contact with numerous people throughout the organization's broad infrastructure. His ties with the Montgomery Improvement Association and the SCLC, however, focused on his friendship with Martin Luther King Jr., who became the embodiment of these two significant groups. King embraced Carey as a confidante, fund-raiser, and liaison with the FBI's notorious J. Edgar Hoover. Carey had long-standing relationships with notable black spokesmen A. Philip Randolph and Paul Robeson as well as the NAACP's White and Wilkins, but he described King as his "friend." Carey visited the Kings in their home months before Rosa Parks ignited the Montgomery movement, and the two ministers made guest appearances in each other's pulpits. "When I need help," Carey wrote, "I can count on Martin Luther King, and when he needs help he can count on me." The personal contacts between Carey and King evidenced a closeness that was missing from Carey's associations with other civil rights leaders except for Powell. Moreover, Carey admired King and other activists' courage and commitment to nonviolent direct action, observing, "The world cannot understand the courage of a Negro-American who will go to school to learn how to be beaten and bow his head before a rain of blows and then hold it up erect like a man. The world cannot understand the courage of a white American who will start out on one leg and two crutches to walk 50 miles to set things right in Selma and in Saginaw. Black and white, Jew and Gentile, priests and nuns, ministers and laymen, rich and poor, educated and untrained, high and low—all have formed one solid phalanx."[19]

King and Carey cemented their friendship when the Chicagoan accepted a speaking invitation at a June 1955 citizenship rally at the all-black Alabama State College in Montgomery. Local black professionals, including King, the new pastor at Dexter Avenue Baptist Church, fully supported the effort. King pronounced the benediction at an Alpha Phi Alpha fraternity event and spent time with Carey, discussing public theology and President Eisenhower's Committee on Government Employment Policy. Carey subsequently wrote to King, "I can't tell you how very much I enjoyed the afternoon and night that I spent with you and your charming wife, Coretta and the distinguished Dr. M. L. [King], Sr." A few months later, after Parks's December 1, 1955, refusal to relinquish her seat on a bus sparked the bus boycott, King invited Carey to serve as chair of a Chicago committee to help "the Negro citizens of Montgomery." Since the local bus company was a subsidiary of the Chicago-based National City Lines, King urged Carey and other Chicago leaders, including AME Zion bishop William J. Walls; the Reverend Joseph H. Jackson of the National Baptist Convention, U.S.A.; and Congressman Dawson to convey the boycotters' grievances to "the hearts and minds" of company officials. Perhaps more important, they needed to be aware that most of the Montgomery bus profits came from African Americans.[20]

Carey offered financial support to the Montgomery Improvement Association, promising an offering from Quinn Chapel and other area churches. At the same time, Carey remained sensitive to the need to avoid providing southern white critics with ammunition to argue that the boycott "was either being financed by northern money or directed by outside influence." King shrugged off Carey's concerns, noting the association's "pressing need" for funds. The result was the National Day of Deliverance Prayer Meeting, sponsored by Carey, the NAACP, Powell, Bishop William Y. Bell of the Christian Methodist Episcopal Church, and the Reverend William H. Jernagin of the Fraternal Council of Negro Churches, among others. King's assistant, the Reverend Ralph D. Abernathy, attended the Chicago rally and returned to Montgomery with $2,500 plus a special offering of $250 from Quinn Chapel.[21]

Carey's support of King and the Montgomery Improvement Association also surfaced at other times during the 381-day boycott. Carey viewed his backing of the boycott as complementing his position as a federal official fighting employment discrimination. When Coretta Scott King, a talented soprano, came to Chicago to perform at a fund-raiser, Carey urged Quinn Chapel's congregants to attend. After the Supreme Court ordered the desegregation of Montgomery's buses, Carey commended King for taking "upon his shoulders the mantle of tremendous responsibility" and for embodying African Americans' "press for first class citizenship."[22]

Carey recognized that the grassroots activism that King helped to channel into the Montgomery Bus Boycott was an effective strategy for improving the condition of blacks, while King respected the insider role of such politically connected clergy as Carey and Powell. This mutual regard was evident in King's invitation to speak at Quinn Chapel's 110th anniversary celebration in July 1957 and in the Alabama minister's "very happy" acceptance. King visited the Carey home and met Hazel and Carolyn, just as Carey had met King's family. King later declared himself impressed with Carey's "great work in a great church." King reciprocated by inviting Carey to address the Montgomery Improvement Association's Institute on Non-Violence and Social Change: Carey's "presence and participation [would] do much to lend dignity and effectiveness to [the] program of developing leaders for the struggle in the South." After Carey's speech, King observed that audience members "are still talking about the magnificent job you did."[23]

Soon after King and other southern pastors founded the SCLC in January 1957, King wrote to tell his friend Carey that the new organization's "primary aims are those of mutual planning, financial assistance, moral support and the carrying out of common projects across the south in the struggle for civil rights." He assured Carey that the SCLC would not supplant the NAACP but would "implement through non-violent action the decisions the NAACP has won in the courts." The organization's first major project, the Crusade for Citizenship, was set to start in January 1958 and sought "to double the number" of African American voters and to raise two hundred thousand dollars to establish an Atlanta headquarters, from which field workers would blanket the South to conduct voter education. King asked Carey to join the initiative's national advisory committee because "your name would lend prestige in helping us carry out the objectives of the Crusade." King also solicited Carey's "advice and counsel" and endorsement of his "non-violent movement." When Carey learned that King would be in Chicago in January 1958, he hoped their schedules would allow them "to break bread together or at least pass the time." King proposed that they meet either in Chicago or in Washington, D.C., where Carey's government employment committee was convening, and the two became confidantes. In contrast, Powell, though initially supportive of King's movement, seemed unable to adjust to his new type of grassroots leadership, and the two Baptist clergymen grew increasingly estranged.[24]

Carey served as a mentor for the younger King, sharing with him material from speeches. Carey offered King biblically based reflections about brotherhood and peace and provided him with copies of various talks, including Carey's 1960 World Methodist Conference address delivered in Oslo, Norway, and probably his 1952 Republican National Convention speech, from which King borrowed the refrain about freedom ringing from mountaintops that he rearticulated in the "I Have a Dream" speech at the 1963 March on Washington. King acknowledged this debt when he remarked that he had "heard a powerful orator say" that black freedom could be described through convincing allegories, demonstrating his high regard for Carey's homiletic abilities. A few months later, Carey and three other black ministers signed on as contributors to a volume of sermons for which the majority of orations would come from white clergymen; he and the editor agreed that an address from King should be included and suggested that he send the sermon he had delivered at the National Conference on Religion and Race or the speech given at a Hebrew Union event in Chicago, "which a number of Rabbi friends have told me was 'tremendous.'" This request demonstrates the back-and-forth nature of the collaboration between these two clerical colleagues.[25]

King came to Quinn Chapel as often as his schedule allowed. He was honored at a dinner there in 1958 and returned on February 12, 1960, which Carey declared "Alpha Day" in honor of King, a fellow member of Alpha Phi Alpha fraternity. A previous engagement prevented King from accepting Carey's invitation to preach at the church in January 1963, but the SCLC leader hoped to be able to return to Quinn Chapel "sometime in the near future." Carey invited Coretta Scott King to speak at Quinn Chapel's Women's Day in 1962 and turned to Martin Luther King Sr., the pastor of Atlanta's Ebenezer Baptist Church, the following year. Carey boasted that he had known the elder King before his son "hit the headlines" and described his visit to Quinn Chapel as "one of the high points of my whole pastoral experience." Daddy King too enjoyed the visit, noting that Carey's "strong leadership to this church was evident throughout the service." C. T. Vivian, SCLC's director of affiliates, preached at Carey's church in June 1965. Carey's attachment to the Kings sustained his role as a major player in civil rights affairs even after the GOP lost the White House in 1960. At the same time, the younger King hoped to leverage Carey's connections to persons of significant influence in both political parties to benefit the movement.[26]

By the 1960s, Carey preferred the SCLC's conspicuous activism to the approach taken by the NUL and the NAACP, to which his value had dropped along with his insider political access. In Carey, King found a like-minded minister whose church and civic experiences gave great value to the advice and counsel he provided to SCLC. A May 1963 invitation to preach at St. John AME Church in Birmingham, Alabama, allowed Carey to see firsthand the development of a major SCLC campaign in the nation's "most segregated city." In the wake of the recent protests and the Birmingham police's use of water cannons and dogs on demonstrators, Carey wanted "to see as much and learn as much of the situation there as time and circumstance will permit." He asked pastor C. E. Thomas (a future bishop) to take him "by the spots of significance [to] talk to whom ever is available." During his talk, St. John members "roared when I told them that 'the [state] Troopers scrutinized me and I scrutinized them—and they didn't say anything to me and I didn't say anything to them.'" Carey gained more exposure to the risks of civil rights activism when he visited Jackson, Mississippi, the following July. Twenty-four youth were arrested for distributing flyers advertising his appearance, and he visited the home of Medgar Evers's widow, Myrlie, and saw "the hole in the wall through which the bullet passed that killed her husband." Evers's assassination the preceding month greatly affected not only Carey but also his sister, Annabel Carey Prescott. Because Evers had been scheduled to speak at Quinn Chapel, the congregation sent $100 to his widow for the "personal use" of herself and the Evers children. Prescott also sent money on behalf of a white colleague, with a note explaining that the gift represented the "thousands" who supported "the cause for which your husband sacrificed his life." Two years later, Carey sent $352 from Quinn Chapel for the Selma-to-Montgomery march for black voting rights.[27]

In the fall of 1965, King invited Carey to join the board of directors of the American Foundation on Nonviolence, of which King served as honorary chair and to which he had donated twenty-five thousand dollars from his Nobel Peace Prize to fund voter registration, leadership training in nonviolence, and efforts to fight "murder, violence, brutalities" against southern civil rights workers. Further evidence of King's esteem for the Chicago pastor came when Randolph T. Black-well, the SCLC's program director, invited Carey to attend the group's 1965 annual convention in Birmingham: "Because of your work and great interest in the cause of human rights, I am instructed by Dr. Martin Luther King, Jr. to extend this special invitation." Carey's "heavy schedule" prevented him from accepting, but he noted, "I am always available for special service."[28]

Such "special service" included intervening with J. Edgar Hoover and the FBI on King's behalf. From the late 1950s until King's assassination in 1968, the FBI sought to undermine his integrity as an African American spokesman. Hoover spearheaded efforts to prove that King had communist connections, that he was sexually immoral, and that he had embezzled SCLC funds. Carey's tenure on the President's Committee on Government Employment Policy had brought him into contact with Hoover, and the two men had a cordial and collegial relationship. Carey liked to meet prominent people and convert them into allies for the civil rights cause, and he hoped to realize that goal with Hoover. Hoover instructed the administrators in charge of FBI field offices to attend committee conferences and cooperate with its antidiscrimination initiatives. Carey found Hoover's attitude "very gratifying" and asked his permission to quote from his complimentary let-ter in the committee's annual report. This cooperation continued through 1959, when "fine reports" emerged about meetings between committee staffers and FBI field officers in Houston and Oklahoma City. Carey thanked Hoover for being "of inestimable value to our morale, and to me, as Chairman, an unfailing source of comfort." Carey thus thought that he could be an honest broker between the King and Hoover and still sustain his high standing with both the FBI and the SCLC.[29]

It is hard to believe that Carey was unaware of Hoover's fearsome reputation as an anticommunist crusader and as a collector of incendiary information on public figures. So why did Carey, whose ample FBI files revealed no moral or fiduciary failings, deem it important to ingratiate himself with the FBI director? Perhaps he enjoyed proximity to power or sought protection either for himself or some rela-tive or friend with potential legal troubles. Whatever his motivation, the various encounters between the two men illustrate the minister's desire to solidify his link to the director. Carey and guests toured the FBI headquarters in 1958 but did not meet Hoover; the following year, however, when Carey returned with three family members, the group met with Hoover and witnessed a "firearms demonstration." Carey commented that Hoover had been "gracious and considerate" during previ-ous encounters and that "the Director was one of the outstanding figures in gov-ernment." He added that Hoover had acquired "three more fans of undiminished enthusiasm in the Carey household." When Carey saw the movie *The FBI Story* later that year, he told the director that it constituted "a very personal experience" and testified to the public's high regard for Hoover and "the intricate, complex, and exacting institution" that he had built. Carey's "generous comments" again flattered Hoover and drew his hearty thanks.[30]

In 1960, Carey's Quinn Chapel sponsored a special dinner to honor the FBI director. Why Carey chose Hoover, hardly a person known for his religious faith, is difficult to determine, and the selection of Hoover surely puzzled parishioners. The program received generous publicity and included Bishop Gomez, the AME prelate in the Midwest, and Joseph Bibb, Illinois's state director of public safety. Since congressional business prevented the presence of Senator Dirksen, Harold E. Rainville substituted for his boss.[31]

Hoover challenged the audience to recognize that "moral breakdown" afflicted American society. He advocated the elimination of "moral slums" and observed that "courage and determination" were needed to save "freedom and decency" in the United States. The plaque Carey prepared for Hoover praised him for building the FBI into an efficient agency and "for securing the national safety by seeking out the enemies of the Republic and shoring up the defenses of the Nation." Carey expressed appreciation for the attendance of Hoover's associate director, Clyde Tolson: "The opportunity of getting to know you has been a pleasant one for me." Hoover received a "standing ovation," and Carey was "almost overwhelmed by comments" praising the speech. Carey also promised to donate the "profit" from the event to "something suitable to honor" Hoover.[32]

In 1960, in exchange for the goodwill evidenced by the FBI director's cooperation with Carey's committee, Carey warned Hoover about a possible congressional investigation of the FBI's employment policies regarding African Americans. A committee headed by Democratic congressman James Roosevelt of California, son of Franklin Roosevelt, was examining how many African American agents the agency employed and whether they were permanent or temporary. Cartha De Loach, with whom Carey already had an amiable relationship, answered on Hoover's behalf. The FBI "definitely" employed African American agents, and on numerous occasions, according to De Loach, Hoover had "commended these Agents for the excellent services they have performed for the FBI." Moreover, De Loach noted, "The Director has a Negro Special Agent in his office and thinks very highly of him." No African American agents had temporary status, and no applicant had been rejected because of race. Carey accepted De Loach's testimony, indicating, "We should forget the matter" of black employment in the agency." In 1962, Carey congratulated Hoover on "the spread in *Ebony* magazine on 'The Negro in the FBI.'"[33]

Hoover apparently considered Carey a like-minded anticommunist. The FBI had compiled files on Carey in connection with his Eisenhower administration appointments, describing him as "a highly controversial lawyer, a politician, and minister" who associated with several leftist groups and with "known and suspected communist sympathizers." Nevertheless, Hoover did not believe that Carey was a security risk but rather thought him "a most vocal and aggressive champion of the cause of obtaining equal rights for the Negro." By 1962, this benign assessment caused Hoover to endorse Carey for membership on the Subversive Activities Control Board: the FBI director "had always believed a person of the substantial background of Dr. Carey" should be affiliated with the board.[34]

Carey reinforced Hoover's favorable view of his patriotism by commending the director's anticommunist writings. In 1960, Carey was "very pleased" to receive an autographed copy of Hoover's book, *Masters of Deceit*, which discussed communist infiltration into the United States. Carey "enjoyed reading many of its passages" and subsequently promised to read "with special pleasure" Hoover's 1962 *A Study of Communism*, which Carey anticipated would provide a "treasure of information and insight." In March 1963, Carey was pleased to learn that Hoover would not retire from the FBI but would continue his "sterling leadership."[35]

The FBI commenced its wiretaps on King in November 1963. In March 1964, as African Americans criticized the FBI for lax protection of civil rights activists and for slow investigations of civil rights violations, Carey commended Hoover's efforts, earning the director's thanks for a "generous evaluation" of the agency and a salute to FBI "accomplishments in connection with minority groups."[36]

In May 1965, however, "Dr. King told Dr. Carey that the FBI was trying to discredit him and might release stories to the press regarding his personal life in the near future." According to a government report, Carey contended that King had not asked him to talk with the FBI but rather "that he had volunteered to 'see what he could do.' Dr. King gave his assent." Carey believed that his credibility with Hoover would enable him to "enlist the sympathies of the FBI in not letting any effort to discredit King occur." Given Carey's earlier access to Hoover, he must have been surprised when the director was unavailable to meet with him. After Carey called for an appointment, an internal memorandum to De Loach affirmed that the minister "is very friendly with the Bureau," that he had "toured" the agency, and that he was "well known" to high level Hoover assistants. However, Carey "refused to divulge the information he desired to discuss with the Director," and the memorandum recommended "that the Director should not take time from his extremely busy schedule to see Dr. Carey on this occasion. It is suggested that we advise Dr. Carey that it will be impossible for the Director to see him." Instead, Hoover's gatekeepers suggested that Carey meet with De Loach, and Carey acquiesced.[37]

Carey forthrightly declared his intention to prevent any forthcoming effort to circulate salacious information about the civil rights leader. King "indicated every evidence of great disturbance" over this matter, and Carey hoped that De Loach would intervene to prevent any attacks on the character of "a good man." Carey described King as a "'symbol' to the Negro race today" and a "safety valve" whose "articulate voice was preventing more of the militant and violent Negroes from committing serious acts in the United States." De Loach told Carey that because of his familiarity with the agency, he should know "that the FBI had plenty to do without being responsible for a discrediting campaign against Reverend King," a contention Carey seemingly accepted. According to De Loach, Carey "agreed that [King] did not know [the FBI] better and stated that he had doubted King's allegations from the very beginning." Furthermore, De Loach told Carey, King had "very unfairly" criticized FBI agents' allegedly inadequate investigations of civil rights violations in the South. Moreover, according to De Loach, King had met with Hoover and denied making such charges but received "some very good advice insofar as his moral responsibilities were concerned." De Loach also stressed that "extremists on both sides"—a group in which he clearly included King—attacked the FBI. "Dr. Carey," he noted, "showed great interest and indicated that he would be one that would attempt to remedy that situation."[38]

Carey relayed the substance of his conversation with De Loach to King and then reported to FBI headquarters that he had encouraged King to "make a greater effort to praise the FBI for its excellent work in the civil rights field." The NAACP's Wilkins, CORE's Farmer, and the SCLC's Abernathy also urged FBI officials to abandon their campaign to embarrass King, and De Loach believed that the agency held the upper hand since King "is becoming very disturbed and worried about his background else he would not go to such great effort to have people approach the FBI." When told "flatly" about "King's derelictions insofar as false allegations against us are concerned and of the fact that King and other civil rights workers owed the FBI a debt of gratitude they would never be able to repay," Carey and the other black leaders "backed down," refusing or too afraid to challenge Hoover.[39]

Having adopted the agency's perspective on King, Carey sought to use his FBI ties for personal advancement. During the De Loach meeting, according to FBI sources, Carey changed the subject away from King "to be very immodest for a second." After reminding De Loach that he was pastor of Quinn Chapel, a lawyer, and president of the Illinois Savings and Loan Association, Carey stated that "he felt he had done a great deal for the [Johnson] Administration" and that he hoped Hoover "would say a good word for him to the President." De Loach responded that Hoover regarded Carey "very highly and would naturally keep his request in mind, although it might be presumptuous for the Director to make such recommendations to the White House." Carey understood and "again pledged his loyalty and friendship." De Loach gave his boss a complete report, noting that he had not committed "the FBI in any manner insofar as not exposing King is concerned." The director responded, "Well handled."[40]

King did not know of Carey's other objectives in meeting with the FBI or of his abandonment of King's cause, and the SCLC leader and his group believed that Carey had served them well. He received two hundred dollars from SCLC headquarters as reimbursement for the trip to Washington, accepting the money and telling King's lieutenants, "You fellows can certainly count on me as one of your strongest spiritual supporters and I hope I never fail when you need me." Unaware that Carey had disbelieved King's charge that the FBI aimed to destroy him, Abernathy described Carey "as one of our greatest friends."[41]

In 1962, Al Raby and other activists had organized Chicago's Coordination Council of Community Organizations, which worked to desegregate the city's public schools and housing. In 1965 and 1966, King periodically participated in some of these protests, with which Carey was tangentially involved. Carey knew about King's ties to Raby and invited the SCLC leader to preach at Quinn Chapel on July 25, 1965, and some open-housing rallies were held at Quinn Chapel. When Raby threatened to block traffic to dramatize the city's racial problems, King agreed to cooperate, leading Mayor Daley to seek to dissociate the SCLC leader from the demonstrations. The mayor called on black clergy, especially Carey, to convince King to separate himself from Raby. In exchange for Carey's assistance, Daley dangled the carrot of a judgeship.[42]

In 1966, the Democratic Party nominated Carey as judge of the Circuit Court of Cook County and another AME lawyer, Glen T. Johnson, as associate judge. Delighted delegates at the Chicago Annual Conference endorsed both men. As usual, anyone running on the Daley machine's ticket was certain of victory: Carey received 952,717 votes and finally realized his goal of a seat on the bench. He shared the news with Hoover, who offered his "heartiest congratulations."[43]

Carey's commitment to the civil rights movement became increasingly symbolic. His desire for the destruction of de jure and de facto racial discrimination, though undiminished, shifted from substantive involvement to simple gestures of support. He used the Quinn Chapel pulpit to host and pay tribute to civil rights activists. Clyde Kennard, a former University of Chicago student who was arrested for trying to register at the segregated University of Southern Mississippi, was invited to speak at the church on the 1963 Men's Day, with Carey anticipating "a touching and soul-stirring message." Comedian and activist Dick Gregory provided Kennard's introduction. For the featured speaker at the same year's Women's Day, Carey chose Daisy Bates, "a distinguished officer" in Bethel AME Church in Little Rock, Arkansas, and a leader of the state's NAACP who had been instrumental in the desegregation of the city's Central High School. Carey observed that Bates "has made history in a dramatic fashion in these last few years of the civil rights struggle" and "has a fascinating story to tell."[44] On one level, these associations demonstrated Carey's ongoing civil rights commitments; on another level, however, these activities masked his heightened focus on his purely careerist objectives.

Whereas in earlier years he had held important offices on the municipal and federal levels, the end of the Eisenhower administration and his failed campaigns for two Cook County judgeships left him with only a pastorate and the presidency of a savings and loan. For some, these two positions would have been plenty, but for Carey, they were not enough. Public involvement and public notice seemed his lifeblood, and he was lost without a political position. Early in 1966, he confided to a friend that he appeared to have no prospects despite having become a Democrat: "My political future—Nothing special. Nobody has said nothing and I have not either." On a recent trip to Washington, he had "chatted with" President Johnson, "very pleasantly and innocuous. That was the day of Adam Powell's big hearing on the Poverty Program. I passed by and looked into the jammed room from the corridor. He waved at me during the hearing and folks around wondered again who I was."[45] Carey had always engaged in civil rights activities out of genuine commitment to the cause, but he had also always merged those activities with his personal ambitions. By the mid-1960s, self-promotion seemed increasingly to be his focus.

Carey was not alone in allowing his taste for public office to eclipse his civil rights activism. Powell's biographers have observed the same increased focus on self-promotion under the guise of African American advocacy. As head of the House Education and Labor Committee, Powell was responsible for much legislation that benefited blacks. At the same time, his flamboyant lifestyle, which included Caribbean retreats, multiple marriages and romances, and political hubris separated him from his congressional constituents and his parishioners.[46] Though Carey led a much less salacious personal life, he succumbed to the same careerist temptations. What happened after they became political insiders?

Carey hoped that the favors he solicited from Daley and Hoover would provide influential connections that would benefit blacks. But favors require reciprocity, a high price that Carey, wittingly or unwittingly, seemed inclined to pay. His judgeship and his other government positions would enable him to do much good for African Americans. But a seat on the bench required a dispassionate administration of justice rather than fervent advocacy on behalf of aggrieved members of his congregation and his community. Moreover, getting to the bench and maintaining influence in the federal government caused Carey to make unsettling alliances with Daley and Hoover, and in the end, the costs outweighed the benefits. However much Carey aided the civil rights movement, he also harmed it, at least marginally, through the damaging ties he forged as a political insider.

As a judge, Carey committed to a lower profile in the ministry and to a deeper involvement in jurisprudence. At the two congregations that Carey served, his members frequently validated their pastor's dual roles in church and civic affairs. In 1957, for example, when Dwight D. Eisenhower appointed Carey as chair of the President's Committee on Government Employment Policy, Quinn Chapel parishioners sent their endorsement to the White House. Acknowledging that "this is the first time a Negro-American has been named Chairman of a Presidential Committee,"

Carey's congregants expressed their "grateful appreciation and genuine approval of his selection." The congregation behaved similarly when Carey was elected a judge, presenting him with a "judicial robe and an embossed leather Bible on which to take his oath of office." He was assigned to Cook County's criminal court, where he presided over intense and notorious murder cases. In the "Milk Shake Mary" case, a woman had placed arsenic in a beverage and given it to her hospitalized husband. In another case, a tavern owner set fire to his business, resulting in the deaths of thirteen patrons. Carey's first few months on the bench thus exposed him not to important deliberations on civil rights law but to the ugliest aspects of human behavior.[47]

His connections to Quinn Chapel and the AME Church may have provided Carey with needed relief. Although he took some lumps in denominational politics, he could always count on stroking from the *Christian Recorder*. Proud of his many achievements in both the religious and secular arenas, editor B. J. Nolen regularly featured Carey on the weekly's front page, always noting his preeminent position as pastor at Quinn Chapel. In 1962, Nolen called him an AME "Minister of the Times." Even after Carey declined to run for the bishopric in 1960, Nolen noted that "the great minister at [the] great Quinn Chapel, Chicago . . . would make one of the finest additions to our episcopacy." When Carey spoke on a Chicago television station about black civil rights, Nolen joined "countless hearers in congratulating Dr. Carey for this and innumerable contributions to this nation, race, and the church."[48] Carey continued to rely on fellow AMEs to affirm their respect and admiration for him both as a preacher and a judge.

It was important to Carey that the same public theology that he espoused influenced other ministers in his denomination. Melvin Chester Swann, the pastor at St. Joseph AME Church in Durham, North Carolina, drew Carey's commendation for his involvement in the civil rights movement, which included being jailed. Similarly, the Reverend G. R. Haughton, the pastor of Pearl Street AME Church in Jackson, Mississippi, merited Carey's "undiminished admiration for the gallant warfare which the people are waging. . . under your leadership." The Reverend H. Hartford Brookins had been an admirer from the time he studied at Ohio's Payne Theological Seminary and fulfilled his field education requirement at Carey's Wood-lawn Church. Brookins was "greatly encouraged and helped" by Carey's example and replicated his mentor's pastoral successes by building new edifices at St. Paul in Wichita, Kansas, and at Los Angeles's First Church. Carey reciprocated Brookins's esteem, delivering the keynote address at the 1963 unveiling of architectural plans for the new California church and expressing pride at Brookins's political involvements, which included important roles in the 1963 election of his parishioner, Tom Bradley, as one of the first African Americans on the Los Angeles City Council and in his 1973 election as the city's first African American mayor.[49] Carey endorsed

Brookins's ministry because he embodied an earlier version of Carey himself. Unlike his mentor, however, Brookins was elected a bishop in 1972 and eschewed public office while remaining active as a political broker.

In 1967, Carey's congregation marked its 120th anniversary, staging a series of elaborate events and commissioning a commemorative volume in honor of the milestone. On May 31, however, the fifty-nine-year-old Carey suffered a stroke, remaining hospitalized until early August. By the second week of September, Carey felt strong enough to meet Bishop Joseph Gomez at the Chicago Annual Conference and to read his thirty-seventh pastoral report. His appearance became a moving valedictory.[50]

Standing in the spacious sanctuary of Grant Memorial Church, Carey thanked his bishop, his fellow pastors, and the members of Quinn Chapel for the "tremendous love and prayerful concern" they had shown during his illness. Since starting at Woodlawn in 1931 and then at Quinn Chapel beginning in 1949, he was presenting a report that was "spiritually his best." Carey was proud that his congregation had collected forty-two hundred dollars for the denominational budget and seventy thousand dollars for local operating expenses during 1966–67, exceeding its earlier contributions. Carey, who had been introduced as both pastor and judge, then revealed his deep religiosity. He "told of God's goodness to him," citing several scriptures that testified to God's promises to humankind, and led the assembly in singing the familiar "I'll Be Alright Some Day." The "entire vast congregation was moved to tears by the faith manifested in one of the greatest personalities in African Methodism." Moreover, "as he took his seat this entire great throng arose to their feet and gave [Carey] a hearty applause." Perhaps they already knew that this was Carey's last report as an active pastor; his physician had admonished him to give up his church. At his congregation's request, the Chicago Annual Conference designated him "Minister-Emeritus of Quinn Chapel," a position "of honor without responsibility or compensation." The resolution expressed "the desire of Pastor and people to continue the pastoral relationship which has been mutually enriching." The request was granted and Bishop Gomez subsequently appointed A. Leon Bailey as Carey's replacement. In 1971, when Carey's sister, Eloise Carey Bishop, a longtime resident of New York City, died, Bailey provided the obsequies. The services were held at A. W. Williams's Unity Funeral Parlors in Chicago. Williams, Carey's best friend, and Bailey, the officiating minister, stood with Carey as he parted with his "Alter Mater." Another pastoral successor, Gregory G. M. Ingram, a future bishop who, like Carey, was a Garrett graduate, recalled that his predecessor continued to sit in the pulpit but never offered unsolicited advice or interfered in congregational governance. At the time, Ingram did not realize that Carey had been a nationally prominent person in both church and civic affairs. Carey avoided upstaging those who followed him into the Quinn Chapel pulpit.[51]

According to the Reverend Jesse W. Cotton, whom Carey had mentored at Woodlawn, "his God-given gifts of recall and an excellent memory were not marred greatly by his stroke." Nevertheless, he lightened his load considerably, not only by giving up his ministry but also by surrendering the presidency of the Illinois Savings and Loan Association, which under his stewardship had grown to hold twelve million dollars in assets by 1962. He observed that the institution had "provided the funds which have made possible the building and beautification of churches and businesses" and had "created two dozen new jobs." Perhaps the achievement of which he was most proud was the savings and loans' construction of a three-story debt-free building.[52]

Carey won reelection as a Cook County judge in 1970 and 1976, although he seemed temperamentally unsuited for the criminal court. His pastoral inclinations, useful in serving parishioners and legal clients and in approving loans for worthy community residents, were less applicable on the bench, where mandatory sentences left little room for judicial discretion. He was eventually reassigned to civil court and later to equity court. In 1980, two years after he reached the mandatory retirement age of seventy, the Illinois State Supreme Court twice recalled him to service "to help reduce the backlog of personal injury cases in the Law Jury Division of the Circuit Court." He remained on the bench until March 31, 1981.[53]

Denominational contemporaries, especially in the Midwest, kept Carey in front of AME audiences. Cotton, the pastor at the Institutional Church, invited Carey to preach during the 1970s. In 1971, he delivered an address to celebrate the centennial of Turner Chapel AME Church in Fort Wayne, Indiana. Chicago's St. James AME Church hosted him as its guest preacher in 1978. Robert Thomas Jr., the pastor of Detroit's Ebenezer AME Church and a future bishop, asked Carey to speak at the Michigan congregation's 106th anniversary in 1977. With his wife, Hazel, accompanying him, Carey told a crowd of one thousand, "We are a generation that made the unthinkable thought of and . . . we have moved from a society where a court says that a Black man has no rights a white man must respect to a court which has declared that separate is unequal and unacceptable." Though he was uncomfortable with Black Power and the separatist black ideology that arose during the late 1960s and 1970s, he fully embraced affirmative action and other new remedies to fight racial inequality. "We have moved from a system of quotas to keep Black people out," he said, "to a new quota system to put us in." Carey appreciated all the invitations to speak for both church and community organizations. One from Chicago's Poro College in 1971, he said, was "one of the biggest lifts to my morale since my illness."[54]

Carey died at home on April 20, 1981, at the age of seventy-three. Both the *Chicago Defender* and the *Christian Recorder* noted the broad range of his vocational activities. "Lawyer, judge, politician, diplomat and freedom fighter. Judge Archibald

J. Carey Jr. wore all those hats and many more during his long and distinguished service to his city, state, nation, and race," observed the *Defender*. The paper ran a large picture of Carey in his clerical vestments and identified him as the "longtime pastor of Quinn Chapel AME Church." An even larger image showed Carey with Mayor Daley. The *Recorder* described Carey as a "great preacher, pastor, [AME] connectional leader and Illinois judge."[55]

Carey's funeral, like his father's fifty years earlier, was held in the cavernous sanctuary of Quinn Chapel. The roster of honorary pallbearers included members of Alpha Phi Alpha Fraternity, Sigma Pi Phi Fraternity (The Boule), the Circuit Court of Chicago, the Original Forty Club, and other exclusive organizations that attested to Carey's elite affiliations among both blacks and whites. Hazel Carey chose Bishop Brookins as her husband's eulogist, demonstrating that she viewed him as Carey's leadership heir and the best person to explain his ministry and his public theology.[56]

EPILOGUE

Both Archibald J. Carey Sr. and Archibald J. Carey Jr. were heirs to a tradition of activism and officeholding among black ministers dating from Reconstruction. Headiness from the prestige and influence that came from these accomplishments may have blinded both father and son to the dangers that these involvements posed. Moreover, holding public office sometimes made it difficult to disentangle personal ambition from the public good of those whom they represented. Their desire to benefit blacks was unambiguously actualized through their presence in the public square. African Americans were better off because of the Careys, but both men at times were caught in the damaging cross fire intrinsic to their high-level political involvements.

The precepts of John Wesley's "practical divinity" pushed Methodist ministers such as the Careys into civic affairs. When Wesleyan preachers, both black and white, fought slavery in the eighteenth and nineteenth centuries and battled racial segregation and discrimination in the twentieth century, they stood in the public square as advocates for the "new creation." Neither Carey drew explicitly from this lexicon of Wesleyan theology; rather, they invoked the name of Richard Allen, the founder of their denomination, whose lived religion and Methodist consciousness envisioned a just and equitable American society. The Careys understood Allen's involvements as a theology of black liberation that was singularly focused on freedom from slavery and segregation and whose roots lay in a merged Wesleyan/black liberationist ethos.[1]

Despite controversy, the Careys found it easy to embrace a belief in public square involvements. More difficult, however, was the task of negotiating the compromises embedded in getting to and staying in public office and avoiding becoming apologists for allies in both party and government. Despite these difficulties, both Careys broke with the Republican Party when it failed to support African American aspirations. The senior Carey allied himself with Democrats who were willing to back black equality; the younger Carey spoke favorably of Progressive Henry A. Wallace in the 1948 presidential election and surrendered his long-standing Republican affiliation after President Lyndon B. Johnson demonstrated his commitment to African American equality by engineering the passage of the Civil Rights Act of 1964.[2]

The Careys made no attempt to build a "righteous kingdom" in American society. Rather, they tried to align government with the goals of black equality. They worked to nudge public officials on the municipal, state, and federal levels to enforce just and equitable treatment of African Americans in accordance with both scriptural mandates and constitutional principles. Though the Careys waded knee-deep in partisan politics, neither became a "patriot preacher" or a "court prophet."[3] They used party membership to address the broad objectives of African American advancement. Although party leaders tried to exploit the Careys' church influence by seeking their followers' votes, father and son always remained clear that political organizations should serve the goals of black liberation. The Careys were strikingly disinterested in changing or redefining the republican ideas that underlay American government except in those areas that affected African Americans' welfare. They saw government not as a means to realize a Christian commonwealth but as an ally to correct egregious wrongs against blacks.

Addressing the urgent issues confronting African Americans required the Careys to mobilize their congregants to support Social Gospel initiatives and to vote to change government policy. At times, parishioners' votes enabled the Careys to obtain benefits for their congregations and communities. At other times, this quest for personal and community benefits moved both Careys to tolerate political parties or leaders who disrespected African Americans or denigrated the importance of civil rights. The elder Carey looked the other way when Chicago mayor William Hale Thompson waged only a weak fight against public and private racial discrimination; his son had questionable interactions with J. Edgar Hoover at the same time that the FBI director was trying to destroy Martin Luther King Jr. These alliances suggest that both father and son were willing to jeopardize their moral legitimacy to gain favor from powerful whites. Nevertheless, the two men left a legacy of ministerial activism that empowered African Americans and demonstrated that their votes could advance and affirm their civil rights and fully integrate them into the American body politic. Their practice of public theology offered a standard by which their contemporaries could judge the efficacy of clergy involvement in the public square.

NOTES

Abbreviations

ACP Jr.	Adam Clayton Powell Jr.
ACR	*AME Church Review*
AJC Jr.	Archibald J. Carey Jr.
AJC Jr. Papers	Archibald J. Carey Jr. Papers, Chicago Historical Society, Chicago
AJC Sr.	Archibald J. Carey Sr.
AJC Sr. Papers	Archibald J. Carey Sr. Papers, Chicago Historical Society, Chicago
AME Archives	Archives of the Department of Research and Scholarship, AME Church, AME Sunday School Union, Nashville
CD	*Chicago Defender*
CR	*Christian Recorder*
Dirksen Papers	Everett M. Dirksen Papers, Chicago Office File, Dirksen Congressional Center, Pekin, Illinois
EMD	Everett M. Dirksen
FBI File	Archibald J. Carey Jr. File, Federal Bureau of Investigation, Department of Justice, Washington, D.C., FOIPA nos. 1036946-000, 1050204-000
HAJ	Homer A. Jack
JEH	J. Edgar Hoover
MLK Jr.	Martin Luther King Jr.
NAACP Records	Records of the National Association for the Advancement of Colored People, Manuscript Division, Library of Congress, Washington, D.C.
Rickey Papers	Branch Rickey Papers, Manuscript Division, Library of Congress, Washington, D.C.
VJW	Val J. Washington
WHCF-AF	White House Central Files, 1953–61, Alphabetical File, AJC Jr. File, Dwight D. Eisenhower Library, Abilene, Kansas
WHCF-GF	White House Central Files, 1953–61, General File, Dwight D. Eisenhower Library, Abilene, Kansas
WHCF-OF	White House Central Files, 1953–61, Official File, Dwight D. Eisenhower Library, Abilene, Kansas

Introduction

1. *Journal of the Twenty-ninth Quadrennial Session of the General Conference of the AME Church, May 2–16, 1932, Cleveland, Ohio*, 202, AME Archives; Wesley J. Gaines, *The Gospel Ministry: A Series of Lectures* (Philadelphia: Rodgers, 1899), 59–61.

2. W. J. Walls to AJC Jr., March 5, 1949, AJC Jr. Papers, Box 7, Folder 43; *CR*, June 6, 1961.

3. Eric L. McDaniel, *Politics in the Pews: The Political Mobilization of Black Churches* (Ann Arbor: University of Michigan Press, 2008), 13, 16.

4. Richard Neuhaus, *The Naked Public Square: Religion and Democracy in America* (Grand Rapids, Mich.: Eerdmans, 1984).

5. See, for example, Gayraud S. Wilmore, *Black Religion and Black Radicalism* (Maryknoll, N.Y.: Orbis, 1973); Charles V. Hamilton, *The Black Preacher in America* (New York: Morrow, 1972).

6. David Howard-Pitney, "'To Form a More Perfect Union': African Americans and American Civil Religion," in *New Day Begun: African American Churches and Civic Culture in Post–Civil Rights America*, ed. R. Drew Smith (Durham, N.C.: Duke University Press, 2003), 93.

7. Eric Foner, *Freedom's Lawmakers: A Directory of Black Officeholders during Reconstruction* (New York: Oxford University Press, 1993), xiv; Thomas Holt, *Black over White: Negro Political Leadership in South Carolina during Reconstruction* (Urbana: University of Illinois Press, 1977), 1, 229–41; Reginald F. Hildebrand, "Richard Harvey Cain, African Methodism, and the Gospel of Freedom in South Carolina," *ACR*, January–March 2001, 39–45; Bernard E. Powers Jr., "'I Go to Set the Captives Free': The Activism of Richard Harvey Cain, Nationalist Churchman and Reconstruction Era Leader," in *The Southern Elite and Social Change*, ed. Randy Finley and Thomas A. DeBlack (Fayetteville: University of Arkansas Press, 2002), 34–52, 186–89.

8. Holt, *Black over White*; Canter Brown Jr., "George Washington Witherspoon: Florida's Second Generation of Black Political Leadership," *ACR*, January–March 2003, 70, 72.

9. Daniel A. Payne, *Recollections of Seventy Years* (reprint; New York: Arno, 1969), 262, 332; Daniel A. Payne, *History of the African Methodist Episcopal Church* (Nashville: AME Sunday School Union, 1891), 470–71; Canter Brown Jr., "George Washington Witherspoon," 70.

10. See Evelyn Brooks Higginbotham, *Righteous Discontent: The Women's Movement in the Black Baptist Church, 1880–1920* (Cambridge: Harvard University Press, 1993); Glenda E. Gilmore, *Gender and Jim Crow: Women and the Politics of White Supremacy in North Carolina, 1896–1920* (Chapel Hill: University of North Carolina Press, 1996).

11. E. Franklin Frazier, *Black Bourgeoisie* (New York: Collier, 1962), 193. I have written on another member of this "responsible elite" in "George E. Cannon: Black Churchman, Physician, and Republican Politician," *Journal of Presbyterian History*, Winter 1973, 411–32.

12. Hanes Walton to author, June 24, 2004.

13. Paul A. Djupe and Christopher Gilbert, *The Prophetic Pulpit: Clergy, Churches, and Communities in American Politics* (New York: Rowman and Littlefield, 2003), 219; Mary R. Sawyer, "Theocratic, Prophetic, and Ecumenical: Political Roles of African American Clergy," in *Christian Clergy in American Politics*, ed. Sue E. S. Crawford and Laura R. Olson (Baltimore: Johns Hopkins University Press, 2001), 67.

14. Thomas Langford, "John Wesley and Theological Method," in *Rethinking Wesley's Theology for Contemporary Methodism*, ed. Randy Maddox (Nashville, Tenn.: Kingswood, 1998), 35; Theodore Runyon, *The New Creation: John Wesley's Theology Today* (Nashville, Tenn.: Abingdon, 1998), 13–14.

15. James H. Cone, *Black Theology and Black Power* (Maryknoll, N.Y.: Orbis, 1969), 35, 37, 95–96. For the depth of Allen's Wesleyan consciousness, see Dennis C. Dickerson, *A Liberated Past: Explorations in AME Church History* (Nashville, Tenn.: AME Sunday School Union, 2003),

17–26; Dennis C. Dickerson, "Scripture and Hymnody in the Conversion of Richard Allen," *ACR*, January–March 2008, 57–60.

16. AJC Jr., "A New Resource," AJC Jr. Papers, Box 48, Folder 336.

17. Several significant monographs have recently chronicled the careers of African American ministers and have examined them in the context of the transformation of twentieth-century black religious culture. Books about black Brooklyn, Detroit, and Chicago clergy especially show how the rise of a black proletarian presence in northern urban and industrial areas challenged preachers to focus on issues of employment, housing, public education, and political empowerment. In *Black Religious Intellectuals: The Fight for Equality from Jim Crow to the Twenty-first Century* (New York: Routledge, 2002), Clarence Taylor offers a typology for understanding various activist black clergy in the post–World War II era. African American Christian liberals, radicals, and Pentecostals opposed racial segregation and discrimination but adopted different attitudes and postures for attacking these injustices. Afro-Christian liberals, whether sympathetic to Democrats or Republicans, accepted the New Deal welfare state and fought for the equal treatment of blacks in federal programs. Black Christian radicals, while lauding Franklin D. Roosevelt's New Deal and Harry Truman's Fair Deal, believed that these measures fell short in addressing the social and economic ills afflicting the African American population. These clergy aligned themselves with Marxists, socialists, and other radicals in pursuing a restructuring of American society to benefit the working class. Black Pentecostals, however, believed that an emphasis on spirituality prepared African Americans for improvements in their temporal condition. Individual and moral rehabilitation, more than movement activities, provided the best routes to black equality. Clarence Taylor also explores one of these themes in *Knocking at Our Own Door: Milton Galamison and the Struggle to Integrate New York City Schools* (New York: Columbia University Press, 1997). In his eclectic embrace of insurgent Reformation, Marxist, and reformist American figures, Galamison, an African American Presbyterian pastor at Brooklyn's Siloam Presbyterian Church, used their writings to develop his critique of racism and worker exploitation, fitting Taylor's definition of the black Christian radical. From his pulpit, Galamison became a local NAACP leader, a strategist in the assault on de facto public school segregation, and an opponent of job discrimination in public works. In *Faith in the City: Preaching Radical Social Change in Detroit* (Ann Arbor: University of Michigan Press, 2007), Angela D. Dillard focuses on activist clergy beginning in the 1930s who laid foundations for their insurgent successors in the 1960s. The proletarianization of southern black migrants and their unionization in Detroit shaped the "radicalism" of Charles A. Hill, a Baptist pastor starting in the 1930s, and the Afrocentrism of Albert Cleage, a Congregational minister who founded the nationalist Shrine of the Black Madonna in the 1960s. Like Galamison in Brooklyn, these two radical African American clergy affiliated with movements aimed at improving the employment, housing, and political condition. Another Detroit minister, C. L. Franklin, however, belonged in the Afro-liberal Christian category. Nick Salvatore examines this black folk preacher in *Singing in a Strange Land: C. L. Franklin, the Black Church, and the Transformation of America* (New York: Little, Brown, 2005). Franklin, a pulpit, gospel, and radio performer, understood and advanced the economic and civil rights interests of his working-class congregation and became a sponsor of popular religious music that blended the sacred and secular tastes of his proletarian followers, thus placing himself at the center of a transformed African American religious culture. In *Passionately Human, No Less Divine: Religion and Culture in Black Chicago, 1915–1952* (Princeton: Princeton University Press, 2005), Wallace Best similarly contends that the remolded religious culture that Franklin helped to forge in Detroit also occurred in the Chicago. New Pentecostal bodies, nondenominational community churches, and grassroots Baptist congregations supplanted established Baptists and African Methodists. Though these insurgent religious bodies catered to southern black migrants, welcomed popular gospel music, and preferred

ecstatic expressions of religiosity, they did not eclipse the Afro-liberal Christian roles and perspectives of such elite preacher/politicians as the Careys.

18. Victor Anderson, "Contour of an American Public Theology," *Journal of Theology*, Summer 2000, 50, 53, 62, 63.

Chapter 1

1. Wesley J. Gaines, *African Methodism in the South: Twenty-five Years of Freedom* (Atlanta: Franklin, 1890), 4–8, 10.

2. Stephen W. Angell, *Bishop Henry McNeal Turner and African American Religion in the South* (Knoxville: University of Tennessee Press, 1992), 67–80; Benjamin W. Arnett, ed., *The Budget of 1904* (Philadelphia: Lampton and Collett, 1904), 161, 163.

3. Gaines, *African Methodism*, 303–4.

4. Ibid., 288, 291–92.

5. "Prominent Citizen File for Park File Name," attached to George S. Cooley to AJC Jr., April 29, 1958, AJC Jr. Papers, Box 34, Folder 235; *Chicago Daily Journal*, April 13, 1927.

6. U.S. Department of Commerce, Bureau of the Census, Ninth Census of the United States, 1870, City of Atlanta, Second Ward, 56–57; Avery O. Craven, *Soil Exhaustion as a Factor in the Agricultural History of Virginia and Maryland, 1606–1860* (Urbana: University of Illinois Press, 1926); U.S. Department of Commerce, Bureau of the Census, Tenth Census of the United States, 1880, City of Atlanta, Humphries Street, 293.

7. U.S. Department of Commerce, Bureau of the Census, Tenth Census, 293; *Minutes of the Fourteenth Session of the North Georgia Annual Conference of the African Methodist Episcopal Church Held in Allen Temple, Atlanta, Ga., from the First to the Eighth of December, 1886* (Atlanta: Harrison, 1887), 3; *Minutes of the North Georgia Annual Conference, African Methodist Episcopal Church, Twentieth Session, November 9, 1892, Greensboro, Georgia*, 67, AME Archives.

8. Gaines, *African Methodism*, 46–47, 223–24; *CR*, March 16, 1876.

9. *CR*, July 15, 1875, January 4, 1877, July 3, 1878.

10. Ibid., March 16, 1882, July 26, 1883; Gaines, *African Methodism*, 147–48.

11. *Minutes of the Fourteenth Session*, 16, 27–28, 34, 36–37; 57–58; tabular statement of churches, statistical tables, *CR*, March 15, 1888.

12. *CR*, December 19, 1889; Gaines, *African Methodism*, 215, 217; *Minutes of the North Georgia Annual Conference, 1892*, 6, 8, 14, 44, 66; *Minutes of the Twenty-first Session of the North Georgia Annual Conference of the AME Church, Held in Trinity AME Church, Marietta, Ga., November 8th to 13th, 1893* (Atlanta: Franklin, 1894), 17, 46, 78–79, 88; *Proceedings of the Scientific and Literary Institute of the Georgia Conferences, Atlanta, Georgia, May 23, 1893*, 18, AME Archives; W. H. Mixon, *History of the African Methodist Episcopal Church in Alabama with Biographical Sketches* (Nashville: AME Sunday School Union, 1902), 132.

13. Gaines, *African Methodism*, 215; Sara J. Duncan, *Progressive Missions in the South and Addresses* (Atlanta: Franklin, 1906), 130; George A. Sewell and Cornelius V. Troup, *Morris Brown College: The First Hundred Years, 1881–1981* (Atlanta: Morris Brown College Press, 1981), 26–27; *Competitor*, August 1920; *Journal of Proceedings of the Fifty-third Session of the Kentucky Conference of the African Methodist Episcopal Church, Held at St. Peter's AME Church, Harrodsburg, Kentucky, from October 6th to 10th, 1920*, 7, AME Archives.

14. See Clarence A. Bacote, *The Story of Atlanta University: A Century of Service, 1865–1965* (Atlanta: Atlanta University Press, 1969); *Minutes of the North Georgia Annual Conference, 1892*, 7; *CR*, January 28, July 27, 1893; *Minutes of the Twenty-first Session*, 80.

15. *Minutes of the Twenty-first Session*, 9, 15, 17, 20, 88–89.

16. *CR*, July 5, 1894; *Minutes of the North Georgia Annual Conference of the AME Church, November 7, 1894, in Athens, Georgia*, 63, AME Archives.

17. *Minutes of the North Georgia Annual Conference, 1894*, 19, 49–50, 55.

18. Ibid., 56–57.

19. Ibid., 63; *CR*, December 20, 1894.

20. Foner, *Freedom's Lawmakers*, xi, xiv.

21. Elizabeth Studley Nathans, *Losing the Peace: Georgia Republicans and Reconstruction, 1865–1871* (Baton Rouge: Louisiana State University Press, 1968), 34, 123–26, 222, 226–27.

22. Foner, *Freedom's Lawmakers*, xxi; Angell, *Bishop Henry McNeal Turner*, 82.

23. Foner, *Freedom's Lawmakers*, 7, 27, 53–54, 63, 74, 162, 227, 203–4.

24. Clarence A. Bacote, "The Negro in Georgia Politics, 1880–1908" (Ph.D. diss., University of Chicago, 1955), 52–53, 73.

25. Joseph Logsdon, "The Reverend A. J. Carey and the Negro in Chicago Politics" (master's thesis, University of Chicago, 1961), 6, 8; *Chicago Daily Journal*, April 13, 1927; "Dr. Archibald J. Carey," *Half-Century Magazine*, September 1919, 9.

26. M. M. Ponton, *The Life and Times of Henry M. Turner* (Atlanta: Caldwell, 1917), 53; Foner, *Freedom's Lawmakers*, 58.

27. *CR*, October 10, 1895.

28. Ibid., October 10, 1895, September 2, 1897.

29. Ibid., March 3, 31, 1898.

30. Ibid., October 1, 1896, September 1, August 12, 1897.

31. *Chicago Daily Journal*, April 3, 1927; *CR*, June 10, August 12, 1897.

32. *CR*, February 25, August 12, 1897, March 3, 1898.

33. Logsdon, "Reverend A. J. Carey," 8; *Chicago Daily Journal*, April 13, 1927.

34. AJC Jr., Speech, n.d., AJC Jr. Papers, Box 50, Folder 356.

Chapter 2

1. See Allan H. Spear, *Black Chicago: The Making of a Negro Ghetto, 1890–1920* (Chicago: University of Chicago Press, 1967), 51–89; David W. Wills, "Archibald J. Carey, Sr. and Ida B. Wells-Barnett: Religion and Politics in Black Chicago, 1900–1931," *ACR*, July–September 2004, 104.

2. Harold F. Gosnell, *Negro Politicians: The Rise of Negro Politics in Chicago* (Chicago: University of Chicago Press, 1967), 16.

3. Wallace D. Best, "Passionately Human, No Less Divine: Racial Ideology and Religious Culture in the Black Churches of Chicago, 1915–1963" (Ph.D. diss., Northwestern University, 2000), 4, quoted in Spear, *Black Chicago*, 178.

4. "Dr. Archibald J. Carey," 9.

5. Best, "Passionately Human," 82, 95; AJC Jr., *Quinn Chapel African Methodist Episcopal Church, 120th Anniversary Record, 1847–1967*, 25 (courtesy of Robert Thomas Jr.).

6. AJC Jr., *Quinn Chapel . . . Anniversary Record*, 25.

7. Richard R. Wright Jr., *Eighty-seven Years behind the Black Curtain: An Autobiography* (Philadelphia: Rare Book, 1965), 90; AJC Jr., *Quinn Chapel . . . Anniversary Record*, 25; *CR*, February 22, November 11, 1900.

8. *CD*, January 9, 1915, February 19, 26, 1916, August 24, 1918; "Dr. Archibald J. Carey," 9; *New York Age*, October 4, September 30, 1909; Richard R. Wright Jr., *Eighty-seven Years*, 94.

9. *CD*, September 28, 1918.

10. Ibid., February 23, 1918, April 5, 1919, March 13, 1920; "Dr. Archibald J. Carey," 9.

11. Ralph E. Luker, *The Social Gospel in Black and White* (Chapel Hill: University of North Carolina Press, 1991), 172–73.

12. Reverdy C. Ransom, *The Pilgrimage of Harriet Ransom's Son* (Nashville: AME Sunday School Union, n.d.), 103–10.

13. W. E. B. Du Bois, *The Souls of Black Folk* (New York: New American Library, 1969), 212–13.

14. Ransom, *Pilgrimage*, 83–84, 105–10, 228–57.

15. *CR*, January 25, 1900; Wills, "Archibald J. Carey," 99–100.

16. Ransom, *Pilgrimage*, 88, 111–12, 115; Wills, "Archibald J. Carey," 101. Ransom outlived Carey by nearly thirty years, giving Ransom the last word on their relationship. Moreover, his autobiography, *The Pilgrimage of Harriet Ransom's Son*, paints a favorable and self-serving account of his Chicago years and portrays Carey as singularly ambitious and addicted to power and dominance. Annetta L. Gomez-Jefferson's superb *The Sage of Tawawa: Reverdy Cassius Ransom, 1861–1959* (Kent, Ohio: Kent State University Press, 2002), 66, presents disputes between Ransom and Carey and Murray from Ransom's perspective. Similarly, Wills, "Archibald J. Carey," 94–95, follows Ransom's narrative, blaming Carey for attempts to replace Ransom in Chicago's church and civic affairs. Ransom was right about Carey's undignified and at times rude and ruthless self-promotion but erred in ignoring Carey's broader and more complicated objectives, presenting him as wholly egocentric and bereft of any motivations except those that advanced his narrow personal interests.

17. Ransom, *Pilgrimage*, 88; *CR*, June 8, September 9, 1899.

18. Ransom, *Pilgrimage*, 111; Richard R. Wright Jr., *Eighty-seven Years*, 90, 94, 108, 114; Logsdon, "Reverend A. J. Carey," 16–18.

19. Spear, *Black Chicago*, 64.

20. See Richard R. Wright Jr., *Eighty-seven Years*, 168–73. See also Kenneth H. Hill, "The Political Behavior of African Methodist Church Members" (Ph.D. diss., University of Michigan, 1988).

21. *CR*, September 14, 1899, December 11, 1902; *CD*, January 2, 1915.

22. *General Program of the Sessions and Anniversaries of the General Conference of the African Methodist Episcopal Church Held in Quinn Chapel AME Church, Chicago, Dr. A. J. Carey, Pastor, Beginning May 2, 1904, 3, 30–31, AME Archives; AJC Jr., Quinn Chapel . . . Anniversary Record, 25; Proceedings of the Twenty-second Quadrennial Conference of the African Methodist Episcopal Church, Chicago, May 2, 1904*, 160, AME Archives.

23. *Journal of the Twenty-third Quadrennial Session of the General Conference of the African Methodist Episcopal Church, Norfolk, Virginia, May 4th–21st, 1908*, 93, 172, 188, AME Archives; *Journal of the Twenty-fourth Quadrennial Session of the General Conference of the African Methodist Episcopal Church, Kansas City, Missouri, May 6th to 23rd, 1912*, 162, 179, 190, AME Archives.

24. *Journal of Proceedings of the Thirty-fourth Annual Session of the Macon, Georgia, Conference of the African Methodist Episcopal Church Held at Turner Tabernacle AME Church, Macon, Georgia, November 17–21, 1915*, 33–34, 42–43, AME Archives.

25. *CD*, May 6, 27, 1916; *Journal of the Twenty-fifth Quadrennial Session (Being the Centennial Session) of the General Conference of the African Methodist Episcopal Church, Philadelphia, Penn., May 3rd to May 23rd, 1916*, 27, AME Archives.

26. *CD*, February 23, November 23, 1918; *Journal of the Twenty-sixth Quadrennial Session of the General Conference of the African Methodist Episcopal Church, Held in St. Louis, Missouri, May 3rd to 18th, 1920*, 29, 72, AME Archives.

27. Ransom, *Pilgrimage*, 111, 135; *CD*, October 16, 1915, September 28, 1917, January 31, 1920; *Chicago Whip*, October 9, 1920; "Prominent Citizen File for Park File Name," attached to George S.

Cooley to AJC Jr., April 28, 1958, AJC Jr. Papers, Box 34, Folder 235. Cook refused the Des Moines appointment and instead led most of Bethel's members out of the AME denomination, establishing an independent congregation, the Metropolitan Community Church Center.

28. *CD*, September 27, 1919, May 15, 1920; *Chicago Whip*, April 24, 1920.

29. Ibid., May 23, 1920.

30. Francis J. Grimké, "The Afro-American Pulpit in Relation to Race Elevation," in *The Works of Francis James Grimké*, ed. Carter G. Woodson (Washington, D.C.: Associated, 1942), 1:228.

31. W. E. B. Du Bois to Alexander Walters, n.d., in *The Correspondence of W. E. B. Du Bois*, vol. 1, *Selections, 1877–1934*, ed. Herbert Aptheker (Amherst: University of Massachusetts Press, 1973), 93; Helen Buckler, *Daniel Hale Williams: Negro Surgeon* (New York: Pitman, 1968), 230–51.

32. Spear, *Black Chicago*, 64–65, 113, 118.

33. Ransom, *Pilgrimage*, 161–67, 196–97; AJC Sr. to Booker T. Washington, October 28, 1903, in *The Booker T. Washington Papers*, ed. Louis R. Harlan and Raymond W. Smock (Urbana: University of Illinois Press, 1972–89), 7:315–16.

34. Secretary of the Executive Committee to Alberta Moore Smith, April 12, 1901, Booker T. Washington and T. Thomas Fortune to National Negro Business League, Meeting Minutes, 1901, all in Booker T. Washington Papers (microfilm), Pt. 3, National Negro Business League, cont. 1053–55; Gosnell, *Negro Politicians*, 82–83; Theodore W. Jones to Booker T. Washington, January 28, 1904, in *Booker T. Washington Papers*, ed. Harlan and Smock, 7:417–19.

35. Booker T. Washington to Daniel Hale Williams, January 25, 1908, in *Booker T. Washington Papers*, ed. Harlan and Smock, 9:448; *New York Age*, July 15, 1909, December 15, 1910; "Prominent Citizen File for Park File Name," attached to George S. Cooley to AJC Jr., April 29, 1958, AJC Jr. Papers, Box 34, Folder 235; *CD*, November 20, 1915.

36. Logsdon, "Reverend A. J. Carey," 16; *CD*, March 3, November 24, 1917.

37. *CD*, November 24, 1917, February 16, 1918.

38. Ibid., April 20, June 22, August 31, 1918; Levi J. Coppin, *Unwritten History* (Philadelphia: AME Book Concern, 1919), 341–42.

39. *CD*, April 27, 1918.

40. Logsdon, "Reverend A. J. Carey," 65–68.

41. Ibid., 71–73.

42. *CD*, January 3, 1920.

43. Wills, "Archibald J. Carey," 92, 104–6; Paula J. Giddings, *Ida: A Sword among Lions: Ida B. Wells and the Campaign against Lynching* (New York: Amistad, 2008), 439, 466, 456–58, 523–24, 569; Spear, *Black Chicago*, 69–70.

44. Giddings, *Ida*, 523–24, 569, 625.

45. Ibid., 483, 495, 566–70.

46. Benjamin W. Arnett to William McKinley, October 31, 7, 1899, William McKinley Papers (microfilm), Ser. 3, Reel 69, Manuscript Division, Library of Congress, Washington, D.C.; Benjamin W. Arnett to William McKinley, February 8, 1901, McKinley Papers, Ser. 3, Reel 76; George B. Cortelyou to AJC Sr., August 24, 1900, McKinley Papers, Ser. 2, Reel 49; AJC Jr., *Quinn Chapel . . . Anniversary Record*, 25.

47. Gosnell, *Negro Politicians*, 66, 68.

48. Ibid., 75, 153, 155, 168–69, 181–83.

49. Spear, *Black Chicago*, 78–79.

50. Best, "Passionately Human," 92–93; Logsdon, "Reverend A. J. Carey," 37; Gosnell, *Negro Politicians*, 39, 49–51; *Half-Century Magazine*, April 1917.

51. Ransom, *Pilgrimage*, 88; Gosnell, *Negro Politicians*, 37, 39; Logsdon, "Reverend A. J. Carey," 40.

52. Logsdon, "Reverend A. J. Carey," 41–42; Spear, *Black Chicago*, 84–85; William Howard Taft Pamphlet, AJC Sr. Papers, AJC Sr. Folder.

53. *CD*, April 3, 17, 1915.

54. Ibid., January 15, April 15, 1916.

55. Logsdon, "Reverend A. J. Carey," 46–47, 25.

56. Gosnell, *Negro Politicians*, 50.

57. Logsdon, "Reverend A. J. Carey," 19–20.

58. Gosnell, *Negro Politicians*, 50, 199; *CD*, September 19, 1919.

59. Buckler, *Daniel Hale Williams*, 214; Logsdon, "Reverend A. J. Carey," 28.

60. Logsdon, "Reverend A. J. Carey," 47–48.

61. *CD*, February 19, 1916.

Chapter 3

1. *CD*, March 26, 1921, January 14, July 29, February 4, 11, 1922, January 6, September 15, 1923; *Chicago Whip*, February 4, July 29, 1922.

2. *CD*, May 14, 1921, August 19, 1922; *Journal of the Twenty-seventh Quadrennial Session of the General Conference of the African Methodist Episcopal Church, Held in Louisville, Kentucky, May 5th Including the 21st, 1924*, 42, 103, AME Archives.

3. "Archibald James Carey," biographical profile, AJC Sr. Papers, AJC Sr. Folder; *Proceedings of the Fifth Ecumenical Methodist Conference Held in the Central Hall, Westminster, London, September 6–16, 1921*, 352–56, xxvii–xxxiii, AME Archives.

4. *Journal of Proceedings of the Fifty-third Annual Session*, 12; *Journal of Proceedings of the Fifty-fourth Annual Session of the Kentucky Conference of the African Methodist Episcopal Church Held at St. James AME Church, Ashland, Kentucky, from October 25th to 30th, 1921*, 3–4, AME Archives.

5. Ibid., 9–10, 13; *Proceedings of the Thirty-fourth Session of the Michigan Annual Conference of the African Methodist Episcopal Church Held in Turner AME Church, Fort Wayne, Indiana, September 8–12, 1920*, 17, AME Archives.

6. Ibid., 6, 9.

7. See Dennis C. Dickerson, "Black Ecumenism: Efforts to Establish a United Methodist Episcopal Church, 1918–1932," *Church History* 52 (December 1983): 479–91; *CD*, January 15, July 2, 1927; *Journal of Proceedings of the Fifty-third Annual Session*, 26; *Journal of Proceedings of the Fifty-fourth Annual Session*, 21; *Journal of the Twenty-seventh Quadrennial Session*, 60.

8. *Journal of the Twenty-seventh Quadrennial Session*, 43, 326, 337; *Journal of Proceedings of the Fifty-fourth Annual Session*, 11, 5, 24, 57.

9. Dickerson, *Liberated Past*, 121–36; William H. Heard, "Episcopal Address," in *Journal of the Twenty-seventh Quadrennial Session*, 22.

10. Dickerson, *Liberated Past*, 138–39, 145–58; *CD*, November 11, 1915, August 10, 1918; "Martha Jayne Keys," in *Who's Who in the General Conference of 1924*, comp. Richard R. Wright Jr., 151–52, AME Archives; *Official Programme of the Twenty-seventh General Conference of the African Methodist Episcopal Church Held in Quinn Chapel AME Church, Louisville, Ky., May 5th to 23rd, 1924*, 62, AME Archives; *Journal of the Twenty-eighth Quadrennial Session of the General Conference of the AME Church, May 7–23, 1928, Chicago*, 24, AME Archives.

11. *Journal of Proceedings of the Fifty-fourth Annual Session*, 2, 11, 16, 22, 54–55; Patrick Ann Clay-Joyner, "Independent Project: Women Evangelists in the Kentucky Annual Conference of the AME Church," Payne Theological Seminary, Spring 1991, 13–14. See also Patrick Clay-Joyner, "AME Women

in Ministry in the Kentucky Annual Conference, 1921–1953," *ACR*, April–June 2006, 60–61. The AME Church finally granted women full ordination in 1960, in large part because of decades of effort by Keys.

12. *Journal of the Twenty-seventh Quadrennial Session*, 263–64, 274.

13. *Journal of Proceedings of the Fifty-fourth Annual Session*, 18, 20, 21, 35, 60.

14. *Journal of the Twenty-seventh Quadrennial Session*, 230; *Journal of Proceedings of the Fifty-fourth Annual Session*, 11.

15. *Journal of the Twenty-seventh Quadrennial Session*, 238; *Journal of Proceedings of the Fifty-fourth Annual Session*, 8, 11, 22.

16. *Journal of the Twenty-seventh Quadrennial Session*, 239, 242.

17. *Journal of Proceedings of the Fifty-fourth Annual Session*, 11; *Official Programme*, 41–42.

18. *Official Programme*, 69–70, 75–77; *Journal of the Twenty-seventh Quadrennial Session*, 117, 120.

19. Ransom, *Pilgrimage*, 264–65.

20. *Journal of Proceedings of the Fifty-fourth Annual Session*, 17–18.

21. *Journal of Proceedings of the Fifty-third Annual Session*, 12; *Journal of Proceedings of the Fifty-fourth Annual Session*, 4.

22. *Journal of the Twenty-seventh Quadrennial Session*, 49, 121.

23. *CD*, July 4, 1925; *Chicago Daily Journal*, April 13, 1927; *Minutes of the Forty-second Annual Session of the Kansas Conference, Fifth Episcopal District of the African M. E. Church Held in St. John AME Church, Topeka, Kansas, September 14, 15, 16, 17, 18, 1927*, William T. Vernon Collection, Kansas Collection, University of Kansas Library, Lawrence.

24. Ransom, *Pilgrimage*, 267.

25. *CD*, September 13, 1924, August 20, September 10, 1927; Richard R. Wright Jr., *The Bishops of the African Methodist Episcopal Church* (Nashville: AME Sunday School Union, 1963), 346; *Minutes of the Thirty-ninth Annual Session of the Michigan Conference of the African Methodist Episcopal Church Held in Community AME Church, Jackson, Michigan, September 16–20, 1925*, 15, AME Archives.

26. *CD*, October 13, 1923, June 28, 1924, June 27, July 4, 1925, June 5, 19, 1926; Best, "Passionately Human," chap. 5.

27. *CD*, October 25, November 1, 1924, March 12, 1927; *Chicago Daily Journal*, April 13, 1927.

28. *CD*, August 20, 1927; *Journal of the Twenty-eighth Quadrennial Session*, 54, 185.

29. Ransom, *Pilgrimage*, 268–69.

30. *CD*, April 12, 1924; November 24, 1923, December 7, 1929, August 9, September 13, 1930; *Journal of the Twenty-eighth Quadrennial Session*, 238–39.

31. *Chicago Whip*, June 5, 1920; *CD*, August 9, 1924; "Robert Edmund Wilson," in *Centennial Encyclopedia of the African Methodist Episcopal Church*, comp. Richard R. Wright Jr. (Philadelphia: Book Concern of the AME Church, 1916), 252; *Minutes of the Forty-second Annual Session of the Michigan Conference of the African Methodist Episcopal Church Held at First Community AME Church, Grand Rapids, Michigan, August 29th to September 2nd, 1928*, 24, AME Archives.

32. William Hale Thompson to Charles C. Fitzmorris, "Facts Regarding the Check," June 9, 1927, AJC Sr. Papers; *Journal of the Twenty-eighth Quadrennial Session*, 99.

33. *Chicago Whip*, April 22, 1922; J. G. Robinson, "The Civil Service Commission of Chicago—Bishop A. J. Carey," *ACR*, July 1927, 43, in AJC Sr. Papers.

34. *CD*, September 15, 1923, February 5, March 19, 1927.

35. Ibid., April 16, 1927; J. G. Robinson, "Civil Service Commission of Chicago," 43; Monroe H. Davis, *The Dogmas and Precepts of the Fathers* (Nashville: AME Sunday School Union, 1948), 97.

36. J. G. Robinson, "Civil Service Commission of Chicago," 43–47.

37. *Minutes of the Forty-second Annual Session of the Michigan Conference*, 15–16.

38. "Bishop Carey, Negro Leader, Dies Suddenly," 1931, "Negro Leader Dead," 1931, unidentified newspaper clippings, AJC Sr. Papers; *CD*, March 15, 1930.

39. Ibid., October 4, 25, 1930.

40. AJC Jr., interview by Robert Wright, Chicago, March 24, 1970, Moorland-Spingarn Research Center, Howard University, Washington, D.C.

41. *CD*, April 4, 1931.

42. Ibid., March 28, 1931; Davis, *Dogmas and Precepts*, 97.

43. Richard R. Wright Jr., "Archibald J. Carey," *CR*, April 9, 1931, clipping in AJC Sr. Papers.

44. "The Wilberforce Dilemma: A Critical and Objective Evaluation of Dr. Wesley's Administration," *Wilberforce University Bulletin*, January 1948, 8–10 (courtesy of Annetta L. Gomez-Jefferson); Ransom, *Pilgrimage*, 282.

Chapter 4

1. *CD*, March 28, 1931.

2. Elizabeth Bishop Trussell, interview by author, New York, June 10, 2003; Dorothy F. Patton, interview by author, Washington, D.C., October 21, 2003; *CR*, September 21, 28, 1899.

3. Trussell, interview; *CD*, October 21, 1916; "Obsequies of Eloise Carey Bishop," Unity Funeral Parlors, Chicago, November 1, 1971 (courtesy of Ruth Williams). See also Higginbotham, *Righteous Discontent*, 20–21.

4. *Chicago Whip*, July 3, 1919; "Hutchens Chew Bishop" and "Shelton Hale Bishop," both in *Encyclopedia of African American Religions*, ed. Murphy, Melton, and Ward, 85–87; *CD*, April 5, 1930.

5. Trussell, interview; Patton, interview; Richard R. Wright Jr., *Bishops*, 129.

6. Trussell, interview; Carey, interview; FBI Teletype, July 24, 1953, Washington Field Teletypes, July 29–30, 1953, Cincinnati Teletype, July 31, 1953, New York Teletype, August 3, 1953, Chicago Teletype, July 31, 1953, Report by JWS: JB, August 11, 1953, M. A. Jones to Cartha D. De Loach, November 11, 1959, "Archibald James Carey, Jr. Summary Memorandum Requested by Director's Office," August 20, 1953, May 5, 1957, all in FBI File; Patton, interview.

7. Trussell, interview.

8. George Mason Miller, "'A This Worldly Mission': The Life and Career of Alexander Walters (1858–1917)" (Ph.D. diss., State University of New York, Stony Brook, 1984), 405; "George C. Clement," in *Encyclopedia of African American Religions*, ed. Larry G. Murphy, J. Gordon Melton, and Gary L. Ward (New York: Garland, 1993), 180–81; James Bond to George C. Clement, April 16, 1925, Horace Mann Bond Papers, Ser. 1, Bond Family Papers, Box 2, Folder 9A, Special Collections and Archives, W. E. B. Du Bois Library, University of Massachusetts, Amherst.

9. "George C. Clement," 181–82; Richard G. Foster to Rufus E. Clement, June 30, 1951, Rufus E. Clement Papers, General Correspondence, 1951–52, Box 2, AME Zion Folder, Atlanta University Archives, Robert W. Woodruff Library, Atlanta University, Atlanta; James Clair Taylor to Rufus E. Clement, April 26, 1952, General Correspondence, A–G, Box 2, Clement Papers, AME Zion Church Folder; Adelaide Fassett to Rufus E. Clement, February 1956, Clement to Fassett, February 13, 1956, both in Clement Papers, AME Zion Folder, 1955–56, A. See also Dennis C. Dickerson, "Rufus E. Clement, Zion Methodism, and the Atlanta School Board Election of 1953," *ACR*, January–March 2007, 72–79.

10. Ralph Garlin Clingan, *Against Cheap Grace in a World Come of Age: An Intellectual Biography of Clayton Powell, 1865–1953* (New York: Lang, 2002), xv–xxi; Gary Scott Smith, "Adam Clayton Powell, Sr.," in *African American National Biography*, ed. Henry Louis Gates Jr. and Evelyn Brook Higginbotham (New York: Oxford University Press, 2008), 6:408–9.

11. Charles V. Hamilton, *Adam Clayton Powell, Jr.: The Political Biography of an American Dilemma* (New York: Atheneum, 1991).

12. *CD*, September 28, 1918, April 26, May 3, June 28, 1924, September 13, 1930; unidentified newspaper clipping, AJC Jr. Papers, Box 1, Folder 1; *Journal of the Twenty-seventh Quadrennial Session*, 90.

13. "Archibald J. Carey, Jr.," in *The Encyclopedia of African Methodism*, comp. Richard R. Wright Jr. (Philadelphia: AME Book Concern, 1947), 62; AJC Jr. to Eloise Carey Bishop, January 28, 1947, AJC Jr. Papers, Box 3, Folder 9.

14. Agness Joslyn Kaufman, "Lewis Institute," 1–7, ; Memorandum to FBI Director, July 31, 1953, Bureau Teletype, July 24, 1953, Washington Field Teletype, July 29, 1953, Cincinnati Teletype, July 31, 1953, New York Teletype, August 3, 1953, Chicago Teletype Airtel, July 31, 1953, all in FBI File.

15. AJC Jr., Academic Transcript, Garrett Biblical Institute, Entered Winter 1930/Graduated June 8, 1932, *Catalog of Garrett Biblical Institute, 1929–1930*, 2–4, 22, *Catalog of Garrett Biblical Institute, 1930–1931*, 50, all in United Library, Garrett-Evangelical Theological Seminary and Seabury-Western Theological Seminary, Evanston, Illinois.

16. Chicago-Kent College of Law, Office of Alumni Relations, *C-K Dateline*, http:/www.kentlaw.edu/overview/dateline.html; "Chicago-Kent History: Historic Figures of Chicago-Kent," http://www.kentlaw.edu/history; Chicago-Kent College of Law: Students, http://www.nndb.com/edu/872/000122506/; "Robert S. Abbott," http://www.nndb.com/people/733/000141310/; Richard R. Wright Jr., *Encyclopedia of African Methodism*, 62; Bureau Teletype, July 24, 1953, August 20, 1953, both in FBI File.

17. Richard R. Wright Jr., *Encyclopedia of African Methodism*, 62–63; statistical tables in the appendix of the *Journal of Proceedings of the Forty-fifth Annual Session of the Chicago Conference of the African Methodist Episcopal Church Held in Ebenezer AME Church, Evanston, Illinois, September 21 to 25, 1927*, AME Archives.

18. *Journal and Year Book of the Fifty-sixth Annual Session of the Chicago Annual Conference of the African Methodist Episcopal Church Held at Institutional AME Church, Chicago, September 21, 1938*, 39, AME Archives; Richard R. Wright Jr., *Encyclopedia of African Methodism*, 63; AJC Jr. to Joseph Nicholson, May 15, 1946, AJC Jr. Papers, Box 2, Folder 14; George W. Baber to AJC Jr., December 3, 1940, AJC Jr. Papers, Box 1, Folder 4; AJC Jr. to Henry C. Taylor, October 30, 1944, AJC Jr. Papers, Box 2, Folder 10; Jesse W. Cotton, interview by author, Ormond Beach, Florida, May 29, 2003; Glen Johnson, interview by author, Nashville, Tennessee, November 24, 2003; Timuel Black Jr., interview by author, Chicago, October 28, 2003.

19. AJC Jr., "Record of Service," AJC Jr. Papers, Box 3, Folder 20; AJC Jr. to Charles H. Wesley, June 18, 1943, Wesley to AJC Jr., AJC Jr. Papers, June 24, 1943, Box 2, Folder 8; AJC Jr. to William A. Fountain Jr., June 23, 1947, Fountain to AJC Jr., June 25, 1947, AJC Jr. Papers, Box 4, Folder 14; Carlyle F. Stewart to AJC Jr., July 26, 1939, AJC Jr. Papers, Box 1, Folder 3.

20. *Journal of Proceedings of the Thirty-second Quadrennial Session of the General Conference of the African Methodist Episcopal Church Held with the Arena, Philadelphia, Penna., May 3 to 14, 1944*, 45, AME Archives; Sadie T. M. Alexander to Richard R. Wright Jr., June 15, 1944, 55/20, Sadie T. M. Alexander Papers, 1898–1989, Record Group 55/17, University Archives and Records Center, University of Pennsylvania, Philadelphia (courtesy Ipsita Chaterjea); AJC Jr. to G. W. Reed Jr., January 12, 1945, AJC Jr. to Brother, January 12, 1945, AJC Jr. Papers, Box 2, Folder 11; Noah W. Williams to AJC Jr., December 13, 1944, Sherman L. Greene to AJC Jr., December 23, 1944, John A. Gregg to AJC Jr., December 14, 1944, AJC Jr. to D. H. Sims, December 7, 1944, all in AJC Jr. Papers, Box 2, Folder 10.

21. *CD*, March 21, 28, April 4, 1936, all in AJC Jr. Papers, Box 1, Folder 1; John Dale Russell to Mabel Simpson, October 5, 1939, Edward J. Kelly to John W. Banks, October 4, 1939, Snow F. Grigsby to AJC Jr., October 2, 1939, all in AJC Jr. Papers, Box 1, Folder 3.

22. SAC, WFO (77-44823) to FBI Director, May 10, 1957 (AJC Jr.-SPI), Jones to De Loach, November 19, 1959, AJC Jr. Memorandum, FBI File; Harvard Sitkoff, "Racial Militancy and Interracial Violence in the Second World War," Journal of American History 58 (December 1971): 661–81; Dennis C. Dickerson, *Out of the Crucible: Black Steelworkers in Western Pennsylvania, 1875–1980* (Albany: State

University of New York Press, 1986), 151–81; AJC Jr. to Madison D. Carey Jr., June 21, 1943, AJC Jr. Papers, Box 2, Folder 8; AJC Jr. to Henry Taylor, October 30, 1944, AJC Jr. Papers, Box 2, Folder 10.

23. Cynthia Taylor, "A. Philip Randolph and the Transformation of the Negro Church" (Ph.D. diss., Graduate Theological Union, 2003), 237; M. A. Jones to Cartha D. De Loach, November 19, 1959, "Archibald James Carey Jr.: Summary Memorandum Requested by the Director's Office," FBI File; AJC Jr. to Madison D. Carey Jr., June 21, 1943, AJC Jr. Papers, Box 2, Folder 8.

24. Truman K. Gibson to AJC Jr., January 10, 1941, AJC Jr. Papers, Box 1, Folder 5.

25. William H. Hastie, interview by Jerry N. Hess, January 5, 1972, 5–8, Harry S. Truman Library, Independence, Missouri, hist/hastie.htm; AJC Jr. to Truman K. Gibson Jr., September 8, 1942, AJC Jr. Papers, Box 2, Folder 7.

26. Truman K. Gibson Jr. to AJC Jr., August 31, 1942, AJC Jr. Papers, Box 2, Folder 7.

27. AJC Jr. to Truman K. Gibson Jr., September 8, 11, 1942, AJC Jr. Papers, Box 2, Folder 7; Truman Gibson Jr., interview by author, Chicago, September 21, 2005.

28. Edwin C. Berry to AJC Jr., October 21, 1946, Box 3, Folder 17, AJC Jr. Papers.

29. *Chicago Second Ward News*, May 9, 1936, Part I, Box G-53, NAACP Records; "Marshall Lorenzo Shepard, Sr.," in *Encyclopedia of African American Religions*, ed. Murphy, Melton, and Ward, 691–92; Snow F. Grigsby to AJC Jr., October 2, 1939, AJC Jr. Papers, Box 1, Folder 3; "Dwight Vincent Kyle," in *Encyclopedia of African Methodism*, comp. Richard R. Wright Jr., 590.

30. ACP Jr. to AJC Jr., October 8, 1937, AJC Jr. Papers, Box 1, Folder 2; Adam Clayton Powell Sr. to AJC Jr., February 1, October 24, December 1, 1939, all in AJC Jr. Papers, Box 1, Folder 3; Adam Clayton Powell Sr. to AJC Jr., August 4, 1943, AJC Jr. Papers, Box 2, Folder 9.

31. AJC Jr. to ACP Jr., March 13, 1939, ACP Jr. to AJC Jr., July 15, 1939, both in AJC Jr. Papers, Box 1, Folder 3; ACP Jr. to AJC Jr., February 27, 1943, AJC Jr. Papers, Box 2, Folder 8; AJC Jr., "One World or None," May 19, 1946, AJC Jr. Papers, Box 2, Folder 14; AJC Jr. to Carl Fuqua, June 1, 1965, AJC Jr. Papers, Box 49, Folder 350; Patton, interview.

32. AJC Jr., "Unenforceable Obligations," AJC Jr. Papers, Box 1, Folder 5.

33. W. Thomas Soders to AJC Jr., August 11, 1938, A. L. Foster to AJC Jr., September 29, 1938, both in AJC Jr. Papers, Box 1, Folder 2; AJC Jr. to Dear Friend, February 25, 1947, AJC Jr. Papers, Box 3, Folder 20; AJC Jr., "Record of Public Service," February 25, 1947, AJC Jr. Papers, Box 3, Folder 20.

34. Robert Bagnall to A. L. Weaver, November 7, 1930, Record of Chicago Branch Activities Taken from NAACP Annual Reports, 1913–30, both in NAACP Records, Part I, Box G49; "Your Civil Rights in Chicago Are Being Adequately Protected by the Chicago Branch," 1936, NAACP Records, Part I, Box G53; William Pickens to "My Dear Rev. ———," October 19, 1932, NAACP Records, Part I, Box G50; Alice D. Johns, "Analysis of the Annual Membership Drive for 1945 and Plans for the 1946 Drive," NAACP Records, Part II, Box C45; Lucille Pollock to Sirs, December 10, 1945, NAACP Records, Part II, Box C44; Carey, interview; Christopher Robert Reed, *The Chicago NAACP and the Rise of Black Professional Leadership, 1910–1966* (Bloomington: Indiana University Press, 1997), 159.

35. "Scottsboro Boys to Speak in Chicago," NAACP Records, Part I, Box H6; AJC Jr. and C. A. Hansberry open letter, May 2, 1937, NAACP Records, Part I, Box G53; Walter White to AJC Jr., June 8, 1937, AJC Jr. Papers, Box 1, Folder 2; M. A. Jones to Cartha D. De Loach, November 19, 1959, "Archibald James Carey, Jr., Summary Memorandum Requested by Director's Office," FBI File.

36. Henry W. McGee to Gloster Current, February 24, 1947, NAACP Records, Part II, Box C45; Oscar Brown to AJC Jr., June 8, 1942, AJC Jr. Papers, Box 2, Folder 7; T. G. Nutter to AJC Jr., August 10, 1946, Lillie M. Jackson and Addison V. Pinkney to AJC Jr., August 7, 1946, Lillie M. Jackson and Addison V. Pinkney to AJC Jr., August 27, 1946, all in AJC Jr. Papers, Box 3, Folder 16; Eunice I. Pendergrass to AJC Jr., February 3, 1942, AJC Jr. Papers, Box 1, Folder 6; Neal Harris to Geraldine Tillison, September 3, 1946, Ruth M. Wheeler to AJC Jr., September 7, 1946, J. M. Tinsley to AJC Jr.,

September 23, 1946, all in AJC Jr. Papers, Box 3, Folder 16; AJC Jr. to Joseph W. Nicholson, May 15, 1946, AJC Jr. Papers, Box 2, Folder 14.

37. AJC Jr., "One World or None," 3. See also Dennis C. Dickerson, "African American Religious Intellectuals and the Theological Foundations of the Civil Rights Movement, 1930–1955," *Church History*, June 2005, 217–35.

38. Walter White to Franklin D. Roosevelt Jr., April 22, 1946, Annual Convention 1946 Invitations, NAACP Records, Part II, Box A30; Roy Wilkins to AJC Jr., April 23, 1946, AJC Jr. Papers, Box 2, Folder 13.

39. Gloster B. Current to Walter White, June 4, 1946, Walter White to AJC Jr., June 6, 1946, both in AJC Jr. Papers, Box 2, Folder 14; M. A. Jones to Cartha D. De Loach, November 19, 1959, FBI File.

40. AJC Jr. to Walter White, June 14, 1946, AJC Jr. Papers, Box 2, Folder 14; AJC Jr. to Gloster Current, January 27, 1947, AJC Jr. Papers, Box 3, Folder 19.

41. AJC Jr. to Paul Robeson, May 17, 1946, AJC Jr. Papers, Box 2, Folder 14; M. A. Jones to Cartha D. De Loach, November 19, 1959, "Archibald James Carey, Jr. Summary Memorandum Requested by Director's Office," August 20, 1953, FBI File.

42. See Dickerson, *Liberated Past*, 161–74; George Houser, interview by author, Ramapo, New York, July 16, 2003; James Robinson, interview by author, New York, September 17, 2003; Roy Wilkins to John LaFarge, October 11, 1933, NAACP Records, Part I, Box G51.

43. Houser, interview; Robinson, interview.

44. Bernice Fisher to AJC Jr., December 14, 1942, AJC Jr. Papers, Box 2; Folder 2; Bernice Fisher to AJC Jr., January 24, 1943, AJC Jr. Papers, Box 2, Folder 8; Bernice Fisher to AJC Jr., October 3, 1943, Bernice Fisher to Ernest Tremont Tittle, October 4, 1943, AJC Jr. to Bernice Fisher, October 5, 1943, all in AJC Jr. Papers, Box 2, Folder 9; National CORE Conference Flyer, June 13, 14, 15, 1947, Indiana Methodist Church, Chicago, AJC Jr. Papers, Box 4, Folder 24; AJC Jr. to George M. Houser, June 14, 1949, AJC Jr. Papers, Box 7, Folder 46; Dickerson, *Liberated Past*, 162–65, 168.

45. Houser, interview; Dickerson, *Liberated Past*, 161–62, 171. See also John D'Emilio, *Lost Prophet: The Life and Times of Bayard Rustin* (New York: Free Press, 2003), 54–60, 134–40; AJC Jr., "A New Resource," AJC Jr. Papers, Box 48, Folder 336.

46. Lola Robinson to AJC Jr., November 15, 1943, AJC Jr. Papers, Box 2, Folder 9; AJC Jr. to M. O. Bousfield, October 16, 1946, AJC Jr. Papers, Box 3, Folder 17.

47. James Davis to AJC Jr., June 15, 1937, AJC Jr. Papers, Box 1, Folder 2; Dennis S. Nordin, *The New Deal's Black Congressman: Arthur Wergs Mitchell* (Columbia: University of Missouri Press, 1997), 47–86.

48. AJC Jr. to William F. Waugh, AJC Jr. Papers, November 8, 1946, Box 3, Folder 17.

49. AJC Jr. to Dwight N. Green, June 2, 1943, AJC Jr. Papers, Box 2, Folder 8.

50. Ibid.; Minutes of First Meeting of Committee to Investigate Segregation of Negroes in Industries Having Defense Contracts, February 27, 1942, AJC Jr. Papers, Box 1, Folder 6; AJC Jr. to Dwight N. Green, July 14, 1943, AJC Jr. Papers, Box 2, Folder 9.

51. Frank G. Thompson to AJC Jr., September 25, 1946, AJC Jr. to Thompson, September 27, 1946, both in AJC Jr. Papers, Box 3, Folder 16.

52. Unidentified to AJC Jr., October 7, 1940, AJC Jr. Papers, Box 1, Folder 4; AJC Jr. to Henry C. Taylor, October 30, 1944, AJC Jr. Papers, Box 2, Folder 10; AJC Jr. to Thomas Stephens, October 31, 1946, A. J. Kelly Williams to AJC Jr., November 15, 1946, both in AJC Jr. Papers, Box 3, Folder 17.

53. AJC Jr. to Dwight N. Green, June 2, 1943, AJC Jr. Papers, Box 2, Folder 8; AJC Jr. to Robert A. Taft, January 30, 1946, Taft to AJC Jr., February 6, 1946, both in AJC Jr. Papers, Box 2, Folder 13.

54. Earl B. Dickerson to the Judges of the Supreme Court of the United States, January 23, 1942, Belford Lawson to AJC Jr., February 27, 1942, both in AJC Jr. Papers, Box 1, Folder 6; Robert J.

Blakely with Marcus Shepard, *Earl B. Dickerson: A Voice for Freedom and Equality* (Evanston, Ill.: Northwestern University Press, 2006), 143–47; M. A. Jones to Cartha D. De Loach, November 19, 1959, "Archibald James Carey, Jr. Summary Memorandum," Bureau Teletype, July 24, 1953, Special Inquiry, July 31, 1953, Washington Field to Director and SAC, July 29, 1953, all in FBI File.

55. Scovel Richardson to AJC Jr., January 7, 1947, AJC Jr. to Scovel Richardson, January 8, 1947, both in AJC Jr. Papers, Box 3, Folder 19.

56. Ruth L. (Teena) Williams, interview by author, Chicago, December 9, 2003; "Obsequies of Albert Wycliffe Williams," October 11, 1985 (courtesy of Ruth L. Williams); "Memorial Service for Sydney Phillip Brown," May 24, 1982 (courtesy of Ruth L. Williams); Timuel D. Black Jr., *Bridges of Memory: Chicago's First Wave of Black Migration* (Evanston, Ill.: Northwestern University Press, 2003), 568; Richard R. Wright Jr., *Encyclopedia of African Methodism*, 62.

57. Theodore M. Berry to AJC Jr., April 4, July 3, 1939, AJC Jr. Papers, Box 1, Folder 3.

Chapter 5

1. AJC Jr., "Address to the Connectional Council, February 25, 1953," AJC Jr. Papers, Box 14, Folder 95; AJC Jr., "Because My Time in Office Expires," [1950?], AJC Jr. Papers, Box 10, Folder 68; see also Robert Frederick Burk, *The Eisenhower Administration and Black Civil Rights* (Knoxville: University of Tennessee Press, 1984), 47.

2. *Star of Zion*, April 2, 1931.

3. Sara Walker Jones to AJC Jr., July 18, 1956, AJC Jr. to Jones, July 20, 1956, both in AJC Jr. Papers, Box 28, Folder 190; Unidentified to AJC Jr., n.d., Box 10, Folder 67, AJC Jr. Papers; Patton, interview.

4. R. R. Wright Jr. to AJC Jr., March 31, 1956, AJC Jr. Papers, Box 27, Folder 183; Sherman L. Greene Sr. to AJC Jr., December 28, 1956, Box 29, Folder 199, AJC Jr. Papers; Lutrelle G. Long to AJC Jr., April 11, 1956, AJC Jr. Papers, Box 27, Folder 184.

5. Lutrelle G. Long to AJC Jr., September 12, 1952, AJC Jr. Papers, Box 13, Folder 87; Long to AJC Jr., April 11, 1956, AJC Jr. Papers, Box 27, Folder 184; L. T. Thornhill to AJC Jr., October 12, 1955, AJC Jr. Papers, Box 25, Folder 169; Edward S. Foust, "Greatness and Men: Carey and Hickman," ca. 1952, AJC Jr. Papers, Box 14, Folder 95; Peter G. Crawford to AJC Jr., March 23, 1960, AJC Jr. Papers, Box 40, Folder 280; W. D. Williams to AJC Jr., April 2, 1956, AJC Jr. Papers, Box 27, Folder 184.

6. Mary McLeod Bethune to AJC Jr., April 10, 1953, AJC Jr. Papers, Box 15, Box 102; M. T. Bailey to AJC Jr., September 16, 1959, AJC Jr. Papers, Box 38, Folder 267.

7. AJC Jr. to R. Elwyn Lamb, December 16, 1948, AJC Jr. Papers, Box 6, Folder 37; AJC Jr. to Friend, February 29, 1956, AJC Jr. Papers, Box 27, Folder 181; AJC Jr. to Fred A. Hughes, July 7, 1955, AJC Jr. Papers, Box 20, Folder 133; *Journal and Year Book of the Sixty-fifth Annual Session of the Chicago Annual Conference of the African Methodist Episcopal Church, Held at Quinn Chapel AME Church, Chicago, September 16th through 21st, 1947*, appendix, AME Archives; *Journal and Yearbook of the Sixty-seventh Session of the Chicago Annual Conference of the African Methodist Episcopal Church Held at Grant Memorial AME Church, Chicago, September 13–18, 1949*, appendix, AME Archives.

8. AJC Jr. to Fred A. Hughes, July 7, 1955, AJC Jr. Papers, Box 20, Folder 133; "Dinner for J. Edgar Hoover," AJC Jr. Papers, Box 40, Folder 281; *Journal and Yearbook of the Sixty-seventh Session*, 66–69; AJC Jr., *Quinn Chapel . . . Anniversary Record*, 30–31; Black, *Bridges*, 46–47; J. S. Brookens, "Passing Revue," *ACR*, April–June 1950, 37–38.

9. AJC Jr. to Fred A. Hughes, July 7, 1955, AJC Jr. Papers, Box 20, Folder 133; Statement on Historic Quinn Chapel, ca. 1952, AJC Jr. Papers, Box 14, Folder 95; *Journal and Yearbook of the Seventy-seventh Session of the Chicago Annual Conference of the African Methodist Episcopal Church Held at*

Coppin Memorial AME Church, September 8–13, 1959, in *The Combined Minutes of the Fourth Episcopal District of the African Methodist Episcopal Church, 1959,* 244, AME Archives.

10. Glen Johnson, interview; *Journal and Yearbook of the Sixty-eighth Session of the Chicago Annual Conference of the African Methodist Episcopal Church Held in Institutional AME Church, Chicago, September 12–17, 1950,* appendix, AME Archives; *Journal and Yearbook of the Seventy-first Session of the Chicago Annual Conference of the African Methodist Episcopal Church Held at First AME Church, Gary, Indiana, September 8–13, 1953,* 49, appendix, AME Archives; AJC Jr. to Eloise Carey Bishop, November 29, 1951, AJC Jr. Papers, Box 11, Folder 75.

11. *Journal and Yearbook of the Sixty-eighth Session,* 22; *Journal and Yearbook of the Seventy-seventh Session,* 22; *Journal and Yearbook of the Seventy-fourth Session of the Chicago Annual Conference of the African Methodist Episcopal Church Held at Allen Temple AME Church, Chicago, September, 1956,* 14, 19, AME Archives.

12. *Journal and Year Book of the Sixty-fifth Annual Session,* 27, 40; *Journal and Yearbook of the Sixty-eighth Session,* 14–15, 22.

13. *Journal and Year Book of the Sixty-fifth Annual Session,* 15; Robert Thomas Jr., interview by author, Detroit, September 10, 2003.

14. Russell S. Brown, comp., *Combined Minutes of the General Conferences of the African Methodist Episcopal Church, 1948–1952–1956,* 47, 51, 79, 192, 202, 237, 262–63, AME Archives; S. L. Greene to AJC Jr., January 16, 1956, AJC Jr. Papers, Box 26, Folder 178.

15. AJC Jr. to George W. Baber, February 25, 1952, Baber to AJC Jr., February 28, 1952, Dixon O'Brien to AJC Jr., February 28, 1952, AJC Jr. to Robert Quain, February 27, 1952, all in AJC Jr. Papers, Box 12, Folder 77.

16. AJC Jr., "The Concept for Conquest," AJC Jr. Papers, Box 8, Folder 55; Frank R. Veal to AJC Jr., November 24, 1947, AJC Jr. Papers, Box 4, Folder 26; John A. Gregg to AJC Jr., March 5, 1949, AJC Jr. Papers, Box 7, Folder 43.

17. John H. Lewis to AJC Jr., February 8, 1950, Daniel G. Hill to AJC Jr., December 23, 1949, AJC Jr. to Frederick D. Jordan, December 28, 1949, B. J. Nolen to AJC Jr., December 2, 1949, all in AJC Jr. Papers, Box 8, Folder 52; A. Wayman Ward to AJC Jr., January 20, 1950, AJC Jr. to John Adams, January 11, 1950, both in AJC Jr. Papers, Box 8, Folder 54. See also Dennis C. Dickerson, *Religion, Race, and Region: Research Notes on AME Church History* (Nashville, Tenn.: AME Sunday School Union/ Legacy, 1995), 107–11; "Programme of the Connectional Council of the African Methodist Episcopal Church, Jacksonville, Florida, February 15–17, 1950," AJC Jr. Papers, Box 8, Folder 55.

18. AJC Jr., "The Concept for Conquest," AJC Jr. Papers, Box 8, Folder 55; Jesse E. Beard to AJC Jr., March 31, 1950, AJC Jr. Papers, Box 8, Folder 56.

19. "Programme of the Connectional Council of the African Methodist Episcopal Church, Los Angeles, February 21–23, 1951," AJC Jr., "Connectional Council Address," Los Angeles, February 22, 1951, both in AJC Jr. Papers, Box 11, Folder 70; AJC Jr., "Connectional Council Address," Charleston, South Carolina, February 21, 1952, AJC Jr. Papers, Box 12, Folder 77; AJC Jr., "Connectional Council Address," New Orleans, February 25, 1953, AJC Jr. Papers, Box 14, Folder 95.

20. AJC Jr., "Because My Time in Office Expires."

21. AJC Jr. to H. Ralph Jackson, February 5, 1952, AJC Jr. to Frank R. Veal, February 25, 1952, AJC Jr. Papers, Box 12, Folder 77; AJC Jr. to Jackson, July 5, 1960, AJC Jr. Papers, Box 41, Folder 286; Henderson S. Davis to AJC Jr., February 14, 1957, AJC Jr. Papers, Box 30, Folder 206; Paulette Coleman and Joseph C. McKinney, *Brief History of the Financial Department of the African Methodist Episcopal Church* (Washington, D.C.: Finance Department of the AME Church, 1984), 14–15, 27; *The Official Minutes of the Thirty-fifth Session of the General Conference of the African Methodist Episcopal Church Which Convened in Miami, Florida, May 1956,* 454–88, AME Archives; *Program of the 50th*

Anniversary Observance of the General Board of the African Methodist Episcopal Church, Tuesday, June 27, 2006, North Charleston, South Carolina, AME Archives.

22. AJC Jr. to Sherman L. Greene Sr., September 8, 1958, AJC Jr. Papers, Box 35, Folder 243; AJC Jr. to S. M. Davis, May 8, 1961, AJC Jr. Papers, Box 43, Folder 302; G. Dewey Robinson to AJC Jr., June 9, 1960, AJC Jr. Papers, Box 40, Folder 284; AJC Jr. to Dr. and Mrs. John H. Lewis, June 6, 1958, AJC Jr. Papers, Box 35, Folder 238; Sherman L. Greene Sr. to AJC Jr., May 31, 1958, AJC Jr. Papers, Box 35, Folder 237; Austin Norris to AJC Jr., February 25, 1960, AJC Jr. Papers, Box 40, Folder 278; Decatur Ward Nichols, *Up to Now* (Nashville: AME Sunday School Union, 1988), 20–21..

23. AJC Jr. to Annabel Carey Prescott, July 16, 1957, AJC Jr. Papers, Box 32, Folder 214; *Official Minutes of the Thirty-sixth Session of the General Conference of the AME Church, Los Angeles, May 1960,* 109–10, AME Archives; "For Immediate Release," AJC Jr. Papers, Box 43, Folder 300; H. Ralph Jackson to AJC Jr., June 30, 1960, AJC Jr. Papers, Box 41, Folder 285; AJC Jr. to Jackson, July 5, 1960, AJC Jr. Papers, Box 41, Folder 286.

24. Sherman L. Greene Jr. to AJC Jr., April 10, 1952, AJC Jr. Papers, Box 12, Folder 79; Charles L. Hill to AJC Jr., May 27, 1953, AJC Jr. Papers, Box 15, Folder 104; William R. Wilkes to AJC Jr., March 18, 1954, AJC Jr. Papers, Box 19, Folder 129; Otto J. Baab to AJC Jr., June 18, 1954, AJC Jr. Papers, Box 20, Folder 135.

25. Sherman L. Greene Sr. to AJC Jr., January 5, 1957, AJC Jr. Papers, Box 30, Folder 203; AJC Jr. to Greene, November 30, 1960, AJC Jr. Papers, Box 42, Folder 294; "Speech on Negro Methodists," AJC Jr. Papers, Box 43, Folder 304.

26. AJC Jr. to Alexander J. Allen, March 30, 1954, AJC Jr. Papers, Box 19, Folder 129; AJC Jr. to Allen, November 15, 1956, AJC Jr. Papers, Box 29, Folder 197.

27. AJC Jr. to Dear Friend, February 29, 1956, AJC Jr. Papers, Box 27, Folder 181.

28. Ibid.

29. Ibid.

30. Ibid.; AJC Jr. to Fred Hughes, July 7, 1955, AJC Jr. Papers, Box 5, Folder 164.

31. AJC Jr. to Dear Friend, February 29, 1956, AJC Jr. Papers, Box 27, Folder 181.

32. J. H. Clayborn to AJC Jr., May 18, 1954, AJC Jr. Papers, Box 20, Folder 133.

33. AJC Jr. to Dear Friend, February 29, 1956, AJC Jr. Papers, Box 27, Folder 181; Glen Johnson, interview.

34. Harrison J. Bryant to AJC Jr., November 7, 1952, AJC Jr. Papers, Box 13, Folder 91.

35. "Rufus E. Clement," in *Encyclopedia of African American Religions,* ed. Murphy, Melton, and Ward, 181–82; Stephen Gill Spottswood to Rufus E. Clement, October 30, 1937, Clement to Spottswood, November 5, 1937, both in Atlanta University Presidential Records, 1856–1984, Ser. 9, Rufus E. Clement Records, 1931–69, Box 205, Folder 6, Atlanta University Archives, Robert W. Woodruff Library, Atlanta University, Atlanta; Josephine Humbles Kyles to Clement, May 2, 20, 1938, Clement to Kyles, May 4, 1938, all in Clement Records, Box 205, Folder 5; James W. Eichelberger to Clement, October 27, 1938, Clement to Eichelberger, November 1, 1938, both in Clement Records, Box 212, Folder 15; W. J. Walls to Clement, March 24, 1938, Clement to Walls, March 26, 1938, both in Clement Records, Box 208, Folder 13; L. Powell to Clement, December 6, 1943, Clement to Powell, December 13, 1943, both in Clement Records, Box 279, Folder 17; James Clair Taylor to Rufus E. Clement, April 26, 1952, Rufus E. Clement Papers, General Correspondence, A–G, Box 2, AME Zion Folder, Atlanta University Archives; Richard A. G. Foster to Clement, June 30, 1951, Clement to Foster, July 5, 1951, both in Clement Papers, General Correspondence, 1951–52, Box 2, AME Zion Folder; Adelaide Fassett to Clement, February 1956, Clement to Fassett, February 13, 1956, both in Clement Papers, Box A, AME Zion Folder, 1955–56; AJC Jr. to Rufus E. Clement, May 20, 1953, AJC Jr. Papers, Box 15, Folder 104; Clement to AJC Jr., June 3, 1953, AJC Jr. Papers, Box 15, Folder 105.

36. Richard R. Wright Jr., *Bishops*, 34. For assessments of Wesley and Hill, see Michael R. Winston, "Charles Harris Wesley: 1891–1987: A Eulogy," *ACR*, Fall 2000, 26–34; Arthur Stokes, "Charles Leander Hill: Profile of a Scholar," *ACR*, Fall 2000, 79–82.

37. HAJ to AJC Jr., June 18, 1959, AJC Jr. Papers, Box 38, Folder 262.

38. *Official Minutes of the Thirty-sixth Session*, 25; AJC Jr. to Dear Friend, February 29, 1956, AJC Jr. Papers, Box 27, Folder 181; AJC Jr. to Cameron Hall, June 19, 1961, AJC Jr. Papers, Box 43, Folder 303.

39. Dwight H. Green to AJC Jr., November 12, 1948, AJC Jr. Papers, Box 6, Folder 36; AJC Jr. to VJW, April 27, 1949, AJC Jr. Papers, Box 7, Folder 45; Gibson, interview; Gosnell, *Negro Politicians*, 376; "GOPer Val Washington, Who Helped Eisenhower Put Blacks in Key Posts, Dies," *Jet*, May 15, 1995, http://findarticles.com/p/articles/mi_m1355/is_n1_v88/ai_16951706/?tag=content;col1;; Illinois Commerce Commission, List of Commissioners," http://www.icc.illinois.gov/cc/.

40. Gosnell, *Negro Politicians*, 90–91.

41. AJC Jr., interview by Robert Wright; *Journal and Yearbook of the Sixty-eighth Session*, 130; AJC Jr. to John A. Gregg, January 16, 1947, Box 3, Folder 19, AJC Jr. Papers.

42. AJC Jr. to John A. Gregg, January 16, 1947, AJC Jr. Papers, Box 3, Folder 19; Gregg to AJC Jr., February 3, 1947, AJC Jr. Papers, Box 3, Folder 20.

43. AJC Jr. to Eloise Carey Bishop, January 28, 1947, AJC Jr. Papers, Box 3, Folder 19.

44. AJC Jr., "Record of Public Service."

45. AJC Jr. to Vince M. Townsend, January 23, 1947, AJC Jr. to William Lacey, January 30, 1947, both in AJC Jr. Papers, Box 3, Folder 19; ACP Jr. to AJC Jr., February 3, 1947, AJC Jr. Papers, Box 3, Folder 20.

46. AJC Jr., "Record of Public Service"; *Journal and Yearbook of the Sixty-eighth Session*, 128, 130.

47. Open Letter from Woodlawn Members, AJC Jr. Papers, Box 3, Folder 20; "For Able and Progressive Representation in City Council: Archibald J. Carey for Alderman, Third Ward," April 1, 1947, AJC Jr. Papers, Box 4, Folder 22.

48. AJC Jr. to A. Wayman Ward, April 4, 1947, AJC Jr. Papers, Box 4, Folder 22.

49. McDaniel, *Politics in the Pews*, 5, 10–11, 13, 16.

50. "Salute to: Rev. Archibald J. Carey Jr.," Radio Fellowship Hour, September 5, 1948, AJC Jr. Papers, Box 4, Folder 25; AJC Jr. to Dear Voter, February 28, 1951, AJC Jr. Papers, Box 11, Folder 70; AJC Jr., *Bronze Town*, October 1948, AJC Jr. Papers, Box 5, Folder 35.

51. AJC Jr., *Bronze Town*; AJC Jr. to Robert Merriam, n.d., AJC Jr. Papers, Box 23, Folder 158; AJC Jr. to Dear Voter, February 22, 1951, AJC Jr. Papers, Box 11, Folder 70.

52. AJC Jr. to Edna H. Schramm, September 26, 1947, Secretary to AJC Jr. to HAJ, September 18, 1947, "Enforce Civil Rights," all in AJC Jr. Papers, Box 4, Folder 25.

53. Clement E. Vose, *Caucasians Only: The Supreme Court, the NAACP, and Race Restrictive Covenant Cases* (Berkeley: University of California Press, 1967), 55–56, 58; Oscar C. Brown to NAACP Secretary, February 26, 1945, NAACP Records, Part II, Box C44; AJC Jr., "Record of Public Service."

54. AJC Jr., *Bronze Town*; AJC Jr. to Dorothy C. Patton, August 18, 1947, AJC Jr. Papers, Box 4, Folder 24.

55. AJC Jr. to Dorothy C. Patton, August 18, 1947, Resolution (Chicago Racial Violence), both in AJC Jr. Papers, Box 4, Folder 24.

56. "The Curse of Race Restrictive Covenants," NAACP Records, Part II, Box C45; Vose, *Caucasians Only*, 205–10; "Alderman Carey's Views on the Non-Discrimination Ordinance for Publicly Aided Housing," AJC Jr. Papers, Box 6, Folder 38; AJC Jr. to A. T. Burch, October 7, 1948, AJC Jr. Papers, Box 5, Folder 35; AJC Jr. to VJW, April 4, 1949, AJC Jr. Papers, Box 7, Folder 45.

57. AJC Jr. to A. T. Burch, October 7, 1948, AJC Jr. Papers, Box 5, Folder 35; AJC Jr. to Robert Merriam, n.d., AJC Jr. Papers, Box 23 Folder 158; Sidney Williams to AJC Jr., December 3, 1948, AJC

Jr. Papers, Box 6, Folder 37; "Organizations on Record Supporting the Non-Discrimination in Publicly Aided Housing Ordinance," AJC Jr. Papers, Box 6, Folder 38; Chicago Council against Religious and Racial Discrimination, "Action against Discrimination," AJC Jr. Papers, Box 5, Folder 29; AJC Jr. to HAJ, February 25, 1949, AJC Jr. Papers, Box 6, Folder 41.

58. AJC Jr. to Alfred [sic] Kazan, November 22, 1948, Abraham E. Kazan to AJC Jr., November 26, 1948, both in AJC Jr. Papers, Box 6, Folder 36; AJC Jr. to Alfred K. Stern, September 23, 1948, AJC Jr. Papers, Box 5, Folder 34; Stern to AJC Jr., October 11, 1948, AJC Jr. Papers, Box 5, Folder 35.

59. AJC Jr. to A. T. Burch, October 7, 1948, AJC Jr. Papers, Box 5, Folder 35; AJC Jr. to Harold Eckhart, January 12, 1949, AJC Jr. Papers, Box 6, Folder 39.

60. AJC Jr. to Harold Eckhart, January 12, 1948, AJC Jr. Papers, Box 6, Folder 39; "Alderman Carey's Views."

61. "Alderman Carey's Views."

62. AJC Jr. to Floyd E. Skinner, May 5, 1950, AJC Jr. Papers, Box 9, Folder 58; AJC Jr. to George W. Baber, February 17, 1949, AJC Jr. Papers, Box 6, Folder 41; AJC Jr. to Robert Merriam, n.d., AJC Jr. Papers, Box 23, Folder 158; AJC Jr. to VJW, April 27, 1949, AJC Jr. Papers, Box 7, Folder 45.

63. William J. Walls to AJC Jr., March 5, 1949, HAJ to AJC Jr., March 4, 1949, both in AJC Jr. Papers, Box 7, Folder 43; HAJ to Frank Keenan, March 4, 1949, Keenan to HAJ, March 16, 1949, DG No 63, III/3, Correspondence Folder, 1948–49, HAJ Papers, Swarthmore Peace Collection, Swarthmore College Library, Swarthmore, Pennsylvania; Elmore Baker to AJC Jr., March 4, 1949, M. C. B. Mason to AJC Jr., March 4, 1949, both in AJC Jr. Papers, Box 7, Folder 43; VJW to AJC Jr., April 25, 1949, AJC Jr. to VJW, April 27, 1949, both in AJC Jr. Papers, Box 7, Folder 45.

64. DeHart Hubbard to AJC Jr., March 7, 1949, AJC Jr. Papers, Box 7, Folder 44; Joseph M. Darst to AJC Jr., February 5, 1951, Gale F. Johnston to AJC Jr., February 8, 1951, both in AJC Jr. Papers, Box 11, Folder 69; Martin Meyerson to AJC Jr., April 16, May 10, 1954, AJC Jr. to Meyerson, April 28, 1954, all in AJC Jr. Papers, Box 19, Folder 132.

65. Gerald Bullock to AJC Jr., August 14, 1949, AJC Jr. Papers, Box 7, Folder 47; AJC Jr. to Cromwell Gilbert, September 22, 1950, AJC Jr. Papers, Box 9, Folder 62.

66. AJC Jr. to Eloise Carey Bishop, January 28, 1947, AJC Jr. Papers, Box 3, Folder 19.

67. AJC Jr. to William L. Dawson, January 31, 1950, William Levi Dawson Papers, Box 2, Folder 10, Special Collections and Archives, John Hope and Aurelia E. Franklin Library, Fisk University, Nashville, Tennessee; AJC Jr. to Cromwell Gilbert, September 22, 1950, AJC Jr. Papers, Box 9, Folder 62; "Remarks of Rev. Archibald Carey (Republican Alderman, Chicago), to 2nd National Progressive Party Convention," February 25, 1950, AJC Jr. Papers, Box 8, Folder 55.

68. *Chicago Daily News*, clipping, January 11, 1950, VJW to AJC Jr., January 9, 1950, both in AJC Jr. Papers, Box 8, Folder 54; Black, *Bridges*, 37–38.

69. VJW to AJC Jr., January 9, 1950, AJC Jr. Papers, Box 8, Folder 54; "Civil Rights Double-Talk: The Egg that Truman Laid," 1950, AJC Jr. Papers, Box 10, Folder 64; Leslie Perry to AJC Jr., April 4, 1950, AJC Jr. Papers, Box 9, Folder 57.

70. AJC Jr. to Guy George Gabrielson, August 7, 1950, Gabrielson to AJC Jr., August 11, 1950, both in AJC Jr. Papers, Box 9, Folder 61.

71. "Remarks of Rev. Archibald Carey"; Werner W. Schroeder to AJC Jr., January 4, 1950, AJC Jr. to Schroeder, January 6, 1950, AJC Jr. to William Langer, January 13, 1950, all in AJC Jr. Papers, Box 8, Folder 54.

72. See Harvard Sitkoff, *A New Deal for Blacks: The Emergence of Civil Rights as a National Issue: The Depression Era* (New York: Oxford University Press, 1978).

73. See William C. Berman, *The Politics of Civil Rights in the Truman Administration* (Columbus: Ohio State University Press, 1970); Harvard Sitkoff, "Harry Truman and the Election of 1948: The Coming of Age of Civil Rights in American Politics," *Journal of Southern History* 37 (November 1971):

597–616; Barton J. Bernstein, "The Ambiguous Legacy: The Truman Administration and Civil Rights," in *Politics and Policies of the Truman Administration*, ed. Barton J. Bernstein (Chicago: Quadrangle, 1972).

74. "Civil Rights Double-Talk."

75. J. S. Brookens, "Negro Candidates of the Republican Party," *ACR*, April–June 1950, 11–14.

76. Ibid.; "J. S. Brookens," in *Encyclopedia of African Methodism*, comp. Richard R. Wright Jr., 49.

77. AJC Jr. to VJW, February 28, 1950, VJW to AJC Jr., March 6, 1950, AJC Jr. to Leonard Hall, March 31, 1950, all in AJC Jr. Papers, Box 8, Folder 56.

78. AJC Jr. to Werner W. Schroeder, July 20, 1950, AJC Jr. Papers, Box 9, Folder 60; AJC Jr. to Kent S. Clow, September 18, 1950, AJC Jr. Papers, Box 9, Folder 62; AJC Jr. to VJW, October 11, 1950, AJC Jr. Papers, Box 10, Folder 63; AJC Jr., "Statement of Contributions and Expenses of Campaign for Nomination to Be Candidate to the House of Representatives," 1950, AJC Jr. Papers, Box 10, Folder 68.

79. Perry W. Howard to AJC Jr., September 11, 18, 19, 1950, VJW to AJC Jr., September 8, 1950, AJC Jr. to Howard, September 14, 20, 1950, all in AJC Jr. Papers, Box 9, Folder 62; AJC Jr. to EMD, November 3, 1950, AJC Jr. Papers, Box 10, Folder 64.

80. VJW to AJC Jr., January 24, 31, 1950, AJC Jr. Papers, Box 8, Folder 54; AJC Jr. to VJW, September 7, 1950, AJC Jr. Papers, Box 9, Folder 62; Frank Veal to AJC Jr., July 22, 1950, AJC Jr. Papers, Box 9, Folder 60; "Do You Know?" AJC Jr. Papers, Box 10, Folder 68.

81. "Carey for Congress," AJC Jr. Papers, Box 10, Folder 63; Christopher E. Manning, "The Ties That Bind: The Congressional Career of William L. Dawson and the Limits of Black Electoral Power, 1942–1970" (Ph.D. diss., Northwestern University, 2003), 1:192–93.

82. "Do You Know?"; "Archibald J. Carey for Congress," AJC Jr. Papers, Box 10, Folder 64; "Remarks of Rev. Archibald Carey."

83. AJC Jr. to ACP Jr., January 27, 1950, Louise Dargans to AJC Jr., February 2, 1950, AJC Jr. Papers, Box 8, Folder 54; Dargans to AJC Jr., February 9, 1950, AJC Jr. Papers, Box 8, Folder 55; Hamilton, *Adam Clayton Powell*, 165; *CD*, November 4, 1950.

84. Hamel Hartford Brookins to AJC Jr., February 25, 1950, John H. Lewis to AJC Jr., February 8, 1950, AJC Jr. Papers, Box 8, Folder 55; "AME Endorses Carey for Congress," AJC Jr. Papers, Box 10, Folder 68; *Journal and Yearbook of the Sixty-eighth Session*, 29.

85. Best, *Passionately Human*, 40–42, 66, 115; AJC Jr. to Clarence H. Cobbs, November 27, 1950, AJC Jr. Papers, Box 10, Folder 65; AJC Jr. to Leonard Hall, March 31, 1950, AJC Jr. Papers, Box 8, Folder 56.

86. AJC Jr. to VJW, February 22, 1950, AJC Jr. Papers, Box 8, Folder 55; AJC Jr. to VJW, March 8, 1950, AJC Jr. to Leonard Hall, March 31, 1950, AJC Jr. Papers, Box 8, Folder 56; "Meetings," October 23, 1950, AJC Jr. Papers, Box 10, Folder 63.

87. *CD*, November 4, 1950.

88. AJC Jr. to Guy Gabrielson, December 8, 1950, AJC Jr. Papers, Box 10, Folder 65.

89. AJC Jr. to Bernice Fisher, November 8, 1950, AJC Jr. Papers, Box 10, Folder 64; *CD*, February 24, 1951.

90. AJC Jr. to Benjamin M. Becker, March 1, 1951, AJC Jr. to HAJ, March 1, 1951, both in AJC Jr. Papers, Box 11, Folder 71; Werner W. Schroeder to AJC Jr., February 28, 1951, AJC Jr. Papers, Box 11, Folder 70; HAJ to AJC Jr., January 18, 1950, AJC Jr. Papers, Box 8, Folder 54; William C. Hueston to AJC Jr., October 24, 1951, AJC Jr. to HAJ, March 1, 1951, both in AJC Jr. Papers, Box 11, Folder 75; AJC Jr. to William G. Stratton, December 3, 1954, AJC Jr. to HAJ, March 1, 1951, both in AJC Jr. Papers, Box 21, Folder 146.

91. AJC Jr. to Maxwell M. Raab, October 11, 1954, AJC Jr. to HAJ, March 1, 1951, both in AJC Jr. Papers, Box 20, Folder 142.

92. AJC Jr., Statement, November 22, 1954, AJC Jr. to HAJ, March 1, 1951, both in AJC Jr. Papers, Box 21, Folder 145.

93. "Ralph Howard Metcalfe (1910–1978)," http://bioguide.congress.gov/scripts/biodisplay. pl?index=M000675; Bindley C. Cyrus and Jesse Owens to Fellow Citizen, January 10, 1955, "A Citizen's Salute to Alderman Archibald James Carey Jr.," February 7, 1955, both in AJC Jr. Papers, Box 22, Folder 152; AJC Jr. to Harold E. Rainville, January 27, 1955, Dirksen Papers, Alpha 1955, Chicago Office File; AJC Jr. to William G. Stratton, December 3, 1954, AJC Jr. Papers, Box 21, Folder 146; AJC Jr. to Charles F. Carpenter, March 3, 1955, AJC Jr. Papers, Box 23, Folder 156.

94. "Record of Archibald James Carey, Jr.," ca. February 1955, AJC Jr. Papers, Box 22, Folder 151; AJC Jr. to VJW, February 1, 1955, AJC Jr. Papers, Box 22, Folder 122; AJC Jr. to Bernice Fisher, January 20, 1950, Fisher to AJC Jr., January 24, 1950, both in AJC Jr. Papers, Box 22, Folder 150; Telephone Message from Bernice Fisher, January 26, 1950, AJC Jr. Papers, Box 22, Folder 151.

95. AJC Jr. to A. T. Burch, "Aldermanic Election," February 25, 1955, AJC Jr. Papers, Box 23, Folder 155; CD, April 30, 1955.

96. HAJ to AJC Jr., February 24, 1955, AJC Jr. Papers, Box 23, Folder 155; W. J. Walls to AJC Jr., March 8, 1955, AJC Jr. Papers, Box 23, Folder 156, AJC Jr. to Walls, March 25, 1955, AJC Jr. Papers, Box 23, Folder 157.

Chapter 6

1. AJC Jr. to Clarence H. Cobbs, November 27, 1950, AJC Jr. Papers, Box 10, Folder 65; AJC Jr. to ACP Jr., March 9, 1953, ACP Jr. to AJC Jr. and Hazel Carey, March 5, 1953, AJC Jr. Papers, Box 15, Folder 100; AJC Jr. to Eloise Carey Bishop, January 27, 1947, AJC Jr. Papers, Box 3, Folder 19.

2. SAC, WFO (77-44w23) (P) to FBI Director, June 12, 1962, via Airtel, FBI File.

3. AJC Jr. to EMD, November 3, 1950, AJC Jr. Papers, Box 10, Folder 64; AJC Jr. to EMD, August 3, 1951, AJC Jr. Papers, Box 11, Folder 73; AJC Jr. to EMD, July 28, 1953, AJC Jr. Papers, Box 16, Folder 107; AJC Jr. to EMD, April 15, 1952, AJC Jr. Papers, Box 12, Folder 79.

4. Russell S. Brown, *Combined Minutes*, 237–38.

5. AJC Jr. to Harold Rainville, July 6, 1954, AJC Jr. to EMD, March 16, 1954, both in Dirksen Papers, Alpha 1954.

6. AJC Jr. to EMD, August 16, 1954, AJC Jr. to Clarence Mitchell, August 18, 1954, both in AJC Jr. Papers, Box 20, Folder 139; AJC Jr. to Harold Rainville, May 18, 1954, AJC Jr. to John Preston, May 3, 1954, Rainville to AJC Jr., April 12, 1954, AJC Jr. to Harold Rainville, September 6, January 5, 1954, EMD to AJC Jr., March 9, 1954, December 28, 1953, AJC Jr. to EMD, March 17, 1954, all in Dirksen Papers, Alpha 1954; Rainville to AJC Jr., August 18, 1959, Rainville to Haywood Henry, September 1, 1959, Dirksen Papers, Alpha 1959; EMD to AJC Jr., January 16, 1956, Dirksen Papers, Alpha 1956.

7. VJW to AJC Jr., January 28, 1952, AJC Jr. to VJW, January 28, 1952, AJC Jr. to John H. Johnson, February 26, 1952, all in AJC Jr. Papers, Box 12, Folder 77.

8. Marjorie Letts to AJC Jr., February 5, 1952, AJC Jr. Papers, Box 12, Folder 77.

9. AJC Jr. to Werner W. Schroeder, July 28, 1953, AJC Jr. Papers, Box 16, Folder 107.

10. AJC Jr., "Address of the Honorable AJC Jr., Member of the Chicago City Council, to the Republican National Convention, Chicago, Tuesday Morning, July 8, 1952," AJC Jr. Papers, Box 12, Folder 81 (Courtesy of Kerry Taylor, MLK Jr. Papers, Stanford University, Stanford, California); Eric Sundquist, *King's Dream* (New Haven: Yale University Press, 2009), 98.

11. AJC Jr., "Address of the Honorable AJC Jr., Member of the Chicago City Council, to the Republican National Convention, Chicago, Tuesday Morning, July 8, 1952," AJC Jr. Papers, Box 12, Folder 81.

12. Ibid.

13. AJC Jr. to Eloise Carey Bishop, July 24, 1952, William H. Gray Jr. to AJC Jr., July 24, 1952, both in AJC Jr. Papers, Box 12, Folder 84; Reverdy C. Ransom to AJC Jr., July 28, 1952, AJC Jr. Papers, Box 12, Folder 84.

14. A. Chester Clark to AJC Jr., July 8, 1952, Perry B. Jackson to AJC Jr., July 15, 1952, both in AJC Jr. Papers, Box 12, Folder 82; M. C. Donnell to AJC Jr., July 8, 1952, Roscoe C. Giles to AJC Jr., July 8, 1952, W. Constantine Perry to AJC Jr., July 8, 1952, all in AJC Jr. Papers, Box 12, Folder 81.

15. Frederick Arkin to AJC Jr., July 8, 1952, D. Howard Householder to AJC Jr., July 8, 1952, both in AJC Jr. Papers, Box 12, Folder 81.

16. Barry Goldwater to AJC Jr., July 8, 1952, AJC Jr. Papers, Box 12, Folder 81; Ann Walnum to AJC Jr., July 22, 1952, Elmer S. Kyler to AJC Jr., July 31, 1952, both in AJC Jr. Papers, Box 12, Folder 84.

17. Burk, *Eisenhower Administration*, 16–18; Joseph Gomez to AJC Jr., July 22, 1952, AJC Jr. Papers, Box 12, Folder 84; AJC Jr. to Richard M. Nixon, July 14, 1952, AJC Jr. Papers, Box 12, Folder 83.

18. AJC Jr. to Frank Carlson, August 15, 1952, AJC Jr. Papers, Box 13, Folder 85; "Remarks on General Eisenhower," August 26, 1952, AJC Jr. Papers, Box 13, Folder 86.

19. AJC Jr. to Carlson, August 15, 1952, AJC Jr. Papers, Box 13, Folder 85; Howard Bradley Smith to Dwight D. Eisenhower, August 27, 1952, AJC Jr. Papers, Box 13, Folder 86; Howard Bradley Smith to AJC Jr., September 17, 1952, AJC Jr. Papers, Box 13, Folder 88.

20. Edward T. Ingle to AJC Jr., August 18, 1952, AJC Jr. to VJW, August 19, 1952, AJC Jr. to William J. Love Jr., August 28, 1952, all in AJC Jr. Papers, Box 13, Folder 86; AJC Jr. to William J. Love Jr., September 17, 1952, AJC Jr. Papers, Box 13, Folder 88; AJC Jr. to EMD, March 26, 1958, Dirksen Papers, Alpha 1958.

21. AJC Jr., "My Report," AJC Jr. Papers, Box 13, Folder 88.

22. AJC Jr., "My Report"; Gloria V. Warren, "Edith Sampson," in *Black Women in America: An Historical Encyclopedia*, ed. Darlene Clark Hine, Elsa Barkley Brown, and Rosalyn Terborg-Penn (Bloomington: Indiana University Press, 1993), 2:1002–3.

23. AJC Jr., "Speech," AJC Jr. Papers, Box 13, Folder 90.

24. AJC Jr. to William J. Balmer, October 26, 1952, AJC Jr. Papers, Box 13, Folder 90.

25. Richard M. Nixon to AJC Jr., August 15, 1952, AJC Jr. Papers, Box 13, Folder 85, Sherman Adams to AJC Jr., September 20, 1952, Memo to Mrs. Carey and Miss Taylor, September 25, 1952, "Schedule of Mr. Carey's Out-of-Town Engagements," all in AJC Jr. Papers, Box 13, Folder 88; Membership of Committee, [1950?], AJC Jr. Papers, Box 10, Folder 68; AJC Jr. to VJW, September 18, 1952, AJC Jr. Papers, Box 13, Folder 88.

26. W. B. Banta to AJC Jr., September 10, 1952, AJC Jr. Papers, Box 13, Folder 87; John R. Williams to AJC Jr., October 1, 1952, AJC Jr. Papers, Box 13, Folder 89.

27. AJC Jr. to Charles F. Willis, June 10, 1953, AJC Jr. Papers, Box 15, Folder 105; AJC Jr. to Dwight D. Eisenhower, November 11, 1952, AJC Jr. Papers, Box 14, Folder 92; AJC Jr. to Sherman Adams, December 12, 1952, AJC Jr. Papers, Box 14, Folder 93.

28. AJC Jr. to Sherman Adams, December 12, 1952, AJC Jr. Papers, Box 14, Folder 93.

29. William C. Robison to AJC Jr., February 19, 1953, AJC Jr. Papers, Box 14, Folder 99; AJC Jr. to Eloise Carey Bishop, July 24, 1952, AJC Jr. Papers, Box 12, Folder 84; "Mr. Carey's Out-of-Town Dates," March 13, 1953, AJC Jr. Papers, Box 15, Folder 100; Daniel G. Hill to AJC Jr., June 4, 1953, AJC Jr. Papers, Box 15, Folder 105.

30. AJC Jr. to VJW, March 12, 1953, AJC Jr. Papers, Box 15, Folder 100; Cross Reference Sheet, March 3, 1953, WHCF-AF, Box 520, AJC Jr. File; AJC Jr. to EMD, March 12, 1953, AJC Jr. Papers, Box 15, Folder 100.

31. Unidentified to AJC Jr., December 16, 1952, AJC Jr. Papers, Box 14, Folder 94.

32. Burk, *Eisenhower Administration*, 23–67, 69, 98–99; AJC Jr. to Dwight D. Eisenhower, February 6, 1953, AJC Jr. Papers, Box 15, Folder 100.

33. AJC Jr. to VJW, January 26, 1953, AJC Jr. Papers, Box 14, Folder 97; AJC Jr. to Charles F. Willis Jr., June 10, 1953, AJC Jr. Papers, Box 15, Folder 105.

34. Burk, *Eisenhower Administration*, 28–30; Hamilton, *Adam Clayton Powell*, 212–15.

35. AJC Jr. to Charles F. Willis Jr., June 10, 1953, AJC Jr. to Bernard M. Shanley, June 16, 1953, both in AJC Jr. Papers, Box 15, Folder 105.

36. Burk, *Eisenhower Administration*, 70.

37. Maxwell M. Raab to AJC Jr., June 23, 1953, AJC Jr. to Raab, June 24, 1953, both in AJC Jr. Papers, Box 15, Folder 105.

38. AJC Jr. to Maxwell M. Raab, June 26, 1953, AJC Jr. Papers, Box 15, Folder 15; Raab to AJC Jr., July 6, 1953, AJC Jr. Papers, Box 16, Folder 106.

39. Burk, *Eisenhower Administration*, 69; AJC Jr. to VJW, January 26, 1953, AJC Jr. Papers, Box 14, Folder 97.

40. AJC Jr. to VJW, n.d., VJW to AJC Jr., June 2, 1953, WHCF-AF, Box 956, AJC Jr. File, PPF 673; Burk, *Eisenhower Administration*, 115–16.

41. AJC Jr. to Dwight D. Eisenhower, May 22, 1953, AJC Jr. Papers, Box 15, Folder 103; Burk, *Eisenhower Administration*, 69, 79–80.

42. Burk, *Eisenhower Administration*, 69; AJC Jr. to Sherman Adams, May 6, 1953, AJC Jr. Papers, Box 15, Folder 100; AJC Jr. to Schroeder, July 28, 1953, AJC Jr. Papers, Box 16, Folder 107; *Chicago Sun-Times*, June 11, 1953, clipping, AJC Jr. to Charles F. Willis Jr., June 12, 1953, both in WHCF-AF, Box 520, AJC Jr. File.

43. AJC Jr. to Sherman Adams, May 6, 1953, AJC Jr. Papers, Box 15, Folder 100; AJC Jr. to Dwight D. Eisenhower, May 7, 1953, AJC Jr. to Charles F. Willis Jr., July 17, 1953, AJC Jr. to Maxwell Raab, July 17, 1953, all in WHCF-AF, Box 956, AJC Jr. File, PPF 673.

44. FBI—Special Inquiry, Report Made at Detroit, July 31, 1953 (AJC Jr.), Report Made at Cincinnati, July 31, 1953, FBI Records, U.S. Department of Justice, Chicago, July 31, 1953, Report Made at Washington, D.C., July 31, 1953, Bureau Teletype, July 24, 1953, Washington Field Teletype, July 29–30, 1953, Cincinnati Teletype, July 31, 1953, New York Teletype, August 3, 1953, Chicago Airtel, July 31, 1953, all in FBI File.

45. AJC Jr. to Charles F. Willis Jr., July 26, 1953, AJC Jr. to John Foster Dulles, July 27, 1953, Russell W. Ballard to AJC Jr., July 29, 1953, all in AJC Jr. Papers, Box 16, Folder 107; AJC Jr., "Is the United Nations United?" AJC Jr. Papers, Box 19, Folder 126; "Nominations Sent to the Senate on July 27, 1953," UN Matters, 1953, 1954 (3), John Foster Dulles Papers, 1951–59, Subject Ser., WHCF-AF, Box 520, AJC Jr. File.

46. AJC Jr., "Is the United Nations United?"

47. Geraldine F. Tillison to Reginald J. Holzer, October 15, 1954, AJC Jr. Papers, Box 20, Folder 142; AJC Jr., "The Burmese Item," December 3, 1953, AJC Jr. Papers, Box 18, Folder 119.

48. "Draft Statement for Mr. Carey on Human Rights," September 18, 1953, AJC Jr. Papers, Box 16, Folder 111; "Statement by the Honorable Archibald J. Carey Jr. . . . on the Point of Order Concerning the Propriety of the Committee Chairman's Action in Failing to Accord Proper Recognition to the Representative of China," November 19, 1953, AJC Jr. Papers, Box 17, Folder 117.

49. *New York Amsterdam News*, December 26, 1953, clipping, AJC Jr. to Phylys Greene, December 14, 1953, both in AJC Jr. Papers, Box 18, Folder 121; Geraldine F. Tillison to Reginald J. Holzer, October 5, 1954, AJC Jr. Papers, Box 20, Folder 142.

50. AJC Jr., "One World or None," May 17, 1954, AJC Jr. Papers, Box 20, Folder 133.

51. Charles F. Willis Jr. to Fritz W. Nelson, January 19, 1954, WHCF-AF, Box 520, AJC Jr. File; Clinton A. Brown to Dwight D. Eisenhower, September 9, 1953, WHCF-GF, Box 69, Hon. Archibald

J. Carey Endorsement File (5); Clinton A. Brown to Dwight D. Eisenhower, October 11, 1954, Charles F. Willis Jr. to Clinton A. Brown, October 25, 1954, both in WHCF-GF, Box 69, AJC Jr. Endorsement File—Block.

52. Charles F. Chaplin to Sherman Adams, April 27, 1955, Memorandum: Mr. Gray and Maxwell Raab, June 1 [1955], WHCF-GF, Box 323, AJC Jr. Endorsement File; Edward T. Tait to AJC Jr., December 5, 1955, unidentified newspaper clipping, Maxwell M. Raab to AJC Jr., June 6, 1957, all in WHCF-GF, Box 94, District Courts—First Division—Endorsements, 4-H-1, AJC Jr., District Court Endorsement; Cross Reference Sheet, July 31, 1958, WHCF-AF, Box 520, AJC Jr. File.

53. Press Release—President's Committee on Government Employment Policy, January 18, 1955, AJC Jr. Papers, Box 22, Folder 149.

54. Dwight D. Eisenhower to AJC Jr., January 18, 1955, Memorandum for Governor Adams, January 14, 1955, both in WHCF-OF 103-Q, Box 473, 103-U; AJC Jr. to Dwight D. Eisenhower, January 21, 1955, Maxwell Abbell to Maxwell Raab, January 20, 1955, both in AJC Jr. Papers, Box 22, Folder 150; Raab to AJC Jr., January 26, 1955, AJC Jr. Papers, Box 22, Folder 151; AJC Jr. to ACP Jr., February 9, 1956, AJC Jr. Papers, Box 22, Folder 153.

55. W. Arthur McCoy to Maxwell Raab, November 28, 1956, AJC Jr. Papers, Box 29, Folder 198; "Dr. Carey's Opening Remarks," AJC Jr. Papers, Box 33, Folder 228; Raab to Governor Adams, March 13, 1957, WHCF-OF, Box 474, 103-U.

56. "Dr. Carey's Opening Remarks"; AJC Jr., "Not Good If Detached," AJC Jr. Papers, Box 46, Folder 326.

57. AJC Jr. to E. C. Hatcher, September 13, 1960, AJC Jr. Papers, Box 41, Folder 290; ACP Jr. to Maxwell Abbell, May 5, 31, 1955, AJC Jr. Papers, Box 24, Folder 161; AJC Jr. to ACP Jr., June 14, 1955, AJC Jr. Papers, Box 24, Folder 162; AJC Jr. to Austin Norris, October 17, 1958, Ada Louise Wheatley to AJC Jr., June 14, 1955, both in AJC Jr. Papers, Box 24, Folder 162; Geraldine F. Tillison to Gwendolyn Tise, April 4, 1955, Tise to Tillison, April 11, 1955, both in AJC Jr. Papers, Box 23, Folder 158; "Second Report of the President's Committee on Government Employment Policy," AJC Jr. Papers, Box 34, Folder 230.

58. AJC Jr. to ACP Jr., October 26, 1959, AJC Jr. Papers, Box 39, Folder 269; AJC Jr. to Thomas E. Stephens, March 23, 1959, Dwight D. Eisenhower, "Tape Recorded Statement, Area Conferences of the President's Committee on Government Employment Policy," March 2, 1959, both in WHCF-OF, Box 474, 103 U (5).

59. "Summary Report on Area Conferences in the South and Southwest," 1956, President's Committee on Government Employment Policy, AJC Jr. Papers, Box 28, Folder 187; Press Release, May 28, 1959, National Urban League Records, Part IV, Box 16.

60. AJC Jr. to Ross Clinchy, January 30, 1956, AJC Jr. Papers, Box 26, Folder 179; "Area Conference on Non-Discrimination in Federal Employment," Dallas, Texas, March 21, 1956, President's Committee on Government Policy, AJC Jr. Papers, Box 27, Folder 183; Dennis C. Dickerson, "Finding the Middle Ground: Whitney M. Young Jr., the Urban League, and Texas," *ACR*, July–September 2001, 41–44.

61. Claude Sullivan to AJC Jr., March 26, 1956, Ross Clinchy to AJC Jr., April 3, 1956, "Progress Seen Here on Ike Race Policy," unidentified newspaper clipping, all in AJC Jr. Papers, Box 27, Folder 184.

62. AJC Jr. to Rufus E. Clement, AJC Jr. Papers, February 10, 1959, Box 37, Folder 254; Ross Clinchy to Julius Thomas, June 18, 1959, December 18, 1958, Thomas to Clinchy, July 14, 1959, AJC Jr. to Thomas, March 3, 1959, all in National Urban League Records, Part IV, Box 16, Manuscript Division, Library of Congress, Washington, D.C.

63. Burk, *Eisenhower Administration*, 69–70; James C. Evans to AJC Jr., March 22, 1955, AJC Jr. Papers, Box 23, Folder 157; Secretary to Mr. Carey to James C. Evans, April 13, 1955, AJC Jr. Papers, Box 23, Folder 158; Gwendolyn Tise to AJC Jr., August 5, 1955, AJC Jr. Papers, Box 24, Folder 165;

"Summary of Discussion of Third Meeting of the President's Committee on Government Employment Policy," April 18, 1955, AJC Jr. Papers, Box 23, Folder 159.

64. Alexander J. Allen to AJC Jr., November 20, 1956, AJC Jr. Papers, Box 33, Folder 223; AJC Jr. to Allen, August 1, 1956, Allen to AJC Jr., August 17, 1956, AJC Jr. Papers, Box 28, Folder 191.

65. W. Beverly Carter to AJC Jr., May 19, 1955, AJC Jr. to Carter, May 23, 1955, both in AJC Jr. Papers, Box 24, Folder 161; Carter to AJC Jr., June 6, 1955, AJC Jr. Papers, Box 24, Folder 162; Ross Clinchy to AJC Jr., December 3, 1957, AJC Jr. Papers, Box 33, Folder 225; AJC Jr. to Clinchy, May 1, 1959, AJC Jr. Papers, Box 37, Folder 259.

66. AJC Jr. to Simeon Booker, July 3, 1959, AJC Jr. Papers, Box 38, Folder 263; AJC Jr. to Booker, February 16, 1961, AJC Jr. Papers, Box 43, Folder 300.

67. Shelton B. Granger to R. Maurice Moss, March 30, 1953, National Urban League Records, Part I, Box 109; Joseph A. Hall to R. Maurice Moss, December 15, 1953, Moss to Hall, December 21, 1953, both in National Urban League Records, Part I, Box 87; Hall to AJC Jr., January 22, 1954, AJC Jr. Papers, Box 18, Folder 125; AJC Jr. to Lester B. Granger, December 20, 30, 1955, both in AJC Jr. Papers, Box 26, Folder 175; Maxwell Abbell to Granger, January 6, 1956, AJC Jr. Papers, Box 26, Folder 178.

68. AJC Jr. to Theodore W. Kheel, June 10, 1959, Kheel to AJC Jr., June 9, 1959, both in AJC Jr. Papers, Box 38, Folder 261.

69. "Summary of Discussion at the Twenty-second Meeting of the President's Committee on Government Employment Policy," January 18, 1956, "Summary of Discussion at the Twenty-third Meeting of the President's Committee on Government Employment Policy," January 19, 1956, Maxwell Abbell to Lester B. Granger, January 9, 5, 1956, all in AJC Jr. Papers, Box 26, Folder 178.

70. "Summary of Discussion at the Twenty-second Meeting"; President's Committee on Government Employment Policy, Summary Notes on Conference on Non-Discrimination in the Federal Service, May 24, 1956, AJC Jr. Papers, Box 28, Folder 187; Lewis G. Watts to AJC Jr., October 4, 1957, AJC Jr. Papers, Box 32, Folder 221.

71. Willard L. Brown to President's Committee on Government Employment Policy, August 18, 1955, AJC Jr. to Brown, August 29, 1955, both in AJC Jr. Papers, Box 24, Folder 166; W. Arthur McCoy to Brown, November 23, 1955, AJC Jr. Papers, Box 25, Folder 173; AJC Jr. to Ross Clinchy, May 1, 1959, AJC Jr. Papers, Box 37, Folder 259.

72. Roy Wilkins with Tom Matthews, *Standing Fast: The Autobiography of Roy Wilkins* (New York: Viking, 1982), 262–63; Jesse Thomas Moore Jr., *A Search for Equality: The National Urban League, 1910–1961* (University Park: Pennsylvania State University Press, 1981), 185; Dennis C. Dickerson, *Militant Mediator: Whitney M. Young, Jr.* (Lexington: University Press of Kentucky, 1998), 85.

73. *Journal and Yearbook of the Seventy-sixth Session of the Chicago Annual Conference of the African Methodist Episcopal Church Held at Grant Memorial AME Church, Chicago, September 16–21, 1958*, 241, AME Archives.

74. Ross Clinchy to AJC Jr., February 6, 1959, AJC Jr. Papers, Box 37, Folder 254.

75. AJC Jr. to James Mitchell, April 2, 1959, AJC Jr. Papers, Box 37, Folder 257.

76. AJC Jr. to Thomas E. Stephens, August 19, 1959, H. Colle to Stephens, September 21, 1959, both in WHCF-OF, Box 474, 103 U (7); Minutes of Cabinet Meeting, March 25, 1960 (1), Papers of the President of the United States, 1953–61, Ann Whitman File, Cabinet Ser., Box 15, A75-22, Dwight D. Eisenhower Presidential Library, Abilene, Kansas.

77. The Cabinet—Recommendations from the President's Committee on Government Employment Policy, March 18, 1960, Minutes of Cabinet Meeting, March 25, 1960 (1), both in Papers of the President of the United States, Ann Whitman File, Box 15, A75-22.

78. AJC Jr. to Dwight D. Eisenhower, March 28, 1960, AJC Jr. Papers, Box 40, Folder 280.

79. AJC Jr. to Sherman Adams, January 20, 1958, H. Colle to Thomas E. Stephens, August 19, September 21, 1959, AJC Jr. to Gerald D. Morgan, April 11, 1960, AJC Jr. to Stephens, April 28, June 2, 1960, AJC Jr. to James C. Hagerty, June 2, 1960, all in WHCF-OF, Box 474, 103 U (7).

80. *Chicago Daily News*, clipping, September 11, 1959, WHCF-OF, Box 474, 103 U (7).

81. H. H. Brookins to AJC Jr., June 25, 1958, AJC Jr. Papers, Box 35, Folder 235; Lester B. Granger to AJC Jr., July 3, 1958, AJC Jr. Papers, Box 35, Folder 240; Granger to AJC Jr., July 14, 1959, M. T. Puryear to AJC Jr., October 20, 27, 1959, all in AJC Jr. Papers, Box 38, Folder 263; Julius Thomas to AJC Jr., December 1, 1959, AJC Jr. Papers, Box 39, Folder 271; AJC Jr. to United Press International, December 29, 1960, AJC Jr. Papers, Box 42, Folder 295.

82. AJC Jr. to Lester B. Granger, February 10, 1961, AJC Jr. Papers, Box 43, Folder 300.

83. E. C. Hatcher to AJC Jr., August 20, 1953, AJC Jr. Papers, Box 16, Folder 109; AJC Jr. to Maxwell Raab, September 4, 1953, AJC Jr. Papers, Box 16, Folder 110; Raab to AJC Jr., September 24, 1953, AJC Jr. Papers, Box 16, Folder 111; Cross Reference: Right Rev. E. C. Hatcher, September 4, 1953, WHCF-AF, Box 520, AJC Jr. File.

84. AJC Jr. to E. C. Hatcher, September 7, 1954, AJC Jr. Papers, Box 20, Folder 140; AJC Jr. to Mrs. Robert L. Vann, August 20, 1954, AJC Jr. Papers, Box 20, Folder 139; AJC Jr. to E. Frederic Morrow, September 9, 1955, AJC Jr. Papers, Box 25, Folder 172.

85. Lyman W. Liggins to AJC Jr., October 23, 1953, AJC Jr. Papers, Box 17, Folder 115; AJC Jr. to E. C. Hatcher, September 7, 1954, AJC Jr. Papers, Box 20, Folder 140; AJC Jr. to Mrs. Robert L. Vann, August 20, 1954, AJC Jr. Papers, Box 20, Folder 139; Cross Reference: "Archibald J. Carey Jr.," March 5, 1954, Dwight D. Eisenhower to Sherman L. Greene Sr. and George W. Baber, February 16, 1960, both in WHCF-AF, Box 520, AJC Jr. File.

86. HAJ to AJC Jr., October 26, 1953, George M. Houser to AJC Jr., October 30, 1953, both in AJC Jr. Papers, Box 17, Folder 115; AJC Jr. to HAJ, n.d., AJC Jr. Papers, Box 18, Folder 119; AJC Jr. to HAJ, November 10, 1954, AJC Jr. Papers, Box 21, Folder 144.

87. Geraldine F. Tillison to Reginald J. Holzer, October 5, 1954, AJC Jr. Papers, Box 20, Folder 142; Thomas E. Colgan to Henry Cabot Lodge Jr., February 11, 1954, AJC Jr. to Lodge, February 18, 1954, both in AJC Jr. Papers, Box 19, Folder 127; AJC Jr. to Lodge, September 17, 1956, AJC Jr. Papers, Box 28, Folder 193.

88. A. T. Spaulding to Dwight D. Eisenhower, January 18, 1954, Spaulding to AJC Jr., January 22, 1954, both in AJC Jr. Papers, Box 18, Folder 125; Spaulding to AJC Jr., February 1, 1954, AJC Jr. Papers, Box 19, Folder 126; AJC Jr. to VJW, March 19, 1954, AJC Jr. Papers, Box 19, Folder 129; W. L. Davis and E. S. McCullough to AJC Jr., April 12, 1954, AJC Jr. Papers, Box 19, Folder 131.

89. AJC Jr. to Eisenhower, November 6, 1956, WHCF, Box 520, AJC Jr. File; Burk, *Eisenhower Administration*, 168.

90. AJC Jr., *Why Negro-Americans Should Vote Republican in 1956*, AJC Jr. Papers, Box 29, Folder 198.

91. Ibid.; AJC Jr. to ACP Jr., March 13, 1956, AJC Jr. Papers, Box 27, Folder 182; AJC Jr. to VJW, October 29, 1956, AJC Jr. Papers, Box 29, Folder 196; AJC Jr. to ACP Jr., October 12, 1956, AJC Jr. Papers, Box 29, Folder 195; Hamilton, *Adam Clayton Powell*, 266–68, 273; Burk, *Eisenhower Administration*, 168.

92. Richard M. Nixon to AJC Jr., July 30, 1955, AJC Jr. Papers, Box 24, Folder 166; AJC Jr. to Nixon, February 7, 1956, AJC Jr. Papers, Box 26, Folder 180.

93. E. Frederic Morrow, *Black Man in the White House* (New York: Coward-McCann, 1963), 41; AJC Jr. to Richard M. Nixon, March 9, 1956, AJC Jr. Papers, Box 27, Folder 182.

94. George W. Lee to AJC Jr., September 15, 1956, AJC Jr. to Lee, September 17, 1956, both in AJC Jr. Papers, Box 28, Folder 193; AJC Jr. to VJW, October 29, 1956, AJC Jr. Papers, Box 29, Folder 196.

95. AJC Jr. to Leonard W. Hall, October 31, 1956, AJC Jr. to Jerry McGranahan, October 29, 1956, both in AJC Jr. Papers, Box 29, Folder 196; AJC Jr. to VJW, November 5, 1956, AJC Jr. Papers, Box 29, Folder 197; AJC Jr. to Thalia Thomas, October 11, 1956, AJC Jr. Papers, Box 29, Folder 195.

96. Burk, *Eisenhower Administration*, 169–70; Hamilton, *Adam Clayton Powell*, 272; Morrow, *Black Man*, 106; AJC Jr. to Frank Connell, July 26, 1960, AJC Jr. Papers, Box 41, Folder 287; AJC Jr. to Dwight D. Eisenhower, November 6, 1956, Eisenhower to AJC Jr., November 12, 1956, both in WHCF-AF, Box 520, AJC Jr. File.

97. Burk, *Eisenhower Administration*, 204–26, 244–48; *Journal and Yearbook of the Seventy-seventh Session*, 223, 263–64.

98. Burk, *Eisenhower Administration*, 174–203.

99. AJC Jr., "Proposed Plank for the 1960 Republican Platform," AJC Jr. Papers, Box 41, Folder 287.

100. AJC Jr. to Frank Connell, July 26, 1960, "Suggested Material in the Event of a Floor Fight on the Civil Rights Plank," both in AJC Jr. Papers, Box 41, Folder 287.

101. AJC Jr. to Rosemary Woods, August 9, 1955, AJC Jr. Papers, Box 24, Folder 165; Richard Nixon to AJC Jr., November 8, 1956, AJC Jr. Papers, Box 29, Folder 197; Nixon to AJC Jr., November 29, 1957, AJC Jr. Papers, Box 33, Folder 224; "Dr. Carey's Opening Remarks," AJC Jr. Papers, Box 26, Folder 176; AJC Jr. to A. T. Burch, July 28, 1960, AJC Jr. Papers, Box 41, Folder 287; *Journal and Yearbook of the Seventy-seventh Session*, 259.

102. AJC Jr. to Ezra M. Johnson, July 28, 1960, AJC Jr. Papers, Box 41, Folder 287.

103. Nixon to AJC Jr., August 18, 1960, AJC Jr. to Nixon, August 19, 1956, both in AJC Jr. Papers, Box 41, Folder 289, AJC Jr. Papers.

104. AJC Jr. to Branch Rickey, January 23, February 2, 1962, both in Rickey Papers, Box 7, Folder 1; Morrow, *Black Man*, 295–96.

105. Burk, *Eisenhower Administration*, 71–73; AJC Jr. to Eugene C. Hatcher, September 13, 1960, AJC Jr. Papers, Box 41, Folder 290; *Chicago Daily News*, October 27, 1960, *Chicago Sun-Times*, November 1, 1960, clippings, AJC Jr. to Branch Rickey, November 1, 1960, all in Rickey Papers, Box 7, Folder 1.

106. AJC Jr. to Branch Rickey, January 17, April 23, 1962, Rickey Papers, Box 7, Folder 1; *Journal and Yearbook of the Eightieth Session of the Chicago Annual Conference of the African Methodist Episcopal Church, Held at St. James AME Church, St. Paul, Minnesota, September 4–9, 1962,* in *The Combined Minutes of the Fourth Episcopal District, the African Methodist Episcopal Church, 1962,* 173, AME Archives; AJC Jr. to Joseph Gomez, September 11, 1962, AJC Jr. Papers, Box 45, Folder 316; "Statement by Archibald J. Carey Jr.," October 4, 1962, AJC Jr. Papers, Box 45, Folder 318.

107. AJC Jr. to Joseph Gomez, September 11, 1962, AJC Jr. Papers, Box 45, Folder 316; "Statement by Archibald J. Carey, Jr."

108. AJC Jr. to EMD, July 28, 1953, AJC Jr. Papers, Box 16, Folder 107.

109. AJC Jr. to EMD, September 20, 1963, Rickey Papers, Box 7, Folder 1; EMD to AJC Jr., September 26, 1963, Rickey Papers, Box 7, Folder 1; *Journal and Yearbook of the Eighty-first Session of the Chicago Annual Conference of the African Methodist Episcopal Church Held at Grant Memorial AME Church, Chicago, September 10–15, 1963,* in *The Combined Minutes of the Fourth Episcopal District of the African Methodist Episcopal Church, 1963,* 249, 297, AME Archives.

110. Allan Weber, interview by Dennis C. Dickerson, Virginia Beach, Virginia, December 12, 2003; AJC Jr. to Editor, *Voice of the People* (*Chicago Daily Tribune*), March 20, 1964, AJC Jr. to Charles H. Percy, March 25, 1964, both in AJC Jr. Papers, Box 48, Folder 337.

111. *Official Minutes of the Thirty-seventh Session of the General Conference of the African Methodist Episcopal Church Held in Cincinnati, Ohio, May 1964,* 89, AME Archives; AJC Jr. to EMD, June 24, 1964, Dirksen Papers, Chicago Office File, File 342.

112. AJC Jr., interview by Robert Wright.

113. AJC Jr. to Gerald D. Morgan, June 12, 1964, AJC Jr. Papers, Box 48, Folder 339; AJC Jr. to Branch Rickey, April 23, 1964, Rickey Papers, Box 7, Folder 1; AJC Jr. to Ben Regan, March 6, 1964, AJC Jr. Papers, Box 48, Folder 337.

114. AJC Jr. to Ben Regan, March 6, 1964, AJC Jr. Papers, Box 48, Folder 337; Branch Rickey to AJC Jr., July 21, 1964, Rickey Papers, Box 7, Folder 1.

115. AJC Jr. to Charles H. Percy, July 31, 1964, AJC Jr. Papers, Box 48, Folder 339; AJC Jr. to Rickey, July 20, 1964, Rickey Papers, Box 7, Folder 1.

116. Rickey to AJC Jr., July 21, September 9, 1964, both in Rickey Papers, Box 7, Folder 1.

117. "Len O'Connor Commentary on Archibald J. Carey, Jr.," AJC Jr. Papers, Box 48, Folder 341; *Chicago Daily News*, September 11, 1964, clipping, AJC Jr. Papers, Box 48, Box 341.

118. *Journal and Yearbook of the Seventy-sixth Session*, in *Fourth Episcopal District, Combined Minutes, 1958*, 226–27, AME Archives; AJC Jr. to John M. Johnston, June 13, 1963, AJC Jr. Papers, Box 47, Folder 329.

119. AJC Jr. to Branch Rickey, June 4, 1964, Rickey to AJC Jr., June 9, 1964, both in Rickey Papers, Box 7, Folder 1.

120. AJC Jr. Statement, 1964, AJC Jr. Papers, Box 48, Folder 339; AJC Jr. to Lyndon B. Johnson, September 16, 1964, AJC Jr. Papers, Box 48, Folder 341; AJC Jr. to William L. Dawson, November 28, 1964, AJC Jr. Papers, Box 48, Folder 342.

121. AJC Jr. to Hubert H. Humphrey, September 21, 1964, AJC Jr. Papers, Box 48, Folder 342; AJC Jr. to Humphrey, October 26, 1964, AJC Jr. Papers, Box 49, Folder 343.

122. Modjeska Simpkins to AJC Jr., October 24, 1964, AJC Jr. to Elmer Henderson, October 30, 1964, both in AJC Jr. Papers, Box 49, Folder 343; AJC Jr. to Simpkins, November 7, 1964, AJC Jr. Papers, Box 49, Folder 344.

123. AJC Jr. to William L. Dawson, September 28, 1964, AJC Jr. Papers, Box 48, Folder 342; AJC Jr. to William L. Dawson, June 4, 29, 1965, both in William Levi Dawson Papers, Box 4, Folder 13, Special Collections and Archives, John Hope and Aurelia E. Franklin Library, Fisk University, Nashville, Tennessee.

124. AJC Jr. to Hubert H. Humphrey, October 28, 1964, AJC Jr. Papers, Box 49, Folder 343.

125. AJC Jr. to EMD, April 28, 1966, Dirksen Papers, Chicago Office File, Folder 342.

Chapter 7

1. Dickerson, "African American Religious Intellectuals."

2. AJC Jr. to MLK Jr., February 24, 1956, AJC Jr. Papers, Box 27, Folder 181; ACP Jr., "Address at the Prayer Pilgrimage for Freedom," 1957, in *Rhetoric, Religion, and the Civil Rights Movement, 1954–1964*, ed. Davis W. Houck and David E. Dixon (Waco, Tex.: Baylor University Press, 2006), 245; AJC Jr. to ACP Jr., March 13, 1956, AJC Jr. Papers, Box 27, Folder 182; AJC Jr. to ACP Jr., February 27, March 6, 1956, both in AJC Jr. Papers, Box 27, Folder 183.

3. AJC Jr. to ACP Jr., March 29, 1956, AJC Jr. to Brother, March 28, 1956, both in AJC Jr. Papers, Box 27, Folder 183; AJC Jr. to A. Lincoln James, March 8, 1956, AJC Jr. Papers, Box 27, Folder 182; "A Message to the Churches Regarding Racial Tensions," March 12, 1956, James Henderson, Philip A. Johnson, and John W. Harms to Ministers and Churches of Greater Chicago, March 16, 1956, Shelton Hale Bishop to Bishop and Postcard, March 16, 1956, all in AJC Jr. Papers, Box 27, Folder 183; "For Immediate Release," April 2, 1956, AJC Jr. Papers, Box 27, Folder 184.

4. "News Release: Congressman Adam Powell and Archibald J. Carey—Community Meeting Speakers," June 6, 1957, AJC Jr. Papers, Box 31, Folder 212; "All-Chicago Hour of Prayer and Report

Meeting," April 11, 1956, AJC Jr. Papers, Box 27, Folder 184; AJC Jr. to Clarence H. Cobbs, March 26, 1956, AJC Jr. Papers, Box 27, Folder 185.

5. Bernice Fisher to AJC Jr., July 1, 1953, AJC Jr. Papers, Box 16, Folder 106; Dickerson, *Liberated Past*, 166; Elmer A. Carter to AJC Jr., May 31, 1960, AJC Jr. Papers, Box 40, Folder 483; Fisher to AJC Jr., December 3, 1962, AJC Jr. Papers, Box 46, Folder 322; AJC Jr. to Gardner C. Taylor, May 3, 1966, AJC Jr. Papers, Box 51, Folder 359.

6. "Notes on Homer Jack," AJC Jr. Papers, Box 38, Folder 262; HAJ to AJC Jr., April 9, 1956, AJC Jr. Papers, Box 27, Folder 184; HAJ to AJC Jr., March 31, 1956, HAJ, "The Montgomery Story," *The Progressive*, both in AJC Jr. Papers, Box 27, Folder 183; AJC Jr. to MLK Jr., March 24, 1965, AJC Jr. Papers, Box 49, Folder 347.

7. HAJ to AJC Jr., March 9, 1955, AJC Jr. Papers, Box 23, Folder 156; HAJ to AJC Jr., April 8, 1955, AJC Jr. to John Sherman Cooper, April 12, 1955, both in AJC Jr. Papers, Box 23, Folder 158; HAJ to AJC Jr., November 20, 1956, AJC Jr. to Maxwell Raab, November 23, 1956, both in AJC Jr. Papers, Box 29, Folder 198.

8. HAJ to AJC Jr., May 9, 1955, AJC Jr. Papers, Box 23, Folder 160; HAJ to AJC Jr., November 20, 1956, AJC Jr. to Maxwell Raab, November 23, 1956, both in AJC Jr. Papers, Box 29, Folder 198.

9. HAJ to AJC Jr., November 9, 1954, "Your Invitation to the National C.O.R.E. Council Banquet," November 27, 1954, both in AJC Jr. Papers, Box 21, Folder 144; George M. Houser to AJC Jr., December 2, 1954, "George M. Houser Speaking on Africa," both in AJC Jr. Papers, Box 21, Folder 146; Houser to AJC Jr., May 10, 1955, AJC Jr. Papers, Box 23, Folder 160.

10. George M. Houser to AJC Jr., December 3, 1948, AJC Jr. to Houser, December 7, 1948, both in AJC Jr. Papers, Box 6, Folder 37; Houser to AJC Jr., June 4, 1949, AJC Jr. Papers, Box 7, Folder 46.

11. AJC Jr. to James Farmer, November 11, 1963, AJC Jr. Papers, Box 47, Folder 333; Farmer to AJC Jr., June 12, 1964, AJC Jr. Papers, Box 48, Folder 339.

12. Roy Wilkins to AJC Jr., November 4, 1952, AJC Jr. to Roy Wilkins, November 6, 1952, both in AJC Jr. Papers, Box 13, Folder 91.

13. Roy Wilkins to AJC Jr., November 10, 1952, AJC Jr. Papers, Box 13, Folder 91.

14. Walter White to AJC Jr., April 17, 1953, AJC Jr. Papers, Box 15, Folder 102; AJC Jr. to Henry Lee Moon, June 16, 1953, AJC Jr. Papers, Box 15, Folder 105; George D. Cannon to AJC Jr., June 26, 1958, AJC Jr. Papers, Box 35, Folder 237.

15. George Dows Cannon, "Medicine Plus: The Autobiography of a Black Doctor," 146–48, George Dows Cannon Papers, Schomburg Center for Research in Black Culture, New York Public Library, New York.

16. Lee Lorch to AJC Jr., October 15, 1953, AJC Jr. Papers, Box 17, Folder 114; John W. Lee to AJC Jr., November 2, 1953, AJC Jr. Papers, Box 17, Folder 116.

17. Rufus W. Smith to Lucille Black, October 16, 1948, Mass Action Rally Flyer, both in NAACP Records, Part II, Box C45; Lester Bailey to Walter White, August 6, 1951, NAACP Records, Part II, Box C46; "News from Chicago Branch/NAACP," September 1952, "News from Chicago NAACP," September–December 1952, both in NAACP Records, Part II, Box C47; Frank Horne to AJC Jr., March 1, 1954, AJC Jr. Papers, Box 19, Folder 128; AJC Jr. to Members of the Congregation at Quinn Chapel, December 8, 1957, AJC Jr. Papers, Box 33, Folder 225.

18. Theodore A. Jones to Gloster Current, April 10, 1959, Freedom Fund Dinner program, June 12, 1959, "News from Chicago Branch NAACP," September 21, 1959, all in NAACP Records, Part III, Box C31; S. S. Morris Jr. and Theodore A. Jones to Gloster Current, February 8, 1961, Report of the Executive Secretary, Executive Committee Meeting, February 21, 1961, both in NAACP Records, Part III, Box C32; AJC Jr. to Myrlie Evers, June 17, 1963, AJC Jr. Papers, Box 47, Folder 329; AJC Jr. to Carl Fuqua, June 1, 1965, AJC Jr. Papers, Box 49, Folder 350.

19. AJC Jr., Speech, [1965?], AJC Jr. Papers, Box 50, Folder 356.

20. W. E. Anderson to AJC Jr., May 16, 1955, Alpha Upsilon Lambda Chapter, Alpha Phi Alpha Fraternity, "Citizenship Rally: Operation 5000" Flyer, June 1955, Alabama State College, Montgomery, AJC Jr. Papers, Box 24, Folder 161; AJC Jr. to MLK Jr., June 7, 1955, AJC Jr. Papers, Box 24, Folder 162; MLK Jr. and E. N. French to AJC Jr., December 27, 1955, MLK Jr. to Committee, December 27, 1955, AJC Jr. Papers, Box 29; Folder 199.

21. AJC Jr. to MLK Jr., February 24, 1956, AJC Jr. Papers, Box 27, Folder 181; MLK Jr. to AJC Jr., March 3, 1956, AJC Jr. to MLK Jr., March 5, 1956, both in AJC Jr. Papers, Box 27, Folder 182; AJC Jr. to Geraldine F. Tillison, February 26, 1956, AJC Jr. Papers, Box 27, Folder 181; Ralph D. Abernathy to AJC Jr., April 17, 1956, AJC Jr. Papers, Box 27, Folder 185; AJC Jr. to MLK Jr., March 10, 5, 1956, both in AJC Jr. Papers, Box 27, Folder 184.

22. AJC Jr. to MLK Jr. and Coretta Scott King, October 15, 1956, AJC Jr. Papers, Box 29, Folder 195; AJC Jr., "God Is Where You Find Him," AJC Jr. Papers, Box 43, Folder 300.

23. MLK Jr. to AJC Jr., March 28, 1957, AJC Jr. Papers, Box 31, Folder 208; AJC Jr. to MLK Jr., August 8, 1957, MLK Jr. to AJC Jr., August 5, 1957, both in AJC Jr. Papers, Box 32, Folder 216; MLK Jr. to AJC Jr., October 31, 29, 1957, both in AJC Jr. Papers, Box 33, Folder 222; MLK Jr. to AJC Jr., December 20, 1957, AJC Jr. Papers, Box 33, Folder 226.

24. MLK Jr. to AJC Jr., December 17, 1957, AJC Jr. to MLK Jr., December 23, 1957, both in AJC Jr. Papers, Box 33, Folder 226; Hamilton, *Adam Clayton Powell*, 292–93; MLK Jr. to AJC Jr., January 8, 1958, AJC Jr. Papers, Box 34, Folder 229.

25. AJC Jr. to MLK Jr., December 30, 1957, "Living Philosophies," December 29, 1957, both in AJC Jr. Papers, Box 33, Folder 226; Geraldine F. Tillison to MLK Jr., August 9, [1960], AJC Jr. Papers, Box 44, Folder 205; Dickerson, *Liberated Past*, 176, 179; Sundquist, *King's Dream*, 96; Keith D. Miller, *Voice of Deliverance: The Language of Martin Luther King, Jr., and Its Sources* (New York: Free Press 1992), 12, 146–48; AJC Jr. to MLK Jr., December 6, 1963, AJC Jr. Papers, Box 47, Folder 333.

26. AJC Jr. to MLK Jr., October 16, 1959, MLK Jr. to AJC Jr., October 20, 1959, both in AJC Jr. Papers, Box 38, Folder 268; AJC Jr. to MLK Jr., October 26, 1959, AJC Jr. Papers, Box 39, Folder 269; AJC Jr. to MLK Jr., February 9, 1960, AJC Jr. Papers, Box 40, Folder 277; MLK Jr. to AJC Jr., March 15, 1960, MLK Jr. Papers, Box 22, Folder 16, Boston University Library, Boston (courtesy of Kerry Taylor); MLK Jr. to AJC Jr., December 19, 1962, AJC Jr. Papers, Box 46, Folder 322; AJC Jr., Open Letter, May 23, 1963, AJC Jr. Papers, Box 47, Folder 328; AJC Jr. to Isaac R. Louden, February 15, 1962, AJC Jr. Papers, Box 44, Folder 309; AJC Jr. to Martin Luther King Sr., June 7, 1963, AJC Jr. to S. H. Marcus, June 17, 1963, Martin Luther King Sr. to AJC Jr., June 25, 1963, all in AJC Jr. Papers, Box 47, Folder 329; AJC Jr. to Martin Luther King Sr., June 8, 1963, AJC Jr. Papers, Box 47, Folder 330; Ed Clayton to AJC Jr., March 1, 1965, AJC Jr. Papers, Box 49, Folder 347.

27. AJC Jr. to C. E. Thomas, May 23, 1963, AJC Jr. to Beatrice T. Carter, May 27, 1963, both in AJC Jr. Papers, Box 47, Folder 328; AJC Jr. to Gwen Green, July 19, 1963, AJC Jr. to Myrlie Evers, July 5, 1963, Annabel Carey Prescott to Myrlie Evers, July 5, 1963, all in AJC Jr. Papers, Box 47, Folder 330; AJC Jr. to MLK Jr., March 24, 1965, AJC Jr. Papers, Box 49, Folder 347.

28. MLK Jr. to AJC Jr., November 12, 1965, AJC Jr. Papers, Box 50; Folder 354; Randolph T. Blackwell to AJC Jr., August 3, 1965, AJC Jr. to Blackwell, August 5, 1965, both in AJC Jr. Papers, Box 50, Folder 351.

29. David J. Garrow, *The FBI and Martin Luther King, Jr.: From "Solo" to Memphis* (New York: Norton, 1981); "Second Report of the President's Committee on Government Employment Policy," AJC Jr. Papers, Box 34, Folder 230; AJC Jr. to JEH, November 29, 1957, AJC Jr. Papers, Box 33, Folder 224; AJC Jr. to JEH, November 3, 1959, FBI File.

30. AJC Jr. to JEH, August 21, 1958, June 29, October 27, 1959, M. A. Jones to Cartha De Loach, June 25, 1959, JEH to AJC Jr., November 2, 1959, all in FBI File.

31. "Quinn Chapel African Methodist Episcopal Church Salutes J. Edgar Hoover," Pick-Congress Hotel, Chicago, April 18, 1960, *Chicago Sun-Times*, clipping, April 19, 1960, Frank Reynolds to AJC Jr., April 4, 1960, all in AJC Jr. Papers, Box 40, Folder 281; EMD to AJC Jr., December 16, 1959, Dirksen Papers, Alpha 1959; Geraldine Tillison to Harold E. Rainville, March 15, 1960, Dirksen Papers, Alpha 1960.

32. AJC Jr. to Clyde Tolson, April 19, 1960, AJC Jr. to JEH, April 19, 1960, AJC Jr. Papers, Box 40, Folder 281; AJC Jr. to JEH, September 21, 1960, FBI File.

33. Cartha D. De Loach to John Mohr, June 2, 1960, FBI File; AJC Jr. to Cartha D. De Loach, April 19, 1960, AJC Jr. Papers, Box 40, Folder 281; AJC Jr. to JEH, September 18, 1962, AJC Jr. Papers, Box 45, Folder 317.

34. M. A. Jones to Mr. Nease, October 20, 1958, W. V. Cleveland to Mr. Evans, June 23, 1962, both in FBI File.

35. AJC Jr. to JEH, April 25, 1960, March 15, 1963, both in FBI File; AJC Jr. to JEH, September 18, 1962, AJC Jr. Papers, Box 45, Folder 317.

36. Garrow, *FBI and Martin Luther King, Jr.*, 101–28; JEH to AJC Jr., March 6, 1964, FBI File.

37. *Supplementary Detailed Staff Reports on Intelligence Activities and the Rights of Americans*, book 3, *Final Report of the Select Committee to Study Governmental Operations with Respect to Intelligence Activities, U.S. Senate: Dr. Martin Luther King Jr. Case Study, Carey–De Loach Meeting*, May 19, 1965, M. A. Jones to Cartha De Loach, May 17, 18, 1965, all in FBI File.

38. Cartha De Loach to John Mohr, May 19, 1965, FBI File.

39. Ibid.

40. AJC Jr. to JEH, March 15, 1963, FBI File; Cartha De Loach to John Mohr, May 19, 1965, FBI File.

41. Lillie Hunter to AJC Jr., May 18, 1965, AJC Jr. Papers, Box 49, Folder 349; AJC Jr. to Abernathy, June 10, 1965, Abernathy to AJC Jr., June 8, 1965, both in AJC Jr. Papers, Box 49, Folder 350.

42. David Garrow, *Bearing the Cross: Martin Luther King, Jr., and SCLC* (New York: Morrow, 1986), 431–79, 490–95, 519–25; Ed Riddick to AJC Jr., July 20, 1965, AJC Jr. Papers, Box 50, Folder 351; Ralph David Abernathy, *And the Walls Came Tumbling Down: An Autobiography* (New York: Harper and Row, 1989), 371–72; Glen Johnson, interview.

43. Glen Johnson, interview; *Journal and Yearbook of the Eighty-fourth Session of the Chicago Annual Conference of the African Methodist Episcopal Church Held at Payne Memorial AME Church, Waterloo, Iowa, September 20–25, 1966*, in *Combined Minutes of the 1966 Annual Conferences of the Fourth Episcopal District of the African Methodist Episcopal Church*, 262, AME Archives; AJC Jr. to JEH, February 14, April 10, 1967, JEH to AJC Jr., February 17, 1967, all in FBI File.

44. W. Louis Davis, AJC Jr., and Aelolian Lee to unidentified, May 20, 1963, AJC Jr. Papers, Box 47, Folder 328; AJC Jr. to Daisy Bates, September 7, 1963, AJC Jr. Papers, Box 47, Folder 330; AJC Jr. and Margaret Batteast to unidentified, November 11, 1963, AJC Jr. Papers, Box 47, Folder 333.

45. AJC Jr. to W. Arthur McCoy, April 7, 1966, AJC Jr. Papers, Box 50, Folder 358.

46. Hamilton, *Adam Clayton Powell*, 337–38, 434–78; Will Haygood, *King of the Cats: The Life and Times of Adam Clayton Powell, Jr.* (Boston: Houghton Mifflin, 1993), 231–38, 337–77.

47. AJC Jr., *Quinn Chapel . . . Anniversary Record*, 31; Glen Johnson, interview; Alexander M. Bright and Chester A. Wilkins Sr. to Dwight D. Eisenhower, August 17, 1957, Resolution, August 11, 1957, WHCF-OF, Box 474, 103-U,.

48. *CR*, January 22, March 12, 1963, January 9, 1962, June 6, 1961.

49. AJC Jr. to Melvin Chester Swann, May 31, 1963, AJC Jr. Papers, Box 47, Folder 328; H. H. Brookins to AJC Jr., March 3, 1949, AJC Jr. Papers, Box 7, Folder 43; AJC Jr. to G. R. Haughton, July 19, 1963, AJC Jr. Papers, Box 47, Folder 330; *CR*, March 19, 1963.

50. AJC Jr., *Quinn Chapel . . . Anniversary Record*, 8; Glen Johnson, interview; *Journal and Yearbook of the Eighty-fifth Session of the Chicago Annual Conference of the African Methodist Episcopal Church Held at Grant Memorial AME Church, Chicago, September 12–17, 1967*, in *Combined Minutes of the Fourth Episcopal District of the African Methodist Episcopal Church, 1967*, 246, 285, AME Archives.

51. *Journal and Yearbook of the Eighty-fifth Session*, 246, 285–86, 290; "Obsequies of Eloise Carey Bishop"; Gregory G. M. Ingram, interview by author, Los Angeles, April 7, 2008.

52. AJC Jr., Statement on the Opening of the New Building of Illinois Federal Savings and Loan Association, August 6, 1952, AJC Jr. Papers, Box 45, Folder 315.

53. Glen Johnson, interview; Chicago Annual Conference of the AME Church, Resolution to the Family of the Late Dr. Archibald J. Carey Jr., April 24, 1981 (courtesy of Jesse W. Cotton); Patton, interview; "Obsequies of Archibald J. Carey Jr.," April 24, 1981, Quinn Chapel AME Church, Chicago; "Friends Mourn Archibald Carey," n.d., unidentified newspaper clipping (courtesy of Jesse W. Cotton).

54. *CR*, October 29, 1979, February 12, 1978, December 19, 1977; *150 Years of Triumph: Turner Chapel African Methodist Episcopal Church, 1849–1999* (privately printed, 1999), 35; Cotton, interview; "Obsequies for the Honorable Judge Russell R. DeBow, 1913–1984" (courtesy of Jesse W. Cotton); Patton, interview; *CR*, December 19, 1977; AJC Jr. to Robert O. French, July 2, 1971 (courtesy of Robert O. French).

55. *CD*, April 22, 1981; *CR*, May 4, 1981; Gibson, interview; "Obsequies of Archibald J. Carey Jr."

56. "Obsequies of Archibald J. Carey Jr."

Epilogue

1. See Dennis C. Dickerson, "Toward a Theology of African Methodism: A Conversation with Wesley's Theology," *ACR*, January–March 2006, 38–53.

2. Black, interview. See also Daniel James, "Cannon the Progressive," *New Republic*, October 18, 1948, 14–15.

3. These terms are borrowed from Damon Linker, "The Idolatry of America," *New Republic*, April 23, 2008, 53–54.

SELECT BIBLIOGRAPHY

Primary Sources
MANUSCRIPT COLLECTIONS

Carey, Archibald J., Jr., File. Federal Bureau of Investigation, Department of Justice, Washington, D.C.

Carey, Archibald J., Jr., Papers. Chicago Historical Society, Chicago.

Carey, Archibald J., Sr., Papers. Chicago Historical Society, Chicago.

Clement, Rufus E., Papers. Robert W. Woodruff Library, Atlanta University Center, Atlanta.

Dawson, William Levi, Papers. Special Collections and Archives, John Hope and Aurelia E. Franklin Library, Fisk University, Nashville, Tennessee.

Dirksen, Everett M., Papers. Dirksen Congressional Center, Pekin, Illinois.

Jack, Homer A., Papers. Swarthmore College Peace Collection, Swarthmore, Pennsylvania.

King, Martin Luther, Jr., Papers. Stanford University, Stanford, California.

McKinley, William, Papers (microfilm). Manuscript Division, Library of Congress, Washington, D.C.

National Association for the Advancement of Colored People Records. Manuscript Division, Library of Congress, Washington, D.C.

National Urban League Records. Manuscript Division, Library of Congress, Washington, D.C.

Rickey, Branch, Papers. Manuscript Division, Library of Congress, Washington, D.C.

Washington, Booker T., Papers (microfilm). Manuscript Division, Library of Congress, Washington, D.C.

White House Central Files, Archibald J. Carey Jr. File. Dwight D. Eisenhower Presidential Library, Abilene, Kansas.

CHURCH RECORDS, ARCHIVES OF THE DEPARTMENT OF RESEARCH
AND SCHOLARSHIP, AME CHURCH, AME SUNDAY SCHOOL UNION, NASHVILLE

General Program of the Sessions and Anniversaries of the General Conference of the African Methodist Episcopal Church, 1904.

Minutes of the Chicago Annual Conference of the African Methodist Episcopal Church, 1938, 1947, 1949, 1950, 1953, 1956, 1958, 1959, 1962, 1963, 1966, 1967.

Minutes of the Kansas Annual Conference of the African Methodist Episcopal Church, 1927.

Minutes of the Kentucky Annual Conference of the African Methodist Episcopal Church, 1921.

Minutes of the Macon Georgia Annual Conference of the African Methodist Episcopal Church, 1915.

Minutes of the Michigan Annual Conference of the African Methodist Episcopal Church, 1920, 1925, 1928.

Minutes of the North Georgia Annual Conference of the African Methodist Episcopal Church, 1886, 1892, 1894.

Minutes of the Quadrennial General Conference of the African Methodist Episcopal Church, 1904, 1916, 1920, 1928, 1932, 1944, 1948, 1952, 1956, 1960, 1964.

Official Programme of the General Conference of the African Methodist Episcopal Church, 1924.

Proceedings of the Fifth Ecumenical Methodist Conference, 1921.

Proceedings of the Scientific and Literary Institute of Georgia Annual Conferences of the African Methodist Episcopal Church, 1893.

Quinn Chapel African Methodist Episcopal Church: 120th Anniversary Record, 1976.

NEWSPAPERS AND PERIODICALS

AME Church Review
Chicago Defender
Chicago Daily Journal
Chicago Whip
Christian Recorder
Half-Century Magazine
Star of Zion

INTERVIEWS

Black, Timuel, Jr. Interview by author. Chicago, October 28, 2003.

Carey, Archibald J., Jr. Interview by Robert Wright. Chicago, March 24, 1970. Moorland-Spingarn Research Center, Howard University, Washington, D.C.

Cotton, Jesse W. Interview by author. Ormond Beach, Florida, May 29, 2003.

Gibson, Truman, Jr. Interview by author. Chicago, September 21, 2005.

Houser, George. Interview by author. Ramapo, New York, July 16, 2003.

Johnson, Bennett. Telephone interview by author. Chicago, June 11, 2004.

Johnson, Glen T. Interview by author. Nashville, November 24, 2003.

Patton, Dorothy E. Interview by author. Washington, D.C., October 21, 2003.

Robinson, James. Interview by author. New York City, September 17, 2003.

Thomas, Robert, Jr. Interview by author. Detroit, September 10, 2003.

Trussell, Elizabeth Bishop. Interview by author. New York City, June 10, 2003.

Weber, Allan. Interview by author. Virginia Beach, Virginia, December 12, 2003.

Williams, Ruth L. (Teena). Interview by author. Chicago, December 9, 2003.

Secondary Sources

Anderson, Victor. "Contour of an American Public Theology." *Journal of Theology*, Summer 2000, 49–68.

Angell, Stephen W. *Bishop Henry McNeal Turner and African American Religion in the South*. Knoxville: University of Tennessee Press, 1992.

Berman, William C. *The Politics of Civil Rights in the Truman Administration*. Columbus: Ohio State University Press, 1970.

Best, Wallace D. "Passionately Human, No Less Divine: Racial Ideology and Religious Culture in the Black Churches of Chicago, 1915–1963." Ph.D. diss., Northwestern University, 2000.

Black, Timuel, Jr. *Bridges of Memory: Chicago's First Wave of Black Migration.* Evanston, Ill.: Northwestern University Press, 2003.

Burk, Robert F. *The Eisenhower Administration and Black Civil Rights.* Knoxville: University of Tennessee Press, 1984.

Cone, James H. *Black Theology and Black Power.* Maryknoll, N.Y.: Orbis, 1969.

Crawford, Sue E. S., and Laura R. Olson, eds. *Christian Clergy in American Politics.* Baltimore: Johns Hopkins University Press, 2001.

Dickerson, Dennis C. "African American Religious Intellectuals and the Theological Foundations of the Civil Rights Movement, 1930–1955." *Church History,* June 2005, 217–35.

———. *A Liberated Past: Explorations in AME History.* Nashville, Tenn.: AME Sunday School Union, 2003.

Djupe, Paul, and Christopher P. Gilbert. *The Prophetic Pulpit: Clergy, Churches, and Communities in American Politics.* New York: Rowman and Littlefield, 2003.

Foner, Eric. *Freedom's Lawmakers: A Directory of Black Officeholders during Reconstruction.* New York: Oxford University Press, 1993.

Gaines, Wesley J. *African Methodism in the South: Twenty-five Years of Freedom.* Atlanta: Franklin, 1890.

Garrow, David J. *The FBI and Martin Luther King, Jr.: From "Solo" to Memphis.* New York: Norton, 1981.

Giddings, Paula. *Ida: A Sword among Lions: Ida B. Wells and the Campaign against Lynching.* New York: Amistad, 2008.

Gomez-Jefferson, Annetta L. *The Sage of Tawawa: Reverdy Cassius Ransom, 1861–1959.* Kent, Ohio: Kent State University Press, 2002.

Gosnell, Harold F. *Negro Politicians: The Rise of Negro Politics in Chicago.* Chicago: University of Chicago Press, 1935.

Hamilton, Charles V. *Adam Clayton Powell: The Political Biography of an American Dilemma.* New York: Atheneum, 1991.

Holt, Thomas. *Black over White: Negro Political Leadership in South Carolina during Reconstruction.* Urbana: University of Illinois Press, 1977.

Logsdon, Joseph. "The Reverend Archibald J. Carey and the Negro in Chicago Politics." Master's thesis, University of Chicago, 1961.

Maddox, Randy, ed. *Rethinking Wesley's Theology for Contemporary Methodism.* Nashville, Tenn.: Kingswood, 1998.

McDaniel, Eric L. *Politics in the Pews: The Political Mobilization Of Black Churches.* Ann Arbor: University of Michigan Press, 2008.

Morrow, E. Frederick. *Black Man in the White House.* New York: Coward-McCann, 1963.

Ransom, Reverdy C. *The Pilgrimage of Harriet Ransom's Son.* Nashville: AME Sunday School Union, 1949.

Runyon, Theodore. *The New Creation: John Wesley's Theology Today.* Nashville, Tenn.: Abingdon, 1998.

Smith, R. Drew, ed. *New Day Begun: African American Churches and Civic Culture in Post–Civil Rights America.* Durham, N.C.: Duke University Press, 2003.

Spear, Allan H. *Black Chicago: The Making of a Negro Ghetto, 1890–1920.* Chicago: University of Chicago Press, 1967.

Sundquist, Eric. *King's Dream.* New Haven: Yale University Press, 2009.

Wills, David W. "Archibald J. Carey, Sr. and Ida B. Wells-Barnett: Religion and Politics in Black Chicago, 1900–1931." *AME Church Review,* July–September 2004, 92–107.

Wright, Richard R., Jr. *The Bishops of the African Methodist Episcopal Church.* Nashville: AME Sunday School Union, 1963.

———. *Eighty-seven Years behind the Black Curtain: An Autobiography.* Philadelphia: Rare Book, 1965.

INDEX

Abbell, Maxwell, 135, 136, 138, 139, 140, 142

Abbott, Robert S., 7, 37, 55, 66

Abernathy, Ralph D., 163, 170, 176

Abner, Willoughby, 168

Abraham Schwartz Award, 148

Abyssinian Baptist Church (New York City), 64, 72, 150

Acts, Book of, 46

Adams, Sherman, 124, 125, 130, 131, 136

Addams, Jane, 8, 30, 32

AFL-CIO, 164

Africa, 47, 75, 166

African American clergy, 35; embrace of grassroots mobilization, 163; political involvement, 22; as spokespersons for African Americans, 26; view of role in public square, 72

African Americans, 118, 123; disenfranchisement of, 21, 22, 25; efforts to attain civil rights, 159; growth in number of jobs held by, 137; housing discrimination against, 121; job discrimination against, 137; leaders as members of "talented tenth," 43; in Manhattan, 137; migration from the South in the twentieth century, 26; politics in leadership, 39; as potential candidates for election to Congress, 107; as professional politicians, 26; as Republicans, 22, 103, 121, 124; in WWII army, 69

African Methodism, 22, 23, 90, 94, 180; in Georgia, 19

African Methodism in the South (Wesley J. Gaines), 16

Akron Informer, 129

Alabama, 74, 124

Alabama Annual Conference, 19

Alabama State College, 169

All National Deliverance Day of Prayer, 163

Allen, Alexander J., 91, 139–40

Allen, B. F., 49

Allen, Richard, 4, 10–11, 22, 83, 92, 147

Allen University, 75, 160

Alpha Day, 171

Alpha Phi Alpha fraternity, 82, 169, 171, 182; Theta Chapter of Chicago, 82

AME Church, 4, 8, 10, 24, 27, 30, 32, 47, 57, 63, 67, 83, 84, 85, 147; in Chicago, 13, 45, 46; clergy in politics, 21–22; Connectional Council in Chicago, 69, 86, 88, 89, 110; Council of Bishops, 91; eclipsed by other Christian denominations, 110; Fifth Episcopal District of, 51; Five Million Dollar and Evangelical Campaign, 49; in Florida, 24; Fourteenth Episcopal District of, 35, 48, 49, 50, 51; Fourth District of, 33, 37, 52, 54, 55, 58, 65, 87, 91; Frankfurt District of, 49; in Georgia, 15, 16, 18, 19, 22, 33; Judicial Council, 119; Lexington (Ky.) district of, 48, 49; Marietta (Ga.) district of, 18; Ministerial Alliance in Chicago, 58, 110; Ministers' Alliance, 96; Pension Department, 88; Tennessee district of, 47; Sixth Episcopal District of, 19; South Carolina district of, 25; work to advance black interests in civic affairs, 51

AME Church Review, 50, 51, 57, 88, 106

AME General Conferences, 48, 54, 69; Episcopal Committee of, 33, 34, 87; General Board of,